Fodor's

EXPLORING ROME

FODOR'S TRAVEL PUBLICATIONS, INC.
NEW YORK • TORONTO • LONDON • SYDNEY • AUCKLAND

Published in the United States by Fodor's Travel Publications, Inc.
Published in the United Kingdom by AA Publishing

Fodor's and Fodor's Exploring Guides are trademarks of Fodor's Travel Publications, Inc.

ISBN 0–679–02460–3
First Edition

Fodor's Exploring Rome

Author: **Tim Jepson**
Series Advisor: **Ingrid Morgan**
Series Editor: **Nia Williams**
Copy Editor: **Diana Payne**
Cartography: **The Automobile Association**
Cover Design: **Louise Fili, Fabrizio LaRocca**
Front Cover Silhouette: **Philip Gould/Scope**

Special Sales
Fodor's Travel Publications are available at special discounts for bulk purchases (100 copies or more) for sales promotions or premiums. Special editions, including personalized covers, excerpts of existing guides, and corporate imprints, can be created in large quantities for special needs. For more information write to Special Marketing, Fodor's Travel Publications, 201 East 50th St., New York NY 10022. .

Manufactured in Italy by LEGO SpA, Vicenza.
10 9 8 7 6 5 4 3 2 1

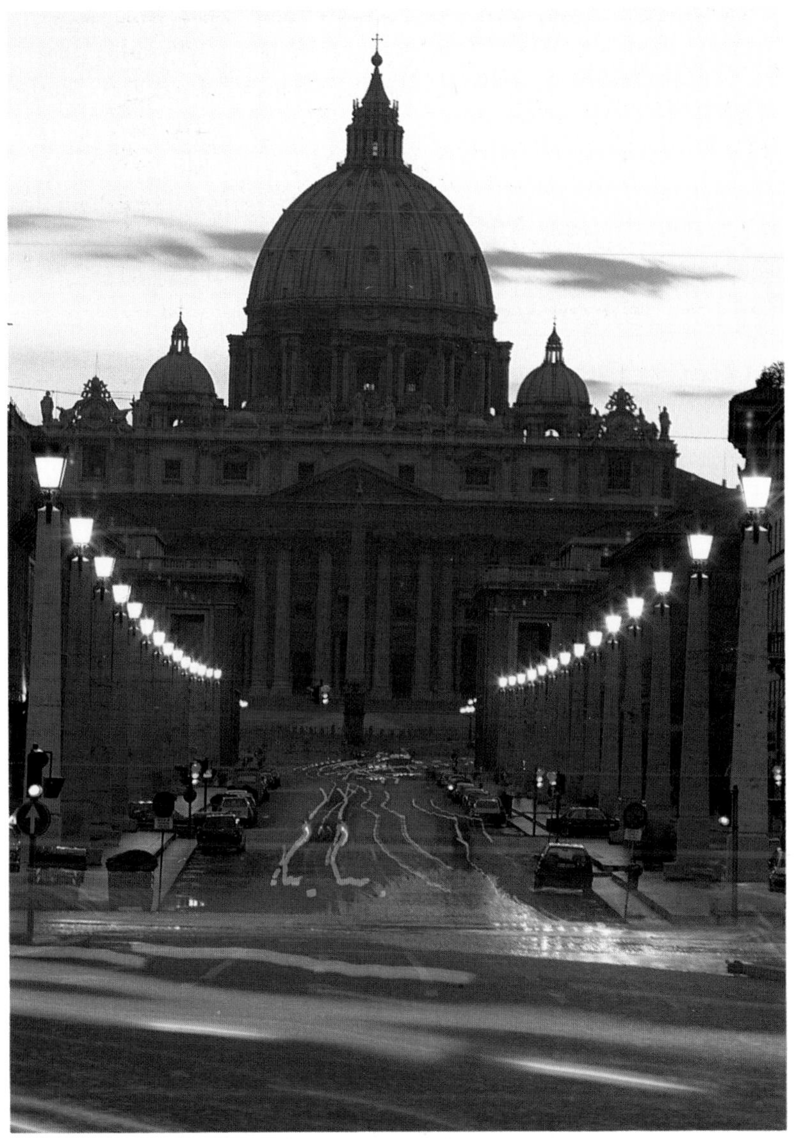

Headlights at night: Rome's drivers and St. Peter's – two of the city's best known features...

Tim Jepson is the author of *Umbria, The Green Heart of Italy, Wild Italy* and *The Rough Guide to Tuscany and Umbria*, and has contributed to *The Rough Guide to Italy* and *Fodor's Italy*. Until 1989 he was the Rome correspondent for the London *Sunday Telegraph*, and he has worked for the Italian section of the BBC World Service.

The Villa Borghese offers a bucolic retreat from the city streets

About this book

This book is divided into three principal sections.

The first part of the book discusses aspects of life today and in the past. The second part covers places to visit, including drives and walks. The Focus on... and Close-up sections, also in this section, look at subjects in greater detail. The third and final part is the Travel Facts chapter, which includes both practical day-to-day information for the traveler, and the Directory, a selective listing of hotels and restaurants.

Some of the places described in this book have been given a special rating:

 Do not miss

 Highly recommended

 See, if you can

General Contents

Maps

Features

Walks

Drives

My Rome by Mario

Mario is a bric-a-brac and furniture dealer who works behind the Campo de' Fiori market.

In Rome we have a saying that *Roma non si cambia mai* – Rome never changes. Most sayings ring true, but this time it's different. On the one hand, we have the same old confusion now as before: the noise and commotion, the sunshine, the impossible bureaucracy, and the sure knowledge that the people in power will never change. But on the other hand, we, like the citizens of so many other cities, have become wooden and inhuman. We care less about others' problems and more about whether they have more than us. People are forgetting how simple pleasures were once able to make a difference to their lives; they are forgetting how to laugh and to sing, to be content with a glass of wine from the Castelli Romani and a plate of *buccatini all'amatriciana*.

Here, in our quarter – which runs from the Tiber to just past the Campo and back, farther up, to the Tiber again close to St. Peter's, we have never had such characters, and by tradition even the police and various local government inspectors tread warily: we are fiercely proud and independent; every street has its own "policeman" and offenders do not dare to cross locals. Here, next door, there sat outside every day, in the same broken chair, for 30 years an old woman they called Rita. They said she'd been stunning in her youth, and earned what she could standing under trees in town touting for business. Downstairs from us – in the typical Roman fashion in which classes rub shoulders – the lawyer who lived on the *piano nobile* (the "noble" floor) paid her, later, to keep her alive. He reckoned that since she knew all the thieves, the best way to avoid getting robbed was to buy her out! She's gone now, old Rita; I hear she's sold her place to a foreigner for three-quarters of a billion lire. Everyone is a gran signore now. Half the people in the market have nice cars. Can you imagine a fruit vendor bowling down the crooked lanes of old Rome in a Mercedes? I know one fellow who parks his car alongside him wherever he goes – but his father's friends found it ideal for playing *scoppa*, a card game, on the hood! Well, come to think of it, maybe we haven't changed so much after all...

Porta Portese market

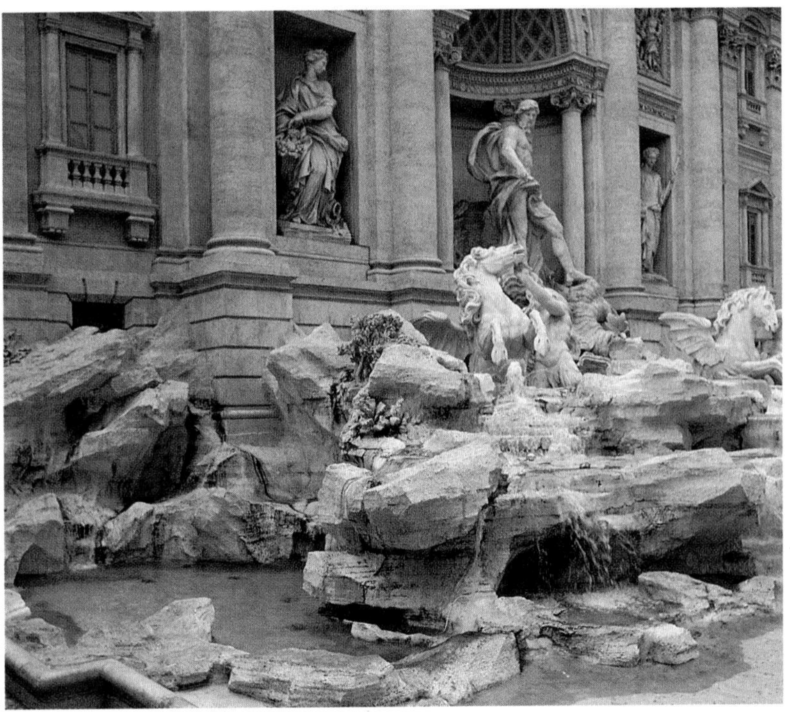

Fontana di Trevi

My Rome
by voices past and present

"In Rome you long for the country; in the country – oh inconstant! – you praise the distant city to the stars"

– Horace

"The frost is over and done, the south wind laughs,
And, to the very tiles of each red roof
A-smoke i' the sunshine, Rome lies gold and glad."

– Robert Browning

"Whoever has nothing else left in life should come to live in Rome; there he will find a land which will nourish his reflections, walks which will always tell him something new. The stone which crumbles under his feet will speak to him, and even the dust which the wind raises under his footsteps will seem to bear with it something of human grandeur."

– François-René de Chateaubriand

"Rome is a world, and it would take years to become a true citizen of it. How lucky those travelers are who take one look and leave."

– Johann Wolfgang von Goethe

"When Rome gets to you with that ancient enchantment, all the negative pronouncements you may have delivered about her disappear, and you only know that it is good luck to be living here."

– Federico Fellini

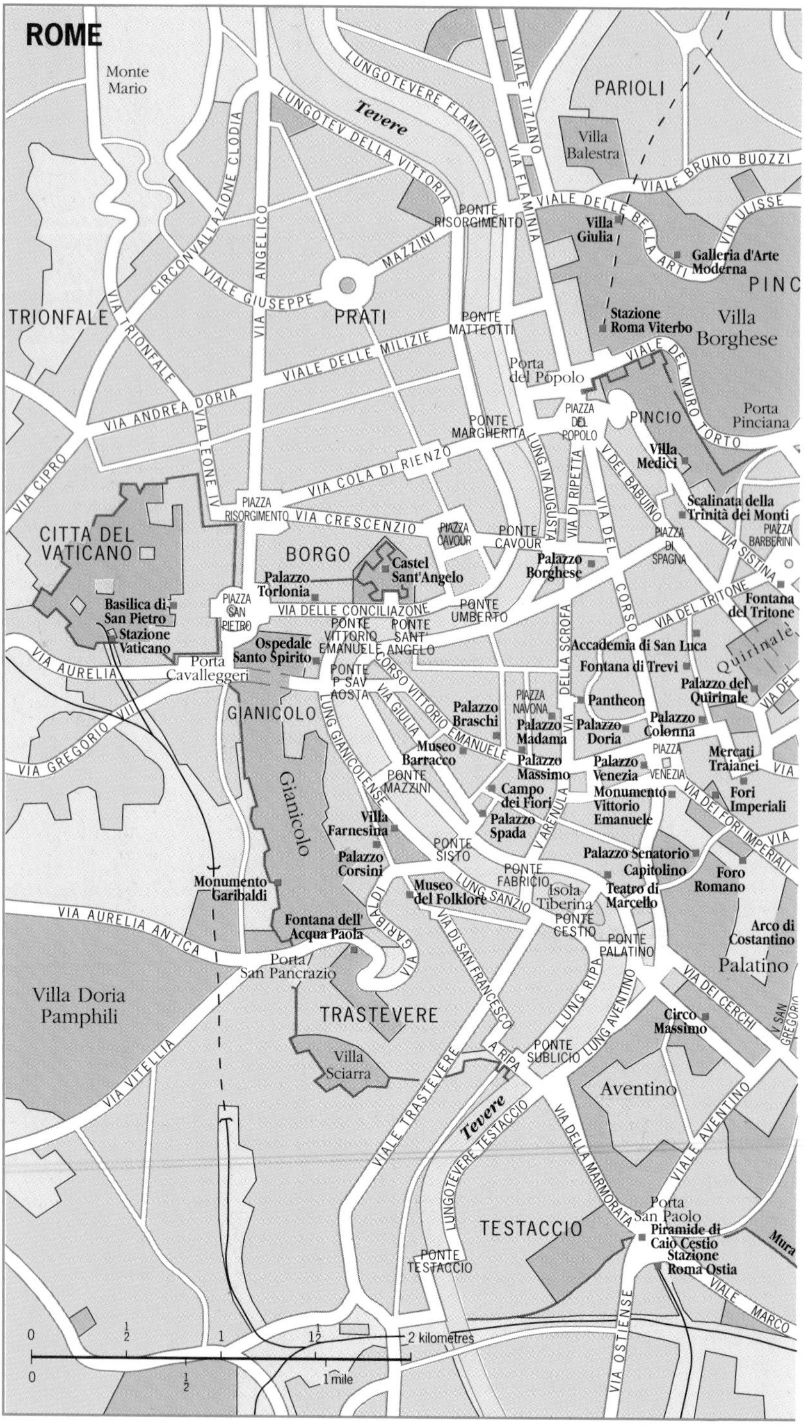

ROME

Monte Mario
Tevere
LUNGOTEVERE FLAMINIO
LUNGOTEV DELLA VITTORIA
VIALE TIZIANO
VIA FLAMINIA
PARIOLI
Villa Balestra
VIALE BRUNO BUOZZI
VIA ULISSE
CIRCONVALLAZIONE CLODIA
VIA ANGELICO
PONTE RISORGIMENTO
VIALE DELLE BELLE ARTI
Villa Giulia
Galleria d'Arte Moderna
PINC
VIALE GIUSEPPE MAZZINI
TRIONFALE
VIA TRIONFALE
PRATI
PONTE MATTEOTTI
Stazione Roma Viterbo
Villa Borghese
VIALE DELLE MILIZIE
Porta del Popolo
VIALE DEL MURO TORTO
VIA ANDREA DORIA
VIA LEONE IV
PONTE MARGHERITA
PIAZZA DEL POPOLO
PINCIO
Porta Pinciana
VIA CIPRO
VIA COLA DI RIENZO
LUNG IN AUGUSTA
VIA DI RIPETTA
VIA DEL CORSO
V DEL BABUINO
Villa Medici
PIAZZA RISORGIMENTO
VIA CRESCENZIO
Scalinata della Trinità dei Monti
CITTA DEL VATICANO
PIAZZA CAVOUR
PONTE CAVOUR
PIAZZA DI SPAGNA
VIA SISTINA
PIAZZA BARBERINI
BORGO
Castel Sant'Angelo
Palazzo Borghese
Palazzo Torlonia
Basilica di San Pietro
PIAZZA SAN PIETRO
VIA DELLE CONCILIAZONE
PONTE UMBERTO
VIA DEL TRITONE
Fontana del Tritone
Stazione Vaticano
PONTE VITTORIO EMANUELE
PONTE SANT' ANGELO
Ospedale Santo Spirito
VIA DELLA SCROFA
Accademia di San Luca
Quirinale
VIA AURELIA
Porta Cavalleggeri
PONTE P SAV AOSTA
CORSO VITTORIO EMANUELE
Fontana di Trevi
Palazzo del Quirinale
VIA DEL
VIA GIULIA
PIAZZA NAVONA
Pantheon
GIANICOLO
VIA GREGORIO VII
LUNG GIANICOLENSE
Palazzo Braschi
Palazzo Madama
Palazzo Doria
Palazzo Colonna
Museo Barracco
PIAZZA VENEZIA
Mercati Traianei
VIA
Gianicolo
PONTE MAZZINI
Palazzo Massimo
Palazzo Venezia
Campo dei Fiori
Monumento Vittorio Emanuele
Fori Imperiali
VIA DEI FORI IMPERIALI
VIA ARENULA
Villa Farnesina
Palazzo Spada
PONTE SISTO
Palazzo Senatorio
Palazzo Corsini
PONTE FABRICIO
Capitolino
Foro Romano
Monumento Garibaldi
Museo del Folklore
LUNG SANZIO
Isola Tiberina
Teatro di Marcello
VIA GARIBALDI
VIA AURELIA ANTICA
Fontana dell' Acqua Paola
PONTE CESTIO
Arco di Costantino
VIA DI SAN FRANCESCO
PONTE PALATINO
Porta San Pancrazio
Palatino
Villa Doria Pamphili
LUNG RIPA
LUNG AVENTINO
VIA DEI CERCHI
TRASTEVERE
Circo Massimo
V SAN GREGORIO
VIA VITELLIA
A RIPA
PONTE SUBLICIO
Villa Sciarra
VIALE TRASTEVERE
Aventino
Tevere
LUNGOTEVERE TESTACCIO
VIA DELLA MARMORATA
VIALE AVENTINO
Porta San Paolo
TESTACCIO
Mura
Piramide di Caio Cestio
Stazione Roma Ostia
PONTE TESTACCIO
VIALE MARCO
VIA OSTIENSE

0 ½ 1 1½ 2 kilometres
0 ½ 1 mile

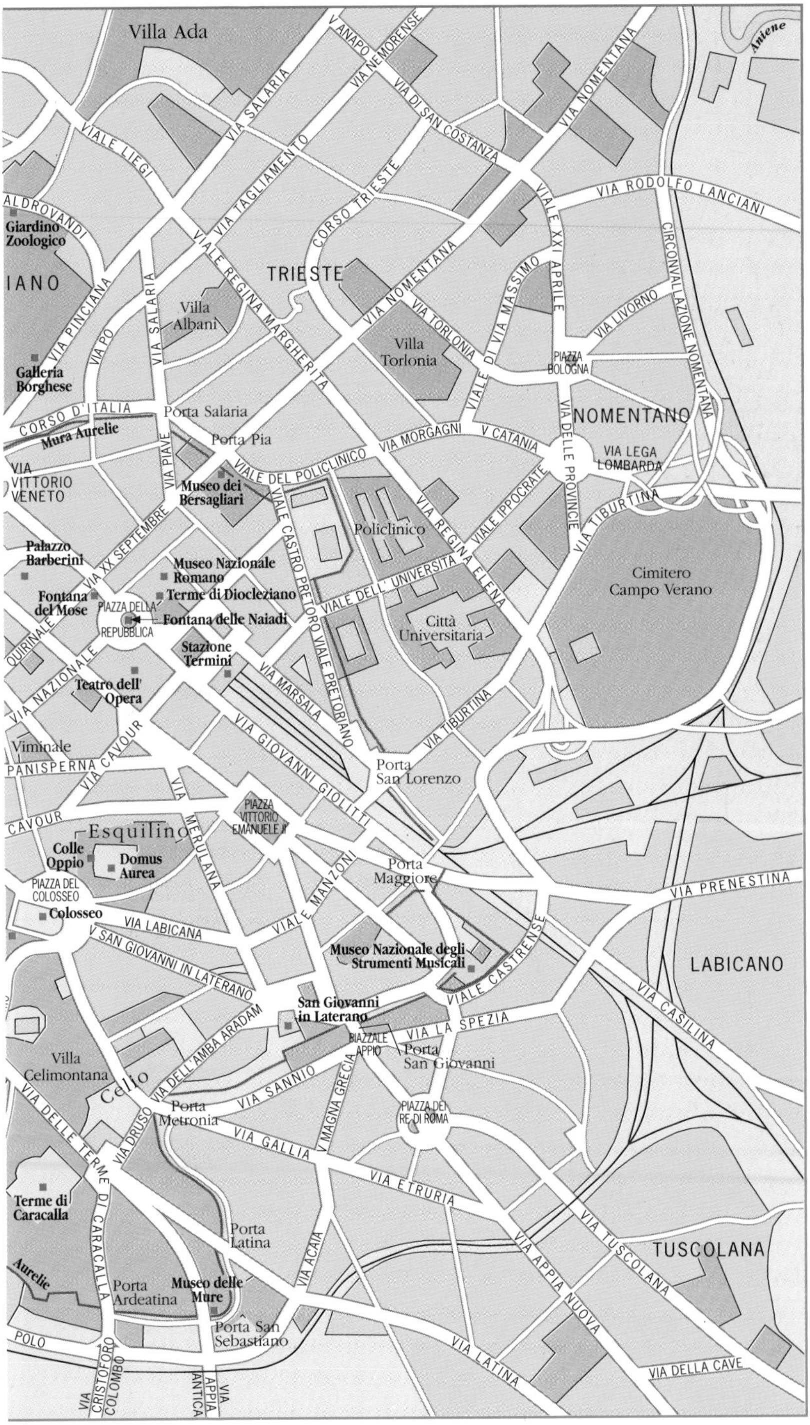

Villa Ada
Aniene
V. ANAPO
VIA NEMORENSE
VIA SALARIA
VIA DI SAN COSTANZA
VIA NOMENTANA
VIALE LIEGI
VIA TAGLIAMENTO
CORSO TRIESTE
VIA RODOLFO LANCIANI
ALDROVANDI
Giardino Zoologico
VIALE REGINA MARGHERITA
TRIESTE
VIALE XXI APRILE
VIA DI VIA MASSIMO
CIRCONVALLAZIONE NOMENTANA
IANO
VIA PINCIANA
VIA SALARIA
Villa Albani
VIA NOMENTANA
VIA TORLONIA
VIA LIVORNO
VIA PO
Villa Torlonia
PIAZZA BOLOGNA
Galleria Borghese
CORSO D'ITALIA
Porta Salaria
VIA DELLE PROVINCIE
NOMENTANO
Mura Aurelie
Porta Pia
VIA MORGAGNI
V. CATANIA
VIA LEGA LOMBARDA
VIA VITTORIO VENETO
VIA PIAVE
VIALE DEL POLICLINICO
Museo dei Bersagliari
VIALE IPPOCRATE
VIA XX SETTEMBRE
VIALE CASTRO PRETORIO
Policlinico
VIA REGINA ELENA
VIA TIBURTINA
Palazzo Barberini
Museo Nazionale Romano
Cimitero Campo Verano
VIALE DELL' UNIVERSITÀ
Fontana del Mose
Terme di Diocleziano
PIAZZA DELLA REPUBBLICA
Fontana delle Naiadi
Città Universitaria
QUIRINALE
Stazione Termini
VIA NAZIONALE
Teatro dell' Opera
VIA MARSALA
VIALE PRETORIANO
VIA TIBURTINA
VIA CAVOUR
VIA GIOVANNI GIOLITTI
Viminale
PANISPERNA
Porta San Lorenzo
VIA MERULANA
PIAZZA VITTORIO EMANUELE II
CAVOUR
Esquilino
Colle Oppio
Domus Aurea
VIALE MANZONI
Porta Maggiore
PIAZZA DEL COLOSSEO
VIA PRENESTINA
Colosseo
VIA LABICANA
V. SAN GIOVANNI IN LATERANO
VIALE CASTRENSE
Museo Nazionale degli Strumenti Musicali
LABICANO
VIA CASILINA
San Giovanni in Laterano
VIA DELL'AMBA ARADAM
PIAZZALE APPIO
VIA LA SPEZIA
Porta San Giovanni
Villa Celimontana
Celio
VIA SANNIO
V. MAGNA GRECIA
VIA DELLE TERME DI CARACALLA
Porta Metronia
PIAZZA DEI RE DI ROMA
VIA DRUSO
VIA GALLIA
VIA ETRURIA
Terme di Caracalla
Porta Latina
VIA APPIA NUOVA
VIA TUSCOLANA
TUSCOLANA
Aurelie
VIA ACAIA
Porta Ardeatina
Museo delle Mure
Porta San Sebastiano
POLO
VIA LATINA
VIA DELLA CAVE
VIA CRISTOFORO COLOMBO
VIA APPIA ANTICA

Agony and Ecstasy

We expect a lot of Rome – seat of empire, mother of civilization, *caput mundi* – the head of the world. It is the city of the Caesars, of romance, of the *dolce vita*, of languorous sunny days, of endless galleries of art, of churches and museums, of fountain-splashed piazzas, and of majestic monuments to its golden age of empire. . . .

<< Stendhal's Syndrome: There is a passage in Stendhal's *Journal* where he alludes to the symptoms of excessive consumption of culture: "If the foreigner who enters St. Peter's tries to see everything, he will develop a furious headache, and presently satiety and pain will render him incapable of any pleasure." >>

The modern reality As well as being a golden city, however,Rome is also the city of unendurable, uncontrollable traffic; the city of frenetic noise and confusion; the city of wanton crowds, obstinate bureaucracy, and groaning inefficiency. The city's brash, 20th-century face is not a pretty one, and to get under its chaotic, rumpled skin requires an iconoclastic approach to the received sightseeing orthodoxy. Plan ahead; don't attempt too much or tackle its streets in the heat of the afternoon. Head-on confrontation with the city, however energetically you join battle, always leaves you the dispirited loser.

Different approach Avoid the temptation to join the obedient trudge around the famous sights. Avoid St. Peter's and the Sistine Chapel; forget the Colosseum and the Pantheon, at least in the beginning; and reflect instead over a quiet cappuccino in Campo dei Fiori, the city's loveliest square. Forgo the Spanish Steps' aimless mob and climb to the Pincio Gardens for a view over the rooftops to St. Peter's. Thus baptized you can prepare for the serious assault on the Vatican museums or the stroll around the Forum; you can face the traffic and the chaos – and perhaps, in time, even come to enjoy them as vital, dynamic aspects of a city that is struggling, as it has for centuries, to incorporate the present into its eternal past.

<< *"I was so moved in the Forum that I almost fell asleep. Rome reminds me of a man who lives by exhibiting to travellers his grandmother's corpse"– James Joyce* >>

Sightseers jostle to put their three coins in the fountain.

■ Romans are a race apart – and one not always highly thought of by many of their fellow Italians. Follow the famous adage and "do as the Romans do," say some fellow Italians, and you may do nothing at all. They are reflecting on outrageous stereotype, of course, but occasionally it is possible to glimpse the unpalatable. . . . .■

Image problem Romans are said to squander the money earned by the rest of the country; they hand down laws but ignore them at their leisure. They are the root of all evil and of all Italy's ills. A distortion of Rome's noble SPQR *(Senatus Populusque Romanus,* the Senate and Roman Populace) – *sono porchi questi Romani* – "they are pigs, these Romans" is the Italians' pithy summation of their capital's citizens. As always there is some truth in the myths. A smile and a little stuttered Italian may well bring you courtesy, but more often than not, you will despair of the Romans.

Under pressure Like many urban dwellers they have adopted harsh measures in the battle to survive. As the city explodes, the problems faced – unemployment, housing, traffic, drugs – have brought still more exaggerated responses from its beleaguered citizens. Romans have to deal not only with too many other Romans, but with a flood tide of tourists. For visitors this can result in a gruff response bordering on rudeness. They excel in the art of *nonmifreghismo* – of "not giving a damn," an oft-heard piece of slang *(non mi frega).*

<< Rome's official population is 2.8 million. Its actual population is probably nearer 4 million, perhaps higher. In recent years figures have been swollen by Italy's first wave of immigrants, mainly from the Philippines, Somalia, Ethiopia, North Africa, and Eastern Europe. >>

Quintessential Romans A handful of Felliniesque survivors can be found. They hark back to an old Rome, when it was a city of 500,000 people – a city whose facilities matched its needs. You see them in the potbellied restaurateurs, the dog-walking old women, the grumpily sarcastic bartenders, the fallen aristocrats, the rough-fingered matriarchs of the market stalls and in the loose jowls and hooked noses that could never be anything but Roman.

Shades of Roman style

■ In many respects Rome is not a religious city at all. Fewer than 10 percent of its population attends Mass, and Catholicism's bugbears – divorce, abortion, and birth control – are as freely available as in most European countries. . . .■

<< The Vatican still has an office for the *Avvocato del Diavolo* – the Devil's Advocate – from which the expression originally derives. His job is to investigate the lives of prospective saints and beatifics to find all the reasons they should not be accepted into the ranks of sainthood. **>>**

Christian center In other ways, however, Rome qualifies as one of the holiest spots on Earth – world capital of Christianity – at least in its Roman Catholic guise; home to hundreds of churches; shrine to saints, martyrs and the apostles Peter and Paul; seat of the pope, supreme spiritual head of 850 million Catholics worldwide.

Historical center This holy heritage stems from historical serendipity, its roots in the fertile ground of ancient Rome's propensity for myth, superstition and pagan observance. The Empire was a collecting ground of cults and religions. Rome was its great melting pot, mixing a heady brew of gods and deities from Greek, Latin and Etruscan ingredients. Wandering the Forum, you might have sampled any one of dozens of recipes for salvation – Mithraism; Judaism; the worship of Isis, Osiris and Atargatis; Christianity; Manichaenism – along with some strange one-shots like the goddess Cybele, whose priests were expected to indulge in ritual self-castration.

Pagan inheritance Christianity was already blooming when Constantine sanctioned its practice in AD 313, but it still owed much to its antecedents. Unable to shake off pagan deities at a stroke, it simply incorporated their trappings. Old festivals were given new names – December's Saturnalia became Christmas, Isis' day of the dead became November's All Souls' Day – and new churches were raised literally from the ruins of old temples. Incense, candles, holy water, even marriage rites, were all commandeered from Roman ceremonies.

The papal influence Overseeing all then, as today, was the pope, St. Peter's spiritual successor. Over and above religious clout, pontiffs enjoyed centuries of political power, administered first from the "Mother of all Churches," San Giovanni in Laterano, and later from St. Peter's. They ruled much of Italy for years, with uneven results, reluctantly relinquishing the Papal States to a newly unified Italy in 1870. Thereafter they sulked in limbo in the Vatican, emerging only in 1929 after Mussolini's Lateran Treaty, which formalized Church and State relations and created the independent Vatican territory.

Today St. Peter's and the pope brood over Rome, but have only indirect power over its morals or its destiny. Divorce and abortion were regularized by the state in the 1970s, and the Vatican now deals mainly with clerical affairs – though it has a corporate side as well, and one prone to occasional financial scandal (illustrated by the $241 million paid out in compensation during the Banco Ambrosiano affair).

Church hierarchy Within the papal administration the pope is followed by the secretary of state, the Curia, or church government, and 10 congregations, each headed by a

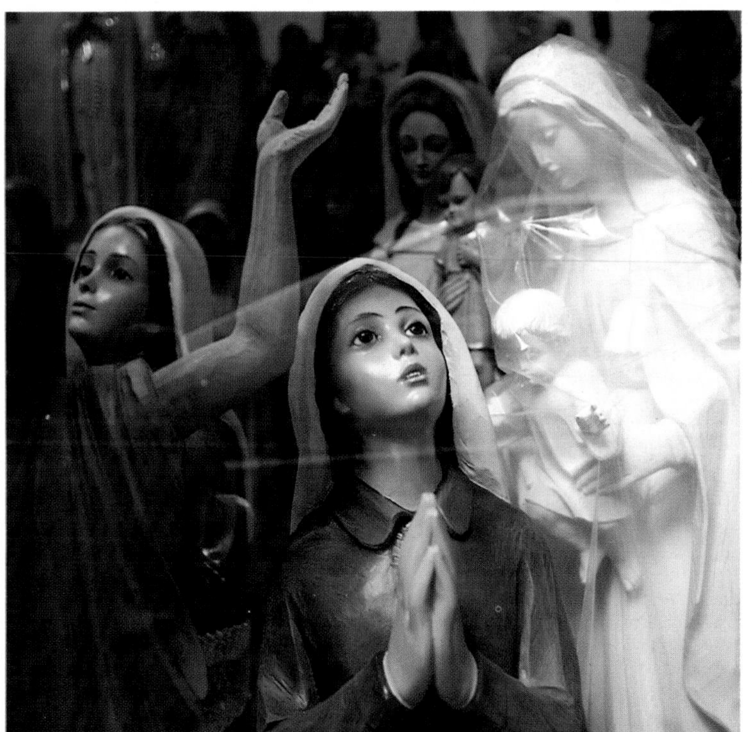

Symbols of religion on sale in the capital of Catholicism

cardinal, to deal with such matters as the Doctrine of the Faith (the Inquisition in earlier incarnations). Once all 10 posts were reserved for Italians – now only one has a native incumbent, a measure of the degree to which the power base of Catholicism has spread to the countries of Africa and Latin America. Few pilgrims from these poorer countries can manage the trip to the Holy City, though all 4,000 bishops worldwide must report to *Rome ad limina Apostolorum* – to the "threshold of the Apostles" – every five years.

Other denominations At the opposite extreme of papal pomp are Rome's Christian charity workers, currently numbering around 5,000 and always on the increase. Nor should one overlook the other religions that set up shop in Catholicism's capital:

<< Papal election is by one of three methods: acclamation – in which divine intervention causes all the cardinals to call one name in unison (not common); by majority vote, with votes cast four times daily until a candidate has a two- thirds majority; or by compromise, in which the recommendation of a commission is accepted. **>>**

Rome is about to see its first mosque (on Via Forte Antenne in Parioli). It boasts some 20,000 Jews and six synagogues and huge numbers of Pentecostals (the largest group after Catholics), Protestant congregations, and even Seventh Day Adventists and the Salvation Army – all of which are a far cry from the pre-19th-century days when the "heathen" had to be buried in unhallowed ground in the dead of night in San Paolo's "Protestant" cemetery.

Politics

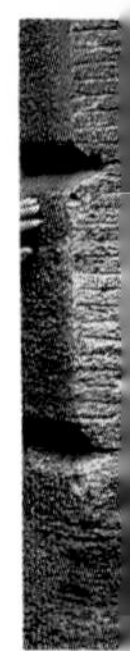

■ It is a matter of little concern, and certainly little pride, to Romans that their city is the seat of Italy's government. Most would rather forget the fact, treating Italian politics with the indifference or weary disdain it largely deserves. Attention in bars and at breakfast tables is more likely to be focused on football than on the latest scandal or umpteenth reshuffling of ministers. Below the surface, however, politics plays an underestimated part in Rome's daily life. . . .■

The city's role in government has an obvious historical inevitability. Mussolini marched on Rome, not on Milan. Memorials and ruins to a time when this city ruled over the (then) known world lie at every turn. For centuries popes ran far-flung dominions from here. When Italy was unified and Rome wrested from the papacy in 1870, there was no question of the new state's capital being elsewhere. The word had its origins in the city's Capitoline Hill. Not that this meant that Rome was remotely suitable for the part. Of a population of 200,000 in 1870, an estimated one-third were beggars, following the upheavals of Napoleonic invasion and local uprisings, and there was little infrastructure and nothing in the way of recent democratic rhetoric. This didn't stop the commandeering of palaces for politicians or the building of bleak ministerial mausoleums for the civil servants.

Flying the flag for a free voice in politics

Symbolic capital But if Rome's role was dubious then, today it is even more open to question. Although it still fulfills a geographic purpose – balanced between Italy's wealthy north and backward south (the existence of this gap is itself an indictment of political impotence) – real power has now moved to the big cities of the north: Milan, Turin and others. It is here that the country's major payoffs, power-broking and arm-twisting take place. What stops the government from following is tradition, vested interest, and the inertia of bricks and cement. At first glance you see little evidence of Rome's political primacy – perhaps the odd cavalcade of ministerial cars carving through the traffic, sirens screaming. Within numberless anonymous buildings, however, many thousands of civil servants are beavering away – in theory at least – on the nation's behalf. Some belong to quite

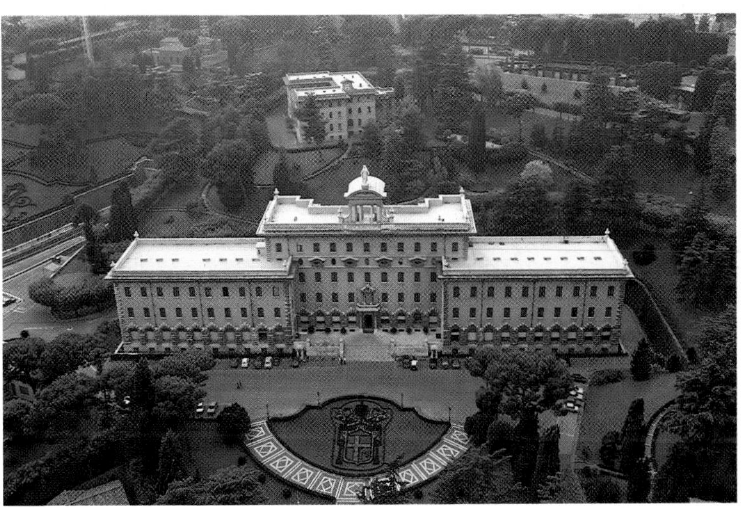

The Vatican Gardens: the Church has an active political role

obvious institutions like the Presidential Palazzo del Quirinale, and the two houses of the Italian Parliament in Palazzo Madama and Palazzo Montecitorio. Others have more obscure hideaways – like the huge ministries tucked away in the suburbs; the headquarters of nationalized industries, or the labyrinthine departments woven into city-center palaces.

Status quo No one should underestimate the numbers – and thus the weight of vested interest – involved. Rome has some 600,000 office workers, most of them in state employ (six times its industrial work force). Dismantling these dinosaurs and firing the civil servants would be political suicide. Nor should Rome's other political monolith be forgotten – the Vatican. Church politics in the capital of Catholicism is as convoluted, perhaps even as nefarious, as its lay counterpart across the Tiber. Monks, priests and cardinals, not to mention another dragoon of civil servants, work quietly to administer an empire whose 2,000-year history has accustomed it to the long view. They can still make mistakes, as the occasional scandal shows, despite having been in the political game longer than anyone. However, the lesson learned has served greater Italian politics well.

Local government Finally, as if the Romans didn't have enough politics to contend with, they also have to put up with Rome's local government, which has the unenviable task of administering the city's day-to-day functioning, a job it tackles mainly by copying on a small scale all the various moves and machinations of state government. There was a time in the 1980s when the Communists had charge of the city, a time looked back on now by people of all political opinion as a sort of golden age. A genuine effort was made to tackle the traffic, transportation was rationalized and improved, restorations were initiated and a popular summer festival was inaugurated. All this went by the board when politics turned full circle and the old guard forced its way back. Tellingly, the last time anything substantial was achieved in Rome, it had little or nothing to do with politics. It was effected by Italy's other prime mover – football, the Italia '90 World Cup – a jamboree that precipitated a huge cleanup, a new railway, roads, face-lifted station and much more. Romans must hope for another international sporting event – it may all happen again.

Crumbling

Conservation has never been Rome's strong point. Parts of the ancient city have been carted off for as long as any one can remember. The barbarians started it, the church builders continued it, and ordinary Romans are finishing off the job. . . .

<< Within a week of Rome's center being closed to traffic, some 6,000 special-access passes had been issued to a mysterious upsurge of "handicapped" drivers. In the "totally prohibited" areas of the *centro storico* 5,000 people have managed to obtain VIP *permessi* to enter at will. >>

Grime-fighting: a losing battle?

Restoring glory No one doubts the burden of Rome's heritage, but until recently efforts to salvage it have been woeful. Now restoration in Rome is finally under way on a large scale. City fathers have found the will, and leading companies have taken to sponsoring a prominent cleanup.

Monuments that emerge gleaming from their tarpaulin shrouds, however, quickly fall prey to the city's appalling air pollution. Most filth comes from domestic heating systems, now less virulent than they were, and from the motor car. Attempts to ban cars seem doomed to failure: it is hard to see the Romans giving up their cars.

Long way to go Look at the Arco di Constantino, the Colonna Traiano, even the Fontana di Trevi, all recently cleaned, for the telltale film of gray. In some cases remains have simply been removed from danger, as with the Campidoglio's statue of Marco Aurelio. In others restoration itself has aroused controversy, as with the cleaning of Michelangelo's frescos in the Sistine Chapel. Elsewhere museums are closed or half derelict – the Museo delle Terme, Santo Stefano Rotondo – awaiting money, political decisions, or both.

The tourism factor Rome's millions of annual tourists are largely but not entirely blameless. Their invasion brings in cash, but increases the pressure on an already-squeezed city. The unending, roaring columns of tour buses at the Vatican and Colosseum are a sobering sight.

Eternal city? Cycles of decay are nothing new. Today, though, the city is at a crisis point. Something must give – one hopes it is the traffic.

Immigration

Immigration may seem a strange thing to highlight in a city's day-to-day life, but it is a phenomenon that has brought about Rome's most visible transformation since around 1988. Over the past few years Italy has experienced its first large-scale immigrations, an ironic turnabout for a country that historically has suffered some of Europe's greatest emigrations to the New World. . . .

Relaxing on a Roman street

Cosmopolitan influx Some say as many as half a million Eastern Europeans, Somalians, Ethiopians, North Africans, Filipinos and Albanians are seeking a new life in the city. Many have blended into its ebb and flow; some, like the Russian Jews, have moved on; others, inevitably, have become marginalized. The most visible example of this underclass is to be found nightly around Termini, where thousands gather to talk, drink, cook, and even set up stalls to sell keepsakes and mementos of their home countries.

So far there has been little overt racism, and Roman reaction has been almost bemused. Unsavory incidents occasionally make the press, and then mass solidarity is shown, as with a Somalian woman insulted on a bus who received a public apology from Rome's mayor. Although these are early days, Italians seem to be accepting immigrants with civilized good grace.

Gypsies This is more than can be said of their reaction to gypsies, who all have the misfortune of being equated in the public eye with the gangs of street urchins that pester tourists in the city center. Most visitors will encounter these fearless, fearsome children sooner or later. The children's usual ploy is to shove a piece of card in your stomach and then rifle your pockets, and they are almost impossible to shake off. Otherwise most gypsies live quietly on the city's fringes.

Their few rogue offspring, however, are probably Rome's most visible sign of crime – if you discount its thousands of illegally parked cars. Otherwise the city's criminal horror stories are largely exaggerated – visitors themselves often invite trouble through carelessness, usually by flaunting expensive cameras, by leaving bags on café tables, or by displaying bulging wallets in back pockets. Take care in crowded streets and buses (wear bags across your chest like Roman women, not over one shoulder) and use common sense when walking at night. Rome does have its share of desperate drug addicts; avoid in particular the parks and Tiber embankments.

La Dolce Vita

For a few heady months Rome was to the 1950s what "swinging London" was to the 1960s – the world's trendsetter, a place inhabited by sunglassed Latin Lotharios and pouting, lean-limbed starlets. Open sports cars flashed down the Via Veneto, and people partied late into Rome's long, lethargic summer nights. Fellini caught it all in *La Dolce Vita,* and the myth was secure. . . .

The reality What really happened, however, was less important than what appeared to happen. Perhaps a few gilded individuals played the part, or perhaps the Romans did have the knack of the soft, sweet, easy life. Times were good, the sun shone, and Italians had money for the first time. For most Romans, though, the *dolce vita* passed them by. Even Fellini's film ended in disillusionment, the waters of the Trevi Fountain failing as the stars met for their famous embrace. Behind them the lights went off to underline the shallow futility of it all. Marcello Mastroianni was left high and dry, and the statuesque Anita Ekberg took her plunging neckline elsewhere.

Lingering memories But if the reality was hollow, the images of the era have lived on in the popular imagination. Modern visitors may be disappointed by the Via Veneto's old stamping grounds, and would-be bathers in the Fontana di Trevi face prompt arrest, but they still look for and find hints of the old days. These hints exist because Rome has always been made for the easy life. The sun shines; the settings are romantic; the evenings are long; and Romans, on the whole, are good-looking people who like to see and be seen. Take a table at the **Bar della Pace** or walk down Via Condotti's parade of exclusive shops for proof that the *dolce vita* is still alive and well.

Indolence, indulgence, romance So too, however, is the ennui that goes with it. It is often possible to detect a strange torpor, apparently unique to the city, as is the peculiar breed who revel in the most extraordinary expenditure – you'll see these over-dressed, bejeweled creatures and their bijou shops at every turn.

Casual visitors should ignore these tanned horrors and delight instead in the aspects of Rome's *dolce vita* still open to all – a few carefree days of cafés and cappuccinos before the return to that other, less *dolce* life at the holiday's end.

Anita Ekberg enjoys La Dolce Vita *in the Trevi Fountain*

Romans are not all stylish – numerous Roman bellies slopping out of ill-fitting T-shirts provide ample evidence to the contrary. But style and fashion sense are bred in the majority from childhood. This is just as well, for in few places are the rigors of creating a *bella figura* so strong. . . .

<< The Romans' propensity for dressing up was already evident in Classical times. In the 2nd century AD Juvenal observed that "in Rome men dress in a showy style beyond their means." (*Satires*) >>

Image is all Flouting this powerful convention is a social taboo, and for Romans there are few things as shamful as standing out from the crowd. Their city is second to Milan in the fashion stakes, with none of its seasonal *sfilate,* or shows, nor their accompanying media razzmatazz. But where Milan scores with its high-profile designers, Rome is the territory of the old-world *stilista* and high-class tailor. It still boasts the doyen of *haute couture,* or *alta moda,* designers, Valentino, who for a king's ransom will run up individually crafted creations. There is also a host of eminent tailors, who for years have catered to the city's ancient aristocracy – Battistoni, Gucci and Locatelli are the most venerable names – all with outlets in Via Condotti, the center of Roman chic.

Big names Other leading Italian names have boutiques nearby. Style doesn't stop at clothes, however, and the hairdressers and beauty salons of Rome can be of extraordinary – and vulgar – opulence. Take a peek at **Sergio Valente** on Via Condotti, complete with movie-star room and private boxes. Shoes, belts, and all manner of accessories of the highest quality and prices are also available to satisfy the most demanding style warriors.

Showing off Neither style nor fashion, however, are the reserve of the rich; Romans dress well, even for the most humble tasks. The younger and more down to earth have their fashion parade in the Via del Corso, a thoroughfare crammed with middle-of-the road clothes shops. There are also the street markets or department stores like **Upim** and **Standa,** whose cheaper clothes the Romans still wear with dash and style.

Roman dress sense starts young

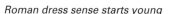

Myth and Legend

The legends of Rome's foundation are far more interesting than the truth – not that historians have been able to agree on what the truth may be. Romulus and Remus is the story everyone knows, twins suckled by a she-wolf on the Palatine, one of whom, Romulus, grew up to be first king of Rome. . . .

<< The Rape of the Sabine Women reputedly occurred in 750 BC, when Romans – short of women – attempted to steal those of the neighboring Sabine tribes. >>

Romulus and Remus Like many other myths, this one was codified by Livy, a 1st-century historian, and by the *Aeneid*, an epic poem by his contemporary, Virgil. Livy's tale begins in the old Latin capital *Alba Longa* with the king Numitor, whose throne was stolen by his brother Amulius. To avoid rival claims, Amulius forced Numitor's only daughter, Rhea Silvia, to become a vestal virgin. The god Mars appeared to Rhea and left her pregnant with Romulus and Remus; Amulius cast the twins adrift in a basket. The gods, however, steered them to safety in the *Velabrum*, the old marshes under the Palatine hill. A she-wolf cared for the twins until they were found by a shepherd. In adulthood Mars appeared to tell them of their destiny, and they founded Rome, said Livy, in 753 BC.

Naming Rome However, both twins then wanted to rule, and neither could agree on a name. Remus favored *Rema*, Romulus preferred *Roma*. Invoking the gods to settle the dispute, Remus saw six vultures over his hill. Romulus, however,

An early view of Rome

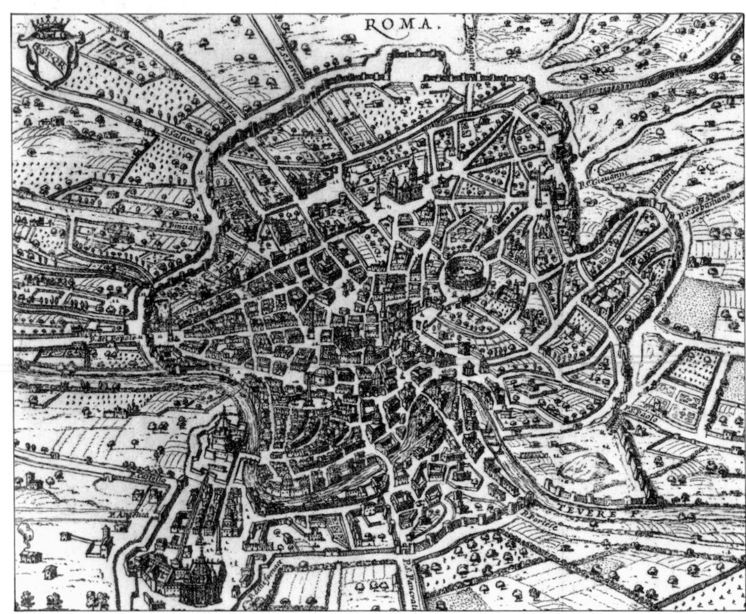

counted 12, and began building his walls on the spot. An incensed Remus jumped over them and was killed by his brother.

Mystery How Rome was founded in truth is unknown. The earliest archaeological remains are pieces of 12th-century BC pottery from the Capitolino. Some claim there were settlements here 2,000 years earlier. The Romans themselves thought that volcanic eruptions in 1000 BC forced them down to the Tiber. By

Palatine Hill, where Romulus and Remus were suckled

the 9th century BC villages were probably established on all Rome's seven hills. They formed a strategic border area between the Etruscans, who controlled much of northern Italy, and the Latins, one of several tribes who shared southern Italy with Greek settlers. The Etruscans probably ruled the settlement, which prospered increasingly from trade and communication routes.

ROME WAS *The Republic*

■ By 509 BC the Romans were powerful enough to throw off the yoke of the Etruscan kings and declare a Republic (*res publica*, a state where in theory the "public were kings"). This republic bore little relation to a modern republic, and from the outset the new order was rived by disputes between the militarist and political elite – or the patricians – and the lower classes – or the plebeians – who were to do much of Rome's fighting but initially shared in few of the spoils. . . .■

<< According to Livy, the event that precipitated the declaration of the Republic was the rape of Lucrezia. Lucrezia was a virtuous Roman matron who was raped by Tarquin the Proud. Devastated by shame, she committed public suicide the next morning. A mob of outraged Romans, led by Lucius Brutus (later to be the Republic's first consul) chased Tarquin from the city and pronounced the Republic the same day. >>

Establishing stability In 494 BC, however, the plebeians succeeded in establishing a magistracy, or *tribune*, to look after their interests. By 450 they were further placated by the Twelve Tables, a public codification of the Republic's laws, drawn up by a temporary 10-man junta called the Decemvirate and displayed in the forum on bronze tablets.

With a measure of stability established, the Romans set out to consolidate their position. The Etruscans were still powerful to the north, but their town of Veii fell in 396 BC, followed by Nepi and Sutri, cities Livy called the "barriers and gateways of Etruria." In the south the Samnites were subdued after 35 years. The greater part of Greek-dominated southern Italy soon followed.

Extending boundaries Rome's expansion, however, soon brought it into conflict with the North African power of Carthage. The Mamertines, a mercenary army ruling Messina, appealed to the Romans for help against the Carthaginians. The Romans obliged and took on their rivals in the so-called First Punic War (264—261BC) winning most of Sicily, together with Corsica and Sardinia.

Rome was now an international power, and any pretext that it had been fighting "defensive campaigns" to secure its position vanished. The motive thereafter was rampant imperial expansion. Conquered lands realized immeasurable riches, balanced budgets, built splendid monuments, oiled the military

Hannibal leads his army and elephants across the Alps

machine, reduced taxes, and provided a social cohesion that united all classes in a common purpose – though imperial booty was never to heal the divisions entirely.

The Punic Wars Events in Sicily, however, had far from removed the Carthaginian threat. Conflict returned in a series of campaigns known as the Second Punic War (214–201 BC). Carthage preempted Rome by sending Hannibal and his famous army – elephants and all – across the Alps to inflict crushing defeats on Rome at Lago Trasimeno and Cannae. Rome retaliated by sending its own charismatic general, Scipio Africanus, to Carthage's territories in Spain and Africa. Overstretched and exhausted, Hannibal was recalled, suffering eventual defeat at Zama in 202 BC. Carthage's final rout came in the Third Punic War (149–146 BC), which left Rome master of Italy, the western Mediterranean, and areas as far flung as Jerusalem and Asia Minor.

Political reform In Rome itself, however, civil strife reemerged on an unprecedented scale. An opposition group known as the Popular party attempted reforms, but inevitably ran up against the vested interests of the senatorial class, a group of rulers, the newly rich and the old landed nobility. The leader of the reformist wing, Tiberius Gracchus, who became a tribune in 133 BC, had radical plans for land reform. Like many Popular party radicals, however, he was quickly assassinated. His brother, Gaius Gracchus, proposed genuine democracy, bringing on his own murder and the declaration of martial law from the Senate. A moderate military strongman, Gaius Marius (100–91BC), was installed amid a growing awareness that the way to political power lay with the army. His influence placated neither side, however, and between 92 and 89 BC the so-called Social Wars marked an explosion of popular revolt.

The Slaves' Revolt With the connivance of the Senate, the conservative general Sulla replaced Marius in 82 BC, who for the first time used the army to settle scores with political opponents. A brutal dictatorship emerged, distinguished by murder, exile, and the destruction of cities that had sided with Marius during Sulla's ascendancy. Among other things, this dictatorship prompted the famous uprising under Spartacus (73–71 BC), a gladiator who led 70,000 slaves and dispossessed farmers to eventual defeat and a grisly death. Thus the senatorial privileges were upheld – though at the cost of any remaining ideals and institutions still clinging to the tattered Republic.

<< Six thousand of Spartacus's followers were crucified on the Via Appia Antica in the aftermath of his revolt. >>

Julius Caesar

■ After Sulla's death power passed to Pompey, an intelligent and apolitical general, and to his corrupt sidekick, Crassus, a rich property magnate. When military demands took Pompey from Rome, a third figure emerged, Julius Caesar, who on Pompey's return joined the partners to form the First Triumvirate (59 BC). . . .■

Career move Originally destined for the priesthood, Caesar joined the army in 81BC to help pay his debts. He worked his way to the post of *Pontifex Maximus*, Rome's high priest, in 63 BC, distinguishing himself with his powers of oratory and his ability as a raiser of funds.

Military campaigns From his position in the Triumvirate, Caesar bought himself the title of consul and began his military initiation. A series of triumphant campaigns followed that confirmed his genius as a general and his political ambition. Between 58 and 49 BC he fought in Germany and Gaul (France) – the Gallic Wars – launching two short invasions of Britain in 55 and 54 BC.

Crossing the Rubicon Caesar's successes irritated Pompey, who turned against his partner, thus giving Caesar the chance to retaliate. Caesar brought his army back to Italy and in 49 BC he crossed the Rubicon, an otherwise inconsequential river near Bologna. In doing so, he committed the offense of bringing an army, without permission, into territory controlled by the Senate. When Caesar reached Rome, Pompey fled and senatorial resistance crumbled. He harried Pompey and his followers through Spain, Greece and Africa, spending six months in Alexandria en route with Cleopatra, the Egyptian queen. In 48 BC he was appointed Rome's absolute ruler.

Caesar's achievements Caesar's rule was dictatorial, but achieved much to heal the scars of almost a century's civil strife. New temples and civic buildings were built and institutions were reformed. He lived in splendor, and claimed a quasi-divine status made manifest in the new Forum of Caesar. Jealousy and envy inevitably mounted, however, and a clique, including his adopted son Brutus, soon developed in the Senate, determined to overthrow him. In 44 BC, on March 15 – the "Ides of March" – the conspirators assassinated Caesar on his way to the Senate, unwittingly paving the way for Rome's imperial age.

A 19th-century engraving of Julius Caesar at the peak of his power

<< Legend has it that Julius Caesar was the first person to be born by cesarean section – the origin of the modern name for this operation. **>>**

■ A year after Caesar's murder Octavius joined Lepidus and Marcus Antonius (Mark Antony) in the so-called Second Triumvirate, a body designed to wage war on Caesar's assassins, but one that soon became a battleground for the future control of Rome. Octavius was Caesar's grandnephew and adopted son, and in time was to become Rome's first emperor (*imperator*) under the name Augustus. Thirteen years, however, were to elapse before he could take his place at the head of the Empire. . . .■

Power struggles In a move guaranteed to arouse tensions, the Triumvirate divided the Empire among them, Octavius taking the west, Lepidus taking Africa, and Mark Antony taking the east. The power struggle quickly came to be dominated by Antony and Octavius, Antony compromising his chances by repeated absences from Rome in the arms of Cleopatra. Octavius, by contrast, built up a military power base, a move that proved critical in the decisive battle of Actium (31BC). Antony was defeated, and both he and Cleopatra committed suicide, leaving Octavius the empire's sole ruler.

The age of Augustus Octavius changed his name to Augustus Caesar and assumed complete powers, his dictatorial stance belied by his modest title *princeps*, or "first citizen." Though the Republic's old institutions were kept up, Augustus occupied most of the key posts personally and retained the others as powerless sinecures.

He then embarked on a series of reforms and building projects that were to create a golden period of Roman history known as the "Augustan Age."

In the military sphere he tightened the Empire's borders, and to the disgust of many generals drew a halt to expansion for its own sake. Gains in one place, he understood, meant losses in another. In Italy he initiated huge public works – roads and aqueducts, for example – and revolutionized the face of Rome itself. In his own words he "found the city brick and left it marble." The present remains of his finest memorials suggest the scope of his achievement: the Foro di Augusto, his Mausoleo, and the Ara Pacis. Arts and literature flourished – Ovid, Virgil, and Horace were writing in this period – and Rome's population passed a million, surpassing Antioch and Alexandria to become the political, artistic, and financial center of the known world.

The Mausoleo di Augusto

The Emperors

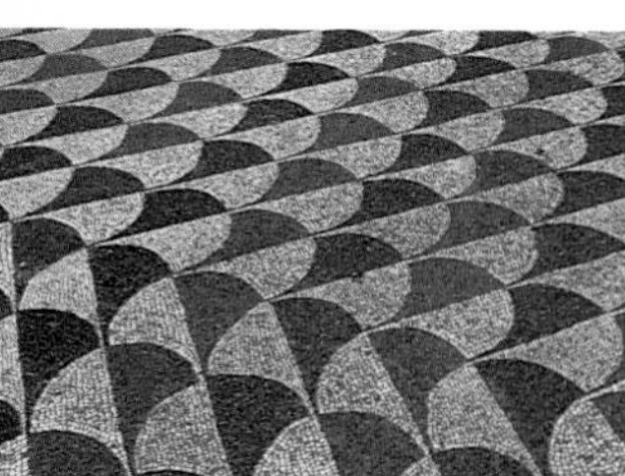

■ Rome's emperors have most resonance for many visitors. Names like Nero, Caligula, Tiberius, and Hadrian evoke both the decadence and splendor of the ancient city. Looking at their magnificent monuments, however, it is hard to believe they were presiding over an empire that in many ways was declining from the day of Augustus's death. . . .■

Power and glory Emperors often did little more than provide excellent gossip and enjoy the spoils of empire; it was usually the army or a beleaguered civil service that kept the wheels of government turning. For 200 years the Empire's wealth supported emperors' indulgences, and Rome apparently both prevailed and prospered. By about the 3rd century, however, the earlier sown seeds of decay were beginning to bear the fruits of chaos.

Augustus (27 BC–AD 14) had called a halt to wanton military expansion and installed a more or less efficient bureaucracy to oversee the Empire's daily running. Rome itself had been transformed, public works were in hand all over Italy, and the arts flourished under men like Ovid, Livy and Horace.

Claudius, emperor of decadence

Decadence and corruption When Augustus died, he was succeeded by **Tiberius** (AD 14–37), a man who ruled with comparative wisdom despite the stories of his many foibles. Gossip and mudslinging were to accompany most of the emperors – often with good reason – and most are recorded in Suetonius's *Lives of the Emperors*.

Claudius (AD 41–54) followed, ushering in an era of decadence started by Tiberius's dalliance with young boys and sexual experiments with goldfish. Southern Britain was conquered in this period, and in AD 42 St. Peter became, in effect, bishop of the city, altering the city's destiny perhaps more than any emperor. Claudius died after eating poisonous mushrooms administered by his wife, Agrippina, and his death made way for his stepson, Nero, one of the most orgiastically renowned emperors.

Nero (AD 54–68) was only 17 when he came to power, and in his youth was still a creature of restrained appetites. He thought of himself as a poet, musician and painter, rather

> **<<** Nero reveled in frivolous expenditures, on one occasion having gilded the Teatro di Pompey inside and out in just a day for the reception of King Tiridates of Armenia. **>>**

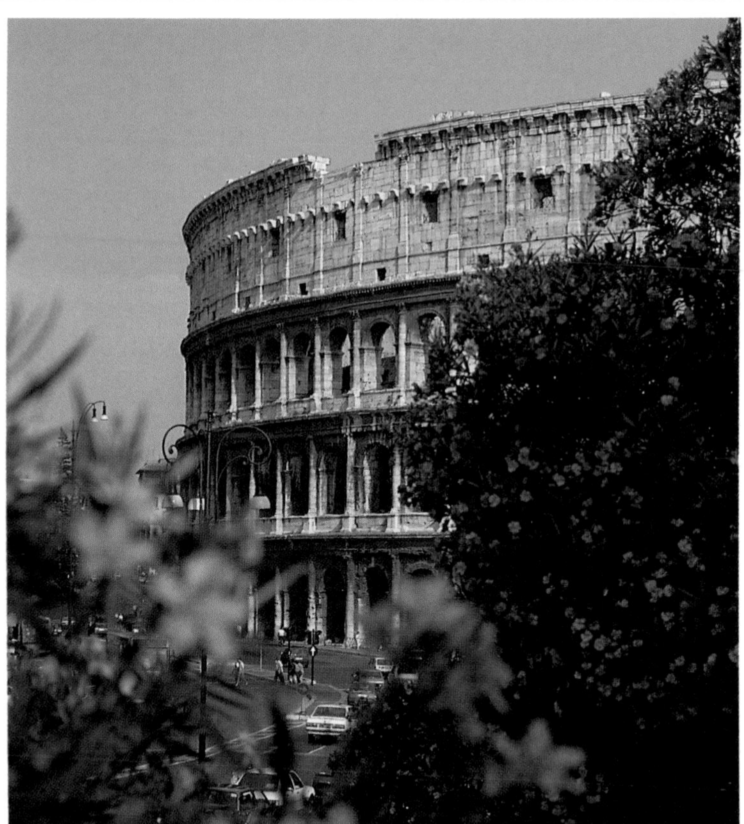

than as a ruler. In time, however, he initiated a reign of terror during which he murdered both his mother Agrippina (AD 59) and his wife Octavia (AD 62). In AD 64 a great fire swept Rome, reputedly started by Nero himself, who is famously said to have "fiddled while Rome burned." Nero blamed the conflagration on the Christians and began a period of brutal persecution that included the martyrdoms of St. Peter and St. Paul (AD 67). He also began rebuilding the city, starting with his *Domus Aurea*, or "Golden House," one of the most extravagant in the city.

Nero's profligacy, coupled with unrest in the provinces, proved to be his undoing, and when threatened by a Senate coup, he committed suicide. Three emperors then followed in a year, stability eventually being restored by the arrival of

A legacy of imperial wealth and power: the Colosseum

Vespasian (AD 69–79), founder of the so-called Flavian dynasty. The Jewish revolt broke out under Vespasian, and in the year of Titus's succession Pompeii and Herculaneum were buried by the eruption of Vesuvius near Naples.

Titus (AD 79–81) continued his father's work on the Colosseum and oversaw the destruction of Jerusalem, an event recorded in his triumphal arch, the Arco di Tito. Another great fire swept the city in AD 80, sparing the Colosseum, which was completed by **Domitian** (AD 81–96), Titus's brother. In the extravagance of the arena, not to mention the bloodletting and debauchery of its entertainment, this huge monument encapsulated the way in which many Romans lived. For each working day of the year citizens also enjoyed a day's holiday. Many, however, were also either poor, unemployed or small-time traders. At times the number on the free monthly "grain ration" – a rudimentary form of social welfare – reached as many as 200,000 in a city of about a million.

Bread and circuses This potentially unruly, idle mob was kept in check with free food and the Colosseum's gory spectacles.

<< The famous phrase *panem et circenses* was coined by the satirist Juvenal (c AD 55–140) to mock the decadent indolence of a population that had sold its real freedom for "bread and circuses." >>

Peace and relative prosperity marked Rome in the 2nd century, a period known as the "Century of the Antonines" after the rule of the five emperors of the Antonine dynasty (Nerva, Trajan, Hadrian, Antoninus, and Marcus Aurelius).

Trajan (AD 98–117) was the first native of Spain to become emperor, having been adopted by his predecessor Nerva (AD 96–98). His regime saw military campaigns that pushed the Empire's borders to their greatest extent. Under the largest army Rome had known – 300,000 strong – the city ruled territory that stretched from Spain to the Caspian Sea and from Britain to North Africa. At home Trajan left his mark in the Foro Traiano – Trajan's Forum – the grandest of the imperial forums.

The Pantheon, built by Hadrian between AD 119 and AD 128

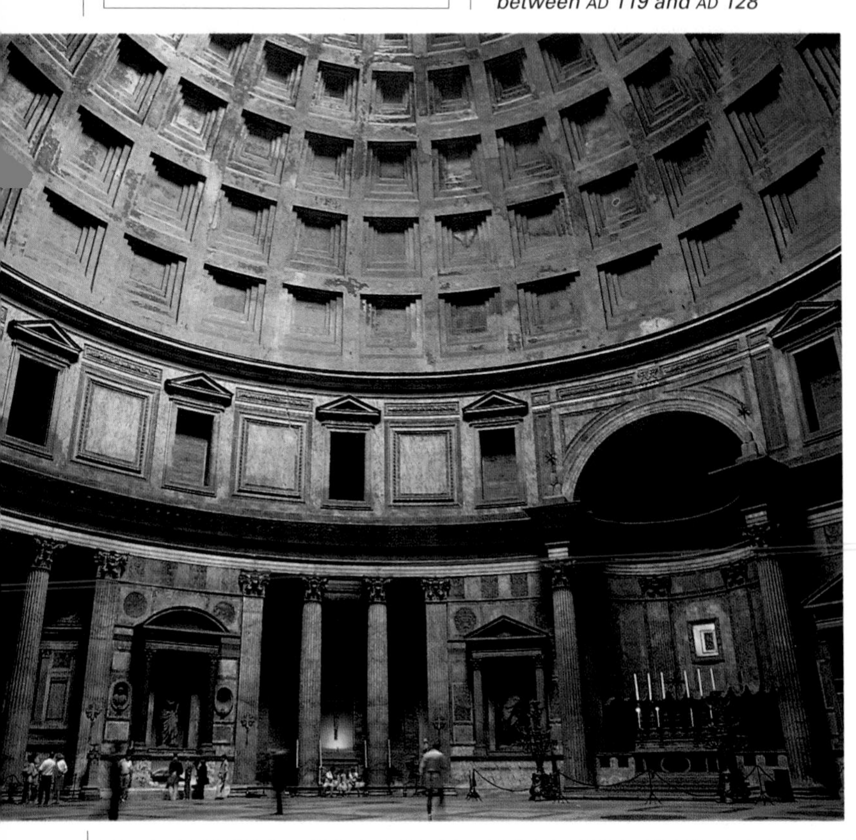

Hadrian, his successor (AD 117–138), another Spaniard, was perhaps the most culturally accomplished and civilized of any of the emperors. He is said to have visited every province in the Empire, and he had an avowed respect for Hellenistic culture, bringing Greek influences to bear on great building projects like the Pantheon, Castel Sant'Angelo, and Villa Adriano. In the military sphere he consolidated the Empire's borders and was responsible for two fortified frontiers – the Limes in Germany and the more famous Hadrian's Wall in Britain.

Marcus Aurelius (AD 161–180) was almost equally accomplished. The so-called Philosopher Emperor was both an aesthete and a capable general. During his reign, however, the threat to the Empire increased from external sources. The first heavy barbarian raids on its borders took place, and there were revolts against the Roman yoke – the Moors in Spain, Caledonians in Britain, the Parthians in Syria, the Chatti in Germany, and many more.

Turning point Aurelius's death marked a turning point in the imperial age. Emperors began to come and go with increasing rapidity. The spoils of conquest began to dry up, slaves could not be found to work, the great estates shriveled, inflation was rife, the economy entered troughs of stagnation, and emperors pawned possessions to finance the state debt. Centuries of expansion at the cost of a sound home economy began to tell. Rome's agricultural base had crumbled long ago; with unlimited free bounty from the Empire there had been little need for homegrown or home-produced goods. Farmland was bought up by Rome's ruling elite or awarded to retired army stalwarts.

Military setbacks These went hand in hand with economic crisis, and emperors increasingly failed to keep a firm grip on the army. Generals spent more time out of Rome in Mediolanum (Milan), the army's headquarters. The army had swollen to half a million men, putting increased strain on an already groaning economy. In AD 193 the praetorian guards – supposedly the emperor's personal troops – went so far as to put the Empire up for auction. The highest bidder, Didius Julianus, lasted just 66 days. Toward the end of the 2nd century, some 50 emperors ruled in the space of 70 years.

Change and decline Familiar names in the imperial ranks become fewer and fewer. **Septimius Severus** (AD 193–211) stands out as the builder of several surviving monuments, such as the Arco di Settimo Severo. His son, **Caracalla** (AD 211–217), built the Terme di Caracalla, but is better known as a psychopathic ruler who murdered his brother, Geta. **Aurelian** (AD 270–275) is remembered for his walls, the first fortifications necessary in Rome in 600 years, a sign of the imminent barbarian incursion.

In AD 286 Diocletian, as well as persecuting Christians and inventing wage and price controls, sought to ease Rome's problems by dividing the Empire into two halves, the east and west, each with separate emperors. This division merely recognized what was already reality, for the huge conquests in the east over the centuries had long left Rome on the Empire's periphery.

Recovery For a while the city enjoyed a period of recovery, notably under **Constantine** (AD 306–337), who united the Empire under a single ruler (defeating his eastern counterpart, Maxentius, at the Battle of Milvian Bridge). In AD 313 he introduced the Edict of Milan, legalizing Christianity, and undertook building projects – the last major ones in imperial Rome – that included the Arco di Constantino and early Christian basilicas, such as St. Peter's and San Giovanni in Laterano. At the same time, however, he moved the capital of the Empire to Byzantium, renamed Constantinople (modern Istanbul), which was more convenient from a strategic and administrative point of view.

■ **Constantine's brief ascendancy was merely a flicker in the empire's decline and fall, which was a gradual process, rather than a sudden collapse precipitated by the attacks of barbarian tribes. . . .■**

Gradual attrition The political mechanics of the disintegration were complicated, revolving essentially around the Goths, Huns and Vandals raiding ever closer to Rome in the absence of defended frontiers. After the death of Emperor Theodosis in AD 395, the Empire was never again united. The western half moved its capital to Ravenna on Italy's east coast. In AD 410 Alaric the Goth broke into Rome, the Western Empire collapsed, and a tremor was felt around the civilized world.

<< *When the whole world perished in one city then I was dumb with silence.* – St Jerome on the sack of Rome, AD 410. **>>**

The last Emperor Other outsiders followed, until in AD 475 Odoacer the Goth displaced the last emperor, Romulus Augustulus, as the city's ruler. For a time stability returned to Rome, though Odoacer ruled from Ravenna. It was cut short by successive raids from the Eastern Empire, still intact, under the Emperor Justinian (AD 538), and from full-blown barbarians like Totila (AD 546) and the Lombards (AD 567).

The rise of the papacy After the empire's fall, the key event in Rome's history was the emergence of the papacy as a temporal power. Many popes were of old noble stock and were able to gain influence in uncertain political times. In this they were bolstered by the arrival of the Franks, a Christian race from Gaul. In a struggle for power within their ranks, Pepin the Short appealed to Pope Stephen III to sanction his right to rule. The pope agreed, anointing the new king with holy oil (AD 754–756), a symbolic gesture of immeasurable consequence.

The Vandals attacking Rome

Politics and power In return the Franks drove the Lombards from Italy and gave parts of central Italy to the papacy, thus establishing the germ of the papal states. Pepin's son, Charlemagne, consolidated the Frankish Empire (better known as the Carolingian Empire) and on Christmas Day AD 800 was crowned Emperor of the Holy Roman Empire by Pope Leo III. By the 11th century the popes had claimed the right to crown emperors, and the northern-based emperors claimed the right to confirm the election of popes. The battle for ascendancy was to dominate Roman and European politics for many centuries to come.

The Middle Ages

Medieval Rome is scarcely imaginable today. Its population was a mere 30,000; most people were crammed into the teeming alleys opposite the Castel Sant'Angelo. Large areas of the ancient city had reverted to wilderness. There were no domes or campaniles, no fountains, none of the airy piazzas that characterize the city today. . . .

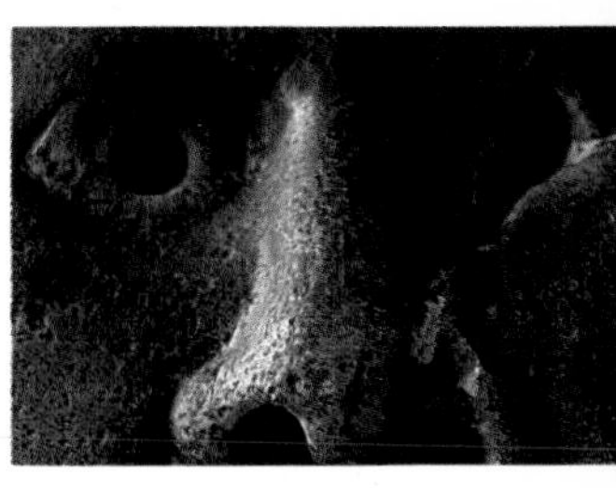

Return to light Rome emerged from the obscurity of the Dark Ages in about the year 1000, the power of the papacy newly bolstered by the support of Charlemagne's successors, the Holy Roman Emperors. Churches were built to reflect its new standing, two of which – Santa Maria sopra Minerva and Santa Maria in Cosmedin – survive as rare memorials to the city's Middle Ages. After the anarchy of the previous two centuries – when nine popes had been murdered – great reforming pontiffs like Gregory VII, better known as **Hildebrand** (1073–85), took control.

Matters thereafter again swayed off course, first with the Normans' brutal sack of Rome in 1084, and then in farces like Rome's military defeat by its tiny neighbor, Tivoli. Between 1144 and 1155 **Arnold of Brescia** was able to create a republic in defiance of both papacy and empire, brought to an end when he was captured by Emperor Frederick I and handed to the papacy for torture and execution. In **Innocent III** (1198–1216), Rome found perhaps its most powerful pope. He gained the upper hand over the Empire and much of Europe.

Political infighting Rome again had its moments in the 13th century – a few new churches and artists like Pietro Cavallini and Arnolfo del Cambio – but was constantly at the mercy of foreign powers, warring nobles, or the age-old rivalry between popes and emperors. Its medieval nemesis, however, proved to be the Great Schism of 1308, when French pressure succeeded in transferring the papacy to Avignon.

<< Rome's 14th-century chaos threw up Cola da Rienzo (1313—54), a self-educated son of a washerwoman, whose militia drove out the warring nobles. From popular hero, however, he turned into demented demagogue and was eventually torn to pieces by a mob on the banks of the Tiber.**>>**

Europe was divided until 1417 over the claims of rival popes. Papal revenues dried up, and with them papal power and patronage, plunging the city into a century of chaos.

Medieval memorial: Santa Maria in Cosmedin

The Renaissance

■ Rome could not lay claim to the Renaissance – that honor went to Florence – and when it came to the city, it came relatively late. In papal patronage, however, it had one of its great driving forces. Commissions and occasional arm-twisting brought the cream of Florentine artists south, so that every great name in the Renaissance pantheon is represented in the city. . . .■

Art in demand The popes and great Roman families needed the artists as much as the artists needed their commissions. They wanted not only memorials to their own greater glory, but also a means to impress church authority upon their flock. There were few better ways than "outstanding sights . . . great buildings . . . and divine monuments," in the words of Nicholas V, an early Renaissance pope (1447–55) who brought **Fra Angelico** to work on his personal chapel in the Vatican. The next great migration was prompted by Sixtus IV, who saw fit to commission a bevy of Tuscan and Umbrian masters (including Perugino, Botticelli and Ghirlandaio) to paint frescoes on the walls of the Sistine Chapel. The city also had its homegrown talent in **Donato Bramante.**

Michelangelo's Pietà, now behind protective glass in St. Peter's

Raphael and Michelangelo All artists took inspiration from the city's classical ruins and the wealth of ancient sculpture being excavated at the time, none more so than Raphael and Michelangelo. **Raphael** arrived from Florence in 1508 to decorate the Vatican apartments of Julius II. **Michelangelo** is best known for his Sistine Chapel frescoes, but he also left architectural schemes and planned several palaces.

Rome's Renaissance highlights
Antonio Filarete: bronze doors at St. Peter's; **Antonio Pollaiuolo:** tombs of Sixtus IV and Innocent VIII in St. Peter's; **Masolino da Panicale:** frescoes in San Clemente; **Fra Angelico:** chapel of Nicholas V (Vatican); **Filipino Lippi:** frescoes in Santa Maria sopra Minerva; **Pinturicchio:** frescoes in Santa Maria del Popolo, the Vatican, and Santa Maria in Aracoeli; **Raphael:** Vatican *stanze*, frescoes in Villa Farnesina and Santa Maria della Pace, altarpieces and paintings in the Galleria Borghese and the Vatican's Pinacoteca; **Bramante:** *Tempietto*, in San Pietro in Montorio and cloister in Santa Maria della Pace; **Michelangelo:** Sistine Chapel, *Pietá* in St. Peter's), *Moses*, in San Pietro in Vincoli, and *Redeemer*, in Santa Maria sopra Minerva.

<< The two classical works that most influenced Renaissance artists were the *Laocoön* and the *Belvedere Torso,* both now in the Vatican museums. **>>**

■ Hardly a street is passed in Rome without some reminder of the city's many dynastic families. Villas and palaces stand as permanent memorials to the host of clans that have been in the front ranks of Italian life for centuries. Some – such as the Pamphili and Borghese – still occupy the city-center palaces built by their ancestors. . . .■

Palazzo Doria Pamphili, built by two merged dynasties

Family histories Although many of these families came to prominence in the Middle Ages, most can trace their roots back 1,000 years earlier. Few, though, would claim to descend from the emperors, whose dynastic ambitions set the tone for the lesser aristocracy to come.

The senatorial class Families were more likely to descend from Rome's senatorial class, a tightly corralled group, who, in the best traditions of Italian politics, kept power within the family's confines. With the rise of Christianity the elevation of popes from leading families became the norm, establishing a continuity of power that continued to the Middle Ages and beyond. **Gregory the Great**, for example, who ruled from AD 540 to 604, was the wealthy offspring of an aristocratic senator.

Power struggles Families, such as the Orsini, Frangipani, and Colonna, begin to crop up in the city's annals as early as the 9th century, fighting one another for power, influence, and the papal throne. Not until 1431, however, and the papacy of Alexander VI, better known as Roderigo Borgia, did the power of the dynastic families reach its zenith. Earlier popes like Boniface VIII, Dante's great villain in the *Inferno*, had shown the way in advancing his Caetani family against the Colonna, but Borgia's worldly corruption was the apotheosis of power building using papal wealth and patronage as the lever. Thereafter, no family worth its salt failed to seize the papal throne. Some were weak, venal individuals like the Pamphili's Innocent X; others were great patrons of the arts, such as the della Roveres' Julius II, the Medicis' Leo X, and the Barberinis' Urban VIII.

<< Evidence of some dynastic clans is hidden in the streets, squares, fountains, churches, and paintings they commissioned. Heraldic trademarks were added to works by artists to glorify their patrons – for example, the three bees of the Barberini (Urban VIII). **>>**

Almost from the first, popes were influential players in the game of Roman politics. The fortunes of the papacy fluctuated over the years, but the papacy always wielded a degree of power. The zenith of its influence – when Rome and the popes were virtually indivisible – occurred in a period of about 200 years spanning the Renaissance and Rome's baroque heyday. . . .

Papal patronage Despite hiccups, like the Reformation and the Sack of Rome in 1527, this was a period of unparalleled wealth and patronage, a time when many of the city's great buildings and works of art were commissioned under papal auspices. The upturn in papal fortunes began with the end of the Great Schism (1378–1417) and the papacy of Martin V, between 1417 and 1431. Martin V gradually reasserted Rome's authority and revived its cultural life, trends continued by **Nicholas V** (1447–55), a pope in the vanguard of Renaissance patronage. Nicholas V's best known legacy are Fra Angelico's frescoes in the Vatican chapel. More shrewd and intelligent popes followed, such as **Sixtus IV** (1471–84), responsible for pieces of rational town planning like the Ponte Sisto (at the time only two Tiber bridges survived from antiquity) and for the Sistine Chapel, which under **Julius II** (1503–13) became one of the age's masterpieces.

Wealth and power Although papal fortunes were borne along on the Renaissance wave, their new prestige was also bolstered by military muscle. Popes aligned themselves alternatively with Spain, France, or the emperor to extend their influence. Papal emissaries like fearsome Cardinal Albornoz bludgeoned the cities of central Italy into submission, making a reality of the papal states that had existed in theory since the days of Charlemagne. When indulgences and the like failed to bring in sufficient revenue, these states were taxed almost to extinction (a greed that was to leave areas like Lazio and Umbria in the doldrums for centuries). **Leo X** (1513–21) summed up the prevailing spirit when he is reported to have said, "Since God has given us the Papacy, let us enjoy it."

Violence and corruption Untold wealth made the papal office supremely attractive, and as never before it became a plaything of Rome's powerful dynastic families. Their candidates were often anything but men of the church, and while remembered as enlightened men of the arts, they were also as worldly, cynical, and corrupt as any Machiavellian prince. Many were also murderous in their ambition, none more so than Alexander VII (1492–1503), better known as the infamous **Roderigo Borgia.** After buying his pontificate through profligate bribery, he then indulged in flagrant nepotism, making his poisonous son, Cesare, a cardinal and his daughter, Lucrezia, a sexual pawn in his political maneuvrings.

Major projects All the while the rebuilding of Rome continued apace, with the construction of hundreds of churches, new roads like the Via Giulia (after Julius II), the restoration of ancient aqueducts, and the jewel in the crown – the raising of the new St. Peter's. These, and hundreds of minor projects like them, laid the papal stamp on the city for good, razing in the process parts of the medieval and ancient Rome that had stood for hundreds of years.

New times The tenor of the times changed after the Sack of Rome in 1527, when German and Spanish

Worshippers attend Mass in the imposing basilica of St. Peter's

mercenaries ran amok in the city for a year. The papacy quickly picked itself up, however, recovering its mettle much as it did in the face of the Reformation – which was partly brought on by its decadent profligacy. Though now politically in thrall to the Spanish, popes enjoyed a successful resurgence during the Counter-Reformation, a comeback epitomized by **Paul III** (1534–39). On a grand scale he convened the Council of Trent, Catholicism's rallying cry, but in Rome his legacy was the approval of the Jesuits, Catholicism's storm troopers, an order that left its mark on Rome in the shape of the great churches of the Gesù and San Andrea della Valle. Although the papacy was increasingly consigned to a political backwater, its wealth and local power continued well into the 17th century, a period that saw another eruption of papal public works. **Sixtus V** (1585–90) began the bout of urban redevelopment, but it reached full fruition under **Urban VIII** (1623–44), who, in tandem with architects like Bernini and Borromini, oversaw Rome's great baroque era of rebuilding.

What was perhaps the swan song of the papacy's golden age was the building of Piazza San Pietro in 1656, a watershed after which Rome declined in the 18th century. In 1798 the French attacked and occupied the city, and in 1809 Napoleon took Pius VII into captivity – the ultimate papal humiliation – and annexed the Papal States.

■ No period in Rome's history left a more lasting architectural stamp than did the 17th century and its taste for the Baroque. In a few years churches that had remained unchanged for centuries were remodeled in a style that virtually wiped the city clean of its Gothic and Romanesque heritage. Today the Baroque's rich decoration and monumental monotony is far from being to all tastes, but it is an essentially Roman phenomenon. . . .■

A certain style Baroque's literal origins are obscure, but the word is thought to derive from the large, irregularly shaped pearls still called *perle baroche* in Italian. The writer Luigi Barzini, in his classic book *The Italians,* explains succinctly how "the term came to be used metaphorically to describe anything pointlessly complicated, otiose, capricious and eccentric." Its political background was one of papal largesse and confidence after the successes of the Counter-Reformation, factors that ensured that at its worst the style would be in thrall to the church, which was unable to produce anything innovative or ideologically subversive. At its best, however, which usually meant in the architectural sphere, it proved capable of great theatricality and an immense spiritual intensity.

An angel on Ponte Sant'Angelo

The big names The baroque's first major architect was **Carlo Maderno** (1556–1629), responsible for the facades of St. Peter's, the Palazzo Barberini, and Santa Susanna. The artists primarily responsible for inaugurating and then dominating its Roman heyday were Gianlorenzo Bernini (1598–1680), Francesco Borromini (1599–1667), and Pietro da Cortona (1596–1669).

Bernini Most dominant of this group was Bernini, a Neapolitan by birth, whose impact not only on the appearance of the city, but on sculpture and architecture – in both of which he excelled – was to have incalculable effects. A youthful prodigy, his early sculptures of **David** and **Apollo and Daphne** in the Villa Borghese were the first important

<< Bernini's masterpiece is *The Ecstasy of St. Teresa* in Santa Maria della Vittoria. The period's emphasis on emotions and stylized drama are all present, as are the sculptor's passion for illusionist techniques and the use of different sources of light. Above all, however, the statue captures the intense spirituality of the saint's ecstatic vision of God. **>>**

statues since Michelangelo's. He went on to design more monumental works, including fountains like the Piazza Navona's Fontana dei Fiumi, and the great piazza in front of St. Peter's, becoming the basilica's overall architectural supremo in 1629. Smaller masterpieces like the church of San Andrea al Quirinale and the Ponte Sant'Angelo's angels are scattered throughout Rome.

Borromini Bernini's great rival, Borromini, was a very different sort of man. In contrast to Bernini's energetic joie de vivre, his was a tortured and introspective soul, eventually driven to suicide, partly out of bitterness at what he saw as his failure to secure the commissions he deserved. In many ways, however, he was the more innovative, even more eccentric architect. The most exhilarating of his works are the churches of Sant'Ivo and San Carlo alle Quattro Fontane, famous for their sophisticated geometry and exotic combinations of shapes. Similar interplays are at work in the Oratorio of the Filippini near the Chiesa Nuova and Piazza Navona's Sant'Agnese in Agone. Often remembered for small-scale projects, Borromini also proved himself to be Bernini's equal in creating the overblown, with his design of the interior of San Giovanni in Laterano.

Pietro da Cortona The third of the triumvirate, Pietro da Cortona, was also an architect, responsible for Santa Maria della Pace's elegant facade. Unlike his partners, however, he was known primarily as a painter. Ornate, illusionist ceiling frescoes were a feature of the age, and in Cortona they found their chief exponent, who painted to greatest effect in the Palazzo Barberini's spectacular *Gran Salone* (1638).

Other noted artists of the genre were Giovanni Gaulli, responsible for the decoration of the Gesù (1679), and Andrea Pozzo, best known for his *trompe l'oeil tour de force* in Sant'Ignazio (1691).

> **<<** The baroque would probably not have been possible without the patronage of the papacy. Three popes from the three leading families of the day dominate all accounts of the period: Urban VIII (1623–44), a Barberini; Innocent X, a Pamphili (1644–55) and Alexander VII (1655–67), a Chigi. **>>**

Gradual decline As papal money dried up and inspiration wavered, however, the baroque's golden age was becoming tarnished as early as the middle of the 17th century. This decline failed, nonetheless, to stop the wholesale destruction of medieval masterpieces in favor of tired Baroque leftovers. The most popular architect of the period's dotage was **Carlo Fontana**. Thereafter the city's architecture largely emulated the city's own decline. Fernando Fuga's designs for Santa Maria Maggiore (1743) and Nicola Salvi's Fontana di Trevi (1762) were notable exceptions.

The Risorgimento

■ The *risorgimento,* or revolution, that was to lead to Italy's unification was started in 1848 by two Giuseppes – Mazzini and Garibaldi – their names immortalized in the streets and piazzas of every Italian town and village. Its seeds, however, were sown earlier in the European upheavals created by the French Revolution and the empire building of Napoleon. . . .■

Foreign control Since the 16th century Italy had been a patchwork of states under the sway of foreign powers – France, Spain and Austria – or in the case of Rome and the Papal States, under the direct control of the popes. It was the maneuvrings of these protagonists and an alliance of the French and Piedmontese that was eventually to bring about unification in 1860.

Republican triumvirate If Italy's revolution was not made in Rome, however, the city was the scene of its finest hour and of its belated apotheosis. Mazzini, an inveterate intriguer, and Garibaldi, a Ligurian sailor with experience of guerilla wars in South America, came together in a wave of unrest that swept the Italian peninsula in 1848. In Rome the Pope fled from the rioting, and the two radicals installed themselves in the city, Mazzini joining its ruling republican triumvirate and Garibaldi taking charge of its defenses. Garibaldi's scratch army held off French troops, sent to bolster the papacy, for many months before accepting defeat.

The new Italy Although the republic failed, the die had been cast, and the protagonists' credentials were established by the fact that 20,000 revolutionaries were expelled from Rome after the uprising. Thereafter the focus of rebellion passed to the state of Piedmont and its prime minister, Count Camillo Cavour. By 1861 Cavour's machinations, Garibaldi's military campaigns, and the playing off of France and Austria succeeded in creating the new kingdom of Italy, a creation tainted only by the fact that it failed to include either Rome or Venice.

> **<<** Between 1860 and 1870, before Rome was liberated, Florence was Italy's provisional capital. **>>**

Inclusion of Rome Pius IX refused to surrender Rome until September 20, 1870, sheltering within a barricaded city protected by a French garrison and bands of papal mercenaries. Only when Prussia defeated France that year was Rome freed from French troops and allowed to take its rightful place at the head of the new country.

Giuseppe Garibaldi

■ Once Rome was established as capital of Italy in 1870, it suffered in the same way as it had suffered under every previous regime. Rulers no sooner rose to power than they began to rebuild the city in their own image. The unification's new Piedmontese heroes were no exception. . . .■

New city The Rome of 1870 was illsuited to its role as state capital, being little more than a moribund provincial town, its glories tarnished by centuries of apathetic papal rule.

From the outset Rome was to be a political capital. A decision was made to keep heavy industry at arm's length – not out of any aesthetic concern – but to prevent it attracting the dangerous "subversion" that might accompany large groups of workers.

Piedmontese quarter Instead whole new quarters were carved out to accommodate the young state's ministries and their army of civil servants. Chief of these was the area around Termini and Piazza Vittorio, modeled on Turin and known as the *quartiere Piedmontese*. Huge areas of parkland in the Villa Ludovisi and Villa Borghese were sacrificed to meet this and other demands of the new capital. Suburbs sprang up around new roads like Via Veneto, Via Nazionale, Via del Tritone, and Corso Vittorio Emanuele – still the city's main routes.

Monuments The chief monument of the period is the huge Altar of the Nation in Piazza Venezia (the Monumento di Vittorio Emanuele), used to persuade Italians that while their new state might be tender in years, its material manifestations were to be vast, symbolic monoliths. The finance ministry in Via XX Settembre, twice the size of the Colosseum, was another such monster.

Less papal influence More successful projects included the tearing down of the ghetto and the regulation of the Tiber using quays copied from the Parisian model. Also implicit in the planning was the desire to marginalize papal power, seen in the new bureaucratic quarters, such as Prati, whose boulevards pointedly had no contact with the nearby Vatican.

One of the inimitable actors in day-to-day Roman life

<< Italy's street names include several dates: XX Settembre (September 20): Italian troops liberated Rome in 1870; XXIV Maggio (May 24): Italy declared war on Austria in 1915; IV Novembre (November 4): the Italian armistice and victory in 1918 after World War I; XXV Aprile (April 25): Rome was liberated by the Allied forces in 1944. **>>**

Fascism and Liberation

■ **Mussolini's march on Rome in 1922 and his seizure of power marked the beginning of over 20 years of Fascist rule in Italy. To a large extent Rome absorbed his megalomania, as it had many before him, but still suffered the spate of building that has accompanied delusions of imperial grandeur since the days of Caesar. . . .**■

Visible legacy Most obvious are the roads through the center of the old city – Via dei Fori Imperiali and Via della Concilazione – the cause of controversy even to this day. Little else, however, survives of the dream to restore Rome as the *caput mundi*, the new head – as Mussolini saw it – of a "Latin bloc of states, encompassing the Iberian peninsula and stretching across to Latin America." Many of the more grandiose building schemes, such as EUR, a model satellite city, were either abandoned or scaled down and were not completed until after the war.

Shifting boundaries Mussolini did succeed in adjusting the lines of Rome's political map. In 1929 he concluded the Lateran Treaty, which recognized the Vatican State and formalized Church and State relations for decades to come. His achievements on the international stage, however, were less exemplary, and Italy's involvement in the Spanish civil war, the Axis with Hitler in 1936, and his doomed imperial dabblings in North Africa all set dangerous precedents. By July 1943 and the overthrow of the Fascists, however, the dictator's war was over, and Rome fell under direct control of the Germans. Allied strikes on the city were restrained, and San Lorenzo was the only church to suffer badly, though at times houses, hospitals and even the Vatican were hit by bombs. As the end drew near, Hitler and Field Marshal Kesselring pulled their troops out, declaring Rome an "open city," a surprising and enlightened move that prevented it from suffering wholesale destruction.

Postwar Italy After liberation (1944) a popular referendum established the Italian Republic (July 2, 1946), and for 15 years thereafter Italy rode the wave of economic boom and prosperity. In Rome this prosperity was marked in popular culture by the films of Fellini, De Sica, and Pasolini and the largely mythical world of *La Dolce Vita*. In practical terms it meant a flood tide of hideous new suburbs (*borgate*) that destroyed the city's hinterland with roads and some 600,000 illegally built houses. City government was chaotic at best and corrupt at worst, a mirror of the Christian Democrat cabal that, with Rome now reestablished as capital, governed Italy from the Eternal City.

A popular pope Maladministration and urban expansion brought with them the predictable problems of vandalism, drug abuse, and worse, but if Rome's social and political life was in a tailspin, its religious and moral outlook – at least from the Vatican's perspective – had perhaps never been better. John XXIII's pontificate (1958–63) was immensely popular with ordinary people, even the Romans, who remember him as the pope who moved early morning bellringing from six to seven o'clock and gave everyone an extra hour's sleep. This sort of touch was typical of John's approach and largely paved the way for the Second Vatican Council (1962–65), a meeting in Rome of some 6,000 bishops and other church heads that brought much-needed church reforms.

Rome's heyday Elsewhere, the zenith of Rome's postwar heyday was in 1960, when Rome hosted the

Olympic Games, an event that merely added to Rome's position as a premier destination for the new phenomenon of mass tourism. Economic swings characterized the 1960s, together with the radical student movements common elsewhere, though in Rome they came later and with more virulence. Violent clashes outside the city's university complex were everyday occurrences, though they were nothing to the political terrorism that marked Italy's *anni di piombo* in the 1970s – the years of lead, so called because of the period's weight of bullets, but also evocative of the gloomy and apocalyptic tenor of the time. Although Rome largely escaped the worst terrorist outrages, it did see the kidnapping and eventual murder of prime minister Aldo Moro in 1978.

Future plans Rome's own administration became Communist for the first time in 1976, and for a while effectively grasped the nettles of housing, traffic, and urban decrepitude. This interlude in the city's decline into chaos was short-lived, however, and despite current high-sounding plans seems unlikely to be repeated. One of these plans, Roma Capitale, claims to plan for the millenium and envisages offices and ministries leaving the city, the extension of the metro, a clampdown on building, and the establishment of a large archaeological park. Similar plans for ordering the Eternal City have come and gone for over 2,000 years. Most have failed or been superseded.

The capital at its most poetic: in a dramatic summer sunset

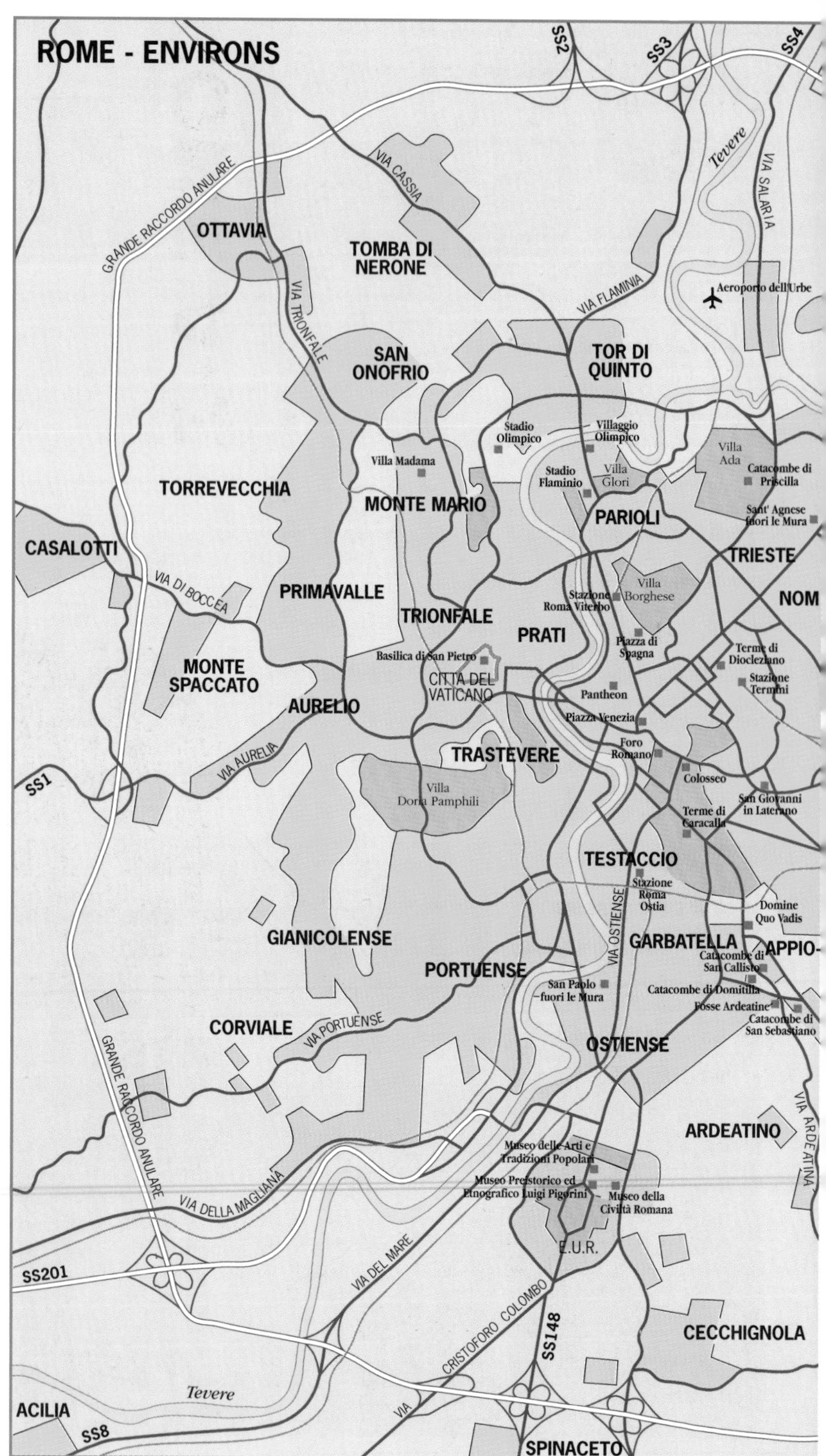
ROME - ENVIRONS
SS2
SS3
SS4
Tevere
VIA SALARIA
VIA CASSIA
GRANDE RACCORDO ANULARE
OTTAVIA
TOMBA DI NERONE
VIA FLAMINIA
Aeroporto dell'Urbe
VIA TRIONFALE
SAN ONOFRIO
TOR DI QUINTO
Stadio Olimpico
Villaggio Olimpico
Villa Ada
Villa Madama
Stadio Flaminio
Villa Glori
Catacombe di Priscilla
TORREVECCHIA
MONTE MARIO
PARIOLI
Sant' Agnese fuori le Mura
CASALOTTI
TRIESTE
VIA DI BOCCEA
PRIMAVALLE
Stazione Roma Viterbo
Villa Borghese
NOM
TRIONFALE
PRATI
Piazza di Spagna
Terme di Diocleziano
Basilica di San Pietro
MONTE SPACCATO
CITTA DEL VATICANO
Stazione Termini
Pantheon
AURELIO
Piazza Venezia
VIA AURELIA
Foro Romano
SS1
TRASTEVERE
Colosseo
Villa Doria Pamphili
San Giovanni in Laterano
Terme di Caracalla
TESTACCIO
Stazione Roma Ostia
VIA OSTIENSE
Domine Quo Vadis
GIANICOLENSE
GARBATELLA
APPIO-
Catacombe di San Callisto
PORTUENSE
San Paolo fuori le Mura
Catacombe di Domitilla
Fosse Ardeatine
Catacombe di San Sebastiano
CORVIALE
VIA PORTUENSE
OSTIENSE
VIA ARDEATINA
ARDEATINO
Museo delle Arti e Tradizioni Popolari
Museo Preistorico ed Etnografico Luigi Pigorini
Museo della Civiltà Romana
VIA DELLA MAGLIANA
E.U.R.
SS201
VIA DEL MARE
VIA CRISTOFORO COLOMBO
SS148
CECCHIGNOLA
Tevere
ACILIA
SS8
SPINACETO

ROME A–Z

A1
0 1 2 3 4 5 km
0 1 2 3 miles
GRANDE RACCORDO ANULARE
TUFELLO
VIA NOMENTANA
MONTE SACRO
SETTECAMINI
SS5
Aniene
A24
PIETRALATA
VIA TIBURTINA
ENTANO
PORTONACCIO
Campo Verano
TOR SAPIENZA
VIA PRENESTINA
LABICANO
CENTOCELLE
VIA CASILINA
TUSCOLANO
LATINO
SS6
VIA TUSCOLANA
CINECITTA
TORRE NOVA
Circo Massenzio
Tomba di Cecilia Metella
APPIO-PIGNATELLI
A2
VIA APPIA NUOVA
VIA APPIA ANTICA
SS215
CASAL MORENA
GRANDE RACCORDO ANULARE
SS511
CIAMPINO
Aeroporto di Ciampino
SS7

Areas of the City

The Palatino, heart of the ancient capital

Rome belongs to no single historical period, and its quarters are a lavish medley of ancient, medieval, Renaissance and modern buildings. In its earliest days the nascent metropolis gathered around seven famous hills – the Aventino, Capitolino, Esquilino, Caelio, Palatino, Quirinale and Viminale.

Its heart then was the Palatino and the Roman Forum and the area around them, first defined by the *pomerium*, the city's sacred boundary. This district and the Seven Hills were enclosed by the Servian Wall in the 4th century BC and by the more wide-sweeping Aurelian Wall six centuries later. To a certain extent this district still defines the city's most visited areas. Also intact are districts created by Augustus, who divided the city into 22 *rioni*, a series of wards in the manner of Paris's *arrondissements*.

Neither the *rioni* nor the Seven Hills, long ago swallowed up by urban expansion, adequately describe the present city. Its modern hub is **Piazza Venezia**, a junction of major streets that strike off to the four points of the compass: **Via del Corso**, which leads north to Piazza del Popolo; **Corso Vittorio Emanuele**, which cuts west toward St. Peter's; **Via dei Fori Imperiale**, which heads south for the Colosseum; and **Via Nazionale**, which strikes west toward Stazione Termini.

The ***centro storico***, the "historical center," is not, confusingly, the Roman Forum and the ancient heart of Rome, but a warren of streets that made up the core of the city from the Middle Ages until the last century. Neatly contained by Via del Corso and the bend of the Tiber, it can be loosely divided into two areas.

The **Renaissance quarter** lies south of Corso Vittorio Emanuele, centering on **Campo dei Fiori**; **Piazza Farnese;** and the elegant **Via Guilia**, in its 16th-century heyday the most fashionable street in Rome. Within this quarter, in the streets east of Via Arenula, lies one of the city's most captivating areas, the old Jewish **Ghetto**. Pope Paul IV ordered the city's 8,000-strong Jewish community, who until then had largely lived across the Tiber, into the old *rione* of Sant'Angelo in 1555. The ghetto's walls were torn down in 1849, but it still has a distinctive atmosphere. It is home to a large synagogue and several noted Romano-Jewish restaurants.

The **medieval quarter** is north of Corso Vittorio Emanuele, centered on Piazza Navona and the Pantheon and more properly known as the **Campo Marzio,** or *Campus Martius*, after the days when it was an open plain, the "field of Mars," and a great Roman quarter of the city.

Across the river is **Trastevere** ("across the Tiber"), one of the city's better defined districts. Rome's poorest 19th-century slum, and still a little seedy in places, it is none the less also one of its most charming areas – especially for aimless wandering, restaurants, and evening entertainment. Similar in some ways is the historic working-class area of **Testaccio**, south of Trastevere, which centers on Porta San Paolo and the Piramide. Once the site of the city's vast slaughterhouse, it is now a newly fashionable area of restaurants and nightclubs.

A remnant of past glories at the forum

To the north of Trastevere, on the Tiber's left, or west, bank is **Vatican City**, centered on St. Peter's, an independent state under papal control. To its east lies another self-contained *rione*, known as the Borgo, renowned for its old-fashioned air and assortment of cheap restaurants. North of the Vatican and the Borgo stretches **Prati**, a quiet, largely 19th-century district of middle-class suburbs, numerous small hotels, and plenty of less expensive shopping streets. Adjacent to Prati, but across the Tiber to the east, is **Parioli**, a cool, leafy area bordered by the Villa Borghese, home of exclusive clubs, luxurious hotels, and currently one of Rome's more desirable residential districts.

Other named districts include **Piazza di Spagna**, a popular, central tourist area, and **San Lorenzo**, a vibrant, turn-of-the-century suburb between Termini and the university, popular with the young and known for its reasonable restaurants and unpretentious atmosphere. **EUR** is a curious region in the city's southwestern suburbs, initiated by Mussolini as a "new Rome", and filled with huge buildings largely used as offices and company headquarters.

Much of the city's skyline, still dominated by St. Peter's, barely noted the passing of the 20th century

The rods, or *fasces* of the *lictors* were symbols of obedience to the law. Fascism was later named to imbue it with a sense of this ancient imperial authority.

 **Ara Pacis Augustae**

Via di Ripetta–Piazza Augusto Imperatore

Sheltered by a glass-plated pavilion, the *Ara Pacis Augustae*, the Altar of Peace, was built between 13 and 9 BC on the orders of the Senate as a memorial to Augustus's victories in Gaul and Spain and in celebration of the peace he brought to the Empire after years of conquest and civil war. The altar, guarded by lion-sphinxes, is raised on a pyramid of 10 steps; the large **screen** surrounding the altar, carved from dazzling Carrara marble, contains some of the most beautiful Roman bas-reliefs in the city.

The **Upper Level** consists largely of figures from mythology and historical characters. The panel at the screen's eastern end depicts an allegorical scene of the earth goddess Tellus (a symbol of Italy), a swan, a cow, a lamb, and a damaged portrait of the goddess Roma. The deities of Air and Water flank Tellus (shown as an adoring mother with two children), Air sailing on a swan, Water on a sea monster. The other main mythological scenes are a partly ruined relief of the *Lupercalia*, or the feast of Pan, and Aeneas making a sacrifice to the Penates (the household gods).

On the long, eastern frieze is a superb processional scene depicting the altar's ceremonial consecration. Leading the procession are 12 *lictors* with their rods or *fasces*, symbols of authority, followed by Augustus himself, taller than the others (the carving here is damaged), and the four *flamine*, strangely hatted priestly figures who were responsible for lighting Rome's ceremonial fires (see the Tempio di Vesta, **Foro Romano**). Following are figures believed to be Augustus's son-in-law Agrippa; his wife, Livia; his niece Antonia; his daughter, Julia; and Julia's husband, Tiberius. Alongside are the young Germanicas and Claudius and an assortment of friends. On the river (west) side of the screen are priests, magistrates, senators, and the Pontifex Maximus, or high priest, recognizable by the toga partly covering his head.

Arco di Constantino

The Lower Level has no narrative panels, but is richly decorated with reliefs of foliage – patterns of acanthus, ivy, laurel and vines – as well as birds, butterflies and snakes.

Open: Tuesday to Saturday, 9–1:30, Sunday, 9–1. April to October also open Tuesday, Thursday, and Saturday 3:30–7. Closed Monday. Admission charge.

<<...It is singular that so useless a thing should give such great pleasure; the style of the triumphal arch is an architectural conquest.>> – Stendhal, *Roman Journal* (1828)

▶▶▷ Arco di Constantino

Piazza del Colosseo

Recently restored and cleaned to dazzling effect, the Arco di Constantino, which was once at the head of the Via Sacra, now stands in glorious isolation alongside the Colosseum. Erected in AD 315 on the orders of the Senate, it was designed to honor Constantine's victory over Maxentius at the Battle of Milvian Bridge in AD 312. Not only the best preserved of Rome's triumphal arches, it is also the largest (69 feet high, 85 feet wide, and 23 feet deep) and one of the last great monuments of ancient Rome.

Partly out of pragmatism, but also in an attempt to link Constantine's regime to the glories of the past, the best of the arch's decorative **reliefs** were removed from older monuments. Few, therefore, relate to Constantine or his exploits. One, for example, showing a boar hunt and a sacrifice to Apollo, dates from the reign of Hadrian. Another, the bristling battle scenes in the central arch, shows Trajan at war with the Dacians. The carvings from Constantine's own era, mainly the medallions above the arches, suffer somewhat by comparison, suggesting the decline that had taken place in the arts of 4th-century Rome. The triumphal arch was part of a long-standing practice by which the Roman Senate sought to honor emperors and victorious generals. Like the basilica, it was a peculiarly Roman contribution to architecture, but only three survive in Rome itself with anything approaching their original splendor: the Arco di Tito, Arco di Settimo Severo, and the Arco di Constantino. Their influence has been immense, as London's Marble Arch and Paris's Arc de Triomphe testify.

The face-lifted Arco di Constantino

▶▶▷ Arco di Settimo Severo

Western end of the Roman Forum

Beautifully proportioned with extensive decorations that have benefited from recent restoration, this arch commemorated the 10th anniversary of Emperor Severus's reign (AD 203) and the minor victories of his sons, Geta and Caracalla, over the Parthians, Arabians and Assyrians. Four large marble reliefs depict graphic episodes from these wars, the figures in each standing proud from the background, along with various goddesses of victory clasping trophies and a large inscription eulogizing Severus and his sons, Geta and Caracalla. This arch greatly influenced future architects, both ancient and modern, but the reclining statues in the spandrels facing the Campidoglio, themselves probably of Greek inspiration, were the models for hundreds of such figures above the portals of Renaissance palaces and country houses throughout Europe.

When Caracalla murdered his brother, he placed Geta *in damnatio memoriae* – "in exile from memory" – and all the arch's references to him were effaced in favor of homilies to Caracalla. The holes of the original lettering can still be seen in the inscription's fourth line.

A view of the Via Sacra from Arco di Tito

▶▶▷ Arco di Tito

Eastern end of the Roman Forum

Situated on the *Velia*, a hilly spur of the Palatino, and close to the end of the Via Sacra, this arch's site is superb and its view toward the Colosseum, a Roman classic. The oldest of the city's triumphal arches, it was erected in AD 81 by the Emperor Domitian in homage to Titus, his brother and predecessor. Titus was the son of the Emperor Vespasian and the general who captured Jerusalem in AD 70, a victory that concluded one of Rome's hardest-fought campaigns and set the seal on the defeat of the Jewish people in Palestine. Even today, many Jews refuse to walk through an arch built as a monument to their downfall.

Its chief beauties are the sculptural reliefs on the inner side of the arch, masterpieces of Roman carving, each representing part of Titus's triumphal return to Rome. On one side the symbolic figure of Roma leads the imperial quadriga; on the other side Titus is shown in his chariot with soldiers bearing spoils from Jerusalem's Holy of Holies.

Included are its silver trumpets, the golden temple of the shewbread, and the seven-branched candelabra – which gave the arch its medieval name, the Arch of the Seven Lamps.

What became of these treasures? Roman Jews claim they were tossed into the Tiber; others contend that they were kept in Vespasian's Temple of Peace until AD 410, when they were carried off by Alaric after the Goths' sack of Rome. When Alaric died in Calabria, his men supposedly buried him and his booty and diverted the River Busento over the grave. Another story has them looted by the Vandals, taken to North Africa, retrieved by Belisarius, and delivered to Constantinople.

Aventino

The most southerly of Rome's original Seven Hills, the Aventino (or Aventine) is one of the city's most genteel residential neighborhoods, but during Republican times, it was home to the lower, plebeian class. The lower orders were separated from their patrician superiors on the Palatino by the Vallis Murcia, the valley that contains the **Circo Massimo** (see page 62). Greek merchants also settled here, bringing "dangerous" democratic notions.

The walk to the Aventine from **Piazza della Bocca della Verità** through the gardens of the Parco Sant'Alessio is delightful. There are tremendous views of the Roman skyline across the Tiber and beautiful spots to sit in the scented shade of orange trees alongside **Santa Sabina,** a church that on its own is worth the climb (see page 172). Immediately beyond the church is Piazza dei Cavalieri di Malta, designed in the 18th century by the engraver Piranesi, and most famous for its exceptional, if quirky view from the Knight's Priory on the right. Through the keyhole of its main door you can see the dome of St. Peter's perfectly framed by an avenue of trees.

Basilica Aemilia

Foro Romano

On the right as you enter the **Foro Romano**, this now heavily ruined basilica was said by Pliny to have been one of the world's three most beautiful buildings. It illustrates how buildings in the forum changed roles over the years. In the 5th century BC, this area was a row of butcher's shops, taken over in time by the city's moneylenders. In 179 BC the Censor M. Aemilius Lepidus, son of Aemilius Paulus, built the forum's second basilica over the shops, such acts of private enterprise being rewarded with the right to have the building named in one's honor. The moneylenders were allowed to stay – but concealed behind a special portico.

During Alaric's attack in AD 410, some of the moneylenders supposedly stayed in the basilica to do business with the invading Goths. You can still see bronze coins fused into marble pavement, perhaps the result of the Goths' violent dislike of the bankers' reception.

Keeping cool the Roman way

The forum seen from the Palatino

The basilica, like the triumphal arch, was a particularly Roman architectural conceit. It consisted of a single, large colonnaded hall that was most often used as a courtroom center for business and commerce. Several Roman basilicas were later converted into Christian churches, and as late as the 13th century the form was still being used as the model for many Italian churches.

Between the *Arx* and the *Capitolium*, the peaks of the Capitoline Hill, ran a shallow valley known as the *Asylum*. Before the foundation of the Republic in 510 BC, early settlers came here to invoke the protection of Romulus, the legendary first king of Rome, and to be granted "asylum", the derivation of the English word.

Campidoglio

Capitoline Hill

The Campidoglio, or Capitol, was the smallest but most famous of Rome's Seven Hills – the seat of power, the city's religious center, and for centuries the heart of the civilized world. Today, its contours are disturbed by the **Monumento Vittorio Emanuele** and by the church of **Santa Maria in Aracoeli**, though in its day it rose to two separate summits, each crowned by the city's most important temples. On the northern ridge (the *Arx*) rose the fortress Citadel, together with the Temple of Juno Moneta, close to the site of the original *moneta* – mint – (from which the word *money* derives). On the other (the *Capitolium*) stood the Capitol itself, the Temple of Jupiter Optimus Maximus Capitolinus. It was here that the Senate's newly elected consuls took their vows, and victorious generals came in procession to offer thanks to the gods.

Piazza del Campidoglio Little survives of the Capitol's earliest monuments, and most of what you see today centers on the **Piazza del Campidoglio**, a majestic piazza designed by Michelangelo for Emperor Charles V's triumphal entry into Rome in 1536 (see page 119). The best approach is the one intended for the emperor, the gentle ramp, or *cordonata*, up from Via del Teatro di Marcello, decked with wisteria and elegantly guarded by two Roman statues of Castor and Pollux. The square is bounded by three palaces, the Palazzo Senatorio (at the far end), now Rome's town hall; the Palazzo dei Conservatori (on the right); and the Palazzo Nuovo (on the left). The last two together form the **Museo Capitolino**, one of the city's finest museums of art and antiquities.

Castor and Pollux guard the Piazza del Campidoglio

Sitting at the feet of a Campidoglio resident

Palazzo Nuovo The smaller but richer part of the collection is held by the Palazzo Nuovo, but a single ticket entitles you to visit both wings of the museum. Its courtyard contains an immense river god, Marforio, one of Rome's *pasquinades* or "talking statues" (see page 120). Nearby are two equally famous sarcophagi, one depicting scenes from the life of Achilles, the other battle scenes between the Romans and Gauls.

The six rooms on the palace's **upper floor** contain numerous masterpieces of classical sculpture. Look in particular for the headless *Capitoline Venus*, housed in a room of her own – a Roman copy of a 2nd-century BC Hellenistic original; the *Dying Gaul* a copy of a 3rd-century BC Greek bronze; two Greek works, *Amor and Psyche* and the *Drunken Old Woman*; the *Young Satyr*, a copy of an original by Praxiteles; and *Infant Hercules*, said to be a portrait of the young Caracalla. Also here is the *Sala dei Imperatori* (the Room of the Emperors).

Palazzo dei Conservatori Across the piazza, the Palazzo dei Conservatori contains further classical pieces, not least the courtyard's fragments of a colossal statue of the Emperor Constantine. Upstairs on the first floor the greatest treasures are the ravishing *Spinario*, a Greek bronze from the 1st century BC of a boy removing a thorn from his foot and the *Capitoline Wolf*, an Etruscan bronze dating from the 6th century. Lightning damaged the wolf's hindquarters in 65 BC, and the figures of Romulus and Remus were added by Antonio Pollaiuolo in 1510. Also outstanding are the reliefs taken from the *Arco di Marco Aurelio*, with scenes showing the emperor's works of mercy and devotion, as well as his victorious receptions in Rome. Look, also, for the *Capitoline Tensa*, a reconstructed chariot in bronze, and the *Esquiline Venus*, a Roman interpretation of a Greek female nude.

Triumphant emperors and generals painted their faces red to imitate Jupiter as they rode in ceremonial procession to offer thanks to the Capitol's deities. Behind them a slave traditionally followed whispering *respice post te! Hominem esse te memento* – "Remember that you are but a man."

A face from the past: the Museo Capitolino

Pinacoteca Capitolina A small but distinguished collection of paintings complements the museum in the Pinacoteca Capitolina on the second floor. These include Titian's *Baptism of Christ*; Guercino's huge *Burial of St. Petronilla*, which was painted for St Peter's; Rubens's version of *Romulus and Remus Suckled by the She-Wolf;* Caravaggio's *Gypsy and the Fortune-Teller*; Van Dyck's double portrait of *The Painters Lucas and Cornelius de Wael;* as well as works by Tintoretto, Reni, Veronese, and portraits by Bellini and Velàzquez, among others. In another room is the *Rape of the Sabines* (1629), one of several influential narrative paintings by Pietro da Cortona.

Open: daily except Monday, 9–1:30, Tuesday, Thursday, and Saturday also 5–8. Admission charge, but free on the last Sunday of the month.

▶▶▷ Campo dei Fiori

The Campo dei Fiori, or "field of flowers," is one of Rome's most captivating piazzas, and the scene of its most picturesque food and flower market (*open*: Monday to Saturday, 6–1:30). A busy and vibrant survivor of old Rome, filled with stall holders, workmen, down-at-the-heels locals, tramps, foreigners, and students, this is one of the most interesting spots to sit back with a cappuccino and take a break from sight-seeing. The best place to observe the often nefarious street life is the infamous wine bar in the piazza's southwest corner. The **Om Shanti** bar in the opposite corner is another local favorite. Cheap restaurants, crumbling *palazzi,* and secondhand clothes shops line the square.

Before the 16th century the Campo was an exclusive residential and business district. Later it became a place of public execution. One victim was Giordano Bruno, burned for heresy in 1600, and now celebrated by the grim, cowled statue in the center of the piazza. His secular outlook typified the square, which has never been dedicated to any cult and still has no church.

Fruit at the Campo dei Fiori

▶▷▷ Campo Marzio

Ancient Rome's *Campus Martius* – the "field of Mars" – today embraces Rome's medieval quarter, bounded on one side by the Tiber and on the other by the Via del Corso.

In the 1st century Marcus Agrippa, both friend and associate of Augustus, turned it into one of the city's greatest monumental quarters. Among the new baths, theaters, arches, and arenas, all of which were laid out in a landscaped park setting, were the Baths of Agrippa; the Basilica of Neptune; and the original Pantheon, later replaced by Hadrian's new **Pantheon**. A great fire destroyed much of Agrippa's work in AD 80, though the real turning point in the Campo's fortunes arrived in AD 537 when Witigus the Goth cut Rome's aqueducts while besieging Belisarius. The lack of water forced citizens down on to the Campo, where they could more easily draw supplies from the Tiber, and thereafter an area that had never previously been lived in came to be the city's heart for centuries to come.

A Greek geographer, visiting Rome in the 7th century BC, thought the Campo Marzio the city's finest area, writing "Superior to all is the Campus Martius . . . the greatness of the plain itself is wonderful, all open for horse and chariot racing and for the great multitudes who take exercise in ball games, in the circus and in gymnastics."

▶▶▶ Castel Sant'Angelo

Lungotevere Castello

It is impossible to miss the huge bulwarks of the Castel Sant'Angelo. Throughout the centuries it has had an extraordinarily varied history, serving as a tomb, a papal fortress, barracks, a prison, and now a museum.

Mausoleum The original structure still forms the basis of the present complex and was started in AD 130 by the Emperor Hadrian as a mausoleum for himself, his family, and his imperial successors. It was finished in AD 139 by his adoptive son and successor, Antoninus Pius, and modified by the Emperor Settimo Severo in AD 193. The design was based on the **Mausoleo di Augusto**, itself probably a copy of earlier Etruscan mausoleums.

Built in travertine and white marble veneer, the tomb was a circular structure 210 feet in diameter and 66 feet high, supported by a solid square base 279 feet across. On top of the drum was a soil tumulus planted with cypresses, and crowning it was a gilded chariot, driven by a vast statue of Hadrian in the guise of the sun god Apollo. Girding the entire structure were statues from Hadrian's vast collection.

The mausoleum continued to be used as the resting place of emperors until the death of Settimo Severo at the beginning of the 3rd century. In AD 271, when Rome was threatened by Germanic invaders from the north, Aurelian incorporated it into the city's defenses. In time it became Rome's Citadel and the city's strongest fortress for over a thousand years.

The original name of Castel Sant' Angelo was the *Hadrianium*. It was altered in 590 after a vision by Pope Gregory the Great, who, while leading a procession through Rome to pray for the end of a plague, saw an angel sheathing a sword, an act thought to symbolize the end of the pestilence. A chapel was promptly built on the spot, and the fortress renamed, though the bronze statue of St. Michael crowning the battlements today was added only in 1753.

Papal fortress In 847 Leo IV created the so-called Leonine City, walling the Vatican and Borgo district and converting the castle into a papal fortress and residence. By 1277 Pope Nicholas III had linked the castle with the Vatican by way of a covered passage known as the *passetto*. One of the more belligerent popes, the Borgia Alexander VI (1492–1503), fortified the passage and reinforced the Castel by building four corner bastions.

Castel Sant'Angelo courtyard

In the 16th century, under Paul III, the interior was decorated and the marble angel by Raffaello da Montelupo (now in the castle's Cortile di Onore) was placed at the summit.

Prison For much of the Renaissance, sections of the fortress were used as a prison, and executions took place on its walls. Graphic accounts survive of the tortures inflicted in its dungeons and of the famous prisoners, such as Benvenuto Cellini, Cesare Borgia, and Beatrice Cenci, incarcerated in its notorious San Marocco cell. Later it reverted to a papal pleasure palace. From 1849 until 1870 it was occupied by French troops and then became a barracks. Plans to restore the shell were laid in 1901, and in 1933 it was opened as a museum.

Museum The Castel's long history has left its original structure overlaid with an intricate complex of additions and alterations. This makes orientation difficult, and the museum – which is spread over four floors – hard to explore with any logic.

Today's entrance to the Castel is also the door to the original tomb, and from here a shallow spiral ramp links the building's levels, leading first to Hadrian's *funerary chamber*. Much of this chamber is in a fine state of preservation and includes patches of its original black-and-white mosaic decoration.

The second level opens first into the Cortile di Onore, decorated with neat piles of marble, cannonballs, and the marble angel removed from the summit in 1753. Rooms off the main courtyard contain collections of arms from the Bronze Age to the present day. The most interesting feature is the facade belonging to the **Chapel of Leo X**, one of Michelangelo's least-known works.

Various other rooms are threaded into the area, most of them lavish papal apartments named after the popes

The Ponte Sant'Angelo, the bridge below the Castel Sant'Angelo – one of Rome's prettiest – was built in AD 134 to link the mausoleum to the city. Bernini's famous angels (1688) dubbed his "Breezy Maniacs" because they seem to be doing manic battle with the wind, line the top of the bridge. They replaced a row of 18 gallows erected in 1500. On the right bank was also the Tor di Nona, a prison tower often used for nocturnal executions. Like Castel Sant'Angelo, it kept a noose on permanent display.

responsible for their decoration. Some contain superb frescoes – *The Angel of Justice* by Perin del Vaga (in the Hall of Justice), grotesques painted for Pope Paul III in 1547 (the Hall of Apollo), and a *Madonna and Saints* by Luca Signorelli and a triptych by Taddeo Gaddi in the small room beyond. Others have more obscure details, such as the bathroom of Clement VII and its dainty grotesques by Giulio Romano, or the Cortile di Alessandro VI, distinguished by the beautiful well head emblazoned with the Borgia coat of arms. On the eastern side of this floor are further prison cells, including the one believed to have harbored Benvenuto Cellini.

Steps to the third floor bring you to the **Loggia of Paul III,** which was designed by Sangallo the Younger, and this leads in turn to the Gallery of Pius IV, which surrounds the whole building and offers glorious views over the Tiber and the city on one side, and to Monte Mario and the Vatican on the other side. The Loggia of Julius II halfway around was designed by Bernini and is close to a welcoming little bar with views of the Ponte Sant'Angelo. Nearby is the entrance to the papal apartments of Paul III (the Sala Paolina), which were designed to be used only in emergencies, but were nonetheless extravagantly finished in stucco, *trompe l'oeil,* and a wealth of frescoes. Adjacent rooms are similarly decorated, but make a special point of seeing the **Sala della Biblioteca**, a magnificent library, and the adjacent Room of the Secret Archives, located in the core of the building and the home of papal treasure until it was moved to the Vatican in 1870.

Before leaving, be sure to climb to the terrace at the summit of the fortress for panoramic views of the city, particularly of St. Peter's.

Open: Monday 2–4; Tuesday to Saturday 9–2; Sunday 9–1:30. Admission charge.

A museum with the walls of a fortress . . .

The "Breezy Maniacs" of the Ponte Sant'Angelo

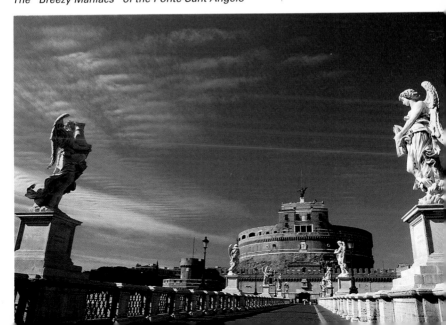

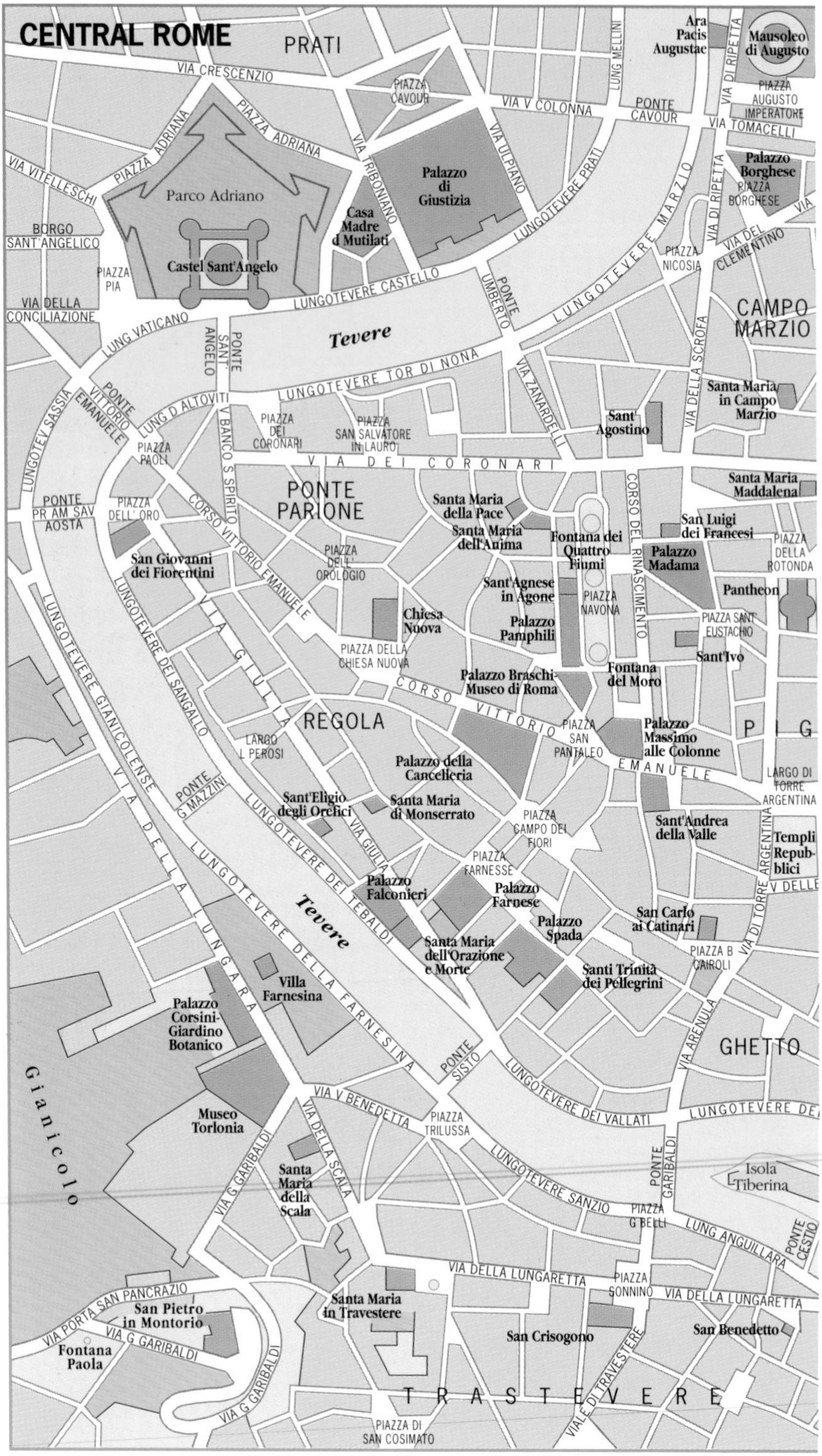

CENTRAL ROME

PRATI
Via Crescenzio
Piazza Cavour
Via V Colonna
Lung Mellini
Ara Pacis Augustae
Mausoleo di Augusto
Via di Ripetta
Piazza Augusto Imperatore
Ponte Cavour
Via Tomacelli
Piazza Adriana
Via Vitelleschi
Parco Adriano
Via Tribioniano
Palazzo di Giustizia
Via Ulpiano
Lungotevere Prati
Palazzo Borghese
Piazza Borghese
Borgo Sant'Angelico
Casa Madre d Mutilati
Castel Sant'Angelo
Piazza Pia
Lungotevere Marzio
Via di Ripetta
Via del Clementino
Piazza Nicosia
Via della Conciliazione
Lungotevere Castello
Ponte Umberto
Campo Marzio
Lung Vaticano
Ponte Sant' Angelo
Tevere
Lungotevere
Lungotevere Tor di Nona
Via della Scrofa
Ponte Vittorio Emanuele
Lung d Altoviti
Via Zanardelli
Santa Maria in Campo Marzio
Piazza dei Coronari
Piazza San Salvatore in Lauro
Sant' Agostino
Lungotev Sassia
Piazza Paoli
V Banco S Spirito
Via dei Coronari
Ponte Pr Am Sav Aosta
Piazza dell' Oro
Ponte Parione
Corso Vittorio Emanuele
Santa Maria della Pace
Corso del Rinascimento
Santa Maria Maddalena
Santa Maria dell'Anima
Fontana dei Quattro Fiumi
San Luigi dei Francesi
Piazza della Rotonda
San Giovanni dei Fiorentini
Piazza dell' Orologio
Palazzo Madama
Sant'Agnese in Agone
Pantheon
Piazza Navona
Chiesa Nuova
Palazzo Pamphili
Piazza Sant' Eustachio
Lungotevere dei Sangallo
Via Giulia
Piazza della Chiesa Nuova
Sant'Ivo
Lungotevere Gianicolense
Palazzo Braschi-Museo di Roma
Fontana del Moro
Corso Vittorio Emanuele
Regola
Piazza San Pantaleo
Palazzo Massimo alle Colonne
Pig
Largo L Perosi
Palazzo della Cancelleria
Largo di Torre Argentina
Ponte G Mazzini
Sant'Eligio degli Orefici
Santa Maria di Monserrato
Piazza Campo dei Fiori
Sant'Andrea della Valle
Templi Repub-blici
Via della Lungara
Lungotevere dei Tebaldi
Piazza Farnese
Via di Torre Argentina
V delle
Palazzo Falconieri
Palazzo Farnese
Palazzo Spada
San Carlo ai Catinari
Tevere
Santa Maria dell'Orazione e Morte
Piazza B Cairoli
Santi Trinità dei Pellegrini
Villa Farnesina
Lungotevere della Farnesina
Palazzo Corsini-Giardino Botanico
Via Arenula
Ghetto
Ponte Sisto
Lungotevere dei Vallati
Lungotevere de
Gianicolo
Via V Benedetta
Piazza Trilussa
Museo Torlonia
Via della Scala
Santa Maria della Scala
Via G Garibaldi
Lungotevere Sanzio
Ponte Garibaldi
Isola Tiberina
Piazza G Belli
Lung Anguillara
Ponte Cestio
Via della Lungaretta
Piazza Sonnino
Via della Lungaretta
Via Porta San Pancrazio
San Pietro in Montorio
Santa Maria in Travestere
Via G Garibaldi
San Crisogono
San Benedetto
Fontana Paola
Viale di Trastevere
Via G Garibaldi
Trastevere
Piazza di San Cosimato

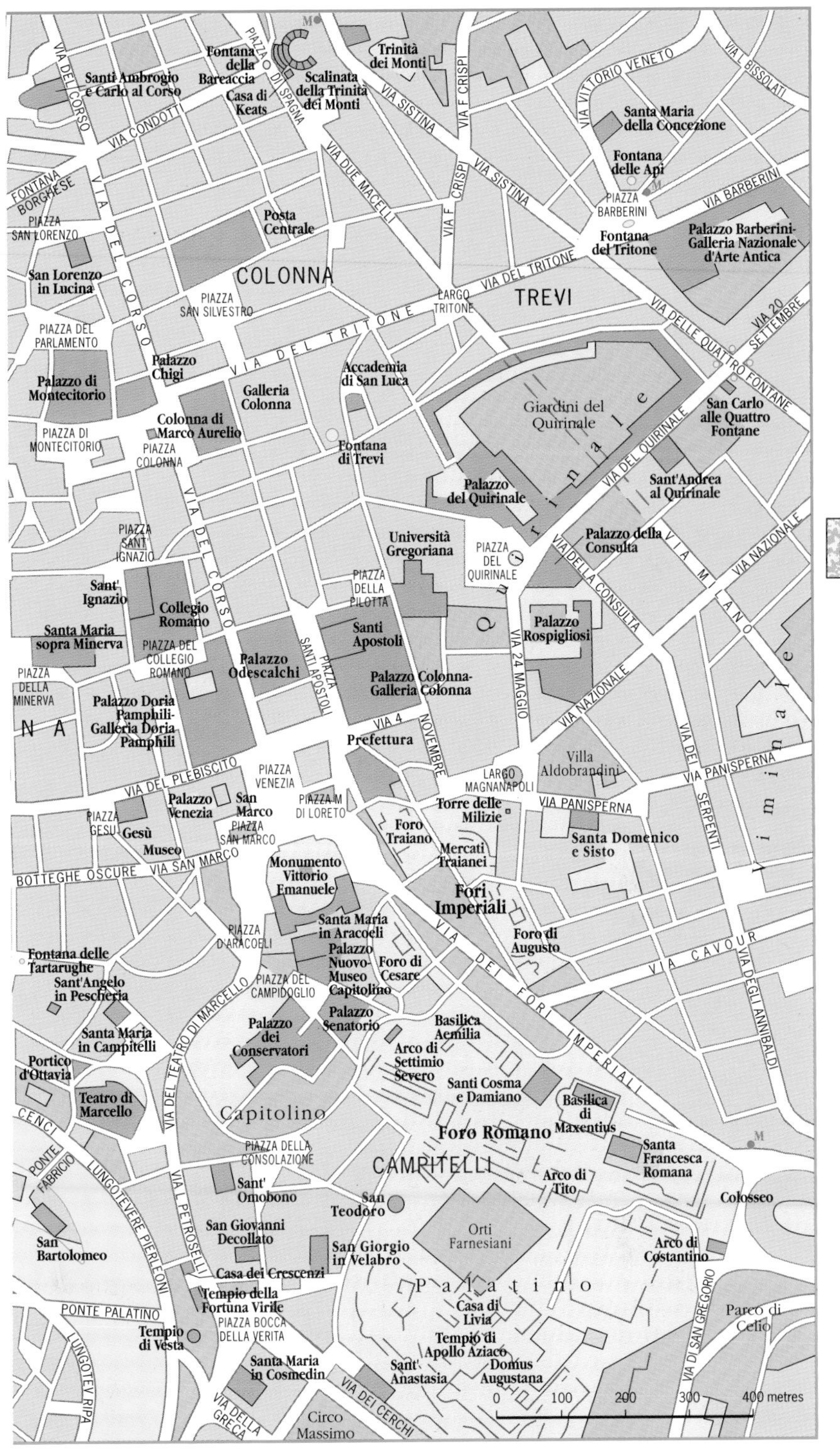
Santi Ambrogio e Carlo al Corso
Fontana della Barcaccia
Casa di Keats
Scalinata della Trinità dei Monti
Trinità dei Monti
Santa Maria della Concezione
Fontana delle Api
Piazza Barberini
Fontana del Tritone
Palazzo Barberini-Galleria Nazionale d'Arte Antica
Posta Centrale
Colonna
Trevi
San Lorenzo in Lucina
Piazza San Lorenzo
Piazza San Silvestro
Piazza del Parlamento
Palazzo Chigi
Palazzo di Montecitorio
Piazza di Montecitorio
Galleria Colonna
Colonna di Marco Aurelio
Piazza Colonna
Accademia di San Luca
Fontana di Trevi
Giardini del Quirinale
Palazzo del Quirinale
San Carlo alle Quattro Fontane
Sant'Andrea al Quirinale
Palazzo della Consulta
Università Gregoriana
Piazza del Quirinale
Piazza Sant' Ignazio
Sant' Ignazio
Collegio Romano
Santa Maria sopra Minerva
Piazza del Collegio Romano
Piazza della Minerva
Palazzo Odescalchi
Santi Apostoli
Piazza della Pilotta
Palazzo Colonna-Galleria Colonna
Palazzo Rospigliosi
Palazzo Doria Pamphili-Galleria Doria Pamphili
Prefettura
Villa Aldobrandini
Largo Magnanapoli
Palazzo Venezia
San Marco
Piazza Venezia
Piazza M di Loreto
Torre delle Milizie
Foro Traiano
Mercati Traianei
Santa Domenico e Sisto
Gesù
Piazza Gesù
Museo
Piazza San Marco
Monumento Vittorio Emanuele
Fori Imperiali
Santa Maria in Aracoeli
Piazza d'Aracoeli
Foro di Augusto
Fontana delle Tartarughe
Sant'Angelo in Pescheria
Palazzo Nuovo-Museo Capitolino
Foro di Cesare
Piazza del Campidoglio
Palazzo Senatorio
Santa Maria in Campitelli
Palazzo dei Conservatori
Basilica Aemilia
Arco di Settimio Severo
Portico d'Ottavia
Teatro di Marcello
Santi Cosma e Damiano
Basilica di Maxentius
Capitolino
Foro Romano
Santa Francesca Romana
Piazza della Consolazione
Campitelli
Arco di Tito
Sant' Omobono
San Teodoro
Orti Farnesiani
Colosseo
San Bartolomeo
San Giovanni Decollato
San Giorgio in Velabro
Arco di Costantino
Casa dei Crescenzi
Palatino
Tempio della Fortuna Virile
Casa di Livia
Parco di Celio
Tempio di Vesta
Piazza Bocca della Verita
Tempio di Apollo Aziaco
Santa Maria in Cosmedin
Sant' Anastasia
Domus Augustana
Circo Massimo
Via del Corso
Via Condotti
Piazza di Spagna
Via Sistina
Via F. Crispi
Via Vittorio Veneto
Via L. Bissolati
Via Due Macelli
Via Barberini
Via del Tritone
Largo Tritone
Via delle Quattro Fontane
Via 20 Settembre
Via del Quirinale
Via della Consulta
Via Nazionale
Via 24 Maggio
Via 4 Novembre
Via del Plebiscito
Via Panisperna
Via dei Serpenti
Via San Marco
Botteghe Oscure
Via dei Fori Imperiali
Via Cavour
Via degli Annibaldi
Via del Teatro di Marcello
Via L. Petroselli
Lungotevere Pierleoni
Ponte Fabricio
Ponte Palatino
Lungotev Ripa
Via della Greca
Via dei Cerchi
Via di San Gregorio
Fontana Borghese
Quirinale
Viminale
Via Milano
0 100 200 300 400 metres

▶▶▷ Catacombe di Domitilla

Via delle Sette Chiese

This 17 km labyrinth of galleries on four levels developed from an early hypogeum, or underground tomb, was built by the family of Domitilla and later used as the burial place for countless thousands of Christians. Domitilla's identity is hazy, but she was probably a Flavian and a distant Christian relative of the Emperors Vespasian and Domitian (AD 81–96). Later canonized, she was buried with her two martyred servants, Nereus and Achilleus.

A 4th-century basilica built over the site was destroyed by earthquakes, though impressive fragments form part of the guided tour. The town also includes a rare bas-relief showing the martyrdom of St. Achilleus, and the **Cappella di Santa Petronilla**, marked by a fresco of the saint thought to have been St. Peter's adopted daughter. Among the catacombs' inscriptions and early Christian paintings are the *Epiphany*, the *Raising of Lazarus*, a portrait of *St Paul*, and one of the first-known depictions of *Christ as the Good Shepherd.*

Open: guided tours daily 8:30–noon and 2:30–5. Closed Tuesday. Admission charge.

To reach the catacombs of St. Priscilla, take bus 56 from Piazza Barerini or the 57 from Termini. Ring the bell on the convent door for entry to the catacombs. The galleries consist of two levels, but tours, conducted by Benedictine nuns, visit only the upper one, which is the more ancient.

▶▶▶ Catacombe di Priscilla

Via Salaria 430

These are among Rome's oldest catacombs and are probably named after Priscilla, part of a wealthy, 1st-century AD senatorial family, the Acilii, who owned much of the area around the present-day Villa Ada. Priscilla was killed on the orders of Domitian, and her grave became something of a fashionable spot to be buried – so much so that several popes were laid to rest here. This may explain the high quality of its paintings, particularly those in the *cubiculum*, a small chapel that

According to a Roman law inherited from the Etruscans, all burials had to be outside the *pomerium*, the city's sacred boundary. This law first led to the crowding of cemeteries and elaborate tombs on consular roads outside the city – roads like the Via Appia and the Via Salaria.

San Sebastiano

contains the earliest-known depiction of the Madonna and Child, *The Virgin and Child with Isaiah* (second half of the 2nd century). Alongside it is another fresco, *The Good Shepherd with Two Sheep*, which like its neighbor is an example of a curious technique that combines stucco with painting. Also noteworthy is the Greek Chapel, so called because of the Greek inscriptions on the wall. Among the frescoes here is the first known representation of *The Breaking of the Bread at the Last Supper*.

Open: daily 8:30–noon and 2:30–5, closed Monday. Admission charge.

The Catacombe di San Callisto are the most visited of Rome's catacombs, and in summer you may have to line up to join one of the guided tours (open: daily 8:30–noon and 2:30–5, closed Wednesday. Admission charge).

▶▶▷ Catacombe di San Callisto

Via Appia Antica

These are Rome's largest and best-known catacombs, excavated to five levels in which 20 km of galleries and some 170,000 burial places have been unearthed. Visitors are admitted only to the second level, a maze of claustrophobic tunnels containing numerous *loculi*, or burial niches, carved out of the soft *tufa* (volcanic rock), usually in tiers five or six deep. Interspersed are occasional *arcosolia*, more sophisticated tombs topped with an arch and crude decoration. In places, larger chapels, called *cubicula*, were built to house whole families. Most important of them is the **Crypt of the Popes**, the tombs of six 3rd-century popes, many of them martyred – St. Urban I (died 230), St. Pontian (died 235), St. Anteros (died 236), St. Fabian (died 250), St. Lucius (died 254), and St. Eutychian (died 284). Each tomb is identified by Greek inscriptions and ringed with lovely spiral columns on the side walls.

During the Red Brigade's terrorist kidnapping of the Italian Prime Minister, Aldo Moro, in 1978, police identified the catacombs of San Callisto as one of the gang's possible hiding places.

To the left of these tombs is the **Crypt of St. Cecilia**, burial place of the young saint after her martyrdom in AD 230. The grave was uncovered in AD 821 by Pope Paschal I, who transferred her remains to the church of Santa Cecilia in Trastevere (see page 136). The walls are wonderfully decorated with frescoes of the *Raising of Lazarus* and the *Miracle of the Loaves and Fishes*. Elsewhere are interesting examples of graffiti, some of the earliest examples of Christian iconography – signs and symbols proclaiming the Christian faith, simple Greek inscriptions and crudely scratched drawings.

The Catacombe di San Callisto

▶▷▷ Catacombe di San Sebastiano

Via Appia Antica

Having always been accessible – and prey therefore to theft and damage – the appeal of these tombs is more muted. The site was a 1st-century BC pagan cemetery and burial place of the famous, arrow-riddled St. Sebastian. During the Valerian persecutions of 258, the bodies of St. Peter and St. Paul are believed to have been brought here for safe keeping. Inscriptions on the walls invoking the saints lend substance to the claims, and the bodies may have been kept here as long as 40 years. The area's spot is the pagan tomb of Clodius Hermes, decorated with well-kept stuccos, and the nearby *triclinium*, where funerary banquets were held.

Open: guided tours daily 9–noon and 2:30–5, closed Thursday. Admission charge.

Born in Florence, Filippo Neri lived in Rome for 60 years and inspired such devotion that he has been called the patron saint and second apostle of Rome. His cheerful, often eccentric behavior, allied with charisma and a shrewd wit, was especially attractive to his young followers. Initiates had to sing or write poetry. Filippo himself took delight in insulting the pope and in forcing his followers to work as laborers on his church as acts of humility. One Roman prince was turned down because he refused to walk in Rome with a foxtail fixed to his rear.

▶▷▷ Chiesa Nuova

Piazza della Chiesa Nuova, Corso Vittorio Emanuele II

The so-called Chiesa Nuova, or "new church," replaced an earlier 12th-century chapel on the site dedicated to St. John. It is known also as Santa Maria in Vallicella – the church in the little valley. Pope Gregory XIII gave this older church to San Filippo Neri, one of the period's most appealing characters, in recognition of his founding of the Oratorians, or Filippini. Like the Jesuits, this was one of several religious orders established in the 16th century during the Counter-Reformation.

Work quickly started on a new church, which was consecrated in 1599, four years after the death of Filippo. By this time the saint's request for a restrained building had been deliberately overlooked. The facade, in particular, by Fausto Rughesi, completed in 1606, is a massive and majestic affair, accentuated by the soaring central dome and the huddle of houses on either side.

Inside, Filippo's wish that the church should be simply whitewashed was also quietly forgotten. In 1647 Pietro da Cortona was commissioned to fresco the nave, dome, and apse, an undertaking that, working on and off, took him 20 years to complete. The result is an elaborate and sumptuous baroque cycle, the *Life and Apotheosis of Aeneas*, which competes with the church's other artistic treasures, an altarpiece and flanking pair of paintings by Rubens that were painted on slate to reduce the effects of reflected light. Equally important are Cortona's *Presentation* and *Visitation*, located respectively, in the left transept and fourth chapel of the left aisle.

The church's most overwhelming items are its glorious pair of shuddering, gilt-covered organs on opposite sides of the nave.

Soaring majesty: the Chiesa Nuova

Oratorio dei Filippini This stands outside the church to the left and dates from 1637 to 1652. Filippo's headquarters are fronted by an idiosyncratic curved facade designed by **Borromini.** Here Filippo's followers held their musical services.

During these services the musical form known as the *oratorio* was developed. Today the building is quiet and houses the Capitoline archive and the Biblioteca Vallecelliana, Rome's greatest library for history and antiquities.

Around the corner of the building is the **Piazza del Orologio**, where Borromini's genius and obsession with curved surfaces reached their pinnacle in his small but exquisite clock tower.

▶▷▷ Circo Massimo

Viale Aventino

All that now remains of the Circo Massimo, once a vast arena that could hold over 300,000 people, is a large open space and the grassy banks of its old seats. Created to satisfy the Roman passion for chariot racing, and a prototype for all subsequent race courses, the circus was started around 326 BC and then rebuilt and modified numerous times before its last recorded use under Totila the Ostrogoth in AD 549.

Masterpieces reproduced on the streets

History The circus started life in the Mursia, the natural hollow between the Palatine and Aventine hills. The Etruscan king, Tarquinius Superbus, added its first terraces and a temple to the fertility goddess Ceres on the Palatine overlooking the Circo Massimo. Healthy competition was also believed to feed the courage of soldiers, as well as appease their god, Mars, a deity of both war and agriculture.

Development Shops and taverns soon mushroomed in arcades around the course, and obsequiousness to the gods gave way to astrological symbolism. An obelisk was raised on the *spina* (backbone), the arena's dividing wall to represent the sun, along with 12 *carceri* (cells), or starting stalls for the chariots, each of which was accorded a sign of the zodiac. The races' seven laps recalled the planets or days of the week and were recorded on the *spina* by moving wooden eggs and, later, bronze dolphins.

Augustus formalized seating on class lines, building an imperial balcony (or *pulvinar)* linked to his villa on the Palatine. Below it, in the general seating, or *cavea,* senators were arrayed on the uppermost marble tiers, lesser worthies huddled on wooden seats below, and the lower ranks fought for standing room in the open stands. More bloodthirsty entertainments followed in time: the slaughter of thousands of wild animals and public executions under the papacy.

Most of the old structure has been used as a quarry over the centuries, and today all that remains is the *spina,* marked by a grass ridge and cypress trees; the ruins of the imperial box, still jutting from the Palatine; and the open space of the arena, now a public park (dangerous after dark).

The sexes were unsegregated at the Circo, unlike the Colosseum, and Ovid, for one, recorded that the races were an excellent place for a spot of romantic dalliance: "No call here for the secret language of fingers: nor need you depend on a furtive nod . . . when you are set upon a new affair".

Races in the Circo Massimo involved either two-horsed chariots *(bigae)* or the more dangerous four-horsed version, the *quadrigae.* By the time of Caligula there were as many as 24 races a day, and meetings could go on for as long as 15 days.

The Sarmatian tribes, a wild Slavic race whose women joined battle, were some of Aurelius's favorite opponents. In his *Memoirs,* he mused: "A spider prides itself on capturing a fly; one man on catching a hare, another on netting a sprat, another on taking wild boars, another Sarmatians."

Opposite the Colonna is a large newsstand (or *edicola),* Rome's best for foreign newspapers and magazines. Around from the newsstand is *Rizzoli,* the city's largest bookshop.

▶▷▷ Colonna di Marcos Aurelios

Piazza Colonna

Like Trajan's Column – on which it is modeled – and Rome's triumphal arches, the Column of Marcus Aurelius is a monument to military achievement. Raised on the orders of the Senate between AD 180 and AD 196, it celebrated Aurelius's victory over northern European tribes like the Sarmatians (AD 174–175) and Marcomanni (AD 171–173). The pillar – 138 feet high and 12 feet in diameter – consists of 27 cunningly disguised drums of Carraran marble, its entire surface carved with a continuous spiral frieze of bas-reliefs commemorating episodes from the victorious battles. Restored recently to a dazzling whiteness, the reliefs' script has revealed a wealth of intimate documentary detail on the military and social life of the period. It also depicts Aurelius no less than 59 times, but oddly enough it never actually shows him in battle.

A 190-step interior staircase, all too often closed, opens on to a platform at the top, where the statue is that of St. Paul, crafted by Domenico Fontana in 1589 to replace the earlier figure of Marcus Aurelius. Fontana also restored the base, confusing its original dedication to Aurelius with a new inscription to his uncle, Antoninus Pius. The column is even now sometimes mistakenly called the Antonine column.

Colosseo see pages 66–68.

▶▷▷ Domus Aurea/Colle Oppio

Via Labicana

In its time, the **Domus Aurea** (Nero's Golden House) was one of the most fantastic, if vulgar palaces Rome had ever seen. Now little remains; that which does has been closed to the public for many years. The **Colle Oppio**, main site of the monolith, is today one of Rome's most delightful neighborhood parks.

Nero's folly Following the great fire of 64 BC, during which Nero famously "fiddled while Rome burned," the demented emperor appropriated huge areas of central Rome for his proposed pleasure dome. The complex was eventually to spread over a quarter of the city, covering the Esquiline, Palatine, and Coelian hills.

Close to the Golden House itself, so called because it was swathed in gold leaf, was an artificial lake (now the **Colosseum),** watched over by a 115-foot statue of the emperor – surpassing the famous Colossus of Rhodes, and the largest statue ever made in antiquity. The approach was an avenue over a mile long, shaded by triple colonnades. Within, indoor baths were fed direct either by seawater or from sulfurous springs, while finely carved ivory ceilings concealed openings that sprayed a fine veil of perfume or wild flowers on to the rooms below.

The Colle Oppio today Work stopped on the extravagance when Nero died in AD 68, and subsequent emperors demolished large portions of the palace in favor of such projects as the Colosseum. Most of the

Domus itself was swallowed up by Trajan's baths (AD 104–109). Rome's first truly monumental bath complex, its plan was copied by all that followed.

It was only during excavations in the 1490s that one wing of the palace came to light. Its exquisite frescoes attracted numerous Renaissance painters, among them Raphael, who was so impressed that he used their motifs in the famous Vatican *stanze* (see **Vatican,** pages 184–194). The figures became known as *grottesche,* after the grottoes in which they were found. In 1506, another renowned work, the *Laocoön* (now in the Vatican) was also retrieved from the Domus Aurea. Trajan's baths have never been excavated, and other works of art are probably buried in the Colle Oppio.

▶▶▷ Esquilino

The Esquilino, or Esquiline Hill, was one of the original Seven Hills of Rome, and today, unlike some of its neighbors, it still retains the outlines of its former lofty contours. However, its two original summits, the *Cispius* and *Oppius,* are not particularly clear. The former is crowned by one of Rome's great patriarchal churches, **Santa Maria Maggiore** (see pages 151–154) and was the site of several important pagan temples. The latter, well to the south, contains the ruins of the **Domus Aurea** (Nero's Golden House, see page 64); the Terme di Traiano (The Baths of Trajan); and the large, appealing park spread over the **Colle Oppio**.

The entrance to the ruins of the Domus Aurea are at Via Labicana 136. It is hardly ever open, and any visits are as guided tours. The park of the Colle Oppio is always open, but has a deserved nocturnal reputation as a haunt of prostitutes and drug addicts.

One of the most decadent rooms in Nero's *domus* was the domed octagonal hall, surrounded by waterfalls and used for sumptuous banquets, where a revolving table ensured that guests never had to rise from a reclining position to reach their food. According to Suetonius, moreover, the entire room revolved day and night in time with the heavens.

Santa Maria Maggiore

▶▶▶ Colosseo

Neither pictures, photographs, nor the many superlatives heaped on the Colosseum can prepare you for the awe-inspiring spectacle of Rome's most famous monument. It is easy to visualize the combat of gladiators and hear the roar of the Roman crowd. Even though only half the original structure remains and is ringed by thundering traffic, it lives up to its promise as the city's most majestic sight.

The idea for the arena came in AD 72 from the Emperor Vespasian, who intended it to be built on land previously set aside for Nero's **Domus Aurea**. At the time of his death in AD 79, however, it remained unfinished and was inaugurated by his son, Titus, in AD 80 with a gala that saw 5,000 animals slaughtered and was followed by 100 days of continuous games. It received its finishing touches during the reign of Domitian (AD 81–96), who like his predecessors was part of the Flavian dynasty. This dynasty gave the stadium its original name, the *Amphitheatrum Flavium* – the Flavian Amphitheater.

The inspiration for the scheme came from the **Teatro di Marcello** (see page 174). The site, chosen for its proximity to the Roman Forum and the Palatine, posed massive engineering problems, chief of which was its marshy surroundings, a legacy of the Domus Aurea's artificial lake, which had to be drained to make way for the amphitheater. Engineers laid down huge drains (many still in use), together with a ring of *pozzalana,* a cement foundation made from volcanic sand some 23 feet thick. The weight of the building, whose original circumference was a third of a mile, was spread between a series of circular *tufa* (volcanic rock) walls and a fan of barrel vaults that supported the terraces and corridors between. Jewish slaves, brought to Rome after the Judaean revolt, provided unwilling labor.

A unique wedding setting: the Colosseum

An impressive model for stadiums of the future

Trendsetting design For all its immense size, few would deny the amphitheater's architectural beauty or its functional simplicity, which has provided the models for large stadiums ever since. A potentially rowdy crowd could leave their seats within minutes via the numbered *vomitoria,* or exits. On the upper story, a huge sailcloth awning (the *velarium*), supported by some 240 masts, protected spectators from the sun. For the most part, the genius of the building's architecture speaks for itself, though odd details are worth noticing, such as the half-columns on the exterior arcades, which – like the Teatro di Marcello – are Doric at ground level, Ionic on the first arcade and Corinthian on the second.

However, if the Colosseum's beauty is unequivocal, its original purpose was more double-edged. Juvenal observed that Romans sold their power in return for bread and circuses – the lures of free food and entertainment. Contrary to popular myth, the latter's gory manifestations probably did not include the martyrdom of many Christians – despite the bronze commemorative cross in the center of the arena; the great era of religious persecution under Nero took place before the arena was built. Gladitorial contests first took place among the Samnites in the 4th century, and the Etruscans are also believed to have indulged in ritual combat. Traditionally the encounters were to prepare soldiers for battle, to raise their morale and harden them to the sight of death, but in time they degenerated to the level of sport.

All manner of decadent variations on a theme were introduced to satisfy the crowds. Criminals, slaves and gladiators, some of them volunteers, fought each other – usually to the death; women grappled with dwarfs,

The Colosseum is the largest surviving Roman structure: 187 feet high, 610 feet long, 512 feet across with seating for up to 87,000. Some 420 species of flowers once grew in its ruins, many introduced with animal fodder in classical times.

and even mock sea battles took place in the arena, which could be flooded in minutes by closing off the underground drains. Gambling on the outcome of mortal combats was rife, and spectators could even win themselves a slave in an imperial lottery.

The Colosseum's name may have been coined simply because of its huge size or may have come from the *Colossus of Nero*, the largest bronze statue ever made (now lost), which stood close by. Its first recorded mention comes in a manuscript attributed to the Venerable Bede in the 7th century. In it Bede quoted the prophecy made famous by Byron's translation in *Childe Harold's Pilgrimage: While stands the Colisseum, Rome shall stand; When falls the Colisseum, Rome shall fall: And when Rome falls – the world.*

Who sat where The crowds for such events were rigidly divided by class, with the emperor, his Imperial court, and high officials (including the Vestal Virgins) in the lower tiers; Rome's aristocratic families on the second; and the common herd in the third. Women, who by all accounts largely avoided the carnage, were expected to occupy the uppermost tiers. A special official, or *designator*, was employed to keep people in their allotted places. Spectators often exercised power of life and death over the combatants, replying to a wounded man's appeal for mercy (the raising of a finger on his left hand) either with the waving of handkerchiefs or – for the less fortunate – with the famous signal of the down-turned thumb. The survivors often had their throats cut in any case, and even the dead were poked with red-hot irons to make sure they had actually expired.

Gladiatorial tussles were finally outlawed in AD 438, and the last animal show was recorded in AD 523. As a result of successive earthquakes during the Dark Ages, much of the arena fell into ruin. In AD 664, Constans II removed the metal clamps that had bound the Colosseum's travertine blocks, leaving the holes that pock-mark the building and mystify many visitors. Later the Frangipani family built a fortress into the arena, which in time became a huge quarry. This fortress was unashamedly pillaged for masonry to build the Palazzo Venezia, Palazzo Barberini, and Palazzo Farnese as well as any number of Rome's bridges, churches and minor palaces.

Volcanic rock was used to build the vast Colosseum walls

In memoriam Pope Benedict XIV brought an end to the desecration in 1744, when he consecrated the site and set up the Stations of the Cross in memory of the Christians supposedly martyred there. Pius VIII (1800–1823), together with later popes and the city's French administrators, began the process of restoration by buttressing the outer arches and excavating the labyrinth of walls and passages in the arena area. In their day these passages provided underground cages for animals, storerooms, prisons, and training or changing rooms for the gladiators.

They were covered with wooden boards and a layer of sand, useful both to provide sure footing and to act as a sponge for the blood (the Latin for sand is *arena).*

There are fine views from the Colosseum's higher levels over the Roman Forum, and its small museum illustrates the seating arrangements and operation of grand events in its heyday.

The best time to visit is early in the morning or late in the afternoon, and at night the entire building is floodlit to spectacular effect.

Open: daily, 9–7 (Sunday and Wednesday, 9–1:30). Winter, 9–4. Admission charge to upper levels.

Water show: Fontana della Barcaccia

▶▷▷ **Fontana delle Api**

Piazza Barberini

This small fountain is one of Bernini's most captivating creations. The piazza takes its name from the great Florentine family, and the fountain was commissioned in honor of Urban VIII, one of the clan's leading lights. In particular it was coined to mark the 21st anniversary of his accession to the papacy in 1644. The fountain was completed before the event, and an inscription was made in anticipation, claiming that the fountain was dedicated in the 22nd year of the pope's reign. Many saw this as a bad omen, rightly in the event, because Urban died soon after – eight days before the 22nd year of his pontificate. The fountain itself centers on a scallop shell – a favorite Bernini conceit – at which three large bees (*api*), taken from the Barberini coat of arms, have settled to drink.

▶▷▷ **Fontana della Barcaccia**

Piazza di Spagna

Most people sooner or later loll around the Barcaccia fountain (literally the "fountain of the worthless boat"), crowded with thousands of others watching the world go by at the foot of the Spanish Steps (the **Scalinata della Trinità dei Monti**). Urban VIII commissioned the work in 1627, but there is much dispute as to whether it was the brainchild of Pietro Bernini or his more famous son, Gianlorenzo.

Whatever the provenance, the design is wonderfully eccentric and represents a half-sunken boat with water spilling sluggishly from bow and stern. The low water pressure of the Acqua Vergine aqueduct feeding the fountain precludes a more dramatic display. Urban was responsible for restoring the area's old Roman aqueduct, and inevitably his family's emblems – the Barberini bees and suns – adorn the fountain on every side.

A drink with the bees: Fontana delle Api

The story goes that it fell to one Prospero da Brescia to sculpt the figure of Moses on the Fontana del Mose (page 70), a thankless task, given the towering achievement of Michelangelo's Moses in the church of San Pietro in Vincoli. The critical mauling given to the work on its completion is said to have pushed him to an early grave – perhaps even to suicide. According to the critic Venturi, it was the most shameful parody of Michelangelo's work in Rome. In fact Prospero was only a hapless assistant to the fountain's true perpetrator, the sculptor Leonardo Sormani.

Some say the work was prompted by the tumultuous Christmas flood of 1598 that left a boat stranded nearby; others that it is a reminder this was a part of the city that was frequently flooded by the Tiber. Other possibilities are that it represents the ship of the Church or marks the supposed site of Domitian's water stadium where sea battles were reenacted in the days of the Empire.

▶▶▷ **Fontana del Moro**

Piazza Navona

The third of Piazza Navona's fountains, at the piazza's southern end, the "Moor Fountain" is the work of Giacomo della Porta (1575). The central figure of the so-called Moor (actually a marine divinity) grappling with a dolphin was added by Antonio Mori, from a design by Bernini. The encircling tritons are 19th-century copies of 16th-century originals.

▷▷▷ **Fontana del Mose**

Piazza San Bernardo

The Moses fountain, named after its huge central figure, is also known as the Fontana dell'Acqua Felice (the "Fountain of the Happy Water") – and was commissioned by Sixtus V in 1587. Before he became pope, Sixtus was called Felice Peretti, hence the name. The first of the big post-Renaissance fountains, it was designed to show off the pope's newly restored aqueduct, the *Acqua Alessandrina*. Size for its own sake is the fountain's only distinguishing feature.

▷▷▷ **Fontana delle Naiadi**

Piazza della Repubblica

Of little historical fame, and in one of the city's less inspiring piazzas, the Naiads's Fountain (1901) nonetheless rates as one of the most erotic works of art on public display anywhere. Water plays seductively

Fontana dei Quattro Fiumi

Seductive sculpture: Fontana delle Naiadi

over frolicking and suggestively clad women, each entwined in a marine creature's phallic tentacles so as to leave little to the imagination. The city fathers felt the poses too lascivious for public consumption, and the wraps were taken off only after a massive public protest.

▷▷▷ Fontana Paola

Via Garibaldi

A glorious fountain, arranged over a monumental facade of five arches and six granite columns, the Paola was built between 1610 and 1612 for Pope Paul V's recently restored Trajan aqueduct. Water on the resurrected causeway was brought from as far away as the **Lago di Bracciano** (see page 227), and in ancient Rome was used to power the mills that ground the city's flour. The columns in the fountain were removed from the facade of the original St. Peter's; other marbles were plundered from the Temple of Minerva in the Foro di Nerva (see pages 75–76, **Fori Imperiali**).

The best time to catch the fountain is during a walk on the **Gianicolo** above Trastevere, combined with a visit to **San Pietro in Montorio.**

▶▶▷ Fontana dei Quattro Fiumi

Piazza Navona

Bernini's greatest fountain, the so-called Fountain of the Four Rivers, is also his best known because of its position at the heart of **Piazza Navona**. The spirited and majestic work was commissioned by Innocent X in 1648 as part of his plan to improve the approach to the **Palazzo Doria Pamphili.**

The four rivers are symbolized by four massive figures perched on a crag of travertine. Each one represents all four rivers of Paradise – the Nile, Ganges, Danube and Plate – and the four known corners of the world: Africa, Asia, Europe and America. However, only the horse representing the Danube was personally carved by Bernini. The obelisk was designed to make the fountain stand out. The dove on top is a symbol of Innocent's Pamphili family.

The commission for the Fontana dei Quattro Fiumi was not a popular one among Romans at the time. Pope Innocent X levied a tax on citizens' bread to raise the vast sum of gold (29,000 *scudi*) needed to pay for it. Both he and his sister-in-law, Olympia Maidalchini, who swung the commission in Bernini's favor, were violently and publicly vilified.

Detail from Fontana dei Quattro Fiumi

▶▷▷ Fontana delle Tartarughe

Piazza Mattei

Far and away Rome's most charming fountain, the "Fountain of the Tortoises" was designed by Giacomo della Porta in 1581 and sculpted by Taddeo Landini, a Florentine artist, which perhaps explains the whimsy of the piece, unusual for Rome. It revolves around four bronze boys, each grasping a dolphin that jets water into marble shells, and several bronze tortoises each held in the boys' hands and drinking from the fountain's upper basin. The tortoises – the fountain's touch of genius – were a 17th-century addition, added, inevitably, by Bernini.

▶▷▷ Fontana del Tritone

Piazza Barberini

Among the greatest of Bernini's baroque conceits, the "Fountain of Triton" (1643) overshadows his other fountain in Piazza Barberini, the **Fontana delle Api**. Like its neighbor, the fountain was commissioned by the Barberini Pope Urban VIII, and the family crest is as much in evidence. The inspired design was one of Bernini's earliest aquatic efforts, and in its use of travertine – rather than the usual marble – was a novelty at the time. It consists of four dolphins supporting twin scallop shells (each emblazoned with the Barberini arms), a sea throne for the magnificent figure of Triton, who blows water through a conch shell held to his lips.

▶▶▶ Fontana di Trevi

Piazza Fontana di Trevi

The Fontana di Trevi is the most spectacular of Rome's fountains, immortalized by Anita Ekberg's midnight dip in Fellini's classic film, *La Dolce Vita*. Lesser Hollywood offerings, such as *Three Coins in the Fountain* and *Roman Holiday,* have used the fountain to more kitsch effect, but coming round a corner to discover its watery display – "silvery to the eye and ear," as Charles Dickens wrote – is one of the city's most memorable pleasures. It's a favorite meeting place, so on most days, especially Sunday, the area can be very crowded, making late evening, when things are quieter and the fountain is floodlit, the best time to visit.

The first fountain to take the waters of the *Acqua Vergine* was built in 1453 for Pope Nicholas V. He paid for it with a tax on wine, leading the Romans to sneer that "he took our wine to give us water." It looked, however, said one 18th-century historian, like "a dilapidated village well," and before long a competition was instigated among 16 sculptors to come up with something better.

The new fountain This was commissioned by Pope Clement XII and supervised by Nicolo Salvi between 1732 and 1762. The long project and the time spent in the winter chill supervising it are believed to have brought about his premature death. He was not, however, the key designer, and some scholars believe Bernini worked on the project for Urban VIII as early as 1644. Others also now attribute the work's central idea

– combining a fountain with a palace facade – to Pietro da Cortona. Its name probably comes from *tre vie* ("three roads") after the three streets that converge here out of the warren of lanes.

The fountain's facade forms the east wing of the Palazzo Poli and was modeled on the ancient **Arco di Constantino** of all things. The figure of Oceanus (Neptune) dominates the proceedings, supported by tritons to either side; the one on the left struggling to control his horse represents a stormy sea; his partner on the right, blowing into a conch shell, symbolizes the ocean in repose. The statues in niches to either side of Neptune are allegories of Health and Abundance, overseen by figures on the pediment who represent the four seasons. The circle of seats in front is a later addition.

Coins in the fountain Most people know the tradition of throwing a coin into the fountain if they want to return to Rome. It continues a tradition of the ancient Romans, who threw coins into certain fountains to appease the gods, a practice later adopted by Christians, who threw coins onto the tomb of St. Peter. For many years, it was enough simply to drink the Trevi's waters to guarantee a return trip; now the received wisdom is that a coin has to be thrown over the left shoulder for the desired effect. Few visitors can resist the temptation, and huge sums are raked out weekly. In theory it all goes to charity, though as ever in Rome things are not actually that simple, and there have been several scandals in which the coins have wound up in the wrong hands.

The fountain is fed by the *Acqua Vergine* aqueduct, built by Augustus in 19 BC and reputed to have the sweetest waters in Rome. The name comes from a legend in which a young girl (*vergine*) showed the original spring to a group of thirsty Roman soldiers, a story you can see illustrated on the fountain to the right of Oceanus.

Under cover by the Fontana di Trevi

Fountains and Water

■ Cars, raised voices and the gentle splash of water – these are Rome's distinguishing sounds. The city has more fountains – and more beautiful ones at that – than any city in the world. Few piazzas are without one, whether a solitary affair gurgling quietly to itself, a masterpiece like Bernini's Fontana dei Fiumi, or a vast erotic caprice like the one relieving Piazza della Repubblica's tawdry sprawl. . . .■

Water everywhere Rome can afford to be extravagant – its water is either flowing with wanton ease from hundreds of street-corner taps, or gushing into sinks in countless bars that perversely keep their taps jammed open.

<< The water from any of Rome's hundreds of street-corner fountains is fine to drink, still as "clear, sweet and fresh" as it was in Petrarch's day. It's not unusual to see Romans filling up huge carafes to take home from the more renowned fountains. **>>**

The seemingly bottomless reservoir comes from the mountains to the east, from the Colli Albani, or from ranges like the Simbruini in the foothills of the Apennines, whose very name – literally *sub imbribus* – derives from the Latin for heavy rain. The fountains to see above all others are the Fontana di Trevi, the Fontana delle Tartarughe, the Fontana dei Quattro Fiumi and the Fontana delle Naiadi.

The city's real aquatic lifelines, however, are its aqueducts, 11 of which date from classical times. The best known are the Acqua Vergine, built by Augustus; Trajan's Acqua Paola; and the Acqua Felice, championed by Severus. There is, however, one sour note – the horrendously polluted Tiber. Until the 1950s people fished and swam here, but it is no longer Virgil's Tiber of the blue water, the river most dear to heaven.

<< Many households in Rome have a separate drinking tap, the prized *acqua diretta*, whose waters come directly from the aqueduct, and Romans still argue over the merits of the various springs that feed them. **>>**

One mouthful these days, say the Romans, is enough to kill you. The river itself has long aroused little but contempt: "A ditch" (Herman Melville, 1757); "A scurvy draught" (David Garrick, 1763); "An inconsiderable stream" (Tobias Smollett, 1765); "A menacing serpent, with no more life than the Dead Sea" (Federico Fellini, 1972).

Unmoved by the Naiadi

Remnants of glory: Fori Imperiali

 **Fori Imperiali**

Via dei Fori Imperiali

The Fori Imperiali, or Imperial Forums, are so called to distinguish them from the **Foro Romano**, or Roman Forum, close by. By the end of the Republican era, it was clear that the Roman Forum between the Capitoline and Palatine hills was too small to accommodate the social, commercial and administrative development demanded by the burgeoning Empire. Nor was the old forum capable of accommodating the grandiose schemes through which successive emperors sought to immortalize themselves in bricks and mortar.

Foro di Cesare Julius Caesar was the first to acquire land beyond the confines of the forum for an area that became known as the Forum of Caesar, or the *Forum Julium*. Built between 54 and 46 BC, at the emperor's own expense, its principal buildings were the temple of Venus Genetrix and the Basilica Argentaria, which housed money changers and the exchange. Two-thirds of the site are buried under the Via dei Fori Imperiali, and only three damaged columns survive as memorials to its former glory.

Foro di Augusto Little also remains of the Forum of Augustus, which under Augustus's prompting continued Caesar's expansion north of the Roman Forum. "I found Rome brick and left it marble," was to be the emperor's famous boast. Its best-preserved relics are three columns from the Tempio di Mars Ultor ("Mars the Avenger"), which Augustus founded in 2 BC to commemorate the Battle of Philippi in 42 BC. This was the encounter that saw the defeat of Brutus and Cassius (driving them to suicide) and the avenging of Caesar's murder. The temple housed several of Caesar's possessions, including his sword.

Most of the Fori Imperiali lie either to one side or under the Via dei Fori Imperiali, the huge road that Mussolini scythed through the forums in 1932. Little research was done before construction, and untold archaeological treasures now lie buried beneath the tarmac. One day the Rome authorities have promised to start excavations, but it is difficult to see how they would deal with the traffic chaos caused by the closure of what is now the city's major thoroughfare.

During construction of the Via dei Fori Imperiali, Mussolini placed a statue of each emperor before his respective forum. Every year on the Ides of March, the anniversary of Julius Caesar's death, an unknown hand leaves a bouquet of flowers alongside Caesar's statue.

Detail shown on the Colonna Traiano

Behind the temple is a huge wall that separated the forum from *hoi polloi* of the Suburra, a teeming slum suburb frequently swept by fire. West of the temple stands the **Casa dei Cavalieri di Rodi** (House of the Knights of Rhodes), a 12th-century building cannibalized from an earlier classical structure. Its loggia gives memorable views over the whole forum, and from the atrium – the fossil of an Augustan palace – you can wander to the **Antiquarium,** whose sculptures include a fine head of Jupiter and a crop of wonderfully carved capitals.

Foro di Nerva Laid out by an emperor who ruled for just two years (AD 96–98), much of this forum now languishes under modern streets or was rifled by Pope Paul V to provide stone for aqueducts and papal conceits. However, two arresting columns and a lovely frieze survive, once part of a temple to Minerva. All have been recently restored, bringing out the reliefs that describe the myth of Arachne – who challenged the weaving art of Minerva and was transformed into a spider for her presumption.

Foro di Vespasiano South of Via dei Fori Imperiali and easily overlooked, the Forum of Vespasian was built from AD 71 to 75 (after the Forum of Augustus) using money and materials garnered from the Jewish wars. The most interesting section still on view – all but a fraction of the area is buried under modern roads – is the church of **Santi Cosmo e Damiano** (see page 139), quartered within one of the forum's basilicas.

Foro Traiano Trajan's Forum (built AD 107–113) is by far the grandest of the five imperial forums and can be reached via the lower level of the **Mercati Traianei** (see page 98) or seen from above on Via dei Fori Imperiali. Today all too little remains, hardly suggesting a complex that for centuries was held in awe as one of the architectural wonders of the world. Broken columns and wistful piles of stones are the only monuments to the temple of Trajan, once among the city's mightiest.

Colonna Traiano At least one masterpiece in Trajan's Forum has stood "firm in its pristine majesty." Built in AD 113 to celebrate two victorious campaigns against the Dacians (tribes who occupied modern-day Romania), its 18 drums of Greek marble are carved with a spiraling frieze of some 2,500 figures, actors in battle scenes that have provided a wealth of documentary detail about Roman arms and modes of warfare. In its day the column was gilded and the figures brightly painted, and all are on view at close quarters from the roof gardens of the nearby Greek and Latin libraries. Now the interior staircase and viewing platform are rarely open.

Trajan's ashes were once kept in a golden urn at the base of the column – the first time anyone had been buried within the bounds of the *pomerium*, the city's sacred boundary. A statue of the emperor stood at its summit for years, but was replaced by a more suitable Christian icon, St. Peter.

▶▶▶ Foro Romano

The heart of republican Rome and the center of an empire that embraced most of the known world, the Foro Romano, or Roman Forum, is one of the world's most important historical sites. Originally it was simply a marshy hollow between the Palatine and Capitoline Hills, an Iron Age cemetery – no more than a field crossed by a muddy track – known as the *forum* (from a word that meant 'outside the walls'). Later it became a dumping ground for the shepherds' settlements on the hills, later still a marketplace and common ground for early tribes. It entered the annals of myth, if not of history, as the arena where Romulus, first king of Rome, reputedly concluded peace with the Sabines in 753 BC.

One of the great sights of the Roman Forum: the Basilica di Maxentius, begun in AD 306

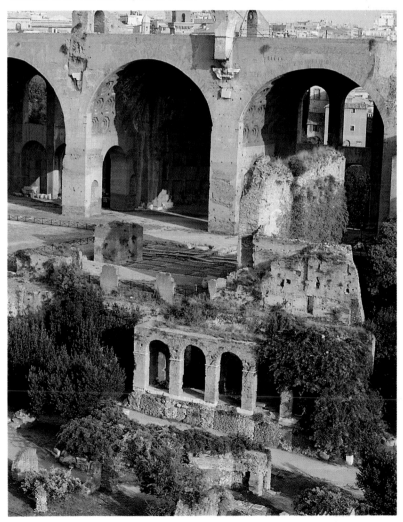

Two little-visited churches stand north of the Forum of Trajan, small gems that pleasantly frame the eastern edge of Piazza Venezia. The first is Santa Maria di Loreto, a High Renaissance confection begun by Antonio da Sangallo that houses du Quesnoy's influential baroque masterpiece, a statue of *Santa Susanna* (1633). The second, *Santissimo Nome di Maria*, was added in the 18th century.

The guide to the monuments of the Roman Forum follows a roughly circular, anticlockwise tour from the entrance and ticket office on Via dei Fori Imperiali. Before any tour of the Roman Forum, be sure to take in its general layout from the vantage points on Via del Campidoglio and the northern side of Piazza del Campidoglio.

Early development After drainage, probably the first buildings to appear were market stalls or temples, followed over the centuries by all the structures of civic, social and political life. As Rome blossomed, consuls, senators and emperors embellished the Empire's epicenter with temples, courts and basilicas, each vying to outdo the other in the magnificence of their efforts. However, after centuries of glorious and unparalleled growth, the tide turned, and by the 2nd century the importance enjoyed by the forum in its Republican heyday had begun to ebb. Political power moved to the Palatine's imperial palaces, commerce to Trajan's Market, and gestures of grandiloquence to the new Fori Imperiali. Churches and fortresses grew up amid the ruin brought on by the fall of Rome, much of the area becoming a rubble-strewn quarry for building stone. By the 16th century the forum had turned full circle and was once again little more than a field.

The forum today To visit the forum now for the first time can be a disappointment. Too much has been plundered or destroyed over the centuries to re-create its ancient splendor from the remaining jumble of stones. In some areas whole monuments have still to be properly excavated, and the dread hand of restoration can put sites out of bounds – sometimes for years.

To add to the confusion, the forum's ruins are not a simple archaeological slice from a single period. The area was built on over 1,100 years, and buildings were pulled down, altered, buried, moved or simply forgotten. The result is a mish-mash of monuments that are tinged with the romance of all ruins, but puzzling. If your imagination is working overtime and you use a methodical approach, these disparate fragments can still be assembled into a picture of past glory.

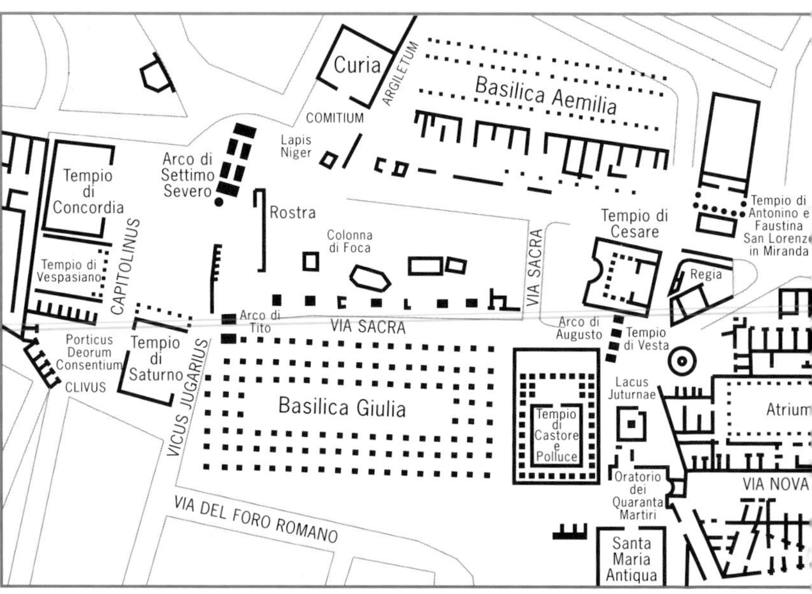

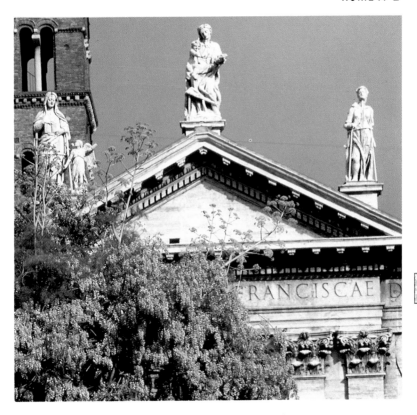

The church of San Francesca Romana, built in the 10th century and still a distinctive part of the Forum

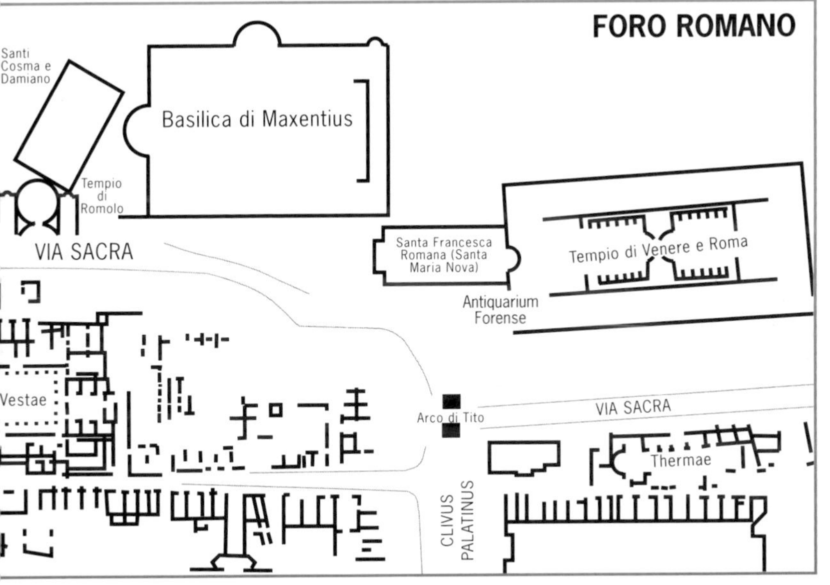

The Roman Forum is open from April to September, 9–7 on Monday and Wednesday to Saturday; Tuesday and Sunday, 9–1: October to March, 9–3 on Monday, and Wednesday to Saturday; Tuesday and Sunday, 9–1.

Tempio di Antonio e Faustina The first site after the ticket office, and one of the forum's best preserved ruins, this temple was built in AD 141 by Emperor Antoninus Pius to honor the virtue of his deified wife, Faustina. According to Roman gossip, however, the so-called pious emperor was the only man in the city not to know of his wife's constant infidelities. The temple owes its state of preservation to the fact that it was converted into a church in the 11th century – the rarely opened **San Lorenzo in Miranda**. Six large Corinthian columns of the portico survive, supporting a superb frieze of griffons and caging the church within. The body of the building rests well above the surroundings, clearly suggesting the original ground level of the *Campo Vaccino* before excavations. The columns bear all the scars of age, some inflicted by the chains of Christian church builders who attempted to pull them down.

Via Sacra Below the temple lies the Via Sacra (Sacred Way), Rome's most ancient street, a narrow thoroughfare that bisects the forum and links most of its monuments. Most of the time it was a workaday place, busy with people going about their daily business, but at other times, it was a scene of the city's many triumphal processions, thronged with citizens watching returning legions and victorious generals parading their prisoners and the booty of the Empire. As often as not, the *triumphator,* or emperor himself, took part, decked in the imperial purple, his face painted red to emulate the god Mars and riding in a chariot which was pulled by four white horses.

Taking stock of the Foro Romano

Basilica Aemilia An extensive but almost completely ruined building, used as a business center and money exchange, the Basilica Aemilia (see page 51) was the forum's first basilica and, according to Pliny, one of its most beautiful buildings. Its parlous state is largely the result of Alaric's sack of Rome in AD 410.

Argiletum East of the Basilica Aemilia, the Via Sacra was joined by the Argiletum, another important and busy street, lined with numerous bookshops. Close to the intersection of the two streets stood a temple – now vanished – to the two-faced god, Janus. Traditionally the temple's two doors stood open while Rome was at war and were closed during times of peace, reputed to have occurred only three times in 1,000 years.

Comitium Much of the open space between the Argiletum and the Curia, the building alongside the Basilica Aemilia, was taken up by the Comitium, probably the forum's earliest public meeting place and the heart of civic administration during the Republic. This was the hub of city life, the scene of religious and triumphant processions, sacrifices, and important funerals. Here orators harangued bystanders, and the heads of the city's 30 neighborhoods, known as the *Comitia Curiata*, met to debate and cast their votes. From its law courts the *praetor,* seated on his *tribunal,* handed down judgments before the populace.

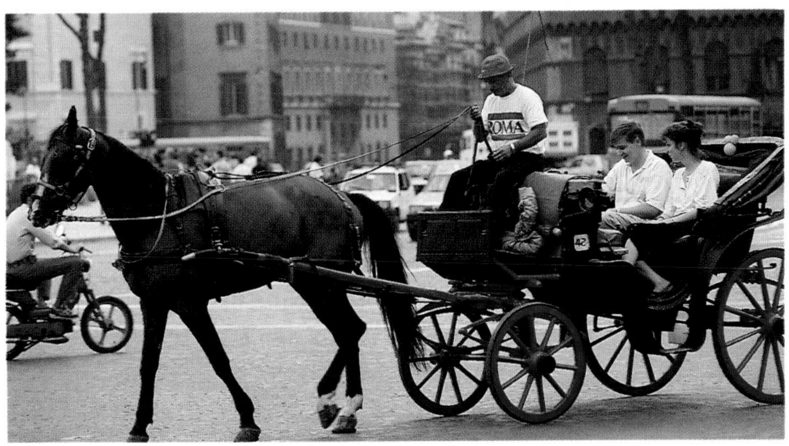

Horse-drawn sightseeing in city traffic

Curia The Curia (or "Senate House") is one of the forum's best-preserved buildings, albeit without the original marble and stucco decoration. This was the meeting place of the Roman Senate, with accommodations for some 300 senators, and was probably here in some shape or form from the time of the first kings. The present structure dates from 80 BC, but was added to by Julius Caesar and completed by Augustus in 29 BC. It was restored by Diocletian after a fire in AD 283, by which time the Senate had lost most of its power, though it continued to be used for several centuries more.

In the 7th century the building was adapted to become the church of Sant'Adriano, which preserved it from further destruction. The current bronze doors are copies of the originals, which Borromini borrowed and modified to use in the main doorway of San Giovanni in Laterano.

The Curia's **interior** (open only occasionally) is as austere as its exterior, all extraneous additions having been removed between 1931 and 1937. Parts of the Roman pavement survive, along with steps where the senators sat on marble seats, though the most interesting features are the Anaglyphs, or *Plutei di Traiano*, two travertine slabs found outside the building with reliefs depicting the emperor and people of Rome.

The Imperial Rostra To the left of the Comitium, below the **Arco di Settimo Severo** (see page 49), runs an ill-defined wall of brick, all that remains of the Rostra, or orator's platform, once in front of the Curia, but removed to its present site by Julius Caesar. It was here, at least by Shakespeare's reckoning, that Mark Antony made his impassioned speech after the murder of Caesar ("Friends, Romans, countrymen . . . "). Little remains of its original marble cladding, and nothing of the bronze beaks, or *rostra,* of ships – used to ram and scuttle other ships – captured at the Battle of Antium in 338 BC. These rostra were used to decorate the podium and gave the platform and modern-day Rostra its name. When the

The Cloaca Massima is the system of sewers that drains the Foro Romano. It was built in the 1st century BC and can still be seen today where it empties into the Tiber below Piazza Bocca della Verità.

The Tarpeian Rock was the forum's most infamous spot, a crag on the edge of the Capitoline Hill off which condemned criminals were thrown to their deaths. Tarpeia was an early Roman maiden who betrayed Rome to the Sabines. In return she asked for all that Sabine warriors wore on their left arms – expecting their gold bracelets. The Sabines, however, crushed her to death with their shields – which they wore on their left arms.

Mass-produced masterpieces ignoring the forum

great orator Cicero was assassinated, his head and hands were cut off and thrown onto the *Rostra,* from which he had often addressed the Romans.

Colonna di Foca Immediately in front of the Rostra stands a lone Corinthian column – the Colonna di Foca (the Column of Phocas). It was the last monument erected in the forum in ancient times, stolen from an earlier building and raised by Smaragdus in AD 608 to honor the usurping Byzantine emperor, Nikephorus Phocas – partly because he presented the Pantheon to Pope Boniface IV.

Close to the Rostra, but now vanished, once stood a bronze column erected by Augustus, intended as a symbolic milepost from which all roads in the Empire ran and from which all distances were theoretically measured.

Lapis Niger The Lapis Niger, or "Black Stone," a slab of black marble, lies in the *Comitium* to the right of the Arco di Settimo Severo, protected by a low roof. This is perhaps the forum's most precious relic and according to Roman legend is supposed to conceal the tomb of Romulus, founder of Rome. The site is highly venerable and may well have been a chthonic shrine to the god Vulcan. In 1899 excavations revealed a chamber below the shrine (today reached by a modern staircase) concealing a tufa altar; the accumulated ashes of numerous sacrifices; and a *stele,* or headstone, inscribed with a 6th-century BC Latin inscription (the oldest ever found) warning against profaning the sacred site.

Tempio di Concordia Beyond the Arco di Settimo Severo, this now-sorry pile, built to mark the peace between patricians and plebeians, preserves only its 4th-century BC platform. It was restored by Tiberius at the beginning of the 1st century AD and later used as a museum for Greek sculptures and paintings.

Tempio di Vespasiano These three elegant Corinthian columns – passed to posterity from the temple erected to the Emperor Vespasian by his son Domitian in AD 79. Almost alone, these columns marked the site of the forum over the centuries while the rest lay buried under silt and rubble.

Porticus Deorum Consentium Just behind the temple are 12 modest columns that mark the gateway dedicated to the *Consentes,* the 12 Olympian gods. Julian's restoration of the portico in AD 367 represented the last work on a pagan temple in Rome.

Tempio di Saturno Left of the Tempio di Vespasiano and across the *Clivus Capitolinus* – a spur of the Via Sacra serving the western edge of the forum – are eight red and gray granite columns that make up the Tempio di Saturno. Much of the ruin dates from reconstructions in 42 BC and AD 284, the latter so badly executed that one of the columns was replaced upside down.

The original temple was one of the earliest in the forum (479 BC), built after the expulsion of the Tarquins but dedicated for some time after to an Etruscan god of the crops. The Romans later used it to honor Saturn, god of agriculture, a deity almost certainly derived from an Etruscan divinity. It became one of the most venerated in Republican Rome, Saturn's agricultural acumen being seen as the source of the city's wealth – possibly the reason it was chosen as the site of Rome's state treasury. Huge reserves of gold and silver were kept here, ostensibly to be used only *in extremis*, but raided over the years by Julius Caesar, Mark Antony and others.

Basilica Giulia Only the obvious ground plan of this huge basilica remains, a building that served as a central courthouse and the meeting place of the four civic tribunals. It was started by Julius Caesar in 54 BC, after whom it is named, perhaps to complement the **Basilica Aemilia** across the Via Sacra. Augustus completed the work in AD 12, though today's ruins date mostly from Diocletian's rebuilding in AD 305. Look out for the board games carved into some of its surviving steps.

Tempio di Castore e Polluce The first temple to the twins was built in 484 BC by the son of the dictator, Aulus Postumius. He was prompted by their supposed intervention in the Battle of Lake Regillus in 499 BC, an encounter that put an end to the efforts of the Tarquin dynasty to reassert its sovereignty over Rome. The Romans, and their cavalry in particular, were outnumbered, but promised the twin gods – then pledged to the Tarquins – a vast temple should they deign to change sides. Remarkably the gods did so, and the Romans appeared with news of the victory soon afterwards, watering their horses at the **Lacus Juturnae**, a natural spring and meeting place for Rome's gossipmongers. The marble-edged rectangular pool is still visible alongside the ruins.

The temple was also a lodge for the city's *equites,* or knights (later to become a business class), who kept their booty in its basement strongboxes. The Empire's

Saturn's festival, *Saturnalia,* was celebrated in December and was one of the forerunners of Christmas. For a week the world and its values were turned upside down. Slaves were waited on by their masters, authority was mocked with impunity, and nonstop feasting and debauchery were the order of the day.

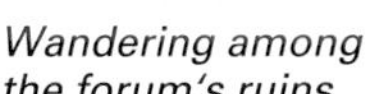

Wandering among the forum's ruins

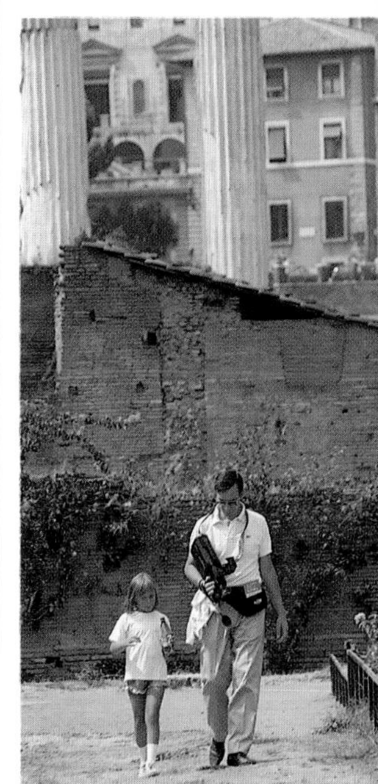

The forum bequeathed a host of words to posterity, many of which have entered the English language. Among them are rostrum, forum, committee, republic, plebeian, civic, census, plebiscite, suffrage, magistrate, pontificate, dictator, censor, and forensic. The Palatino above the forum produced prince and palace, and the Campidoglio, mint, money, capitol and asylum.

weights and measures standards were also kept here. The shrine was rebuilt several times, most notably by Tiberius (1st century), responsible for the three surviving columns, popularly known as the *tre sorelle* – the "three sisters."

Santa Maria Antiqua South of the Tempio di Castore e Polluce and beyond the Lacus Juturnae are a few stones from the Arco di Augusto and the restored remains of a shrine to Juturna, a goddess of healing waters. Close by is the Oratorio dei Quaranta Martiri, a tiny chapel converted from a 1st-century building that preserves 8th-century frescoes – just visible through the gate – recording 40 Armenian soldiers who were forced to wade to their death in an icy lake during the reign of Diocletian.

Immediately beyond is Santa Maria Antiqua, a badly damaged (and usually closed) church, but the oldest and most important Christian building in the forum. It was converted from an earlier imperial building some time between the 5th and 6th centuries and then richly decorated on the orders of several 8th-century popes. In front of the church runs the **Via Nova**, many of whose cobbles still survive.

Tempio di Cesare North of the church, back toward the Via Sacra, are the remains of a temple to Julius Caesar. The emperor's body was brought here after his famous assassination in the Teatro di Pompey and was cremated after an impassioned Mark Antony read his will and persuaded the Romans to ignore religious injunctions forbidding burial in the forum.

Caesar's successor, Augustus, built the temple to the deified emperor 15 years later (29 BC). The altar, which has remained intact, was originally decorated with the prow of Antony and Cleopatra's ship and is said to mark the site of the actual cremation.

The Tempio di Vespasiano

Regia Only the foundations of the Regia survive, the forum's oldest cult building (7th century BC) and once the seat of the chief priest or *Pontifex Maximus*. In its first incarnation it was linked with Mars, the chief god of the Romans before they turned to Jupiter, a deity of Etruscan extraction.

Tempio di Vesta Close by is another very ancient temple, the circular Tempio di Vesta, or the Temple of the Vestal Virgins, a building that arouses the salacious curiosity of most visitors. Apart from the Virgins, only the Regia's *Pontifex Maximus* was allowed to enter its precincts, home to the "sacred flame" of Rome, a vital symbol of the state's continuity. Romans placed great store by their eternal fire and extinguished their fires on the first day of their new year (March 1) before lighting new ones with tapers from the temple's flame.

The original building was probably wooden and modeled on the circular configuration of huts from the forum's earliest settlement. The temple retained its form, right up to the ruins left today, the remnants of a rebuilding in the reign of Settimo Severo (AD 193–211).

Atrium Vestae The Atrium Vestae, or House of the Vestal Virgins, stands alongside the Tempio di Vesta, and was also built in its present guise by Settimo Severo. More a palace than a house, in its day it was equipped with some 50 rooms facing on to a central courtyard, now planted as a rose garden, together with some of the original pools that have been restored and filled. Here, too, there are 3rd-century statues of the Vestals, including one with the name removed – the Vestal Claudia, who converted to Christianity.

Vestal Virgins were the guardians of Rome's sacred flame. Chosen before they reached the age of 14, they were plucked from Rome's finest patrician families, with a maximum of six serving at any one time. Anything up to 30 years were spent in service. Thereafter they were free to retire on a state pension. A vestal's blood could not be spilt, so the loss of virginity was punished by burial alive. They were held in the highest esteem and enjoyed numerous privileges, including the power of mercy over condemned prisoners. They survived until the end of the 4th century, well beyond the Empire's adoption of Christianity.

Tempio di Romolo Scholars know much about virtually nonexistent ruins, but little, ironically, of this small but magnificently preserved circular temple. Its porphyry columns and old bronze doors date from AD 309, and were probably built by Maxentius in honor of his son Romulus, who died young.

Basilica di Maxentius The three vast, coffered vaults of the Basilica di Maxentius, begun in AD 306, are among the most awe-inspiring sights in the forum. Originally over 328 feet long, only a single aisle of the nave survives. The arches were the inspiration for many Renaissance architects. One column from the complex survives, now raised in front of **Santa Maria Maggiore**.

San Francesca Romana Abutted on to the Temple of Venus and Rome, but only accessible from Via dei Fori Imperiali, is San Francesca Romana (also known as Santa Maria Nova), a 10th-century structure whose 1163 Romanesque campanile is one of the forum's key landmarks. Its convent and cloisters contain the **Forum Antiquarium** (open daily, 9–noon, closed Monday), a small, old-fashioned museum on two floors with models of the forum's Iron Age settlements, carvings from the forum, and an ancient fresco of the Virgin removed from San Maria Antiqua (see above).

The forum from the Palatine Hill

San Francesca Romana contains paving stones that bear the imprint of St. Peter's and St. Paul's kneecaps. Simon Magus, a leading Rome magician, challenged the saints to a test of levitation. Neither could rise to the challenge, but Magus roared skyward. However, his victory was short lived because he then plummeted to his death. The saints, however, prayed so hard for their own levitation that they left dents in the stone.

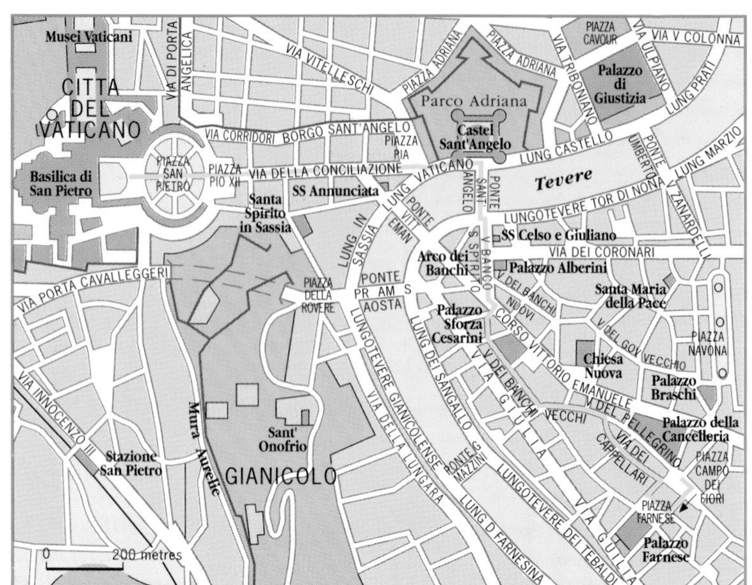

Walk Campo dei Fiori to Piazza San Pietro

Start from Campo dei Fiori.
Rome's most picturesque medieval square , the 'field of flower', has a food and flower market every morning except Sunday. Cheap cafés and restaurants line its sides.

Walk through the Campo dei Fiori into Piazza Farnese.
Piazza Farnese is dominated by **Palazzo Farnese**, Rome's finest Renaissance palace; designed by Sangallo and Michelangelo, it is now the French Embassy. The piazza's fountains were found in the Terme di Caracalla.

Return to Campo dei Fiori and take Via dei Cappellari. Turn left into Via del Pellegrino. Turn right at Via dei Banchi Vecchi and follow it to Corso Vittorio Emanuele II.
Via dei Cappellari is an atmospheric dark, narrow alley, evoking medieval Rome.

Cross the Corso and walk straight down Via Banco San Spirito. Walk over the Ponte Sant'Angelo to Castel Sant'Angelo.

Note the lovely **Ponte Sant' Angelo's** decorations of copies of angels. **Castel Sant'Angelo was the Emperor Hadrian's tomb, and was later converted into a papel fortress. It** now houses an excellent museum.

Turn left on Lungotevere Vaticano and then right onto Via della Conciliazione. Follow to Piazza San Pietro and St. Peter's.
Carved out in the 1930s, Via della Conciliazione obliterated an entire medieval quarter and is Rome's most vilified street. Like Bernini's **Piazza San Pietro, it** was designed to provide a grand entrance to **St. Peter's**.

● **Stroll** *Wander from Piazza Navona, via the alley to the left of the Tre Scalini café and follow it round past the Bar della Pace to Via dei Coronari. Or from Campo dei Fiori follow Via del Governo Vecchio and Via dei Banchi Nuovi to the Ponte Sant'Angelo. Alternatively, explore the lanes of the ghetto as far as Piazza Venezia.*

Walk A circular route from Piazza Navona

Start from Piazza Navona. Take Via dei Coronari to Via della Scrofa. Turn right to Via del Corso.

Piazza Navona is dominated by Bernini's **Fontana dei Fiumi** and Borromini's church of **Sant'Agnese.** Try a coffee in the **Bar Colombia** at No. 88.

Cross the Corso and follow Via della Croce to Piazza di Spagna. Turn left on Via del Babuino to reach Piazza del Popolo.

Via della Croce is famed for its food shops; note the beautiful old bar **Isabeilli** at No. 76.

Go up Via G d'Annunzio and Viale Trinit à dei Monti to the Pincio gardens. Descend the Spanish Steps and Via Condotti, turn left at Via del Gambero and cross Piazza San Silvestro to arrive at the Fontana di Trevi.

The **Spanish Steps** are the focus of exclusive shopping streets like **Via Condotti.**

Take Via del Corso toward the Pantheon. Take Via Palombella to Piazza Sant'Eustachio, turning left in front of Sant'Ivo. Cross Corso del Rinascimento and return to Piazza Navona.

A Piazza Navona character

Sant'Ivo is one of Borromini's most eccentric churches, dominated by its strange spiral lantern.

●**Stroll** *Try a stroll up the Spanish Steps and into the Pincio gardens or from Piazza di Spagni to the Fontana di Trevi and the Pantheon.*

Numerous myths attach to Canova's erotic statue of Paolina Borghese, doubtless because of the knowing sensuality of its subject – bare breasted, hips half-draped in veils and reclining with haughty yet come-hither languor on a Roman sofa. Paolina was as slyly seductive in life as in art and excited much gossip through her jewels, her clothes, a long line of lovers, the servants she used as footstools, and the black retainer who carried her from the bath.

▶▶▶ Galleria Borghese

Villa Borghese

The Galleria Borghese is housed in the Casino, or summerhouse, of the Villa Borghese (see page 200), and contains the greatest of Rome's patrician art collections. Only the collections of the Vatican museums are grander (see pages 183–197). Most of its paintings and its sculptures were accumulated by Cardinal Scipione Borghese, the nephew of Pope Paul V, a patron of Bernini – who dominates much of the gallery – and the greatest collector of his day. Even with a shortfall of 200 works later sold to France, the gallery remains full of masterpieces. The collection was bought for the state in 1902.

Subsidence in 1985 closed the upper of the gallery's two floors for some years, and you may find opening times unpredictable as a result. Even so, the ground floor's sculpture alone more than merits a visit, and to do justice to the entire gallery requires at least two visits. Much of the collection is haphazardly arranged, but it is also comparatively small, so you can see the highlights – picked out below – uncluttered by second-rate works.

The Ground Floor Room I contains the collection's most famous work, Canova's bewitching statue of Paolina Borghese (1804), Napoleon's sister and husband of Camillo Borghese (see panel).

Canova's sensual portrayal of Paolina Borghese

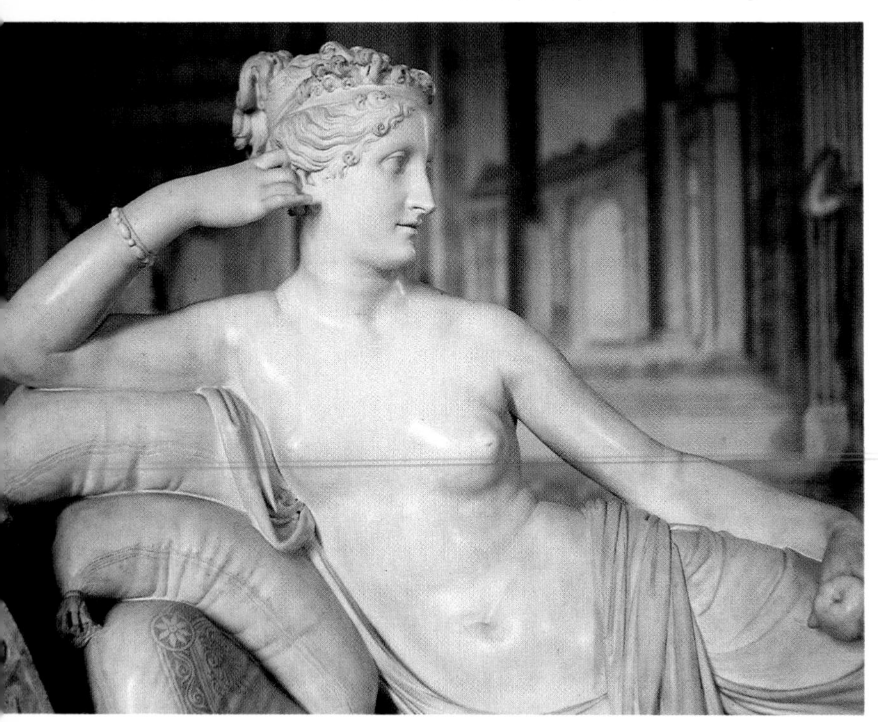

Room II contains *David* by Bernini (1623–24), one of the earliest Baroque sculptures and a virtuoso piece whose face is reputed to be a self-portrait of the artist (sculpted while his patron, Cardinal Scipione, held the mirror for his protégé). In the same room are panels from ancient sarcophagi illustrating the Labors of Hercules.

Room III contains what may be Bernini's masterpiece, *Apollo and Daphne* (1622–25), which describes Daphne's flight from Apollo at the moment she turned into a laurel tree to avoid the god's clutches. Here, as in most of the gallery's Berninis, the sculptor's technical proficiency realizes Baroque's ambitious quest to imbue marble with the drama, movement, and tone of living flesh. The lines at its base are an Ovidean warning against the pursuit of pleasure, an ironic addition, given Scipione's proclivities as a *bon viveur.*

Room IV is known as the Sala degli Imperatori for its bleak collection of alabaster and porphyry busts of the emperors. The sorry parade is redeemed by Bernini's *Rape of Prosperine* (1621–22), an early but technically flawless work in which Bernini's virtuoso way with marble contrasts the muscle of the King of the Underworld with the tender flesh of his victim.

Bernini may have revealed himself in his portrayal of David

Room V is a small room containing some sculptures including the *Athene Parthenos* by Phidias.

Room VI contains slightly lesser works by Bernini, a late, unfinished figure of *Truth Unveiled by Time* (1652) and *Aeneas and Anchises* escaping from the burning Troy (notice Anchises clutching the Palladium, one of the sacred relics of Rome guarded by the Vestal Virgins).

Room VII and Room VIII are built around pieces of classical sculpture, the latter containing the collection's finest ancient work, the figure of *A Dancing Faun*, a Roman copy of a Greek original.

The Upper Floor To reach the gallery's upper floor, home to the finest of the collection's paintings, retrace your steps to Room IV and take the spiral staircase.

Room IX contains a Raphael masterpiece, the *Deposition* (1507), an almost Mannerist work influenced by Leonardo and Michelangelo. It was commissioned by Atalanta Baglioni in memory of her murdered son, a member of the despotic and violent clan that ruled Perugia for much of the 15th century. Other fine paintings in the room include a *Crucifixion with Saints Jerome and Christopher* by Pinturicchio, a *Portrait of a Woman* by Raphael (possibly his fiancée, Maddalena Strozzi), a *Portrait of a Man* by Raphael (attributed to Holbein before restoration), and a *Madonna and Saint with John the Baptist* by Lorenzo di Credi.

Rooms X–XIII contain works, including *The Baptism* by Bronzino, *Venus and the Angel* by Cranach, *Tobias and the Angel* by Savoldo, and Domenichino's *Sybil.*

Ornate ceiling in the Galleria Borghese

Room XIV is among the gallery's more noted salons, famous chiefly for its Caravaggios, which include the early *Boy with a Basket of Fruit* and the so-called *Sick Bacchus*, both remarkable for their realistic treatment of fruit and leaves, and the *Madonna dei Palafrenieri* (in which the Madonna crushes a serpent, a symbol of heresy) and *David and Goliath* in which Goliath, like Bacchus, is believed to have been a portrait of the artist. Scipione Borghese had a keen eye for talent and bought several of the Caravaggios when they were turned down by those who had originally commissioned them. The room also houses further works by Bernini, namely, *Jupiter Suckled by the Goat Amalthea* (1615), completed when the sculptor was just 17, and two busts of his patron, *Scipione Borghese*. Bernini produced two portraits because a crack appeared over the eyebrow of the first just as it was nearing completion. In a remarkable flurry he finished a second in only two weeks.

The museum entrance is off Via Pinciana on Via Raimondi. *Open:* Monday, 9–2, Tuesday to Saturday 9–7, Sunday 9–1. Admission free for the duration of renovation work. At times entrance is restricted to 25 people every 30 minutes, but there is rarely a wait if you visit in the afternoon.

Rooms XV–XIX The paintings of these rooms – a powerful *Deposition* (1605) by Rubens and works by Barocci, Dosso Dossi and Jacopo Bassano – pale alongside the sheer grace, not to say eroticism of Correggio's magnificent *Danae*.

Room XX The last room in the gallery, this is reserved for the collection's acknowledged masterpiece, the celebrated *Sacred and Profane Love* by Titian. An early, tranquil and beautifully colored if rather mysterious work, it was painted in 1512 for the Aurelia family. The source of the iconography is in doubt – over the years the painting has also been called, among other things,

Venus and Medea and *Heavenly and Earthly Love*; most critics believe it represents an allegory of spring, lifted from the same eerie dream romance, the *Hypnerotomachia di Polifilo*, that provided Bernini with the image of his elephant and obelisk in Piazza Minerva. Other fine, if overshadowed works line the room, including a *Madonna and Child* by Giovanni Bellini, Veronese's *St. John the Baptist, The Portrait of an Italian Gentleman* by Antonello da Messina (a prototype of the genre), and another Titian, the damaged *Venus Blindfolding Cupid.*

▷▷▷ Galleria d'Arte Moderna

Viale delle Belle Arti 131

A large, 35-room gallery, this patchy collection offers a survey of Italian and foreign art since 1800, the most notable of the non-Italians represented being Dégas, Cézanne, Kandinsky, Henry Moore, Max Ernst and Jackson Pollock. Of most interest among the largely indistinguishable Italians are the *Macchiaioli*, a group of rural Tuscan painters similar in style to the French Impressionists. The 20th-century Italian wing has recently been renovated, considerably livening up the collection, which includes sculpture by Marino Marini and Giacomo Manzù and paintings by the Futurist Umberto Boccioni and Giorgio de Chirico.

The gallery is also used to stage major exhibitions, so be sure to check listings in daily newspapers for news of events.

Open: Tuesday to Saturday, 9–2; Wednesday to Friday, 3–7:30; Sunday, 9–1; closed Monday. Admission charge.

▷▷▷ Ghetto

Via Arenula–Teatro di Marcello

Rome's is the oldest Jewish community in Europe, having enjoyed over 2,000 years of continuous existence. Today this old quarter contains some of Rome's quietest and most pleasant backstreets, and walking here in the evening or during the calm of siesta is a peaceful and unmitigated pleasure.

History The ghetto was created in 1555 by one of the more unpleasant Counter-Reformation popes, Paul IV, who was one of the dreaded Inquisition's founding fathers. Until 1555 Jews were prominent members of Roman society, many of them were merchants or bankers, and some even physicians to the popes. After this date, however, the restrictions on Jews precluded the right to own land or to practice any trade other than dealing in furniture, scrap iron, and old clothing. People were even restricted in the jewelery they could carry – three rings for women, one for men – and all were forced to wear distinguishing yellow hats outside the ghetto.

Some 5,000 people were crammed into the ghetto, and all had to attend sermons for their conversion to Christianity. A few impositions were relaxed after the death of Paul in 1559, and others were abolished under Napoleonic rule, but a large number remained in force until as late as 1870.

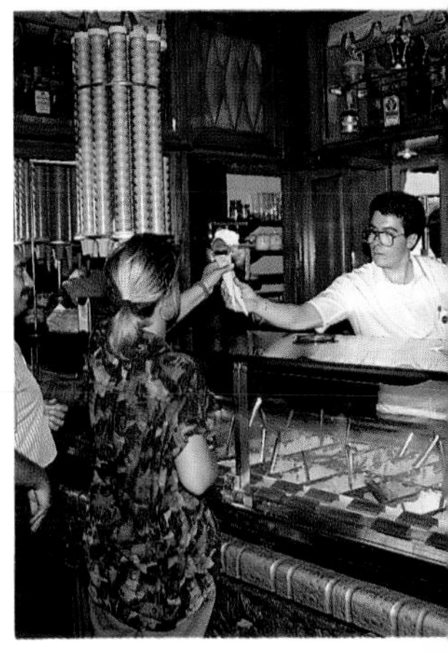

Rome's antidote to a surfeit of sightseeing – Italian ice cream

Jews initially suffered little under Italian Fascism, some 200 having joined Mussolini's March to Rome in 1922. Racial laws were introduced in 1938 under pressure from Hitler, and even then were largely ignored by the general public. Deportations to the concentration camps began after the Italian armistice in 1943 and the Nazi occupation of Rome. Over 2,000 Roman Jews were rounded up, of whom only 15 survived. Many Jews were hidden by Italians, especially by the clergy, though the Vatican is haunted by controversy to this day for apparently failing to take a firmer stand against the persecution.

Take time out on the Pincio for a coffee or ice cream in the refined confines of the café Casina Valadier. It's a precious and overpriced spot, but has a wonderful view and is invariably busy on fine days and full of sun-soaking Italians.

Every day at noon, in one of Rome's more eccentric ceremonies, a cannon is loosed from Piazza Garibaldi, producing a puff of smoke visible from afar and a boom that echoes throughout the city.

▶▷▷ Giardino di Pincio

The Pincio Gardens, some of the most beguiling in Rome, are a short walk from the Spanish Steps to the south (from where you should take Via Trinità dei Monti) and adjoin the parkland of the **Villa Borghese** to the north. The area was known as the *Collis Hortorum*, the "hill of gardens," in Roman times, and the present park, built between 1809 and 1814 by Giuseppe Valadier, lies over the terraced gardens of Lucullus, a 1st-century BC general and epicure (among his spoils of war he brought the first cherries to Europe). In the 4th century the spot was owned by the Pinci family, hence the present name.

▶▷▷ Gianicolo

The closest thing to a genuine hill in Rome, and yet not one of the city's original Seven Hills, the Gianicolo, or "Janiculum hill," forms a green, tree-topped ridge along the western limit of the old capital. Its name comes from the god Janus, whom the ancients believed – erroneously – to have founded a city on the spot. Much of it has been beautifully preserved as public park-land, but it is also home to three sights that combine neatly with the worthwhile walk to the hill: the **Fontana Paola**, Bramante's **Tempietto** and the church of **San Pietro in Montorio**. The best approach on foot is from Trastevere on Via Garibaldi or on the 41 bus from St. Peter's and Corso Vittorio Emanuele II.

The highest point (269 feet) at Porta San Pancrazio saw one of the decisive battles fought by Garibaldi's legion against the French in the Roman Republic of 1849. Garibaldi's heavily outnumbered men were defeated only after weeks of unrelenting French pressure, and the episode has gone down in the history books as one of the Risorgimento's finest hours. A short way away in Piazza Giuseppe Garibaldi stands a bronze statue of the eponymous hero. Nearby is another bronze of his wife, Anita, pregnant and heroic throughout the trials of 1849, and shown on a rearing horse with pistol in one hand and baby in the other.

Sunset over Gianicolo

An island of calm: Isola Tiberina

▶▷▷ **Isola Tiberina**

The Tiber island provides an oasis of calm in the thunder of Rome's traffic. Lying on a bend in the Tiber with **Trastevere** on one bank and the **ghetto** on the other, its position as a stepping stone made it an obvious spot to ford the river. Today two ancient and remarkably well-preserved bridges still connect it to the mainland. The finer of the pair, the **Ponte Fabrico**, which links north to the **Teatro di Marcello**, was built in 62 BC, making it Rome's oldest surviving bridge. The other, the **Ponte Cestio**, was raised in 46 BC and rebuilt in the 19th century using the original stone.

History The island has an association with healing that goes back to 289 BC, when, according to legend, the Sibylline oracles instructed Romans – then in the throes of a terrible plague – to visit the famous Greek Temple of Aesculapius at Epidauros. One of the healing god's sacred snakes was brought back to Rome, where it slid from the boat, swam upstream, and made the island its home. Since this was clearly a sign of divine intent, a temple was built, later superseded by the 10th-century church of **San Bartolomeo** (see page 134).

Today a hospital is still the largest of the island's handful of buildings. Dating from 1538, the Ospedale Fatebenefratelli ("hospital of the do-well brothers") is a modern institution with a word-of-mouth reputation as the best Roman hospital to visit in an emergency.

The island's walkways are favorites for strolling, sunbathing and fishing – though the chances of catching anything in the famously polluted Tiber must surely be minimal. In the annual floods of spring and autumn, however, much of the periphery of the island is submerged, often to an alarming degree. The island has just one shop – which sells only mattresses – and a single bar, Alfonso's, perfect for a quiet drink. Look out for the bronze statues on the north bank, the work of locally famous Padre Martini, one of three Franciscans who still serve San Bartolomeo.

Off the northern tip of the Isola Tiberina stands the single arch of the *Ponte Rotto* (the "Broken Bridge"), all that remains of the *Pons Aemilius*, a wooden bridge started in 179 BC and finished in stone in 142 BC – Rome's first ever stone-arch bridge.

Some say the island grew on the centuries of waste from grain cargoes unloaded nearby. Earlier legend claims it was formed when an overladen ship sank in midstream. The island's tapered ends indeed suggest a boat, and the Romans, in a fit of whimsy, built a stone stern and prow for it – of which remains can still be seen – and raised an obelisk in the middle for a mast.

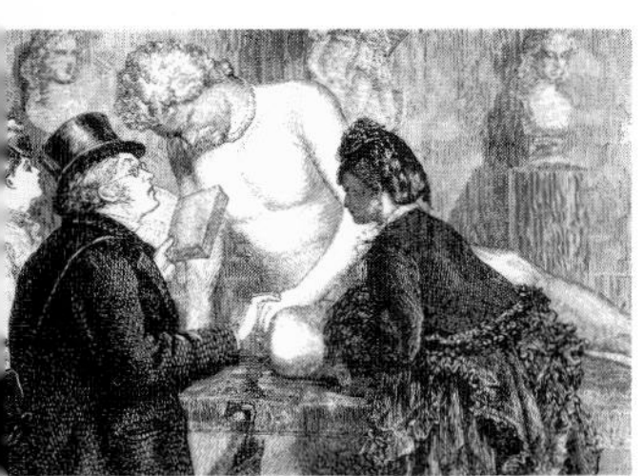

Among Rome's many ghosts are the poets, painters and men of letters drawn to the city by its siren call of ruins, romance and the echoes of one of the greatest empires the world has known. Few visitors went away without recording their impressions. If every stone in the city has its story, then it has been told and retold by the literary giants of the day. . . .

Early "tourists" For centuries Rome's visitors were bent solely on pillage, plunder or pilgrimage, and travel for its own sake scarcely existed. The Middle Ages had just one famous guidebook for pilgrims, the *Mirabilia Urbis Romae*. By the end of the 18th century, however, a flood of books on Italy had appeared in most European languages, the most famous being *Murray's Handbook* for *Travellers in Central Italy* (published simultaneously in four languages). By the 19th century the round of European cities without which no gentleman's (in rare cases, no lady's) education was complete had become almost formalized as the "Grand Tour." Naples was its traditional finale, but Rome was the undoubted star turn.

Grand tourists In many ways it is easier to list those who stayed away or retired from the fray before reaching Rome than to record those who reached the Eternal City. According to Robert Browning, for example, his fellow poet Tennyson turned back at Florence when he realized that nowhere in the city stocked his favorite brand of tobacco. Shakespeare never came, despite his plays' many Roman references, nor did Proust, William Blake or Edgar Allan Poe. Almost everyone else did.

The reasons they came are many – there are the obvious ones of art, history, creative inspiration, health, beauty and scholarship, and the more obscure ones like escape from failure; doomed relationships; the strictures of the home country; and, above all, the lure of love and lust, hundreds being emboldened by the idea of a warm climate stimulating the passions to greater heights, an idea summarized in Byron's *Don Juan*: "What men call gallantry, and gods adultery," he wrote, "Is much more common where the climate's sultry."

What they found The journey to the promised land was fraught with incident and difficulty. Joseph Addison arrived at Calais and promptly fell into the harbor; Petrarch was kicked by a horse and badly injured; Horace Walpole's dog was eaten by a wolf; Casanova was sexually assaulted by a policeman;

Announcing a Grand Tour, 1866

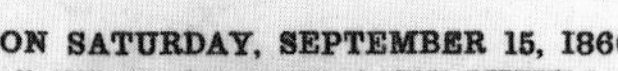

ON SATURDAY, SEPTEMBER 15, 1866,
Mr. COOK will leave London for PARIS, and on MONDAY EVENING, Sept. 17, will depart from Paris for

VENICE

Going through the best parts of

SWITZERLAND

OVER THE ST. GOTHARD,

BY THE

LAKES OF LUGANO & COMO,

RETURNING BY

Milan, Lago Maggiore, and the Simplon.

VENICE is expected to be freed from Austrian Rule by about the 20th of September, and this Trip is arranged to afford an opportunity of witnessing the rejoicings of the Emancipated Venetian People.

FARES FROM LONDON TO VENICE AND BACK,
FIRST CLASS £15 15s., SECOND CLASS £12 12s.

For the convenience of those who wish to be free from all charges, Mr. Cook will pay all ordinary Hotel Expenses, for three weeks for £10.

COOK'S TOURIST TICKETS FOR ONE or TWO MONTHS
May be had any day up to the end of October, for Ordinary and Express Trains and Steamers, to individuals or parties, for

PARIS, SWITZERLAND & ITALY;

Also, Monthly Tickets from London to Hastings, Brighton, Portsmouth, the Isle of Wight, Jersey, Normandy, and Brittany; to the English Lakes, Scarborough, Matlock, Buxton &c.; and to Scotland and Ireland.

Cook's Tourist Tickets to and from the UNITED STATES and CANADA are now issued weekly, by Six Lines of Steamers.

See full particulars in COOK'S EXCURSIONIST, 2d, by post 3d., which may be had through all Booksellers and News Agents, from COOK'S TOURIST OFFICE, 98, Fleet-street, London; or from 63, Granby-street, Leicester.

N B.—All letters of inquiry to contain stamped directed envelope for answer, and to be addressed as above.

[T. COOK, Printer, London and Leicester.

The horrors of foreign food: water with an unwelcome ingredient . . .

and Tobias Smollett, surely the most miserable man ever to travel, found dirt, disease and disappointment at every turn. Italian women en route, for example, he thought the "most haughty, insolent, capricious, and revengeful females on the face of the earth"; accommodations he found universally "execrable"; he "fared wretchedly at supper"; and in Rome itself services were offered only with the "most disagreeable importunity." Keats came for his health and died in the city; James Boswell contracted venereal disease and crab lice within a month; Goethe wisely observed that "every foreigner judges by the standard he brings with him," but left the "First City of the World" transformed, convinced that the experience would be "a guide and education for a lifetime"; Edward Gibbon found inspiration for the epic *Decline and Fall of the Roman Empire* while "musing amidst the ruins of the Capitol"; Shelley ran from "the shadows of his first marriage... the tumult of humankind, and the chilling fogs and rains of our own country"; and talents as diverse as Poussin, Franz Liszt and Nietzsche produced their best work in the city. The turning point of the Grand Tour came perhaps in 1864, when a certain Thomas Cook ran the first organized tour from London to Naples, providing travel, accommodations, food and entertainment for some 50 people, thus sounding both the death knell of travel in the grand manner and ushering in the era of mass tourism that still washes unrelentingly over Rome.

▶▷▷ **Keats-Shelley Memorial**

Piazza di Spagna

In a house to the right of the Spanish Steps is an essential place of pilgrimage for even the most faint-hearted romantic. The poet John Keats died here on February 23, 1821, aged just 25, having been sent to Rome in September of the previous year to seek a cure from consumption. Keats stayed in the rented home of his friend, the artist Joseph Severn, but by all accounts little enjoyed his stay in the city, calling it "a posthumous life" and lamenting that he "already seemed to feel the flowers growing over him."

Since 1909 the house has been a working library for students of Keats and Shelley (who also died in Italy, drowned off the coast near Viareggio, a copy of Keats in his pocket). Numerous books, pamphlets and essays lie scattered around the beautifully kept rooms, which are dotted with a wealth of occasionally quaint, occasionally fascinating literary mementoes. You can see Keats's death mask, resigned, even beatific after the misery of his final months; a lock of his hair; Shelley's half-burnt cheekbone (he was cremated by his friends in a bizarre beach ceremony); and what the museum describes as the "most sacred relic of English literature"— a silver reliquary containing strands of Milton's and Elizabeth Barrett Browning's hair, owned, in turn, by Addison, Dr. Johnson, Leigh Hunt and Robert Browning.

Open: Monday to Friday 9–1, 2:30–5:30 (June to September 3:30–6). Closed weekends and one week in August. Admission charge.

▷▷▷ **Largo di Torre Argentina**

Largo di Torre Argentina—Corso V Emanuele

More commonly known as Largo Argentina, for most people this large piazza on Corso Vittorio Emanuele is little more than a frantic mix of cars, buses and exhaust fumes. At its center, however, easily seen, are the remains of the city's four oldest **Republican temples** (4th–1st century BC). So little was known about the ruins – not even the gods to which they were dedicated – that a story popular in the 1930s claimed that Mussolini wanted some ruins and had random stones dragged here to provide them.

On the Largo's west side is the 18th-century Teatro Argentina, present home of the *Teatro di Roma*, the city's leading theater company. It was here that the first performance of Rossini's *Barber of Seville* was booed and whistled off the stage at its first performance in 1816. The composer's enemy, Paolina Bonaparte, had packed the hall with hecklers, but on the second night a less partisan audience marched in torchlit procession to tell a distraught Rossini how much they had enjoyed the opera.

English poets remembered: Keats-Shelley Memorial

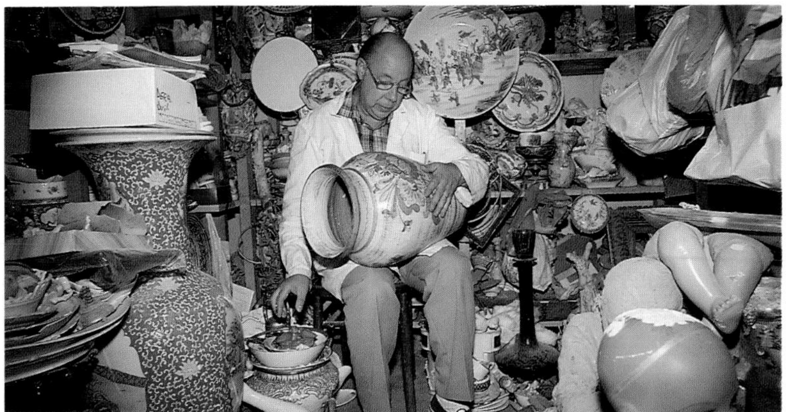

Restoring the ornaments of Rome

▶▷▷ Mausoleo di Augusto

Piazza Augusto Imperatore

The Mausoleum of Augustus is among the city's more overlooked ancient monuments. From a distance the vast circular drum still retains some of the monumental dignity of the **Castel Sant'Angelo** – the tomb of Hadrian – for which it was a model, and whose mixed historical fortunes it shares.

Augustus started the tomb some years before his death, choosing a spot in the **Campo Marzio** for its flat land and proximity to the city center. In its basic form it copied the huge earth tumuli that had distinguished Etruscan and Mediterranean necropoli since prehistoric times. Two Egyptian obelisks guarded the entrance, now outside Santa Maria Maggiore and in Piazza del Quirinale. A pair of bronze tablets alongside, the *Res Gestae*, recorded the triumphs of Augustus's reign. Both are now lost, though their texts are recorded in contemporary inscriptions. A 49-foot statue of the emperor crowned the edifice, which was also ringed by elaborate parks and gardens.

The interior, now closed to the public, contains three distinct niches, one presumed to have been for Augustus himself, who died in August, AD 14 (the month is named after him) and for his wife, Livia. The other two probably contained the ashes of his sister Octavia and his nephews Gaius and Lucius Caesar. His designated heir, Marcellus, who died young, was the first to be buried here, and at least 15 other urns – including six emperors – were interred over the centuries.

In the Middle Ages the Colonna family turned the site into a fortress, later demolished by Gregory IX, and in 1354 it was the spot where Cola di Rienzo was burnt by the Roman mob. After centuries of service as an ornamental garden, it became a bullring in the 18th century, until bullfighting was banned in 1829. Thereafter it was used for circuses and concert recitals. Proper excavations were initiated between 1926 and 1936 by Mussolini, who entertained thoughts of his own ashes reposing here in Augustus's reflected glory.

H. V. Morton had little time for the Mausoleo, describing it as "one of those miserable ruins which refuses to disintegrate," a spot fit only for "lame cats to seek refuge from small boys." *(A Traveller in Rome)*

Close to Trajan's Market is the Torre delle Milizie, a medieval tower built on a Byzantine base. For years a clearly anachronistic legend claimed it was from this high vantage point that Nero fiddled as Rome burned.

▶▷▷ Mercati Traianei

Via Quattro Novembre

Although Trajan's Markets rightly belong to the Foro di Traiano, the largest and most sumptuous of the **Fori Imperiali** (see page 76), they are entered some way from the forum in Via Quattro Novembre, near the steps of Via Magnanapoli. They were built as a response to the shortcomings of the old Foro Romano, where the shortage of space meant it could not accommodate the upsurge of trade generated by the Empire. Trajan was also concerned to ease social unrest by maintaining control over prices at their source, and this was partly achieved by distributing imperial subsidies.

Completed around the beginning of the 2nd century, the complex centered on a semicircular range of halls arranged on three levels. Two of these survive in excellent condition, albeit in brick and without their original marble facing. Some 150 booths traded all the staples and exotica of the Empire – fruit, flowers, wines and spices – as well as fresh- and saltwater fish, housed live in ponds connected directly to aqueducts on the upper floor.

Look in particular for the stairs to the *Via Biberatica*, a medieval corruption of *pipera,* or *pepper,* from which this street of spice shops took its name. Only the richest Romans could afford pepper and spices, then the rarest and most costly condiments. Also in the upper tier was the *Congiara,* a type of welfare office where food and money were distributed to the poor.

The market's centerpiece is the *exedra,* or apse, a huge curving wall – perhaps used as a large covered market – built by the forum's architect, Apollodorus, to fulfill the complex's other function – that of shoring up the slopes of the Quirinale, a vast spur having been removed to build the market.

Mercati Traianei and the Foro di Traiano

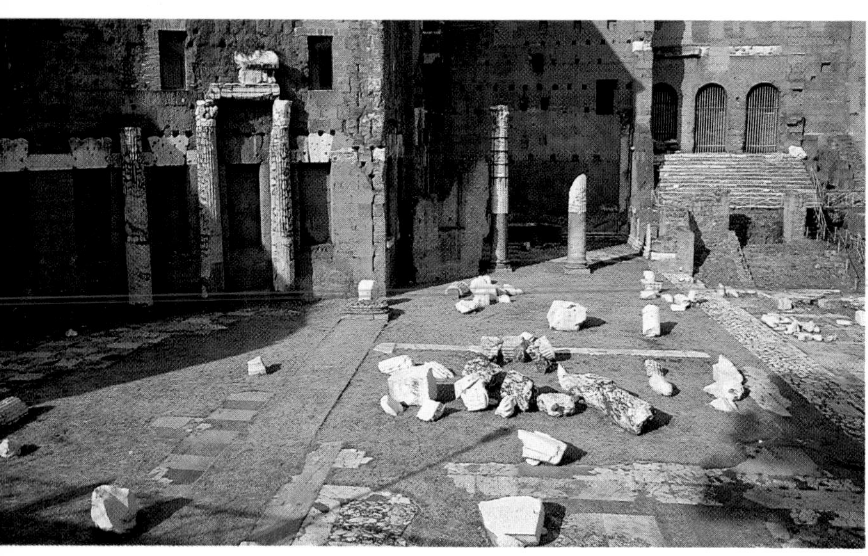

Open: Tuesday to Saturday, 9–1; Tuesday, Thursday, and Saturday also, 4–7; Sunday, 9–1 (closed Monday). Admission charge.

▶▷▷ Monumento Vittorio Emanuele

Piazza Venezia

Opinions differ as to the merits of the vast monument towering over Piazza Venezia, a spectacular landmark, but completely at odds with the character of the surrounding area. To most Romans it is the "typewriter" or the "wedding cake," because of its grandiose tiers and mass of white Brescian marble.

Size and splendor were major prerequisites for what was conceived as the *Altare della Patria*, the "Altar of the Nation" – resting place of the Unknown Soldier and the chief monument to the unification of Italy.

It was built between 1885 and 1911 – the design, by Giuseppe Sacconi, having been chosen from 95 entries submitted during an international competition.

Monumento Vittorio Emanuele

▷▷▷ Museo Nazionale delle Arti e Tradizioni Popolari

EUR, Piazza Marconi 10

It is a shame this museum is out of the way, for its ethnographic record of an Italy that has all but vanished – largely the rural Italy of popular imagination – is fascinating. Its 10 sections are devoted to a huge collection of Italian folk art, and the sections devoted to agriculture, costumes and old musical instruments are particularly interesting.

Open: Tuesday to Saturday, 9–2; Thursday, 4–7; Sunday, 9–1 (closed Monday). Admission charge.

▶▷▷ Museo della Civiltà Romana

EUR, Piazza Giovanni Agnelli

Presented to Rome by FIAT, the excellent Museum of Roman Culture traces the history of the city with the aid of models and reconstructions.

There are moulds taken from the Colonna Traiana in 1861 (see **Fori Imperiali**, page 76), a unique opportunity to study the details of some of the city's finest carvings at close quarters.

Particularly outstanding and informative is the Plastico di Roma, a 1:250 scale model of 4th-century Rome showing every building that then stood within the Aurelian walls.

Open: Tuesday to Saturday, 9–1:30; Thursday, 4–7; Sunday, 9–1 (closed Monday). Admission charge.

All three museums are in EUR (the *Esposizione Universale di Roma*), a bleak new quarter of Rome started by Mussolini. Work stopped after the war, but was restarted for the 1960 Olympic Games. The result is a strange, lifeless suburb of needlessly broad boulevards and stark, often brutal buildings. Long ridiculed, it is now achieving a sort of kitsch cult status among Romans. The quickest and easiest way to reach it is to take the Metropolitan Line B to EUR—Fermi, or use bus 93 from Termini or San Giovanni in Laterano.

▶▷▷ Museo Preistorico ed Etnografico

EUR, Viale Lincoln 1

This museum contains one of the finest collections of its type in the world. It offers a survey of the Stone, Bronze, and Iron Ages, arranged by area, with a special section devoted to Lazio and the Etruscans. The same building contains the **Museo del Alto Medievo**, a necessarily limited insight into Italy during the Dark Ages.

Open: Tuesday to Saturday, 9–2; Sunday, 9–1 (closed Monday). Admission charge.

Surviving detail of Palatine civilization

The Emperor Domitian so feared his own death that he had the interior of his palace, the *Domus Flavia*, lined with slabs of reflective mica to reveal potential assassins creeping up behind him. In the end it was to no avail – he was stabbed to death in the palace's portico.

Tickets for the Foro Romano are also valid for the Palatino. Access is via the flight of steps by the *Atrium Vestae* (the House of the Vestal Virgins); from the large vaulted passage at Santa Maria Antiqua; or on the old cobbled road, the *Clivus Palatinus*, that runs from the Arco di Tito. A separate entrance serves the hill's eastern flanks on Via San Gregorio Magno – the gateway designed by Vignola as the opening to the Orti Farnesiani (the Farnese Gardens).

▶▶▶ Palatino

Via dei Fori Imperiali—Via San Gregorio Magno

The Palatino (Palatine Hill) was the cradle of Roman civilization, predating the site of the Roman Forum, and the first of the original Seven Hills to be inhabited. Rising over 213 feet, close to the Tiber and the Isola Tiberina, it occupied a key strategic site, as well as enjoying the cooling breezes that were to make it a prime residential site for over 1,000 years. It is closely linked with the legend of the city's foundation – it was here that Romulus and Remus were suckled by the she-wolf – and contains Iron Age remains dating back to the 9th century BC. Here, too, in 753 BC, the first boundaries of the emerging city were reputedly drawn (*Roma Quadrata*).

Today it is an atmospheric spot. Orange trees, cistus, oleander and groves of cypress line the paths, with grasses and wild flowers dotted among the ancient stones. It is not, however, a place where you can hope to make even the remotest sense of the ruins. The vicissitudes of history have all but leveled many of its buildings, and elsewhere soil subsidence and the danger of collapse have closed others for years.

History The hill's ascendancy began during the Republic, when prominent citizens, including Agrippa, Cicero and Catullus, started to make their homes here – usually on the westernmost of its three crests, the Germalus. Augustus was born here, but left his birthplace much as he found it, unlike the emperors after him, nearly all of whom built sumptuous palaces wherever they found space. Archaeologists have uncovered the so-called **Casa di Livia** (Livia was Augustus's wife), identified by the stamp of *Julia Aug* on its lead pipes, which in all probability was an extension of Augustus's original house. When open, it has rare traces of Roman wall paintings. Close by are the ruins of the **Tempio di Apollo Aziaco**, built by Augustus in 28 BC to celebrate the Romans' victory at Anzio in 31 BC.

Augustus's successor, Tiberius, cleared much of the Germalus to make way for the **Domus Tiberiana**, little of which has been excavated, being overlaid with the beautiful **Orti Farnesiani** (the Farnese Gardens), which were set out for Cardinal Alessandro Farnese in the 16th century by the great Renaissance architect, Gincomo da Vignola. Caligula, in turn, extended Tiberius's *domus* west toward the Roman Forum, away from the 426-foot Criptoportico *(Cryptoporticus)* on its east, a half-buried, barrel-vaulted corridor built by Nero that linked the various imperial palaces. Legend has it that this was where Caligula was stabbed to death.

Domitian's building program in the 1st century was the most ambitious of all, centering on two major palaces, the **Domus Flavia**, the seat of the imperial government, and the **Domus Augustana**, the emperor's personal palace (also used by successive emperors and by high civic dignitaries right down to Byzantine times). Alongside the palaces Domitian built the **Stadio Domiziano**, some of the Palatine's most extensive ruins, although it is unknown whether it was intended simply as a sunken garden or as a stadium for his personal entertainment.

The best preserved of the Palatine ruins are those of the **Domus Severiana**, the palace of Settimo Severo. Created in the 2nd century, it partly incorporates the massive buttressing used earlier by Domitian to extend the Palatino. Many of its piers and arches supported terme, or baths; others supported a **belvedere**, an extended southern parapet, offering superlative views.

While on the Palatine, you should also hunt out the so-called **Capanna di Romolo** (the Hut of Romulus), the remains of a genuine Iron Age hut, and the **Lupercal**, a few stones that mark an ancient sanctuary, reputedly the sacred grove of the god Lupercus where Romulus and Remus were suckled.

Open: Monday, Wednesday to Saturday, 9–5; Tuesday and Sunday, 9–2. Admission charge.

The word *palatino* probably derives from the shepherd god Pales, one of whose followers is supposed to have discovered Romulus and Remus being suckled by the she-wolf. Rome's official birthday, April 21, is still celebrated on the god's old feast day. From palatino also came the word *palazzo* (palace), after the numerous large buildings raised on the hill.

Making music in the Piazza Navona

▶▶▷ **Palazzo Barberini–Galleria Nazionale d'Arte Antica**

Via delle Quattro Fontane 13

A beautifully appointed palace in its own right, but also home of one of Rome's greatest museums, the Palazzo Barberini was begun in 1625 by Carlo Maderno with the help of Borromini (his nephew) and completed by Bernini in 1633. Modeled on the great palaces of northern Italy, it marks the fullest expression of Rome's high Baroque style, a flowering nowhere more apparent than in the grandiose Gran Salone, the palace's two-story centerpiece. Elsewhere the building is a maze of suites, apartments and staircases, whose labyrinth makes orientation difficult, and whose shifting collections – with works shunted from room to room – guarantee you a convoluted itinerary.

A wealth of Baroque paintings *Antica* in this context means not ancient, but simply old, and refers to the earlier part of the nation's art collection (the later part is in the **Palazzo Corsini**). Bernini's heavy, square staircase ushers you into the villa and it is worth comparing it with Borromini's oval stairwell and gently rising steps in the right-hand wing. Early rooms contain mainly Renaissance paintings; a triptych of the *Ascension, Pentecost, and Last Judgment* by Fra Angelico; a *Madonna and Saints* by the Umbrian artist Nicolò Alunno, also well represented in the Vatican's Pinacoteca; *San Nicola da Tolentino* by Perugino, another Umbrian; and two paintings by Filippo Lippi: a *Madonna and Child*, renowned for the ugliness of the child, and an *Annunciation*, noted for the melting beauty of the Virgin. Close at hand should be these fine works: Lorenzo Lotto's *Portrait of a Young Man* and *St. Catherine and Saints*; Andrea del Sarto's *Holy Family;* and Beccafumi's *Madonna, Child and St. John.*

The gallery's most popular picture by far, however, is Raphael's *La Fornarina*, said to be a portrait of one of the artist's mistresses, later inconclusively identified as a baker's daughter *(fornaio* means baker). It was executed in the year of the painter's death, a demise, it is said, was brought on by his mistress's unrelenting passion. Some killjoy critics dispute the painting's authenticity, however, and claim it was painted by Raphael's follower, Giulio Romano. Alongside is Il Sodoma's *Rape of the Sabines*, followed by a portrait of *Stefano Colonna* by Bronzino and a vivid work by Caravaggio, in which Judith gazes with horror at the severed head of Holofernes.

In subsequent rooms are two small but superb El Grecos, *The Adoration of the Shepherds* and *The Baptism of Christ*, as well as Tintoretto's *Christ and the Woman Taken in Adultery*. The bulk of late 16th- and 17th-century works are less interesting, but in the room given over to Flemish paintings look for Holbein's portrait of *Henry VIII* (possibly a copy), with the king decked out in the finery he wore for his marriage to Anne of Cleves, and for Quentin Massy's dignified *Portrait of Erasmus*, a work that was commissioned by Thomas More in 1517.

Raphael's portrait of La Fornarina

Rich decoration in the Palazzo Barberini

The Gran Salone is the palace's exuberant and almost excessive grand finale. Its centerpiece is Pietro da Cortona's glorious ceiling, the *Allegory of Divine Providence* (1638–39), frescoes that may be too rich for some tastes, but figure among Rome's foremost Baroque masterpieces. Painted for Pope Urban VIII, they are an early example of the period's practice of mindless, even vulgar celebration of a patron's virtues. Here the Barberini pope is shown as an agent of Divine Providence, surrounded by a Heavenly host and apparently being pestered by distended bees – symbols from the Barberini coat of arms that are plastered over much of the palace.

Bar a handful of Canalettos and some pretty views of Rome by Vanvitelli, the 18th-century paintings on the palazzo's upper floor are largely of specialist interest, but you should wander through the rooms to enjoy the sumptuousness of the interior decoration: Meissen china, costumes, Chinese porcelain and plenty of period furnishings. The finest is the suite of rooms redecorated in 1728 for the marriage of a Barberini heiress to a prince of the Colonna family.

Open: daily, 9–2; Sunday, 9–1 (closed Monday). Admission charge.

The Palazzo Barberini was one of many buildings built by the Barberini family in Rome. So many ancient buildings were razed to make way for the dynasty's creations that a pun-epigram was coined by the Romans: *Quod non fecerunt barbari, fecerunt Barberini* – "What was not done by the barbarians was done by the Barberini."

The salons of the Palazzo Borghese's *piano nobile* house one of Rome's most exclusive gentleman's clubs, the Caccia.

The Palazzo della Cancelleria was built by Raffaele Riaro, who is reputed to have won a third of the palace's huge cost in a single night of gambling with Francesco Cybo, nephew of Innocent VIII.

▷▷▷ Palazzo Borghese

Piazza Borghese

This palace's huge but rambling contours have given it the nickname *il cembalo* (the harpsichord). Purchased in 1605 by Cardinal Camillo Borghese, later to become Pope Paul V, it has remained the Borghese family seat to this day. Bernini's chief patron, Cardinal Scipione Borghese, housed his fantastic art collection here (it is now in the Galleria Borghese in the Villa Borghese). This palace was also home to the racy Paolina Borghese, Napoleon's favorite sister, best known for her infidelities and for Canova's famous statue of her (also in the Galleria Borghese). Not open to the public.

▷▷▷ Palazzo Braschi

Corso V Emanuele–Piazza San Pantaleo 10

One of Rome's more drab palaces, the Palazzo Braschi (1792) was built for the nephew of Pope Pius VI. Since 1952 its 52 rooms have housed the **Museo di Roma**, a museum devoted to the history of the city since the Middle Ages, along with a collection of tapestries, costumes, and terracotta sculptures. The favorite exhibit is Pope Pius XI's personal railway carriage, produced in 1857 for his journeys between Rome and Frascati. The palace has long been closed to the public, partly for restoration and partly because of an internecine quarrel between the state and city council. Parts of the permanent collection are occasionally opened for temporary exhibitions.

Open (if restored): daily, 9–2; Tuesday and Thursday also, 5–8; Sunday, 9–1 (closed Monday). Admission charge.

Snack stop: one of Rome's pastry palaces

▷▷▷ Palazzo della Cancelleria

Piazza della Cancelleria—Campo dei Fiori

Remarkably, no one is certain to whom the Palazzo della Cancelleria (1485–1513), praised by many as one of Rome's finest Renaissance palaces, can be attributed. Bramante, for one, is reputed to have had a hand in the superimposed arches of its marvelous courtyard. It is a shame that most of the building's stone was plundered from one of Rome's great ancient monuments, the Teatro di Pompey, originally some 200m away (and the site of Julius Caesar's murder). Today the palace is one of the Vatican's few extraterritorial properties, and its gloomier reaches house papal offices. As a result it is not open to the public, though certain halls are occasionally used for music recitals.

▶▷▷ Palazzo Colonna—Galleria Colonna

Piazza Santi Apostoli–Via della Pilotta 17

The grandiose seat of one of Rome's most venerable patrician families was founded by the Colonna pope, Martin V, in the 15th century, though most of the present palace dates from 1730. Today the only part of the palace open to the public, apart from the church of **Santi Apostoli** (see page 133), is the **Galleria Colonna**, a private art collection of largely Late Renaissance and Baroque works. Highlights of the gallery's six rooms include works by Rubens; Tintoretto; Van Dyck; Veronese; Poussin; Bronzino; landscapes by Gaspard Dughet; and perhaps the prize painting, Annibale Carracci's bucolic scene of a peasant eating beans. Unmissable, too, is the exuberant frescoed ceiling in the gilded Salone (Room 2) that depicts the *Battle of Lepanto*, the famous naval defeat of the Turks in 1571.

Open: Saturday only, 9–1. Closed in August. Admission charge.

▶▶▷ Palazzo Corsini

Via della Lungara 10

The Palazzo Corsini houses the later part of the national art collection. The palace was given to Cardinal Domenico Riario by his uncle, Sixtus IV, in the 15th century, but passed to Queen Christina of Sweden during the 17th century after her abdication and her conversion to Catholicism. (Cynics say she espoused Catholicism because she was hopelessly in love with a cardinal.) The Corsini, a banking family with papal connections, acquired it in the 18th century, instigating a rebuilding program that was never completed.

Among the paintings on display on the upper floor are Guido Reni's famous portrait of *Beatrice Cenci*, praised effusively over the centuries (see panel); a rare portrait of *Bernini* by Baccicia; two Caravaggios: *Narcissus* and *St. John the Baptist*; Rubens's *St. Sebastian;* a *Madonna and Child* by Murillo; two winter scenes by Breughel; and Van Dyck's *Rest on the Flight to Egypt*.

The palace also houses one of Rome's oldest libraries still *in situ*, founded by Lorenzo Corsini in the 18th century.

Open: Tuesday to Friday, 9–6; Saturday, 9–2; Sunday, 9–1 (closed Monday). Admission charge.

Palazzo Corsini's old grounds now house Rome's *Botanical Gardens* (open daily except Sunday, 9–6. Admission free). There is little to see – even less since the disastrous winter of 1984–85, that wiped out many tropical plants – but this is a lovely spot for peace and quiet amid the clamor of Trastevere.

American writer Nathaniel Hawthorne called Reni's portrait of Beatrice Cenci, executed for killing her demonic father, "the saddest picture ever painted or conceived," while his fellow novelist Herman Melville thought it "the sweetest, most touching, but most awful of all feminine heads." It was reputedly painted in Beatrice's cell prior to her execution.

Dynastic wealth: Palazzo Doria Pamphili

▶▶▷ **Palazzo–Galleria Doria Pamphili**
Via del Corso; entrance at Piazza del Collegio Romano 1a
The Palazzo With over 1,000 rooms, five courtyards, and four monumental staircases, the Palazzo Doria Pamphili is one of Rome's largest palaces, now much improved since the time when the Victorian critic John Ruskin described it as "a dull, blue, devilish, dirty hole, though handsome on the outside." Much of it is still lived in or leased by the Doria Pamphili family, a dynasty formed by the joining together of the Doria, a famous Genoa seafaring clan, and the Pamphili, the Rome-based patrician family.

Its core dates from 1435 and was commissioned by Cardinal Fazio Santorio, though it passed through several hands before finding its present owners. Successive generations affected numerous alterations, building on foundations that in places date back to classical times (when they were probably storehouses for the old city).

The Galleria The part of the labyrinth open to the public is given over to the art collection of the **Galleria Doria Pamphili**. Although you should have few problems admiring the palace's innate grandeur, the collection's haphazard arrangement in its four galleries makes seeing the pictures more difficult. Canvases are numbered rather than named, and it's worth investing in a catalog to make sense of the many paintings.

The first gallery contains outstanding works, including Titian's *Salome* (labeled 29) and *Religion Succoured by Spain* (10); *The Allegory of Virtue* (20), a sketch by Correggio; Raphael's *Double Portrait of Two Venetians* (23); and a pair of Caravaggios: *Maddalena* (40) and *Rest on the Flight in Egypt* (42). Here, too, are Lo Spagnoletto's *St. Jerome* (46) and a bust by Alessandro Algardi of *Olimpia Maidalchini*, infamous sister-in-law of Innocent X, the Pamphili pope. Olimpia is supposed to have visited Innocent on his death bed only to steal the last box of money he had been able to hide from her.

The second gallery The main hall of the second gallery has less to recommend it, though the rooms at its end contain small gems in the shape of Giovanni di Paolo's Sienese works, *The Birth and Marriage of the Virgin* (174/176) and the *Adoration of the Shepherds* (200), as well as a *Madonna* by Parmigianino and the *Battle of the Bay of Naples* (317) by Pieter Breughel the Elder.

The third gallery The collection's most treasured work is the Velázquez portrait of Innocent X, given pride of place in a separate small room at the end of the third gallery. It captured the pope's weak and suspicious nature so adroitly that Innocent lamented that it was "too true, too true." Oscar Wilde said much the same, praising it as "quite the grandest portrait in the world – the entire man is there." Its scowling face compares with Bernini's more flattering bust – all smiles and good humor – in the cabinet alongside.

The fourth gallery The gallery's final wing offers 17th-century landscapes by Claude Lorrain and Gaspar Dughet. Before leaving, it is worth joining the guided tours through a sample of the palace's **private apartments** (30 minutes, admission charge). Included are the ballroom; the chapel; the Winter Garden, replete with classical busts, board games for long evenings, and an 18th-century children's sledge; the cosy Smoking Room (built for a homesick English bride); and the Salone Verde, whose 15th-century Tornai tapestry on the *Legend of Alexander the Great* took 40 years to weave. Three good paintings also hang here – an *Annunciation* by Filippo Lippi, Beccafumi's *Holy Family* and a *Deposition* by Hans Memling. In the Andrea Doria room, dedicated to the eponymous admiral, is a famous portrait of the seaman by Sebastiano del Piombo, together with much family memorabilia and Lorenzo Lotto's fine *Portrait of a Gentleman.* Perhaps the most impressive interior, however, is the Salone Giallo (the "Yellow Room"), graced by 12 Gobelin tapestries made for Louis XV.

Open: Tuesday, Friday to Sunday only, 10–1. Admission charge.

Simple surroundings for private worship . . .

The embassy has started to give regular tours of the Palazzo Farnese at 10 every Sunday morning. Visits are also sometimes organized on Wednesday afternoons. To be sure of a place, write well in advance to the Ambassador, French Embassy, Piazza Farnese 64, 00186 Rome.

The French government pays just one lira every 99 years as rent for the Palazzo Farnese. The Italians pay a similarly nominal sum for their embassy in Paris.

▶▷▷ **Palazzo Farnese**

Piazza Farnese

To the oft-expressed disgust of the Romans, the Palazzo Farnese – Rome's first and, in some ways, finest Renaissance palace – has been the French Embassy since 1871 and is not generally open to the public. It was commissioned in 1515 by Cardinal Alessandro Farnese, later Pope Paul III, who used the income from his 16 absentee bishoprics to pay for it, stone from the Colosseum to build it, and the Florentine Antonio da Sangallo the Younger to design it. Sangallo was forced off the project in 1545, having already completed the majority of the main and side facades. Michelangelo added the projecting cornice, together with work on its upper windows and the archway to Via Giulia.

Unless you are lucky enough to join a tour (see panel), you must be content with a glimpse from the piazza of Annibale Carracci's Mannerist masterpiece, the frescoed ceiling of the galleria on the palace's first floor. Executed between 1597 and 1603, the frescoes are a voluptuous riot of color on the theme of all-conquering love. The luckless Caracci, however, is said to have been so dispirited at the miserly fee he received from the Farnese, a fabulously wealthy clan, that he took to the bottle and died shortly afterward.

▷▷▷ **Palazzo Madama**

Corso del Rinascimento

An uninspired 16th-century palace, the Palazzo Madama is today the seat of the Senate, the upper house of the Italian Parliament. It was originally owned by the Orsini family, who were later forced to forfeit it as part of the dowry when Lorenzo de' Medici married Clarice Orsini. Emperor Charles V installed an illegitimate daughter here, Margherita di Parma, devoid of any meaningful title except that of common courtesy – *madama* (madam), hence the palace's name.

Contemplating the Palazzo Farnese's facade

Rome's streets are paved with gold . . .

 **Palazzo Massimo alle Colonne**

Corso Vittorio Emanuele

The soot-blackened Palazzo Massimo alle Colonne, closed to the public, was conceived for the Massimo, a family who trace their lineage back further than any in Rome. The masterpiece of Baldassare Peruzzi, it was built on the site of an earlier Massimo pile, destroyed in 1527 during the Sack of Rome. Peruzzi died before his creation was completed, but he lived long enough to design the eccentric curved facade, unique at the time, and to supervise its audacious arrangement on a narrow and difficult site. Other remarkable Peruzzi touches include the portico's squat Doric columns, flattened as if being squashed by the weight of the building above.

 **Palazzo di Montecitorio**

Piazza di Montecitorio

Since 1871 the Palazzo di Montecitorio has housed the Camera dei Deputati, the seat of the lower house of the Italian Parliament. It was designed by Bernini in 1650 for the Pamphili pope, Innocent X.

 **Palazzo del Quirinale**

Piazza del Quirinale

A palace of staggering size that today is the official residence of the Italian president. If you succeed with Italian bureaucracy and join the hour-long guided tours, you will be privy to a treasure house of art.

Until as late as 1870 it was the popes' summer residence and was even used as a conclave to elect popes, the ceremony taking place in the Cappella Paolina, built to the same plan as the Vatican's Sistine Chapel. Visiting cardinals were put up in the *manica lunga* – the "long sleeve" – a wing designed by Bernini that is some 400m long but only two rooms deep. From 1870 to 1946 the palace was the home of the Italian royal family.

Admission by appointment; apply to the Ufficio Intendenza, Palazzo del Quirinale, 00137 Rome.

You can enter the Palazzo Massimo alle Colonne only once a year – on March16, the day in 1583 that Filippo Neri (see the Chiesa Nuova, page 62) reputedly raised a family scion, one Paolo Massimo, from the dead.

A few doors from the Palazzo Massimo is one of Rome's best little speciality shops – Pisoni. The Pisoni family has been supplying candles in all conceivable shapes and sizes to popes, the nobility, and ordinary Romans for over 200 years.

■ **No single book, let alone a few lines, can do justice to Rome's artistic treasures. Virtually every period in the history of Western art is covered in the city, from the obelisks of ancient Egypt to the surrealism of Giorgio de'Chirico. . . .■**

Sculpture is ancient Rome's main artistic bequest, mostly derived from classical Greece, and is best seen in the Vatican museums and the **Museo Nazionale Romano** at the Terme di Diocleziano. The Romans were also prolific painters, but only traces of their frescoes survive in places like the **Domus Aurea** and the **Casa di Livia** on the Palatino. Much Roman art was also indebted to the Etruscans, whose own civilization is fully explored in the **Museo Etrusco** at the Villa Giulia.

Mosaics Another Roman import, mosaics are one of the surviving features of the city's early Christian art. The best examples are glittering works in the churches of **Santa Pudenziana, Sant'Agnese,** and **Santa Costanza.** They were also burial places, and in the many reliefs and sarcophagi of Christian tombs – mainly now in the Vatican museums – you find some of the period's more enduring sculpture. Lesser pieces largely lost, along with the often sophisticated wall paintings left by Christian artists. You have a glimpse of these artists' work in **San Clemente** and in several of the city's catacombs.

Mosaics were also a central feature in the art of the Early Middle Ages, though by then the Byzantine's stylized influence was uppermost. The best places to admire these later masterpieces are in **Santa Prassede, Santa Maria in Cosmedin, Santa Maria Maggiore,** and **Santa Maria in Trastevere**. Some of the period's greatest artists started in the mosaic tradition – men like Pietro Cavallini and Iacopo Torriti – but moved to painting frescoes with an originality and freedom that looked ahead to the Renaissance.

The Tuscan, Arnolfo del Cambio, achieved similar advances in sculpture, leaving small masterpieces in **St. Peter's** and **San Clemente**. This faint new artistic dawn, however, darkened when the papacy was moved to Avignon in 1308, cutting the papal commissions that had always been the motor of art in the city.

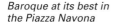

Baroque at its best in the Piazza Navona

The High Renaissance Although Rome's great classical heritage might have been expected to foster the Renaissance, the city had to borrow its next wave of artists from the artistic revival pioneered in Florence. Early works from the period are thin, but in later artists like Raphael and Michelangelo Rome could claim the High Renaissance's greatest exponents. Most other leading figures left paintings scattered around the galleries and churches, many collected in the **Galleria Borghese, Santa Maria del Popolo,** and the Pinacoteca of the Vatican museums (see also page 34).

Art lovers in the Vatican's Raphael Rooms

Mannerism Less familiar, but still talented artists emerged around the time of the Sack of Rome in 1527, a watershed in the city's cultural life. They included men like Giulio Romano, Perin del Vaga, Parmigianino and Rosso Fiorentino, all involved in a new artistic movement later known as Mannerism. Later exponents of the style – Francesco Salviati, Pellegrino Tibaldi and Baldassare Peruzzi – followed, though none could be said to have reversed the city's artistic decline, which reached a nadir with the Counter-Reformation's gloomy outpourings.

New blood and new enthusiasm emerged, however, at the end of the 16th century, with Annibale Carracci and his more radical and notorious rival, Michelangelo Caravaggio. The latter's dramatic realism and revolutionary use of light and shade – less appreciated then than they are today – are seen to best effect in the paintings in the **Galleria Borghese, Santa Maria del Popolo** and **San Luigi dei Francesi.**

Baroque None, however, had quite the effect on Rome's visible face as the giants of the city's Baroque period – Bernini, Borromini and Pietro da Cortona – whose churches, fountains and sculptures are found all over the city. For a crash course in their efforts, visit **St. Peter's,** the **Galleria Borghese, San Carlo ai Catinari, Sant'Andrea al Quirinale** and the Cornaro Chapel in **Santa Maria della Vittoria.**

Baroque, however, was the grand climax of Rome's artistic career, and art in the 18th and 19th centuries was a pale shadow of former glories. Although the neoclassical style was born in the city, with the exception of works by Giambattista Piranesi and Antonio Canova, its masterpieces were executed elsewhere.

Bernini's Rape of Proserpina*, Galleria Borghese*

Palazzo Spada

Piazza Capo di Ferro

The Palazzo Spada, just a stone's throw from the more grandiose Palazzo Farnese, houses a modest art collection, but is best known for the delightful, if overwrought charm of the palace itself. It was built for Cardinal Capo di Ferro in 1540 by Giulio Mersi da Caravaggio, though it was Giulio Mazzoni who added the stucco to the four-story facade between 1556 and 1560.

In 1632 it passed to the wealthy Cardinal Bernardino Spada, primarily responsible for the art collection and indirectly responsible for the palace's most famous architectural foible: a *trompe l'oeil* trick of perspective, built in 1652 to link two courtyards, that can be seen in the garden just outside the entrance to the museum. What appears to be a magnificent twin row of columns leading to a clearing and a sizable statue turns out to be a 9m corridor and a modest, tiny statue, an effect achieved by the narrowing of the corridor and a foreshortening of the columns. For many years it was thought to be a light-hearted touch added by Borromini, who was responsible for restoring parts of the palace, but it is now accredited to an obscure Augustinian priest, Giovanni Mari da Bitonto.

The upstairs gallery consists of four rooms, all of whose paintings are unlabeled, though a free pamphlet offers some guidance. **Room I** is of least interest, dominated by portraits of Cardinal Spada by Guercino and Guido Reni. **Room II** has works by Renaissance Umbrian painters (unusual in Rome), Titian's unfinished *Portrait of a Musician*, further portraits, and a fine *Visitation* by Andrea del Sarto. **Room III** contains Rubens's *Portrait of a Cardinal,* Guercino's large *Death of Dido*, Jan Breughel's *Landscape with Windmills,* as well as fascinating terrestrial and celestial globes (1622) of the eminent Dutch astronomer, Caelius. **Room IV** is left with more obscure paintings by Orazio Gentileschi, Michelangelo Cerquozzi, and Francois du Quesnoy.

The palace is home to the Italian Council of State, and an appointment is required to see its state rooms. Write to the Ufficio Intendenza, Palazzo Spada, Via Capo di Ferro 3, 00186 Rome. *Open:* Monday and Tuesday, 9–2; Wednesday to Saturday, 9–2 and 3–7; Sundays, 9–1. Admission charge.

Trompe l'œil *in the Palazzo Spada*

113

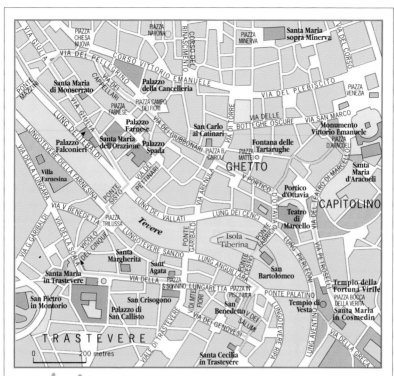

Walk Circular Walk from Piazza Santa Maria in Trastevere

Start in Piazza Santa Maria in Trastevere. Follow Vicolo del Cinque to Piazza Trilussa and cross the Ponte Sisto. Turn left through the arch on to Via Giulia. At Via del Pellegrino turn right to Campo dei Fiori.

The mosaics on the facade of Santa Maria in Trastevere undoubtedly dominate the piazza. Vicolo del Cinque is one of many tiny old streets in Trastevere.

Follow Via dei Giubbonari and cross into the ghetto. Negotiate the many lanes to Piazza d'Aracoeli. Head right down Via del Teatro di Marcello, and at Piazza Bocca della Verità turn right on Lungotevere Pierleoni. Cross the Isola Tiberina and walk to Santa Cecilia in Trastevere.

The old **Jewish ghetto** is central Rome's nicest area to wander. Pass the **Portico d'Ottavia**, fragments of a Classical ruin, and the **Teatro di Marcello**, with medieval houses.

Return to Piazza Santa Maria in Trastevere via Piazza San Sonnino and Via della Lungaretta.

All **Trastevere's** small streets are worth exploring at leisure: there are numerous bars for refreshments. Hunt out Trasté at Via della Lungaretta, a relaxed but refined bar.

Campo dei Fiori market

Walk From Piazza Venezia to San Giovanni in Laterano

Start in Piazza Venezia. Walk up to Piazza del Campidoglio to the right of the Monumento Vittorio Emanuele. Find the lane and steps at the piazza's rear and drop down to Via dei Fori Imperiali. Enter the Roman Forum on the right and walk to the Colosseum.

Monumento Vittorio Emanuele

Explore the **museums** on either side of **Piazza del Campidoglio** and take in the view of the **Roman Forum** beyond the piazza, one of the city's best.

Climb the steps to the right of the Colosseum Metro station, and turn right and then left on Via Terme di Tito. Take the first left to San Pietro in Vincoli. Retrace your steps and turn left on Viale del Monte Oppio. After 200m turn right into the park of the Colle Oppio.

The **Colle Oppio** marks the site of the Domus Aurea and the Terme di Traiano, and is among the city's most pleasant small **parks.**

Cross Via Labicana. Follow Via di San Giovanni in Laterano to San Clemente and then cut up the steps right to Via dei S S Quattro Coronati; follow it to San Giovanni in Laterano. Look into the little church of **S S Quattro Coronati** before climbing to **San Giovanni in Laterano,** the mother church of Rome.

● ***Stroll*** *A good strolling option is to take a route through the Colle Oppio park to San Pietro in Vincoli via Viale del Monte Oppio.*

The world's biggest freestanding dome

▶▶▶ Pantheon

Piazza della Rotonda

The Pantheon is the grandest and best-preserved monument of Roman antiquity. Built in its present form by Hadrian between AD 119 and AD 128, it largely replaced an earlier temple erected in 27 BC by Marcus Agrippa, son-in-law of Augustus. With typical modesty, however, Hadrian retained the original dedication, still boldly picked out in bronze across the pediment: M AGRIPPA L F COS TERTIUM FECIT – Marcus Agrippa, son of Lucius, Consul for the third time, built this. This inscription puzzled historians until 1892, when archaeologists discovered that many of the Pantheon's bricks were date-stamped with Hadrian's seal. Remnants of Agrippa's earlier square temple are now incorporated into the pillared front portico.

From Roman temple . . . Hadrian was personally responsible for the new design, as he was for his other great buildings at Tivoli and the largely vanished Tempio di Venere e Roma near the Colosseum. Like its predecessor the temple was to be dedicated not to all the gods, as the name seems to suggest, but to the "most holy" deities, the 12 Olympian gods of classical Greece. Its design was simplicity itself, involving a single circular and quadrangular element – effectively a Roman dome on a circular base welded to replicate the form of a Greek temple.

. . . to Christian church After the fall of Rome, the Byzantine emperor Phocas presented the building to Boniface IV, who, in turn, consecrated it as a Christian church (AD 609). Thereafter to remove a single stone

In the 16th century Bramante's original plan for St. Peter's proposed to give the basilica an almost exact copy of the Pantheon's dome.

<<It has this great advantage: it requires only two moments to be penetrated by its beauty; you take a few steps, you see the church, and the whole thing is over.>> – Stendhal

<< Simple, erect, severe, austere, sublime –
Shrine of all saints and temple of all gods,
From Jove to Jesus – spared and blest by time;
Looking tranquillity, while falls or nods
Arch, empire, each thing round thee, and man plods
His way through thorns to ashes – glorious dome!
Shalt thou not last? – Time's scythe and tyrants' rods
Shiver upon thee – sanctuary and home
Of art and piety – Pantheon! – pride of Rome. >> – Byron, *Childe Harold's Pilgrimage*

The Venerable Bede claimed the Pantheon was the work of the devil. The *oculus* in the dome, he said, was a hole broken in the roof by demons trying to flee when the church was consecrated by Boniface IV.

constituted a mortal sin, and it is to this injunction that the Pantheon owes its fine state of preservation. It was the first time a pagan temple had been thus converted, Christian emperors having hitherto forbidden the use of this (or any other) temple for worship. Under safe Church care it was rechristened Santa Maria ad Martyres, the dedication to the Virgin and all Christian martyrs taking place on November 1, AD 608 – the origin of All Saints' Day. Large numbers of martyrs' bones were transferred here at the time from the catacombs around the city. The building is still officially a church – hence there is no admission charge.

Changes over the years The building could not pass through history unscathed, however. Although Gregory III plated the concrete dome with lead inside and out, further protecting the building, it was a poor substitute for the bronze that had previously gilded most surfaces. The bulk of the covering was plundered by Emperor Constans II in 667, along with numerous other bronzes and fittings from the city, most of which were returned to Constantinople to be melted down into coins. (Some were waylaid by Arab raiders and wound up in Alexandra, Egypt.) Worse, Bernini, of all people, was instrumental in persuading Pope Urban VIII to remove the bronze that covered the wooden beams of the portico. This bronze found its way into the baldacchino of St. Peter's, with enough left over, it is said, to provide the pope with 60 new cannons. Bernini also added a pair of Baroque spires to Hadrian's dome, protuberances that were popularly known as Bernini's donkey ears until they were removed in 1883.

Today you descend several steps to enter the great **portico** – used in the Middle Ages as a fish market – and into the shadows of 16 massive granite columns. Originally, however, a ramp rose to the entrance, a measure of how much the street level has risen over the centuries. The two great **bronze doors** are miraculous survivors from antiquity, the finest extant from ancient Rome.

The interior and dome If the form of the Pantheon's exterior is magnificent, it is nothing compared with the grandeur of the **interior,** which – with the help of restorations – is the most perfectly preserved of any ancient building in Italy. Of all its features, the breathtaking **dome** is the most captivating and marks the supreme achievement of Roman interior architecture. Its 141-foot span is larger than St. Peter's and until 1960 was the largest freestanding dome anywhere in the world. Its dimensions are crucial to the building's harmony, the dome's diameter being exactly the same as its height from the floor and the side walls precisely half the height (and thus the width) of the dome. In theory, therefore, a perfect sphere could fit neatly into the interior.

The dome's construction (the largest concrete project undertaken before the 20th century) gives an insight into the ingenuity of Rome's civil engineers. Sitting on brick-faced concrete walls some 23 feet across, its lower

Soaring columns in the Pantheon

drum starts at the same width, becoming progressively thinner, and thus lighter, until it is a little over 3 feet thick at its apex. This had the effect of lightening the dome's payload, an effect reinforced by using progressively lighter materials toward its crown. Heavy travertine was mixed with concrete at the base, less sturdy volcanic tufa midway, and feather-light pumice at the summit. Exterior arches were built to retain its huge thrust, along with a boxlike base outside the drum, added when cracks appeared during construction (probably a result of the foundations sinking into the old marsh on which they stood). The artful coffering, or *lacunas,* that indent the dome's interior were made by pouring the concrete over moulds.

Perhaps the most intriguing and, to modern eyes, most puzzling, feature of the dome, however, is the circular 30-foot hole (or *oculus*), which opens the interior to the elements. This was a deliberate part of the original design, allowing sunlight but also rain to pour into the temple. Practically it was used to illuminate the interior, but it also served Hadrian's desire to link the earthly temple with a direct meditation on the heavens.

Immediately off Piazza della Rotonda is La Tazza d'Oro, which by general consent serves Rome's best cup of coffee: Via degli Orfani 84 (Open: 7am–10PM. Closed Sunday).

Refreshments outside the Pantheon

A fountain near the Pantheon

One minute north of the Pantheon is the Gelateria della Parma, Rome's best ice-cream shop. A slick, streamlined affair, it serves over 100 flavors, including such exotica as muesli, avocado, After Eight, kiwi fruit, and pomegranate. It also sells excellent coffee, chocolates, and sticky cakes: Via della Maddalena 20 (*open*: noon–midnight. Closed Wednesday).

Elsewhere the interior is very simple, containing little to suggest that it is a church. The marble floor has been restored, but it conforms to the original design; likewise the eight *aedicules,* or shrines, and six recesses on the circular wall, which once contained the statues of the Olympian gods alongside the figures of Hadrian and Augustus. In the center, illuminated in midsummer by the sun overhead, was a statue of *Jove Ultor*, the Avenging Jupiter.

These days the statues are gone, replaced by an aborted attempt to produce a pantheon of eminent Italians. Raphael is buried here, as are two Italian kings – Vittorio Emanuele I and Umberto I – the tomb of the latter being partly made, in a symbol of restitution, from the cannons cast for Urban VIII out of the portico's stolen bronze.

Open: July to September, daily 9–6; October to June, Monday to Saturday, 9–2; Sunday, 9–1. Admission free.

▶▷▷ Piazza Bocca della Verità

When its usually fierce traffic is quiet, the Piazza Bocca della Verità is one of the loveliest spots in Rome. Views from its green, riverside setting embrace both ancient and Christian buildings: the campanile and Romanesque church of **Santa Maria in Cosmedin,** home of the Bocca della Verità, the "Mouth of Truth," from which the piazza derives its name (see page 150); the Arco di Giano and Arco degli Argentari, both in Via del Velabro off the piazza; the beautifully simple and tranquil church of **San Giorgio in Velabro**; **San Giovanni Decollato**; and two ancient and evocative temples, the **Tempio di Vesta** and **Tempio della Fortuna Virilis** (see page 175).

In the piazza's northwest corner is the **Casa dei Crescenzi**, an unusual medieval house whose inscription claims it was built by Nicolò Crescenzio (a member of Rome's single-most-powerful family in the 11th century), who was trying to re-create the splendor of ancient Rome. To this end he pillaged numerous Roman fragments to incorporate into his classical imitation.

▶▶▶ Piazza del Campidoglio

Occupying a prime site on the ancient ridge of the Campidoglio, or Capitoline Hill (see pages 52–54), the Piazza del Campidoglio is one of the architectural masterpieces of Michelangelo, who was responsible for the square's plan and for the basic design of the palaces that occupy three of its sides. Two of these, the **Palazzo Nuovo** and **Palazzo dei Conservatori** (see page 53) today house the Museo Capitolino, one of the city's most important collections of Greek and Roman antiquities.

The star-shaped inlay of the pavement was intended to emphasize a magnificent bronze equestrian statue (now known to be of Marcus Aurelius) that, until recently, stood at the center of the square. For centuries it stood in front of San Giovanni in Laterano and was believed to represent the Emperor Constantine, whose Christian sympathies probably saved it from destruction. It was moved on the orders of Pope Paul III and against the wishes of Michelangelo.

The Arco degli Argentari (Arch of the Money Changers) was built in AD 204 by the money changers' guild in honor of the Emperor Settimo Severo; his wife Donna; and their two children, Geta and Caracalla. All the family are depicted in relief making a sacrificial offering – all save Caracalla, whose portrait was removed after his murder of Geta.

Star attraction: Piazza del Campidoglio

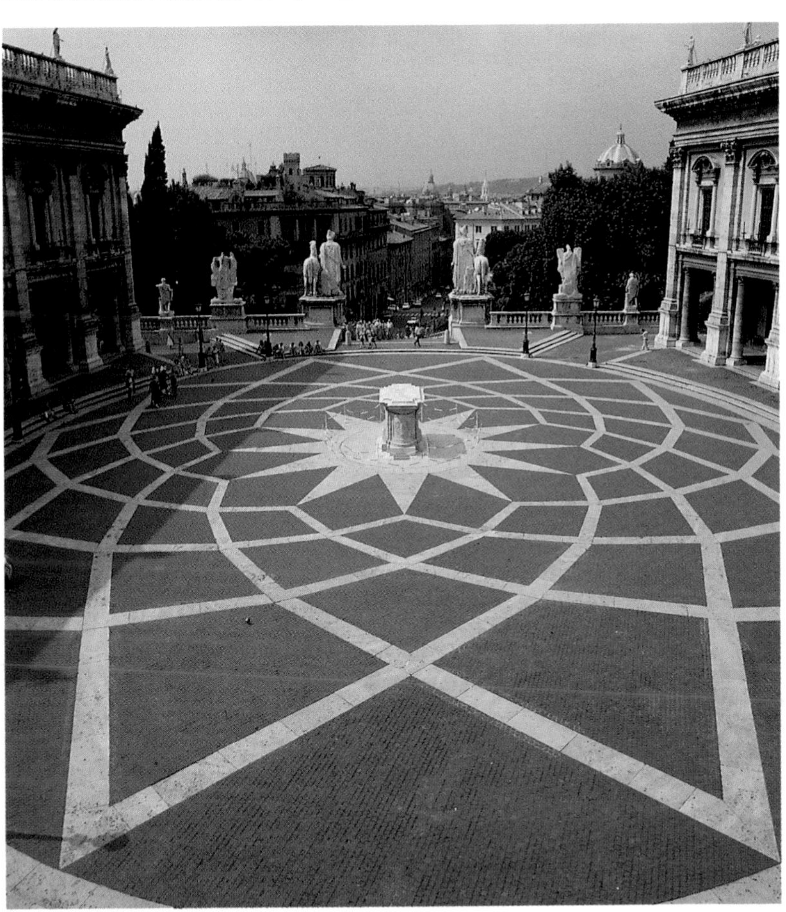

▶▶▶ Piazza Navona

Rome's most exhilarating piazza, Piazza Navona, lays many claims to be the heart of Rome. A wonderful place to walk, sip coffee, or simply watch the world go by, there is no mistaking its vast elliptical shape, which matches exactly the outlines of the *circo,* or stadium, built here by the Emperor Domitian in AD 86. From the arena, originally known as the *Circus Agonalis* – the arena for athletic games – comes the piazza's present name, rendered in medieval Latin first as *in agone*, and then in Rome's strangulated dialect as *'n 'agona*.

The stadium remained intact for many centuries, and in the Middle Ages was used for jousting, horse racing, and water festivals. During the latter, which often took place in the stifling dog days of August, the piazza was flooded and Rome's aristocracy had their gilded carriages pulled around the artificial lake – a direct descendant of the *naumachia,* or mock sea battles, of the Romans. These days, December still sees an almost month-long Epiphany festival – a relentlessly kitsch and commercialized affair – but still a means by which the square's old festive spirit is kept alive.

The piazza suffered its biggest transformation in 1644, when the Pamphili's Innocent X was elected pope and decided to emulate the Barberini, whose papal candidate, Urban VIII, had recently commissioned monuments to the family's greater glory. As a result the square is an unashamed memorial to the Baroque: a cunningly designed church by Borromini, **Sant'Agnese in Agone** (see page 130), and three marvelous fountains – two by Bernini, the **Fontana dei Quattro Fiumi** and **Fontana del Moro** (see pages 70 and 71).

Alongside Sant'Agnese, the **Palazzo Pamphili** (now the Brazilian Embassy) singularly fails as a centerpiece, too large and two dimensional to rival the **Palazzo Barberini,** which it was meant to outshine (see pages 102–103). Borromini was responsible for the interior – the doughty facade was the work of Girolamo Rainaldi (1644) – but it is closed to the public.

Rome's custom of making "talking statues" or *pasquinades,* by hanging messages on them started just off Piazza Navona behind the Palazzo Braschi. In 1501 a cardinal hung the first – a Latin eulogy to St. Mark – on a withered stump of a statue to Menelaus, known for centuries afterward as Pasquino, a Roman tailor reputed to have started the practice of leaving more barbed political comments on the statue. Because the satire was usually directed at the papacy, the threat of death hung over anyone who put up such graffiti.

Hunting for other views on the Piazza Navona

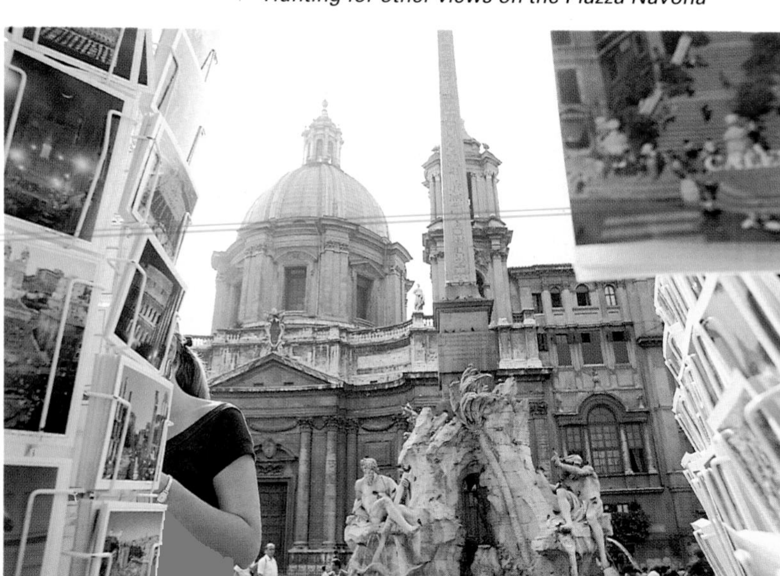

Café Life

■ **Although there are bars on every corner in Rome – functional, stand-up places – the cafés are different. Here, too, you can stand and fight for service, but more often they are places for leisurely, sun-drenched contemplation. You pay extra to relax and be waited on, but a purchase buys the right to read, dream or take in the street life for as long as the mood takes you . . . .** ■

A choice of styles The bars are more for a kick-start espresso, a breakfast *cornetto* (croissant), or a hurried lunchtime snack. Pay the cashier, take your chit to the bar, and you are away. All human life is here, together with all it needs to keep body and soul together. Bars are shops, pubs, phone booths, and social meeting places rolled into one.

<< Giolitti, Via Ufficio del Vicario 40, is venerable and old-fashioned, has great ice cream, and is one of the city's best-known and best-loved cafés. **>>**

Traffic precludes the pavement locations of Paris's boulevards for cafés; in Rome the best ones are in the piazzas. The street-side palaces of the Via Veneto, veritable symbols of the *dolce vita* of the 1950s, are now expensive shadows of their former selves. Self-respecting Romans no longer visit the once-legendary **Café de Paris**, though they may still risk **Doney** across the street or **Harry's Bar** if they are politicians or second-rate actors.

Watch the world go by The tradition of Rome's *dolce far niente* – the sweet doing of nothing – to the accompaniment of sun, coffee, or alcohol, is a long one, dating back to classical times and, more recently, to the Grand Tour. From 1760 the Via Condotti's **Caffè Greco**, which is still going but living on past glories, watered the likes of Goethe, Wagner, Stendhal and most of the famous names since.

<< Camilloni and Eustachio, on Piazza Sant' Eustachio, are neighboring cafés, both claiming the city's best cup of coffee. **>>**

All the cafés recommended here are deservedly well known, usually because they command the best locations or are tinged with the style and respectability bestowed by years of service. Yet if you explore off the main piazzas, there are many more, equally picturesque – and probably cheaper and quieter into the bargain.

<< Colombia, Piazza Navona 88, is the busiest, sunniest, and best of Piazza Navona's many cafés. Tre Scalini, opposite, has famous tartufo chocolate ice cream. **>>**

Once a legend: Café de Paris

Gushing lion on the Piazza del Popolo

▶▶▷ Piazza del Popolo

For centuries travelers entering Rome from the north on the Via Cassia or Via Flaminia, two of Rome's oldest consular roads, would have had their first impression of the city in the Piazza del Popolo. Its name derives from the *popolus*, or hamlet, that stood here in open fields during the Middle Ages.

The Via del Corso, the arrow-straight street that runs south from the piazza, once the Via Lata, has been here since earliest times, leading directly to the Campidoglio and ancient forums. The Via di Ripetta, however, one of the "trident" of roads leading off the square, was built by Leo X as a direct route to the Vatican. The third road, Via del Baubuino, which leads to Piazza di Spagna (see page 124) was added by Clement VII to celebrate the 1525 Jubilee and to balance the existing streets. The square's present gateway, the **Porta del Popolo**, was commissioned by Pius IV in 1561, its three arches designed to mirror the trio of streets opposite.

The piazza's obsession with balance was continued in its twin churches, **Santa Maria dei Miracoli** and **Santa Maria di Monte Santo**, built in 1679 by Rainaldi (with help from Bernini and Fontana) to either side of Via del Corso. Both appear identical, but Rainaldi had a titanic struggle to achieve the effect because the land on which they stand is unequal – one church is round, the other oval. Both are overshadowed, however, by the square's highlight, **Santa Maria del Popolo**, home of one of the richest collections of art of any church in Rome (see page 158).

On Napoleon's prompting, Giuseppe Valadier added the piazza's finishing touches in 1814, creating its present oval shape and the four water-belching lions around the **obelisk** of Pharaoh Rameses II, a 3,200-year-old pillar, first removed by Augustus from Heliopolis for the Circo Maximo and brought to its present site in 1589 by Sixtus V and his architect Domenico Fontana.

Emile Zola described the Via del Corso as a place where "people scrutinized and jostled one another. It was open-air promiscuity, all Rome gathered together in the smallest possible space. . . Its pleasure lay . . . in the forced elbowings which facilitated not only desired meetings but the satisfaction of curiosity, the display of vanity, and the garnering of endless tittle-tattle."

▶▶▶ Piazza San Pietro

It is hard to divorce St. Peter's square – one of the most famous in Christendom – from the great basilica that it frames (see **San Pietro**, pages 165–69), a testament to Bernini's genius in realizing a piazza that had to be both a setting for a vast church and a meeting place for countless thousands of pilgrims. Laid out between 1656 and 1667, a century after St. Peter's, it takes the form of a colossal ellipse (1115 feet by 787 feet), partly enclosed by two huge, semicircular colonnades – designed as arms reaching out symbolically to embrace the pilgrim. Each is four columns deep and contains 284 Doric pillars. The colonnades are topped by 140 statues of the saints, cleverly silhouetted against the sky (all beautifully floodlit at night). The piazza's smaller rectangle in front of the church is known as the Piazza Retta and is guarded by statues of the Apostles Peter and Paul.

The central **obelisk** (84 feet high), was brought from Egypt to Rome by Caligula in AD 39. The fact that it is without hieroglyphics suggests it was made by the Egyptians to Roman specifications. It was erected in the *Circus Neronis*, a stadium similar to the Circo Massimo, now vanished, but that probably occupied the western part of the piazza and much land beyond. Having remained *in situ* through the Middle Ages, the pillar was moved to the piazza in 1586 on the orders of Sixtus V.

Moving the 350-ton column took four months and involved 900 men, 44 winches, and 140 horses. According to legend Sixtus had ordered silence during the final raising for fear of disturbing the workmen. As the ropes appeared to be stretching to breaking point, however, a Genoese sailor is said to have cried "Pour water on them!", and thus saved the day. The pope forgave him and reputedly promised his family the right to supply the palms used in St. Peter's on Palm Sunday; to this day they come from Bordighera, his hometown.

A magnificent setting for a center of pilgrimage

The iron cross on the piazza's obelisk is said to contain part of the True Cross and replaced a golden orb from ancient times that was long considered to contain the ashes of Julius Caesar. Sadly, when the sphere was ordered to be removed by Sixtus V, it was found to be empty.

Either side of the piazza's two fountains (by Carlo Maderno, 1613, and Carlo Fontana, 1677) are a pair of stone discs marking the focus of its ellipse – the point at which the colonnade's sets of four columns appear to line up as a single pillar.

Not to be missed is the wonderfully grotesque Rococo facade of the Palazzetto at Via Gregoriana 30, just a minute's walk from Piazza di Spagna. The door forms the mouth of a monstrous face, and the windows the eyes, a piece of folly designed by Federigo Zuccari in 1591.

▶▶▶ Piazza di Spagna

Be sure to visit this piazza, one of Rome's most popular spots and known to most visitors for the so-called Spanish Steps (the **Scalinata della Trinità dei Monti**, see page 174). The square fully deserves its fame, both for the beautiful elegance of its surroundings and for the marvelous views and walks on hand nearby. Cars are largely kept out of its environs, a spur to the throng of people who gather here to while away the hours.

The piazza dates from the days of Sixtus V, and the name was coined from the **Palazzo di Spagna** in the southwest corner. The palazzo was built in the 17th century as the Spanish Embassy to the Holy See. In time the district became a favorite with artists and those on a Grand Tour – particularly the English, who nicknamed it the "English ghetto." Many illustrious visitors made it their home, including Tennyson; Byron; Liszt; Wagner; Stendhal; Rubens; Balzac; and especially Keats, the English poet who died here and is remembered in the **Keats-Shelley Memorial** alongside the Spanish Steps (see page 96). The hotel trade moved in to meet the demand, and the area has never looked back. Rome's top hotel, the Hassler, still occupies a prime site at the top of the Spanish Steps.

Piazza di Spagna: a favorite night spot

Sights here largely take second place to ambience, but the church of **Trinità dei Monti** (see page 182) is striking, framed against the sky above the piazza; so, too, is the **Villa dei Medici** to its right (see page 203) and not the least, the eccentric **Fontana della Barcaccia** at the foot of the Spanish Steps (see page 69).

Via Condotti and **Via Frattina**, Rome's two most elegant shopping streets (for Gucci, Bulgari, Valentino et al) lead off from the square – not to mention the galleries of nearby Via Baubuino and Via Margutta, legacies of its bohemian heyday. Some of the city's most venerable (and expensive) cafés are also close by: Babington's Tea Rooms, founded in 1896 and self-consciously English in style; and the Caffè Greco, which was founded in 1742 and was once the haunt of notables such as Goethe, Casanova, Byron, Buffalo Bill, among others.

▶▷▷ Piazza Venezia

Few visitors will escape the frenetic madness of Piazza Venezia, one of Europe's busiest traffic junctions, or miss the majestic folly of its **Monumento Vittorio Emanuele II**, the huge white marble monument to Italy's first king on its southern flank (see page 99). It forms the hub of Rome's street system, with Via del Corso striking north (toward the **Piazza del Popolo**); Via Vittorio Emanuele, west (toward **San Pietro**); Via dei Fori Imperiali, south (to the **Colosseo** and **Foro Romano**) and Via Nazionale, east (toward Stazione Termini). In its southeastern corner is the approach to the **Campidoglio** and the church of **Santa Maria in Aracoeli**, magnets that tend to overshadow the piazza's more modest sights.

Abutting the square's west side is the **Palazzo Venezia**, part fortress, part palace, from whose balcony Mussolini used to harangue and incite the crowds during the 1930s. The church of **San Marco** occupies the same complex, best known for its early Byzantine mosaic (see page 148).

The palace was built for Cardinal Pietro Barbo, later Pope Paul II, in 1451 and was Rome's first important Renaissance building. Between 1594 and 1797, however, it belonged to the Venetian Republic, hence its name and the name of the square. One floor now houses the **Museo di Palazzo Venezia** (Sezione Mediovale), a modern and well-presented collection (opened in 1985) that runs the gamut of medieval art, sculpture, weaving, weapons, china, jewelery, and miscellaneous *objets d'art*. Temporary exhibitions are regularly held here, advertized by red velvet banners on the walls outside.

Do not be fooled by the authentic-looking Renaissance palace opposite the Palazzo Venezia: It is a fake built in 1911 after the original was demolished to improve the outlook on to the Monumento Vittorio Emanuele. Make sure to look for a plaque that marks the house in which Michelangelo died in 1564, wantonly demolished at the same time.

Open: Tuesday to Saturday, 9–2 and Thursday, 9–7; Sunday 9–1 (closed Monday). Admission charge.

Mussolini's office in the Sala del Mappamondo was one of the largest Rome could offer – two storys high, 82 feet long and some 49 feet wide. Its dimensions and the long walk to the dictator's desk were intended to intimidate visitors. Women friends of *Il Duce*, by all accounts, were sexually accommodated on its floors and window seats.

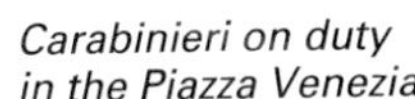

Carabinieri on duty in the Piazza Venezia

Monument and metro station: piramide

Piramide di Caio Cestio
Piazzale Ostiense
The pyramid of Gaius Cestius – or *piramide* to most Romans, who know it mainly as a metro station – is one of Rome's more eccentric monuments: a steeply pitched, albeit miniature pyramid that dates from 12 BC. It was built as the tomb of Cestius, an otherwise unremarkable man who in his time had been praetor, tribune, and member of the *Septemviri Epulones*, the committee of seven responsible for supervising holy festivals. Such is the information on the external inscription, which also records that the structure took only 330 days to build – making it all the more ironic that this memorial to a man of modest fame has survived when grander imperial tombs have vanished – a monument that "defends his death from the oblivion which had utterly effaced his life." Beneath the gleaming marble facing, the pyramid is built in brick, but entry into the interior chamber is restricted to token openings about once every five years.

On the gate's outer flank is a massive block of travertine marking the tomb of Marcus Virgilius Eurysaces (30 BC), a master baker who made a fortune supplying Romans with their daily bread. Its stone circles are said to represent bread pans (or perhaps ovens), while its frieze shows the toga-clad Virgilius directing his slaves in all aspects of bread making.

Porta Maggiore
Piazza di Porta Maggiore
Today the Porta Maggiore stands surrounded by a crush of cars and clanking trams, but in its day it was one of ancient Rome's more imposing edifices. Constructed in AD 52 by the Emperor Claudius, it marked the intersection of two important roads – the Via Casalina (the road to Cassino) and the Via Prenestina (the road to

Praenesta, present-day **Palestrina**; see page 218). Its two vast arches carried twin aqueducts into the city, the *Anio Novus* and the *Aqua Claudia*. Begun by Caligula and completed by Claudius, they were used to bring water to the city from Subiaco, 68 km away. The gateway was not, however, incorporated into the Aurelian walls until AD 279, which explains the discrepancy between its travertine construction and the brick of the adjacent walls.

Most of Rome's surviving gateways were part of the Aurelian Walls, built by the emperor Aurelius in AD 275 to counter the threat of invasion. They were the first walls to have been set up round the city in over 600 years.

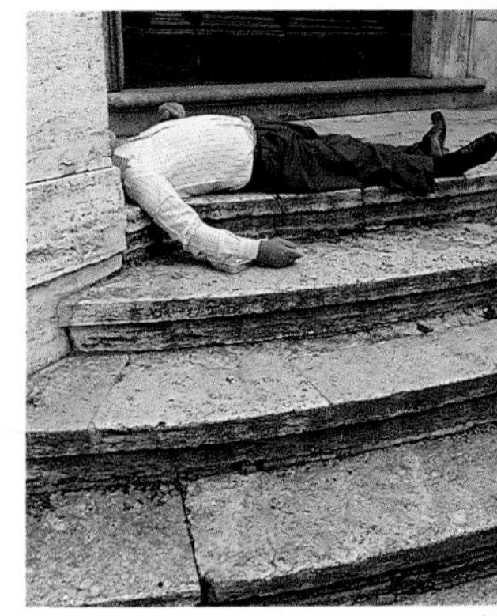

Asleep on the street

▷▷▷ **Porta Pia**

Via XX Settembre

One of the chief gates in the Aurelian walls, the Porta Pia, was known as the Porta Nomentana until 1561 when Pius IV commissioned Michelangelo to design a new facade. Much was reconstructed between 1853 and 1861 by Virginio Vespignani, who was fully responsible for the present outer face. A monument alongside marks the breaches made in the walls by the armies of united Italy as they entered Rome on September 20, 1870 – hence the name of this and many Italian streets – to wrest the city from the pope for the new Italian state. The gate building houses the Museo dei Bersaglieri, which contains military memorabilia.

Open: Tuesday and Thursday 9–1.

▷▷▷ **Porta San Paolo**

Piazza di Porta San Paolo

Gateway to the seaport at Ostia, this portal now takes its name from **San Paolo fuori le Mura,** the basilica to which it leads (see page 164). Its inner face has changed little since Aurelius built it in the 3rd century, though the outer facade was restored by Honorius in AD 402 and Belisarius in the 6th century AD, when the lofty defensive towers were added. The gatehouse conceals the **Museo della Via Ostiense**, with a small collection of finds excavated along the old Via Ostiense.

Open: Tuesday and Saturday only, 9–1. Admission charge.

▶▷▷ **Porta San Sebastiano**

Via Appia Antica

The Porta San Sebastiano, the Porta Appia of antiquity, is the finest of the surviving gateways of the Aurelian walls. Even earlier, as the Porta Capena in the Servian Wall, it was one of the principal entrances to the city – the gateway for the Via Appia Antica, one of the earliest and most vital of Rome's great consular roads (see pages 198–99). Incorporated into the Aurelian walls in the 3rd century, it was refortified a century later by Honorius – with an eye on the Goths' increasing threat to Rome – and again in the 6th century by Narses and Belisarius. Be sure to look at the magnificent outer face of the gate and to pick out the nearby Arco di Druso, which was used in the reign of Caracalla to support an aqueduct.

Porta San Sebastiano's impressive towers are medieval and now contain the Museo delle Mure, a collection that traces the history of the Aurelian walls and the Appia Antica. It also gives you a chance to play at soldiers and clamber along the parapet to Sangallo's Bastione, a stolid piece of medieval military engineering. *Open:* daily 9–1 and Thursday 4–7 (closed Monday). Admission charge.

Food markets have been part of Roman life for centuries

▶▷▷ **Portico d'Ottavia**

Via del Portico d'Ottavia

Strolling around the **ghetto,** you soon stumble across one of the city's least-visited ruins, the Portico of Ottavia, a tantalizing glimpse of a once-great imperial building. What you see today is its *propylaeum,* or entrance, built by Quintus Metellus of Macedonia in 146 BC, overhauled by Augustus in 27 BC (and dedicated to his sister Octavia), and restored by Settimo Severo in AD 203. At one time it fronted a great double colonnade of 300 columns, used by Augustus as part of a covered passageway to link the **Teatro di Pompey** and the **Teatro di Marcello** (see page 174–75). Within its confines – which measured 377 feet by 443 feet – were a library, twin temples to Juno and Jupiter, and a medley of prized decorative statues.

Oddly, given the setting's decorum, the complex was hard up against Rome's bustling food markets, most notably the fish market, the *Forum Piscarium*. For long into the Christian era the legacy lingered, and Octavia's porch continued to be used as a fish stall. To its right you can still see a Latin inscription regulating the length of fish on sale – legend says that if any fish were longer than the inscription, the part above the fin had to be given to the building's caretakers as a tribute.

Today many of the portico's columns and its entablature are enmeshed in the 8th-century church of **Sant' Angelo in Pescheria** – the aptly named Angel of the Fish Market. It was here that Cola di Rienzo and his followers gathered before their ill-fated seizure of the Campidoglio in 1347.

Directly opposite the Portico d'Ottavia is the most authentic of the ghetto's Jewish (but nonkosher) restaurants: **Da Giggetto** (Via di Portico d'Ottavia 21a, closed Monday and July). Solid, old-fashioned, and known for its humorless waiters, Da Giggetto has a menu that includes Jewish-Roman specialties, such as *carciofi alla Giudea* – deep-fried artichokes, stuffed veal, and baked *mozzarella alla carrozza.*

For more refined surroundings and more expensive cuisine, walk up the street to the **Uno,** Rome's only kosher restaurant (Via del Portico d'Ottavia 1e, closed Friday evening and Saturday lunchtime).

River pursuits in the middle of the city

The Protestant Cemetery

What more could there be than to die in Rome, wondered 19th-century Romantics, than to share Chateaubriand's "dearest dream" of "eternal exile among the ruins"? Few places in the city are imbued with its romance, and even the Romans have belatedly become attached to its "heathen" ground – in contrast to the 19th century when burials had to take place at night to avoid provoking attack from outraged Catholics. . . .

<< This must be the most beautiful cemetery in the world . . the cypress trees cast their long shadows upon the most extraordinary collection of exiles ever assembled in one place. – H. V. Morton, *A Traveller in Rome.* >>

The Protestant Cemetery stands close to the **Piramide di Cestio**, a quiet, beautifully tended plot in the shadow of the Aurelian walls, a way station to match the **Keats-Shelley Memorial** on the round of Rome's literary pilgrimage.

Most people come here to see the grave of **John Keats** (1796–1821), to the left as you enter. Buried with him are final letters from his sweetheart Fanny, none of which he could bear to open once he knew he was dying. Alongside is the grave of his friend, the artist Joseph Severn, who outlived him by 65 years.

The remains of **Percy Bysshe Shelley** are also buried here under the inscription *Cor cordium* – "heart of hearts" – and a verse from *The Tempest:*

<< *The Cemetery is an open space among the ruins, covered in winter with violets and daisies. It might make one in love with death to know that one should be buried in so sweet a place.* – Percy Bysshe Shelley, *Preface to Adonais.* >>

Percy Bysshe Shelley

Nothing of him that doth fade,
But doth suffer a sea-change
Into something rich and strange.

The lines were apposite, for Shelley drowned near La Spezia and was cremated on the beach nearby. His friend, Trelawney, brought his heart to Rome and was himself laid to rest alongside the poet 59 years later. Strictly speaking, this is more than an English Protestant cemetery, for some 4,000 non-Catholic Italians and orthodox believers are also buried here. A map from the caretaker helps locate other graves, which include many famous names. **J Addington Symonds** (died 1893), the Renaissance scholar; **Julius Goethe**, the writer's only son; and **Antonio Gramsci**, founder of the Italian Communist party are among them.

Open: daily 8–11:30 and 2:30–4:30. Ring at the gate for entry. Admission free.

Sant'Agnese was one of Christianity's most popular early martyrs – despite the recorded fact that she never took a bath in the 13 years she was alive. Oversights of hygiene apart, she was, according to legend, a beautiful girl, martyred for refusing to marry the son of a pagan governor of the city. Her steadfastness made her a symbol of Christian chastity, and her tomb in Via Nomentana became a place of pilgrimage particularly venerated by Roman women.

Sant'Agostino

▶▷▷ Sant'Agnese in Agone

Piazza Navona

Sant'Agnese was the victim of one of history's more salacious martyrdoms. In AD 304, having refused to renounce her faith, the 13-year-old virgin was thrown into a brothel, one of several houses of ill-repute attracted to the busy environs of Emperor Domitian's stadium (now the **Piazza Navona**). As she was about to be paraded naked, her hair grew to a miraculous length to save her blushes, but not, unfortunately, her life, her martyrdom following soon after close to the bordello.

Her remains were interred in the basilica of **Sant'Agnese fuori le Mura** (see below), but an oratory was built on the site of her death. This oratorio was eventually superseded by the church of Sant'Agnese in Agone, built on the western side of Piazza Navona as a glorified chapel for Pope Innocent X's **Palazzo Pamphili** alongside. Several architects were involved in the work, starting with the father-and-son team of Girolamo and Carlo Rainaldi in 1652. Borromini was called in to revise the Rainaldi plan only for Carlo to be recalled, in turn, to compromise several of Borromini's modifications.

Nevertheless, the main points of interest rest with Borromini, most notably the inspired concave **facade.** The church was to be an important model for later baroque and rococo churches, both in Italy and abroad.

The **interior,** open only rarely, repeats the exterior interplay of architectural nuance – notice how the array of pillars makes the shorter apses appear equal in length to the longer ones – but too much is buried under a lavish jungle of decoration. Several masterpieces of the High Baroque, however, shine through, the brightest being Antonio Raggi's *Martyrdom of St. Cecilia*; Ercole Ferrata's relief, *The Stoning of St. Eremenziana* (Eremenziana was killed after she was found praying at Agnes's tomb); and the heroine's martyrdom, a marble relief in the charmlessly restored oratory, *The Miracle of the Hair of St. Agnes,* Alessandro Algardi's last work.

▶▷▷ Sant'Agnese fuori le Mura

Via Nomentana 349

Sant'Agnese fuori le Mura is as good as its name – St Agnes outside the Walls – and is well away from the center of the city. However, a trip out here becomes worthwhile if you combine it with a visit to the nearby catacombs and church of **Santa Costanza** (see page 139).

The earliest church here was inaugurated in AD 342 by Constantia, daughter (possibly granddaughter) of the Emperor Constantine. It was buttressed into the hillside so as to be directly above the tomb of St. Agnes, martyred close to **Sant'Agnese in Agone** in Piazza Navona (see above). This building was almost completely replaced by the present church, which dates from the time of Pope Honorius I (625–638), and though escaping substantial redesign during the Baroque period, it suffered substantial restoration in 1855.

Mercifully, work left the essence of the 7th-century church intact – the 16 **columns** of the single nave basilica are original, but were removed from an even older classical building, as well as the Greek-style *matroneum* (women's gallery) above them: and, in part, the outstanding **altar canopy** in the apse, an octagonal dome studded with colored marbles (1641) and supported by four ancient porphyry columns. Pride of place goes to the 7th-century **mosaics** in the apse, some of the city's most beautiful and precious Byzantine works. St. Agnes stands in their midst, the sword of her martyrdom at her feet, flanked by the church's builders, Popes Symmachus and Honorius I. Other early Christian reliefs and inscriptions are kept in the entrance and rear of the church.

If the sacristan is on hand, ask to see the 4th-century **catacombs** below the church – in many ways a more intimate insight into subterranean Rome than is offered in the more famous catacombs elsewhere. There are no paintings in the 7 km of tunnels, but you see plenty of *loculi,* or burial niches, which housed the remains.

During a visit of Pius IX to see the restorations of Sant'Agnese in 1855, the floor gave way, but while everyone else was pitched into the basement, the pope is said to have hovered in the air for a while before falling gently to the floor.

▶▷▷ Sant'Agostino

Piazza di Sant'Agostino

Wedged in a little square near Piazza Navona, Sant' Agostino is one of Rome's earliest Renaissance churches, built between 1479 and 1483, probably by Giacomo da Pietrasanta. The interior was extravagantly refurbished in 1750.

Madonna del Parto, *Sant'Agostino*

Sant'Andrea della Valle's dome is second only to St. Peter's in height

On the right as you enter is the *Madonna del Parto* (Madonna of the Childbirth), a statue by Jacopo Sansovino completed in 1521. This statue is much venerated by pregnant women seeking a safe labor, and by couples wanting a child – as the mass of candles, votive offerings, and the Virgin's much-touched and polished left foot testify. The others are the *Madonna di Loreto* (1605) by **Caravaggio,** in the first chapel of the left aisle, whose dirty-footed peasant scandalized opinion when it was unveiled; **Raphael**'s famous *Prophet Isaiah* (1512), painted on to the third column of the left; Jacopo Sansovino's *Madonna and Child with St. Anne* (1512), which stands below the Raphael fresco; and a Byzantine *Madonna,* brought from Constantinople, which gazes down over Bernini's high altar.

Only Catholic and Baroque diehards visited Sant' Andrea in the past, a church that rarely appeared in early guidebooks to Rome. A notable exception was the American writer Nathaniel Hawthorne, who wrote: "I haven't seen, nor expect to see, anything else so entirely and satisfactorily finished as this small oval church – I only wish I could pack it in a large box and send it home."

▶▶▷ Sant'Andrea al Quirinale

Via del Quirinale

Sant'Andrea is one of Rome's Baroque jewels, designed by Bernini, whose son wrote that this was one of his father's favorite churches. **San Carlino**, a church by his great rival Borromini, is on the corner of the same street (see page 134).

The building brims with architectural ideas previously unthought of and hardly touched on since. Eight lateral chapels gather round the walls, united by an elliptical cornice, with the high altar cleverly lit by a well-placed window. Gilding, sumptuous decoration, and the lush red *cottanello* (a marble from Sicily) columns lend the whole space an almost aristocratic elegance, a legacy of its Jesuit patrons, who believed worldly opulence was a means to persuade the faithful of heavenly glory.

The martyrdom of Sant'Andrea (St. Andrew) and his ascension to Heaven is represented in the painting of the high altar and the pediment statue of the saint.

▶▷▷ Sant'Andrea della Valle

Corso Vittorio Emanuele II

Cars now thunder past Sant'Andrea, whose soaring, filthy facade is long overdue for a cleaning, but in Roman times the *valles* (valley) was the site of a quiet lake. The present Baroque monster was begun in 1591 by Francesco Grimaldi and Giacomo della Porta and completed by Carlo Maderno and Carlo Rainaldi – though all four architects borrowed liberally from the massive church of the Gesù, headquarters of the Jesuit order close by.

The church is famous mainly as the fictional setting for Act I of Puccini's *Tosca* (the only opera set in a church) and for possessing Rome's second highest dome after St. Peter's. Nevertheless, two eminent popes are buried here – Pius II (d 1464) and Pius III (d 1503) – both moved here from St. Peter's in 1614. The frescos (1624–28), by Domenichino, in the pendentives of the dome, led Stendhal to comment, "There are days when it seems to me painting can go no further." Lanfranco's paintings in the dome above constitute one of the earliest Baroque ceilings.

▶▷▷ Santi Apostoli

Piazza Santi Apostoli

The nine-column portico is eye-catching, but nothing in Santi Apostoli suggests that the church is almost 1,500 years old. It was probably founded by Pope Pelagius (556–561) after the expulsion of the Goths from Rome, but suffered several disastrous restorations, most notably Francesco and Carlo Fontana's virtual rebuilding (1702 onward), which obliterated precious Renaissance frescoes. The portico incorporates a Roman-era frieze and dates from the 15th century (note its 1807 tomb by Canova, the Byzantine lions and Roman imperial eagle). The remainder of the facade is by Napoleon's architect, Valadier (1827).

Inside, the only relics of the old church are the fluted columns in the **Cappella del Crocifisso** (at the end of the south aisle), and the only art of note is the two tombs flanking the high altar: one a masterpiece by Canova (1787), his first work in Rome.

The Gesù church (1575), down the Corso from Sant' Andrea, was the model for Counter-Reformation churches all over Europe. Both the facade (by Giacomo della Porta) and the hugely ornate interior (by Vignola) were immensely influential. The chief work of art is the ceiling fresco, *Triumph of the Name of Jesus* by Giovanni Gaulli, a contemporary of Bernini, and one of the seminal baroque ceiling paintings, almost garish in its opulence. The other eye-catching feature is Andrea Pozzo's chapel for Ignatius Loyola (1696).

Sharing the load: shopping in the city

San Bartolomeo was martyred by being flayed alive and, by association, is the patron saint of dermatological distress. The court jester and favorite of Henry II of England, Rahare, was praying at the church for relief from a skin complaint when he saw a vision that led to his founding St. Bartholomew's hospital in London.

It is often said that Borromini set out to make San Carlino no bigger than one of the four great piers of St. Peter's. While the dimensions are certainly similar, he was probably limited from the outset by the constraints of the site, owned by a poor and obscure religious order (the Spanish Trinitarians), who had only a tiny piece of land on which to fit their church, cloister and monastery.

Love on Pincio Hill

▶▷▷ **San Bartolomeo**

Isola Tiberina

Guarded by a 12th-century campanile and disguised by a 17th-century facade, San Bartolomeo nevertheless dates from the year 1000. It was built by the German emperor, Otto III, on the site of an ancient temple of Aesculapius, god of the healing arts. It was dedicated to the memory of Otto's friend, St. Adelbert, patron of Bohemia, and only later rededicated. Adelbert is buried in the *cappella farinaio* ("miller's chapel"), so called because its frescoes illustrate the floating flour mills once moored off the island. His image, along with those of Otto and Bartolomeo, also decorates a unique 12th-century wellhead (on the steps to the main altar). The church has been ravaged by flooding over the centuries.

▶▶▷ **San Carlino (San Carlo alle Quattro Fontane)**

Via del Quirinale

Borromini's San Carlino – his first church in Rome – and its near neighbor, Sant'Andrea al Quirinale, by his archrival, Bernini (see page 132) are both supreme expressions of the Baroque idiom, but in vastly different modes. Whereas Bernini is classical and taciturn, Borromini's subtle complexity blurs the distinction between architecture and sculpture, cramming the interior with details, shapes, and symbols, but cleverly binding them with precise geometrical patterns. The facade was his last work in the city (1668), a mass of three-dimensional interplay, brilliantly crammed into a tiny site alongside one of four crossroad fountains.

▶▷▷ **San Carlo ai Catinari**

Piazza B. Cairoli

An oversized but harmonious Baroque church (1612–20) off Largo Argentina, San Carlo ai Catinari is named after the *catinari*, or washtub makers, who had their work-shops nearby. Among the top names of the day who added to its wealth of interior detail – Pietro da Cortona, Guido Reni, Giovanni Lanfranco, Andrea Sacchi – the key works are the *Cardinal Virtues,* painted by Domenichino in the pendentives of the dome in 1630.

Rich and poor alike shop in Rome's many markets, whose colorful stalls and atmospheric bustle can be one of Rome's most enduring memories. Few things beat a stroll around Campo dei Fiori for spectacle; this is the city's oldest and most picturesque open market, selling cascades of fruit and vegetables, flowers and fresh fish. . . .

Close to Termini and less appealing to the eye is **Piazza Vittorio Emanuele**, the city's biggest market. Leather, shoes, clothes and household goods line one side of the square; food and drink in infinite variety line the other. Prices here are Rome's keenest, but there are no concessions to the picturesque – this is the city's workaday market, and in many ways its most entertaining, particularly if you pick among the speciality food stalls, some selling only fresh tuna and others selling mountain cheeses, lemons, rare gamebirds, live crabs, squawking chickens and much more. Look, too, at the Arab *casbah* near the fringes, a response to the many immigrants who have moved into the cheaper quarters by the square (*open:* Monday to Saturday 7–2).

Running Piazza Vittorio a close second is the smaller but better organized market along Via Andrea Dorio *(open:* Tuesday to Saturday 8–1).

Porta Portese, near Porta Sublicio in Trastevere, is the city's most famous flea market (and the largest such market in Europe). Of its 4,000 stalls, only about 10 percent have a license, and there is constant talk of trying to combat its sprawl and the sheer chaos it brings to the area every Sunday *(open:* 6–2.) Visit early (or not at all) to avoid the crowds, most of whom go for the spectacle. Be on guard here for pickpockets.

A smaller and cheaper clothes and junk market operates on Saturdays in Via Sannio in Laterano.

Although they hardly match the larger markets for razzmatazz, try to find the smaller, backstreet markets that attach to each *rione,* or district, of the city. These markets include Piazza San Cosimo (Trastevere), Piazza del Fico (near Piazza Navona), Via del Lavatore (near the Fontana di Trevi), and Vicolo della Moretta (off Via Giulia).

Color and life in the Porta Portese market

Interior of Santa Cecilia in Trastevere

 **Santa Cecilia in Trastevere**

Piazza di Santa Cecilia

Part of Santa Cecilia's considerable charm is in the approach, which takes you through a Baroque gateway and lovely garden – complete with large Roman vase – and on to Ferdinand Fuga's facade (1741), a 12th-century portico of Roman columns, and a fine Romansque campanile to the right. The core of the church is still partly intact but concealed, and the overwhelming sense in the interior today is of Baroque butchery inflicted in restorations between 1725 and 1823.

Several older and excellent pieces of art survived the assault, the most famous of which is Stefano Maderno's statue of *Santa Cecilia* under the high altar. It portrays the saint as she was found, lying on one side wrapped in a golden robe, her tomb – moved here from the catacombs by Paschal in the 9th century – having been reopened in 1599 for reasons unknown. Maderno was present at the opening and made a drawing of the apparently uncorrupted body – though the three cuts of the executioner's sword on the statue's neck are doubtless expressions of artistic license.

Above the altar is a magnificent Gothic *baldacchino,* or canopy, by Arnolfo di Cambio (c 1293), and behind it, in the apse, a luminous 9th-century mosaic showing Paschal (with a square halo) presenting Cecilia and Valerian to Christ, flanked by St. Peter, St. Paul, and two cities – possibly Bethlehem and Jerusalem. In the first chapel on the right of the nave are traces of medieval frescoes, their theme, inevitably, the martyrdom of St. Cecilia, while the **crypt** contains the tombs of Cecilia and other worthies.

The **cloister** adjacent to the church is graced with fragments of Pietro Cavallini's fresco of the *Last Judgment* (1293), the saddest casualty of the church's restorations. This was Cavallini's masterpiece; Cavallini

Cecilia, or *coeli lilia* – the lily of Heaven – was one of Rome's most celebrated early martyrs. She was killed with her husband in the reign of Diocletian around AD 303 (though some historians think she died earlier, under Marcus Aurelius). The Romans first tried to scald and drown her in the family's bath. When they failed, the executioner's three axe blows – all he was allowed under Roman law – failed to remove her head, and she struggled on for three days, converting many to the faith before dying of her wounds.

was a painter who was contemporaneous with Giotto and a seminal figure in the drift of Italian painting away from the stilted formalities of Byzantine art.

Cloister *open:* Tuesday and Thursday 10–noon, Sunday 11–noon. Admission free.

▶▶▶ San Clemente

Via di San Giovanni in Laterano

Whatever you feel about ruins and old churches, on no account should you miss San Clemente, one of the most exhilarating and best-preserved archaeological sites in Rome. It encapsulates the city's Christian history on three distinct levels, first with the remains of its 1st-century *domus,* or palace, and 3rd-century **Mithraic temple**; second with its 4th-century church dedicated to San Clemente (fourth bishop of Rome after St. Peter); and finally with the present church, built between 1110 and 1130 after the Normans' sack of the earlier church in 1084. Furthermore, it boasts valuable works of art from the corresponding epochs, all of which have been under the care of Irish Dominican monks since 1677.

Before entering the church's side door, have a look at the medieval *quadroporticus* near the locked main entrance, a square-colonnaded courtyard abutting the plain Baroque facade. Such features, once common in Rome's basilica churches, are now rare and represent the survival of a building style more common in southern Italy. (**Santa Cecilia in Trastevere** has another notable example.)

The well-preserved church of San Clemente

A converted Jew and Rome's fourth pope, San Clemente was banished by Trajan to the Crimea in the 2nd century for converting too many Christians. He continued to convert in exile and for his pains was tied to an anchor and thrown into the Black Sea. When the waters miraculously receded, he was found in a tomb "built by angels," enabling his body to be returned to Rome.

New converts to the Mithraic cult, which only men could join, were sprinkled with the blood of a freshly slain bull. The cult was extremely popular among soldiers, possibly for the machismo of its rituals – initiations by fire, ice, hunger, and thirst – and perhaps because it elevated loyalty above all other virtues. At the same time its limited appeal – which excluded women and the ruling classes – together with Christian suppression, probably brought its eventual eclipse.

The interior Perhaps the most wonderful medieval ensemble in the city, the interior is dominated by a superlative 6th- to 9th-century *schola cantorum* (**choir screen**) whose low, marble-paneled walls fill much of the nave. Some of its columns came from the Foro Traiano, and all of it was rescued from the earlier church below. Both **pulpits** were also similarly salvaged – note the beautiful Cosmati **candle holder** on one – as were parts of the altar canopy, or *baldacchino*.

Behind the altar is a majestic 12th-century mosaic, probably copied from an original in the earlier church. Against a glittering background, it describes the *Triumph of the Cross*, the cross shown as a branched tree of life supporting birds, animals, palaces – possibly of the Heavenly City – and figures that include the four Doctors of the Church – Jerome, Ambrose, Gregory, and Augustine. Notice the 12 doves, symbols of the Apostles, and the four rivers of Paradise springing from the foot of the cross. Below it lie a marble tabernacle by Arnolfo di Cambio and faded frescoes of the saints, both from the 14th century. The greatest of the painted work in the church, however, are the frescoes on the *Life of St. Catherine* (c 1428) by **Masolino da Panicale,** a rare example of this influential Early Renaissance Florentine (in the left aisle chapel, near the side entrance).

The lower church Steps lead down to the lower church, excavated in 1857, since when its important 8th- to 11th-century **frescoes** have faded badly on exposure to the air. On the right nave you can still make out a 9th-century Christ and a Madonna (or possibly the prostitute Theodora, who became empress when she married Justinian). Opposite are panels on the *Life of Sisinnius,* best known for the inscriptions beneath them, which are perhaps the oldest known examples of written Italian. There are also depictions of the *Ascension, the Marriage at Cana,* and the *Crucifixion.*

The Mithraic temple Finally, drop down into the dank Mithraic temple itself, the best preserved of the 12 or more such shrines so far uncovered in Rome. In the

Below San Clemente: the Mithraic temple

center of the *triclinium*, the temple's banqueting hall, is an altar with a low-relief of Mithrais slaying a bull surrounded by benches. The chamber alongside is thought to be where devotees were instructed before initiation. Part of the labyrinth here is also the remains of a 1,900-year old Roman alley, now 33 feet below street level, from where you can hear the eerie sound of rushing water – a mysterious underground stream that leads to the Cloaca Maxima.

Much down here remains to be uncovered, including Republican-era buildings destroyed in Nero's great fire. Excavations here reveal exciting discoveries yearly – the latest include a 6th-century sacristry used by Pope Gregory I; his adjoining washroom; and, most tantalizing, a terra-cotta sarcophagus with unidentified 1st-century human remains.

▶▷▷ Santi Cosmo e Damiano

Via dei Fori Imperiali

Perched on the edge of the **Foro Romano**, this church was converted in AD 527 by Felix IV from a classical building. The old Tempio di Romolo still provides part of its vestibule, but note that it cannot be entered from the Roman Forum, only through the cloisters of the convent on Via dei Fori Imperiali. Urban VIII restored the interior to dull effect in 1632, but left untouched the magnificent 6th-century **mosaics** that are the church's biggest attraction. In their day these were highly influential and remained so for many later Roman artists.

The scenes in the apse show Saints Peter and Paul presenting Cosmo and Damiano (two Arabian doctors of the church) to Christ, 12 doves as symbols of the Apostles and four rivers as the Gospels. The detail in the triumphal arch shows angels, the symbols of the Evangelists, and Christ as the Lamb. This is one of the first times these images had been used in Christian art.

▶▷▷ Santa Costanza

Via Nomentana

Tucked behind **Sant'Agnese fuori le Mura** (see pages 130–31), tiny Santa Costanza's drab exterior does little to prepare you for the glory of its early Christian interior. The original building, most of which survives, was set aside in the 4th century as a mausoleum for Constantia (daughter of Constantine) and Helen, the wife of Constantine's successor, Julian the Apostate.

The circular interior is supported by 12 double columns, in turn surrounded by a barrel-vaulted ambulatory of 4th-century **mosaics** unequaled in Rome. The white background – in contrast to the gold Byzantine work – sets off the detail and color of the decoration. On show, too, is a copy of Constantia's sarcophagus (the original is now in the Vatican museums; see pages 184–197). Notice its use of pagan icons adapted to Christian use – the lamb and peacock – symbols of innocence and immortality, respectively.

According to church history, Constantia was a nun and Christian, but contemporary accounts describe her as scheming, tyrannical and "insatiable in her thirst for human blood."

▷▷▷ Santa Croce in Gerusalemme

Piazza Santa Croce in Gerusalemme

Santa Croce was built to house pieces of the True Cross, brought from Jerusalem by St. Helena, mother of Constantine, and an indefatigable collector of relics. The church may date back to AD 320, but the only sign of antiquity in its poor Baroque interior is eight old columns in the nave, together with a Cosmatesque pavement, the legacy of a 12th-century restoration that also raised the Romanesque campanile outside.

The cathedral church of San Giovanni in Laterano

The area first belonged to Plautinius Lateranus (hence the name), who was executed by Nero for treason. It eventually passed to Fausta, the wife of Constantine, whose palace incorporated the earlier title, *Domus Faustae in Laterano*. In 313 it provided a meeting place for Constantine and Pope Miltiades and subsequently becoming a focus for Christianity in the city. Constantine raised the first church in the palace over the barracks of his personal guard. From the outset this church housed the *cathedra* (the bishop of Rome's throne) from which the word *cathedral* derives.

▶▶▶ San Giovanni in Laterano

Piazza di San Giovanni in Laterano

San Giovanni in Laterano is Rome's main cathedral church. It is not, as many people think, St. Peter's, which is in the Vatican, a separate sovereign state. It is, however, the pope's titular See in his role as bishop of Rome and, as the inscription across the facade claims, *Mater et caput omnium ecclesiarum urbis et orbis* – "Mother and head of all the churches of the city and of the world."

History Inevitably it has had a long and troubled history, and today little remains of the earliest church, which Vandals destroyed. An 8th-century earthquake destroyed the next, and two fires in the 14th century finished off the third. Until then the church and its palace were the papal residence and had been the scene of such historic events as Charlemagne's baptism in 774. Popes continued to be crowned here until the 19th century, but the papal palace moved to the Vatican after the Great Schism – the hundred or so years after 1305 when the papacy was split between Rome and Avignon.

Architecture For all its rebuilding, the church still has immense appeal and character, though it stands on the edge of some dreary suburbs and, inevitably, in the midst of considerable traffic chaos. The colossal **facade,** quite clearly modeled on St. Peter's, is by Alessandro Galilei and dates from 1735. Impressive in the extreme, though this was not a period known for its architectural finesse, it is most famous for its gigantic statues, long a Roman landmark and visible from as far away as the Gianicolo and Colli Albani. (They represent Christ, John the Baptist, John the Evangelist and the 12 Doctors of the Church.)

On the portico's left stands an ancient statue of Constantine, a less dramatic link with the past than the celebrated central **portal,** whose bronze doors were brought from the original *curia,* or Senate House, of the **Foro Romano** (see pages 77–85). The door on the extreme right, the *Porta Santa* ("Holy Door") opens only on a *jubilee* or Holy Year.

Interior Nothing as venerable survives in the massive interior, which was refashioned by Borromini between 1646 and 1650. Opinions on his efforts vary, though in truth the church's parlous state, requiring structural, as well as decorative work, left him little room to maneuver. In his cool white and gray scheme he respected the earlier building wherever he could, especially in its fabulously ornate **ceiling** and basic form. Sheer size, however, is still the church's abiding impression, though one or two works of genuine beauty relieve it of sterility. The first pillar in the right aisle has a patch of fresco, perhaps by Giotto, depicting Boniface VIII proclaiming the first Holy Year in 1300. In the main crossing stands the **papal altar,** at which only a pope can officiate and which contains part of a wooden table, said to have been used by St. Peter and the earliest popes. The Gothic **tabernacle** (1367) above the altar contains the church's main objects of devotion – reputed to be the skulls of St. Paul and St. Peter. Below, on the steps to the *confessio,* is the **tomb of Martin V,** on which it is a Roman custom to throw a coin. The **mosaic** in the apse is a faithful 19th-century resetting of a 12th-century original by Jacopo Torriti, also responsible for the mosaics in **Santa Maria Maggiore** (see pages 151–154).

Basilica di San Giovanni

Detail from San Giovanni interior

A monument to Pope Sylvester II in the church incorporates what may be part of his original tomb; before the death of a pope it is reputed to sweat and make the sound of rattling bones.

San Giovanni

■ Connected to San Giovanni are three monuments that, in many ways, are more interesting than the main church itself. Two – the baptistery and cloister – are integral parts of the building; the third, the Scala Santa, is housed separately across the street (see page 174). . . .■

The baptistery was the first in Christendom, and its basic octagonal form was copied throughout Italy. It is the only part of the earliest church to have survived, having been built in the first palace over the baths of Fausta, Constantine's wife.

Some of this early building was lost after raids by the Goths, but it was rebuilt by Sixtus III (432–440) in much the state it appears today. Baptism was then by total immersion, hence the practice of using separate baths, or even separate buildings, for the ceremony. The ancient font here is of green Egyptian basalt, surrounded by eight columns of red porphyry, a marble so rare that reserves from the mine were already exhausted by 300 BC. Four **chapels** circle the basin, the best known being the Cappella di Giovanni Battista on the right, guarded by a pair of famous bronze doors that are supposed to "sing" with a low hum when opened.

<< The baptistery is in the right-hand corner of the right aisle, but to reach it, brave the traffic of the piazza outside (left and left again from the entrance) and enter from the rear of the church. (*Open:* daily 8–noon, 3–dusk). **>>**

<< Alessandro Galilei worked for long periods in England, and in his facade's restrained departure from the baroque shows the influence of English architects like Aldrich, Hawksmoor and Sir Christopher Wren. **>>**

The cloisters A small door at the end of the left aisle leads to the cloisters, one of Rome's most enchanting spots and the high point of the city's **Cosmati** tradition – a school of marble workers, renowned throughout Europe, that dealt in both intricate mosaic inlay and large-scale colored pavements. Each of the arcade's hundreds of tiny columns is different. The columns are the work of Jacopo and Pietro Vassalletto (father and son), masters of the Cosmati art, and were executed between 1215 and 1223.
Open: daily 9–1, 2–6. Admission charge.

<< At a height of 102 feet, the Egyptian obelisk outside San Giovanni is the tallest in Rome. It is also the oldest, dating from the 15th century BC, and was brought to Rome in AD 357 by Constantine and raised in the Circo Massimo. **>>**

San Giovanni's baptistery

Basilica di Santi Giovanni e Paolo

▶▷▷ **Santi Giovanni e Paolo**

Via Clivio di Scauro, off San Gregorio

Grisly martyrdom and subsequent sainthood were often the inspiration for Roman churches. In the case of Santi Giovanni e Paolo, a lovely church with one of Rome's rare medieval facades, the saints concerned were military officers under the first Christian emperor, Constantine. They retired from service, but in 362 were called back by the emperor's pagan successor, Julian the Apostate. When they refused to make sacrifices to a pagan god, they were beheaded in their homes, and their bodies buried close by.

The first church in their honor was reputedly raised by a Roman senator called Pammachius, who, on the death of his wife, gave away his wealth, became a Christian, and died in monastic isolation in 410.

Later churches were burned or sacked by the Goths and Normans, and the present building dates from the papacies of Paschal II (1099–1118) and Adrian IV (1154–59). Having escaped the clutches of the Baroque, its medieval outline has remained largely unsullied for 900 years. Some parts have remained unaltered even longer, such as the **upper facade** – five arches on 3rd-century columns – which survives from the 4th-century basilica. The medieval portico below contains further classical remnants: six granite Ionic pillars and a pair of marble Corinthian columns (probably from a temple to Claudius), rounded off with an attractive **Romanesque campanile.**

Skip the unremarkable Baroque **interior** and take the steep staircase on its right-hand side to the **confessio,** a 3rd-century ruin often held to be part of the saints' houses. Commoners' graves and tombs, unusual within the city limits, have also come to light, along with baths, a library and a wine cellar, which might confirm the theory. Several valuable **wall paintings** from the period have also been uncovered, including one outstanding example showing *Persephone* (or another female divinity). Another describes the beheading of two men and a woman, thought to relate to the legend of Crispin, Crispinian, and Benedicta, all martyred after being found at the tomb of Giovanni and Paolo.

Opposite the church is an entrance to the Villa Celimontana, a lovely but little-known city park. There are other entrances on Piazza della Navicella and Via San Paolo della Croce.

In the church grounds are three chapels: Santa Silvia (dedicated to Gregory's mother), San Andrea and Santa Barbara. Santa Silvia, on the left, houses a stone table on which Gregory is said to have fed 12 poor men every day (one day a 13th appeared – an angel) and a group of flamboyant early 17th-century frescoes by Guido Reni. Alongside, San Andrea is graced by Domenichino's more austere work, the *Flagellation of St. Andrew.*

▶▷▷ San Gregorio Magno

Via di San Gregorio

Pope Gregory the Great (590–604) was by all accounts a generous man who gave a third of his wealth to the Church on his election in 590. He also turned part of his vast estate on the Celian Hill into a monastery in 575, and it was here that his successor, Pope Gregory II, founded, somewhat belatedly, the church of San Gregorio to honor his munificent predecessor.

Rebuilding in the 17th and 18th centuries attempted to remodel the church on **Sant'Ignazio** (see below) and removed virtually all trace of Gregory's church. The **facade,** by Giovanni Battista Soria, dates from the 1620s and was one of the earliest expressions of the emerging Roman Baroque. The only remnants of the old church are patchy remains in the interior, most notably the **Cappella di San Gregorio** (far right-hand chapel), which contains a fine altar by Andrea Bregno (1469) and a slab on which Pope Gregory is said to have slept.

▷▷▷ Sant' Ignazio

Via Sant' Ignazio

Sant'Ignazio was built between 1626 and 1650 to

Andrea Pozzo's ceiling fresco, Sant'Ignazio

honor the canonization of Ignatius Loyola (1622), mystic founder of the Jesuit order (created in 1556), and was Rome's second Jesuit church after the Gesù. Both the architect, Orazio Grassi, and the painter responsible for the interior, Andrea Pozzo, were members of the order.

Fronted by an imposing facade, which is modeled on that of the Gesù, the church is nevertheless best known for the magnificence of its interior. Behind the facade's severity, it comes as a wonderful surprise.

The wide nave was engineered to facilitate preaching and to conduct services from one central spot. The lavish decoration of the chapels alongside was part of a determined Counter-Reformation thrust, spearheaded by the Jesuits, to draw the faithful back to the church through rampant earthly splendor. The attempt is best seen in the lapis lazuli tomb of St. Aloysius (Luigi Gonzaga, 1568–91) in the south aisle. The church's dome was never built, but here superlative paintings further bewitched the eye of the believer. Andrea Pozzo's ceiling fresco, *The Entry of St. Ignatius into Paradise,* is a masterpiece of *trompe l'oeil,* persuasively creating the effect of the missing lantern. It was painted to rival a similar work in the Gesù. A marble disc midway down the nave marks the best place to enjoy the illusion's full effect.

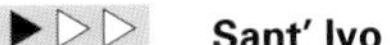

Sant' Ivo

Corso del Rinascimento 40; entrance from the courtyard of Palazzo alla Sapienza

Even by his own ingenious standards, Sant'Ivo (1642–60) is one of Borromini's most accomplished churches. Though hardly on a grand scale, the design makes imaginative use of a limited site in the grounds of the **Palazzo alla Sapienza** (*sapienza* is Italian for "wisdom"), a papal university founded in 1303 as the *Archiginnasio Romano.* The palace's refined Renaissance courtyard, together with Sant'Ivo's facade, are the work of Giacomo della Porta, and also warrant a peek; access to both is restricted and the church itself is restricted to 10 o'clock Mass on Sunday mornings.

Borromini received the commission through the offices of the Barberini pope, Urban VIII, and it was on the Barberini family symbol, the bee, that he reputedly based his extraordinary plan. This symbol is said to account for the strange, twisted **lantern,** perhaps the most eccentric in Rome, whose gilded spiral supposedly emulates a bee's sting. Rather more fancifully, the two intersecting triangles of the interior floor plan recall a bee's shape. Whatever their inspiration, in their repeated appearance they also serve the geometric purpose beloved of Borromini. Hexagons are reiterated throughout, their six points being adapted in the dome to the repetition of concave and convex shapes, themselves another insistent Borromini trademark.

Today Sant'Ivo's interior is a bare, whitewashed lecture hall, and this lack of decoration leaves the basic plan too starkly delineated. Although first impressions are therefore blunted, the spare arrangement still ranks as a masterpiece of the Baroque imagination.

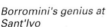

On Via Caravita close to Sant'Ignazio is the Oratorio della Caravita, another Jesuit stronghold, where as recently as 100 years ago whips were issued to the congregation during services. Under cover of darkness the faithful would undress and flagellate themselves, wailing or whimpering *"Ave Maria, ci perdona"* ("Blessed Mary, forgive us").

Borromini's genius at Sant'Ivo

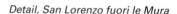

Detail, San Lorenzo fuori le Mura

▶▷▷ San Lorenzo fuori le Mura

Piazza San Lorenzo

San Lorenzo is in an unprepossessing part of the city, wedged between **Campo Verano,** Rome's largest cemetery, and the dull, Fascist-inspired architecture of the university. Nonetheless it is one of the city's seven pilgrimage churches, most distinguished by the strange and fascinating hybrid of styles from different eras.

Constantine built the earliest of these churches around the year 330 on the burial site of the martyred San Lorenzo (see panel). Between 432 and 440 Pope Sixtus III added a second church, dedicated to the Virgin, which backed on to the first. Constantine's church was then enlarged and rebuilt by Pelagius II (579–590). In time the two churches were linked, first, by Adrian I in the 8th century and then, as the number of pilgrims increased, by Honorious III in 1216. In World War II, during Rome's spell as an "open city," San Lorenzo was its only church to be badly bombed.

One of the areas damaged in the raid was the splendid six-column **portico,** since rebuilt. The elegant nave, supported by old Ionic columns, still preserves the shape of Pelagius's basilica, but largely conforms to Honorious's rebuilding. Most of the decoration is colored by Cosmati marble work, in particular the pavement, pulpits, candleholder, and episcopal throne, all dating from the 12th century. The **crypt** contains the relics of Saints Lorenzo, Stefano, and Justino.

Beyond the 13th-century choir the marked difference in styles is inescapable as you enter the Corinthian columns and shadowy arched gallery of Pelagius's church. The columns, carved from a precious *pavonazzo* marble, support an ancient architrave of classical fragments. High up, the mosaic on the triumphal arch dates from the 6th century and shows Pelagius offering the church to Christ. If you can find the sacristan, ask to see the cloister, crammed with a jumble of ancient columns and sarcophagi, as well as the catacombs of St. Cyriaca, Lorenzo's original resting place.

San Lorenzo was a 3rd-century church deacon of some character. When the Roman authorities ordered him to hand over the treasures of the Church, he collected together all the sick and poor people he could muster. The gesture was not appreciated, and he was roasted alive on a grid iron, at one point reputedly telling his executioners that they could turn him over: "I am done on this side." He was buried in catacombs near the present church.

▶▷▷ San Luigi dei Francesi

Piazza di San Luigi dei Francesi

San Luigi dei Francesi (completed in 1589), dedicated to St. Louis (Louis IX of France), is the French national church in Rome. Because it is stranded midway between two of the city's highlights, **Piazza Navona** and the **Pantheon,** many people pass it by in a hurry, untempted by Giacomo della Porta's Renaissance facade (the architect also responsible for the frontage of Borromini's nearby masterpiece, **Sant'Ivo alla Sapienza**). Inside, however, like many a minor Roman church, it contains a single great treasure that merits a stopover: a trio of paintings by **Caravaggio** – "the largest area of canvas painted by Caravaggio, contained in the smallest space in the world," said one critic.

The paintings are at the rear of the church, in the fifth chapel on the left, completely overshadowing an interior once described by the American writer, Nathaniel Hawthorne as "a most shamefully dirty place of worship." The paintings are late works, executed between 1597 and 1602, predominantly dark and dramatic pieces that show Caravaggio's handling of chiaroscuro to virtuoso effect. All three deal with episodes from the life of St. Matthew, starting on the left with the *Calling of St. Matthew*, a somber scene in a strikingly realistic setting (Matthew hears God's call while collecting taxes). The altarpiece in the center, *St. Matthew and the Angel*, is more subdued, an earlier, more shocking version having been rejected by the church authorities. (The wings on the angel are supposed to have been borrowed from a friend in Rome and strapped to the model.) The third canvas on the right is a melodramatic reconstruction of the *Martyrdom of St. Matthew*, which, like all the paintings, was not universally admired at the time.

Contemporaries were far better disposed to the later **frescoes by Domenichino** (1613–14), which tell the *Story of St. Cecilia* (see **Santa Cecilia in Trastevere**, page 136). They are in the second chapel on the right.

The personal life of Michelangelo da Caravaggio (1573–1610) was so full of incident it is extraordinary that he found time to paint at all, let alone produce some of the period's most influential paintings. Wild, dissolute, and larger than life, he fled from Rome after killing a man in a brawl. His canvases were known for their intense realism. To the horror of church authorities, he ignored centuries of iconic tradition and painted religious scenes as they might have appeared at the time, complete with real beggars, prostitutes, thieves and dirty-footed peasants as the models.

Time for a chat in Piazza Navona

San Marco

Piazza Venezia

As so often with Rome's churches, little remains today to suggest the great antiquity of San Marco, one of the city's oldest basilicas.

The dedication is to St. Mark, traditionally held to have written his gospel in Rome, and to Pope Mark, responsible for the original basilica in AD 336 (his relics are under the main altar). Numerous rebuildings took place thereafter, the Baroque meddling of the 18th century inevitably being the most apparent. Marks of previous eras still survive, most notably in the apse's magnificent **mosaic** (833), a legacy of Pope Gregory IV's 9th-century alterations. The mosaic shows Gregory presenting a model of his church to Christ in the company of St. Mark and other saints. The beautiful **gilt ceiling** was added by Paul II from 1455 to 1471, as was the **portico,** built to shelter the pontiff and his acolytes during outdoor ceremonies in bad weather.

On the right-hand wall of San Marco's portico, look for the tomb of Vannozza Cattanei, the mistress of the Borgia pope, Alexander VI, and mother of his three children, including the infamous Cesare and Lucrezia. The tomb used to be in Santa Maria del Popolo, but was moved here in complete secrecy and under mysterious circumstances – no one knows why, when or by whom.

Santa Maria dell'Anima

Via dell'Anima

Pilgrims over the centuries could often find shelter in a hospice and worship in a church belonging to their country of origin. Santa Maria dell'Anima sprang up between 1501 and 1514 to house Germans, then citizens of the Holy Roman Empire, and today is still the national church of Germany in Rome. For a time its bell tower was attributed to Bramante and the lofty facade to Giuliano Sangallo, uncle of the more famous Antonio, attributions now thought dubious. However, the three mock-classical portals are the work of Andrea Sansavino. His *Madonna between Two Souls*, in the tympanum of the central door, gave the church its name. Much of the interior decoration dates from the 19th century, the key exceptions being Guilio Romano's *Holy Family and Saints* on the high altar and Adrian IV's overbearing tomb to its right. Pope Adrian IV (1522–23), a dour, reforming pope (who, to the delight of Romans, lasted only a year in the job) was a native of Utrecht, and the last non-Italian pope before John Paul II.

Climbing up to Santa Maria in Aracoeli

The dazzling interior of Santa Maria in Aracoeli

The church's most highly venerated object is the Santo Bambino, a jewel-encrusted and richly garbed doll supposedly carved from an olive tree from the garden of Gethsemane. Blessed with miraculous healing qualities, it used to be taken around the streets in an old brown coach, securing immediate recognition and – truly miraculous in Rome – instant right of way. Now it only rarely ventures out in a taxi, but is brought from the sacristy at Christmas when children recite songs and poems in its honor.

▶▷▷ **Santa Maria in Aracoeli**

Piazza d'Aracoeli. Entrance from Piazza d'Aracoeli or from behind the (Museo Capitolino) on Piazza del Campidoglio

Santa Maria in Aracoeli occupies a site on the **Campidoglio** (Capitoline Hill) that has been the seat of Rome's most sacred shrines since time immemorial. Augustus set up an altar called the *Ara Filii Dei* or *Ara Coeli* (Altar of Heaven) inscribed *Ecce ara primogeniti Dei* (Behold the altar of the firstborn of God), an inscription now carved on the church's triumphal arch.

The first church here was recorded in AD 574, but even then it was considered old. By the 8th century it had become part of a Benedictine monastery, Santa Maria in Capitolino, in whose cloisters the city elders met, much as the first Roman Senate had met on the same spot in the Temple of Juno Moneta centuries before. The Franciscans took over in 1260, and it is from this time that most of the current structure now dates.

The long, steep flight of steps to the entrance offers a majestic approach to the bare-bricked facade, as well as marvelous views. (It is traditionally climbed by recently married couples.) It was completed in 1348 in thanksgiving for deliverance from the Black Death.

Inside, the **interior**'s overall effect is splendid, from the ancient columns and elaborate chandeliers to the dazzlingly ornate **gilded ceiling** and the Cosmati inlay of the **pavements** and **pulpits.** Its most famous artistic treasures are **Pinturicchio's frescoes** on the *Life of San Bernardino* in the Cappella Bufalini (the first chapel in the right-hand aisle). The Tomb of Luca Savelli in the south transept, built partly around a Roman sarcophagus, is probably by Arnolfo di Cambio, while the third chapel on the left contains Benozzo Gozzoli's fresco, *St. Antony of Padua.* The altarpiece is a 10th-century *Madonna,* backed in the apse by frescoes of Augustus with the Sibyl, whose prophecy prompted his vision of the birth of a child who would overthrow the altar of the gods. Look out for Bregno's colorful monument and a worn tombstone by Donatello to the right of the main door.

In 393 BC the honking of geese in the Arx, the Campidoglio's ancient citadel, saved the Romans from a surprise night attack by Gauls besieging the city. The Romans celebrated the event annually for hundreds of years by leading a chariot-borne goose in triumphal procession around the Roman Forum. They also crucified a dog at the same time, a barbed memorial to all the sleeping watchdogs that failed them that night. The temple to Juno Moneta perhaps later took its name from the geese *(monito* still means "warning" in Italian, which, in turn, yielded the English word *money).*

▶▶▷ Santa Maria della Concezione

Via Vittorio Veneto 27

Behind an innocent facade, and in one of Rome's most unlikely settings – the start of Via Veneto – the crypt of this church contains the skeletons and bones of some 4,000 Capuchin monks. As if in some grotesque baroque parody, they lie arranged over the walls and vaults of five subterranean chapels. However, more macabre than the skeletons, some still dressed in jaunty clothes, are the bones – vertebrae and shoulder blades – crafted into ghoulish chandeliers or lovingly arranged into decorative patterns.

Monks were initially buried here in soil brought especially from Jerusalem; only when space ran out were they left in the open, a practice that continued until as late as 1870. Interment here was a great honor, and in one or two places you can see the remains of children, offspring of noble families who died in childhood. Honor can be yours also if you come to the church on the first Sunday of October. Visitors to the chamber of horrors on this day earn a special indulgence, thanks to a dispensation from Pope Paul VI (1963–78).

The church was built in about 1624 for Cardinal Antonio Barberini, brother of Urban VIII, a Capuchin friar who clearly cared little for his family's usual love of pomp and splendor. His tombstone is set in the pavement before the main altar and bears no name or title, only the cheerful legend, *hic jacet pulvis cinis et nihil*: "Here lie dust, ashes and nothing."

In the 19th century, the church's main sight and, in fact, one of the city's main sights, was Guido Reni's 17th-century painting of *St. Michael Trampling the Devil* (first chapel on the right). It caused an uproar when it was painted, after a contemporary observed that the devil bore an uncanny resemblance to the Pamphili Pope Innocent X, the Pamphili being arch rivals of Reni's Barberini patrons.

Open: daily, 9–noon and 3–6. Admission free, but a donation to the friar on duty is expected.

<<I saw round me skulls upon skulls, so placed one upon another that they formed walls, and therewith several chapels. In these ... were seated perfect skeletons of the most distinguished monks, enveloped in their brown cowls, and with a breviary or a withered bunch of flowers in their hands. Altars, chandeliers, and ornaments were made of shoulder-bones and vertebrae, with bas reliefs of human joints. ... I clung fast to the monk, who whispered a prayer, and then said to me, "Here I also shall some time sleep: wilt thou thus visit me.">> – Hans Christian Andersen, *The Improviasatore* (1833)

▶▶▷ Santa Maria in Cosmedin

Piazza Bocca della Verità

Santa Maria in Cosmedin is most famous for the **Bocca della Verità**, or the "Mouth of Truth," a gnarled, weatherbeaten stone face used by the ancient Romans as a drain cover. The *bocca* is the face's gaping marble mouth, around which a legend sprang up that anyone suspected of lying – particularly women accused of adultery – would have their right hands forced into the mouth. If they dissembled, the mouth would clamp shut and sever their fingers. To give credence to the legend, a priest supposedly hid behind the stone to whack the fingers of those known to be guilty.

Bocca della Verità – the mouth of truth

The simple facade was stripped back to its medieval state in the 1890s and is flanked by a 12th-century **Romanesque bell tower**, the tallest of its age in the city and perhaps the most elegant. The first church was built in the 6th century on the ruins of classical temples dedicated to Hercules and Ceres, and enlarged in 772 by

Pope Adrian I as the church of the Greek community that had grown up in the surrounding area. It was completed in more or less its present state under Calixtus II in 1124.

The **interior** has few artistic treasures, but is a sublime piece of medieval architecture that gathers around the ancient Corinthian columns of the nave. Polychrome Cosmati marble decorates the marvelous **pavement;** the twin *ambos,* or pulpits; the **paschal candlestick**; the bishop's throne (with two marble lions); and the stone screens of the *schola cantorum* (the area set aside for the clergy). All slightly predate the *baldacchino,* or altar canopy, which is signed and dated by Deodato di Cosma, a Cosmati scion (*Deodatus Me Fecit 1294*). The medieval frescoes and mosaics are greatly faded, but in a little room off the right aisle is a captivating **8th-century mosaic** of the *Adoration of the Magi* – almost all that survives of the Greek church.

▶▶▶ Santa Maria Maggiore

Piazza di Santa Maria Maggiore

Santa Maria Maggiore has many claims to being the greatest of Rome's several hundred churches. It is the largest of the 80 churches dedicated to the Virgin, among the city's most important points of pilgrimage, and one of Rome's four great patriarchal basilicas, together with St. Peter's, San Giovanni in Laterano, and San Paolo fuori le Mura. Whereas the other basilicas have been drastically altered over the years or even rebuilt, however, Santa Maria Maggiore remains the finest example of an early Christian basilica in the city. Moreover, it is the only church in Rome where Mass has been celebrated every day without interruption since the 5th century.

The origin of the name Santa Maria in Cosmedin is in doubt, but possibly derives from the Greek *cosmos*, meaning ornament, embellishment or perfect order.

<<This church is a gem of beauty which Time and the Tiber and the vandals of the 16th and 17th centuries have been unable to rob of its glory.>> – O. Potter, *The Colour*

Outside the church of Santa Maria Maggiore

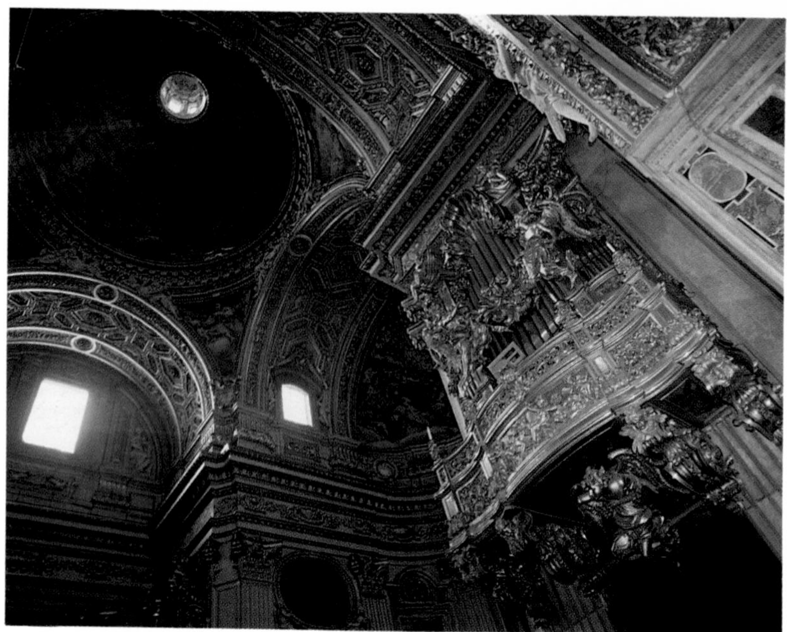

Gilded glory in Santa Maria Maggiore

History According to myth, the Virgin appeared to Pope Liberius on the night of August 5, AD 358, telling him to build a church on the spot where snow was to fall the following day – an unlikely event at the height of a Roman summer. Nevertheless snow fell the following morning on the Esquilino (the Esquiline Hill), marking the outline of a basilica and inaugurating one of the city's more unusual festivals, the feast of the Madonna della Neve on August 5 (Our Lady of the Snow).

Archaeological evidence has not fixed the real date of foundation, but the present church was probably built by Sixtus III in the years after the Council of Ephesus (431), a meeting that reinforced the ever-growing cult of the Virgin. The Esquilino held a temple to the mother-goddess Juno Lucina, then still frequented by Roman women, and in choosing the site Sixtus, and perhaps Liberius before him, substituted a Christian cult for a pagan one, as is often the case.

Interior detail

Architecture The church was extended over the centuries. A new apse was built in the 13th century, and the **campanile** was added in 1377, at 246 feet the tallest in Rome. The coffered **ceiling** was completed at the turn of the 16th century and gilded with some of the first gold to reach Europe from the New World (a gift from Ferdinand of Spain to Pope Alexander VI). At about the same time two large side chapels were added, the Cappella Sistina and the Cappella Paolina. The exterior was completely remodeled in 1740 by Ferdinando Fuga, the same architect, ironically, who was responsible for the painstaking and faithful restoration of the interior.

The church's most majestic profile is from Via Cavour and its broad tiers of steps, but the main **entrance**, constantly besieged by tour buses, is on the opposite side, shadowed by a loggia in whose upper tier you can just make out 12th-century mosaics recalling the legend of Liberius and his miraculous snow. This porch was a favorite spot for the burning of heretical books, a sorry practice thought particularly pleasing to the Virgin. The column here, topped with a statue of the Madonna, is from the Basilica di Maxentius (see Foro Romano), mirrored at the church's rear by the **obelisk** in Piazza del Esquilino, removed from the Mausoleo di Augusto in 1587.

Much of the interior beauty stems from some 40 ancient columns and the **mosaics** in the architrave above: 36 panels of scenes from the Old Testament that date from the time of Sixtus III (5th century). From the same period, but in marked stylistic contrast, are the more visible mosaics in the altar's **triumphal arch** – gold-tinged Byzantine scenes from the *Annunciation* and the *Infancy of Christ*.

The finest mosaics, however, are those in the apse, executed by the Franciscan monk Jacopo Torriti in 1275 and considered the pinnacle of Rome's medieval mosaic tradition.

Sculpture in Santa Maria Maggiore

<< The obvious charm of the church is the elegant grandeur of the nave – its perfect shapeliness and its rich simplicity, its long double row of white marble columns and its high flat roof, embossed with intricate gildings and mouldings. . . . The deeper charm. . . is the sense it gives you, in common with most of the Roman churches, and more than any of them, of having been prayed in for several centuries by an endlessly curious and complex society. >> — Henry James, *Italian Hours*

The art of using colored stone to make mosaics started in Greece in about the 8th century BC. Initially pebbles were used, but by the time the genre reached Rome, marble was the principal medium. Roman and early Christian pieces relied on predominantly black and white stone, but after the fall of the Empire, the Christian tradition increasingly produced the more highly colored gold-edged mosaics associated with the Byzantine style. This style, and its eventual 12th-century mutation, are both on display in Santa Maria Maggiore.

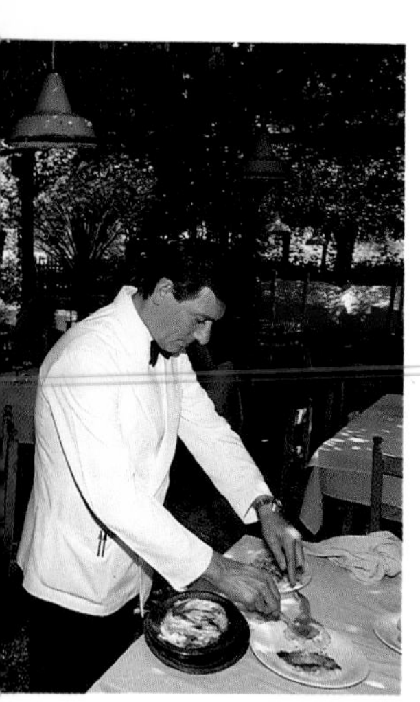

The **Cappella Sistina** opens off the right-hand nave and was built by Domenico Fontana for Pope Sixtus V in 1585. In the process it partly destroyed one of the church's most valuable relics – a *presepio,* or Christmas crib, that, since the 7th century, had stood outside the church in a small *oratorio* (it was the spot where the popes traditionally said Mass each Christmas Eve). In a typical fit of papal vanity, Sixtus ordered Fontana to move the crib into his chapel, at which point it broke irreparably, leaving only Arnolfo di Cambio's celebrated figures of Joseph, the Magi, the ox and the ass intact. All this occurred despite Fontana's careful preparation – the man, after all, was responsible for the immense task of moving the obelisk in **Piazza San Pietro** (see page 123). Ask in the sacristy, and you may persuade someone to open the crypt where they are kept.

Cappella Paolina Opposite the Cappella Sistina, the Cappella Paolina (1611) contains the lavishly embellished tombs of two Borghese popes, Clement VIII and Paul V, who set out with the avowed intention of upstaging Sixtus's tomb across the nave. Although they destroyed nothing, they did appropriate a precious 8th-century altarpiece, a highly revered *Madonna and Child* known as the *Salus Populi Romani,* supposedly painted by St. Luke with the assistance of heavenly angels. The wanton splendor of its surround, which consists of jasper, agate, amethyst, and lapis lazuli, is particularly extravagant even by the Baroque style's excessive standards.

On August 5th every year, white petals fall like snow from the chapel's dome in memory of Liberius's vision and the legendary snowfall.

Take a quick look at the **Cappella Sforza** on the chapel's left, designed by Michelangelo, but completed by Giacomo della Porta – the same, strained partnership responsible for the dome of St. Peter's.

The confessio below the **high altar** contains an overblown statue of Pius IX in prayer before Santa Maria's prize relic, five pieces of wood bound with iron, said to be pieces of Christ's crib from Bethlehem. It is exposed only on the 25th of every month, however, and brought out into the basilica only on Christmas Eve. To the right and rear of the altar is the **tomb of Cardinal Rodriguez** (died 1299), the most beautiful in the church, crafted by Giovanni Cosma with the inspired marble inlay for which all the Cosmati family were famed. In its floor is a memorial to another great artistic dynasty – the family tombs of the Bernini.

▶▶▷ Santa Maria sopra Minerva

Piazza della Minerva

Although it hides behind a plain, ocher-colored Renaissance facade, Santa Maria sopra Minerva has emerged as the only Gothic church in the city. Founded in the 8th century over *(sopra)* the ruins of a temple to Minerva, it was built in its present form in 1280 to a design by Fra Sisto and Fra Ristoro da Campi, two Dominican monks who also designed Florence's famous church of Santa Maria Novella.

Santa Maria sopra Minerva

The **interior** maintains the Florentine link, most notably in the frescoes of Botticelli's Florentine associate, **Filippino Lippi**, lodged in the Cappella Caraffa at the end of the right transept. Painted between 1488 and 1492, they depict the *Annunciation and Assumption of the Virgin* and *Scenes from the Life of St. Thomas Aquinas* (Aquinas was a Dominican), together with the portraits of two young Medicis who later became Popes Leo X and Clement VII. Notice, too, the *Tomb of Guillaume Durand* (1296) on the wall to the chapel's left, a lovely colored work by Giovanni Cosmati.

Left of the altar is another much-revered piece, the statue of *The Redeemer* by Michelangelo (1519–21), an early work much criticized at the time for appearing more like a pagan god than Christ. A sandal was added later to prevent one of its feet being worn away by the kisses of the faithful. Under the altar are the remains of St. Catherine of Siena, one of Italy's national saints, and to its left, in a passage, the t**omb of Fra Angelico**, the great Florentine painter (also a member of the Dominicans).

Other works you should seek out include Agostino di Duccio's *Tomb of Giovanni Arberini* (1473), which incorporates a Roman sarcophagus and a bas-relief, *Hercules and the Lion* (second chapel on the left of the choir); the tomb of Diego da Coca (1477) by Andrea Bregno, frescoed by Melozzo da Forlì (seventh chapel of the right aisle); and a little-known sculpture by **Bernini** (1653), the *Monument to Maria Ruggi* (on the fifth pier from the entrance).

Plaques on the facade of Santa Maria record the high-water marks of the Tiber over the centuries. The worst flood was in 1598, when the river rose 33 feet and claimed thousands of lives.

Santa Maria di Monserrato

Via di Monserrato–Via Giulia 151

Santa Maria di Monserrato is the less arresting of two churches on Via Giulia; the other is **Santa Maria dell'Orazione** (see below). Like the churches of San Luigi dei Francesi (see page 147) and Santa Maria dell'Anima (see page 148), respectively the French and German churches of Rome, it was built as a national church: here the church of the Aragonese; Catalans; and, after 1875, the Spanish. Its erection was prompted by the notorious Borgia pope, Alexander VI, whose family was of Spanish origin. Alexander and another Borgia crook, Pope Calixtus III, are buried here, together with Alfonso XIII, the king of Spain before the declaration of the Spanish Republic in 1931.

From the vine-covered archway at its southern end, Via Giulia is among the most beautiful streets in Rome: a straight, palazzo-lined street designed by Bramante and laid out in 1508 by Pope Julius II, after whom it is named. One of the city's earliest attempts at rational town planning, it cut through the area's hovels and twisted back alleys to provide what at the time was the city center's main approach to St. Peter's. Today, with Via dei Coronari, it is best known for its antiques shops.

Santa Maria dell'Orazione e Morte

Via Giulia

Graphic evidence of Catholicism's individual approach to death is in the wonderfully necrophilic facade of this church, aptly named Our Lady of the Oration and Death. Grinning stone skulls leer down from the frontage; notice also the beaked bird of Osiris, Egyptian god of death, looking grimly down Via Giulia toward the Vatican. A cheerful message accompanies these charming *mementi mori*: "Me today, thee tomorrow."

The sinister iconography belongs to the *Compagnia della Buona Morte* (literally the Company of the Good Death), a pious confraternity who took it upon themselves to collect the unclaimed bodies of the poor, usually people who died on the streets, and dispose of them in a Christian fashion. The church was both its headquarters and its workshop, for at one time three large tunnels, used to store and unload corpses, ran down to the Tiber. All but one were sealed during work on the river's embankment, and in this last passage you can see artful displays of human bones worked into such *bijou* articles as tables and candelabras. As a study of the Italian way of death, compare it with the equally macabre Santa Maria della Concezione on Via Vittorio Veneto (see page 150).

The cloisters of Santa Maria della Pace

Raphael's Sibyls

Santa Maria della Pace

Vicolo della Pace, off Via Piazza della Pace—Via di Parione

This tiny church, tucked away in a dark alley close to **Piazza Navona**, presents an intriguing exterior and a nest of interior artistic treasures. If only it were open more often.

It started life under Sixtus IV in about 1480, possibly to a design by Baccio Pintelli, and was the result of a vow made by Sixtus during the war with Florence. According to legend, a painting of the Virgin (now above the altar) bled when pierced by the sword of a drunken soldier (or by a stone, the story varies). This led the pope, who came in full ceremonial rig to view the miracle, to promise a church to the Virgin if she would bring peace *(pace)* to the warring factions.

The early rectangular church was later overlaid with an octagonal plan, possibly by Bramante, and then exhaustively overhauled for Alexander VI in 1656 by Pietro da Cortona. Although Cortona was better known as a ceiling painter (see **Palazzo Barberini**, pages 102–103), here he conceived the beautiful Baroque facade and the delightful *pronaos*, or circular porch, that together lend the church its greatest charm.

Inside, the Cappella Chigi contains famous **frescoes** by Raphael, a group of *Sibyls* painted for Agostino Chigi in 1514 (first chapel on the right). The group of *Prophets* above the sibyls is perhaps by Timoteo Viti, Raphael's erstwhile teacher. The chapel next door, the Cappella Cesi, is graced with fine High Renaissance sculptural decoration and was designed by Sangallo the Younger. Over the altar of the first chapel on the left is a fine work by Baldassare Peruzzi of the *Madonna with Saints Bridget and Catherine and Cardinal Ponzetti.*

Alongside the church is a much-lauded but in truth rather austere **cloister,** Bramante's first work in Rome and considered the first masterpiece of High Renaissance architecture in the city.

The church is open only on Sunday mornings for Mass. For entry to the cloisters, ring the bell at Via Arco della Pace 5.

Bramante came to Rome in 1499 and refused all commissions for five years, a period during which he concentrated solely on studying and measuring the ruins of antiquity, a labor that revolutionized his style.

Almost next door to Santa Maria della Pace is one of the loveliest and trendiest bars in Rome: Bar della Pace, an oasis of antique calm during the day, but packed to bursting in the evenings: Via della Pace 4.

Santa Maria was supposedly built on the site of Nero's tomb in 1099. A huge walnut tree had grown from the grave, the haunt of deranged crows until the Virgin appeared to Paschal II and ordered him to chop it down. This he did, and then built a chapel. The emperor's ghost supposedly wandered the area, making for the pyramid tomb that contained the remains of his wife. It is now the stylish Rósati café on the corner of Piazza del Popolo, a fashionable spot beloved of the city's artists and literati.

<< What inspiration can anybody get from the cluttered and gaudy mess of the high altar, and the two altars right and left of it, whose columned foppery suggests nothing at all but a sculptor's delight in his own virtuosity? >> – Sean O'Faolain, *Summer in Italy*

Inside Santa Maria in Trastevere

▶▶▷ Santa Maria del Popolo

Piazza del Popolo

Santa Maria del Popolo lures with the promise of its tremendous artistic treasures, though because it sits awkwardly in the corner of Piazza del Popolo you may easily miss it altogether. It was much praised by the trenchant 19th-century critic John Ruskin, who considered the church 'the most perfectly finished and best supported of any after St. Peter's'.

Sixtus IV enlarged the 11th-century chapel (see panel), and **Bramante** extended the apse in 1505. Most work in the interior was directed by **Bernini,** whose efforts have not always been appreciated in the manner of Ruskin. Its greatest works of art are **Pinturicchio's frescoes** behind the high altar, painted between 1485 and 1489 and considered the artist's most accomplished works in Rome. They show the *Coronation of the Virgin,* the *Sibyls,* the *Evangelists,* and the *Fathers of the Church.* In the choir below are two superlative tombs, the masterpieces of sculptor Andrea da Sansovino: the tomb of Cardinal Girolamo Basso (1507) and the tomb of Ascanio Sforza (1505). Pinturicchio is also represented in the first chapel on the right as you enter the church.

The most famous single chapel is the **Cappella Chigi** (1513), commissioned by Agostino Chigi, a wealthy Sienese banker who commissioned Raphael "to convert earthly things into heavenly" in the decoration of his tomb (1526). The artist was responsible for the chapel's entire decoration, including the statues and mosaics, though Bernini could not resist adding oval medallions to both the Chigi tombs The altarpiece, *The Birth of the Virgin,* is by Michelangelo's protégé, Sébastiano del Piombo.

The first chapel of the left transept has the most admired paintings, two masterpieces by Caravaggio: *The Conversion of St. Paul* and *The Crucifixion of St. Peter* (1601–02). Both canvases show a dramatic intensity, using chiaroscuro effects unique at the time. The more orthodox work of Caravaggio's rival and contemporary, Annibale Carracci, is seen in the *Assumption of the Virgin,* hangs over the main altar in the chapel.

▶▶▷ Santa Maria in Trastevere

Piazza di Santa Maria in Trastevere

Trastevere's *al fresco* social life focuses on **Piazza di Santa Maria in Trastevere**, the liveliest and loveliest spot in the area. Children play football here, youths hang around the central fountain, and tourists and locals alike gather in the enticing if overpriced restaurants along the square's main flank. Day or night there is always human interest to divert the eye – some of it not terribly salubrious – though the key to the piazza's appeal is the mosaic-studded facade of the church on its northern edge.

History Santa Maria in Trastevere was the first church in Rome to be dedicated to the Virgin and may even be the oldest place of official Christian worship in the city. Some believe it was the first spot Christians could worship in public, dating its foundation to AD 222, when

Meeting point: Piazza di Santa Maria in Trastevere

a church was dedicated to the pope of the time, St. Calixtus. Legend says this remarkable man toppled out of a window and managed to land head first in a well and drown – just one of the miraculous acts on the road to his canonization.

Another story relates that Christians were in competition for the site with two innkeepers and that the Emperor Severus decided in favor of the church, saying it was better to have a god worshipped in any form, Christian or pagan, than to open another tavern. Yet another claims that a fountain of olive oil sprang up here on the day of Christ's birth (or 38 years before in some versions) and flowed to the Tiber, symbolizing the coming of the grace of God.

The church was rebuilt by Innocent II, a member of a prominent Trastevere family, the Papareschi, and the **Romanesque campanile** was added to the facade in 1143. The portico was tacked on in 1702 by Carlo Fontana, who at the same time replaced the piazza's earlier Bernini fountain. The facade's great importance, as well as its great beauty, derives from its **mosaics,** which show how all major Roman churches would have been decorated during the Middle Ages. This is the only one to have survived both the depredations of time and the ruthlessness of the baroque church builders. Considerable controversy surrounds their authorship, with Pietro Cavallini, responsible for mosaics inside the church (1290), put forward as a possible candidate. Other critics think they were executed earlier – perhaps in the mid-12th century.

Their theme is vague, and the long-held view that the Virgin and her 10 female companions echoed Jesus' parable of the Wise and Foolish Virgins is now in dispute. For example, several of the virgins, appear to be men, and only two are carrying unlighted lamps (not the five mentioned in the parable).

<< Rome is the city of illusion . . . as good a place as any to wait for the end of the world. >> Gore Vidal – quoted in a scene from Fellini's *Roma* (1972), filmed in Piazza di Santa Maria in Trastevere

Well known, but now hackneyed and expensive, Sabatini is the most prominent restaurant in Piazza Santa Maria in Trastevere. Better for a treat is the similarly pricey Paris nearby (Piazza San Caliso 13.)

Rome's only English-language movie theater, the tatty but much-loved Pasquino, is two minutes' walk from Piazza Santa Maria in Trastevere at Vicolo del Piede 19.

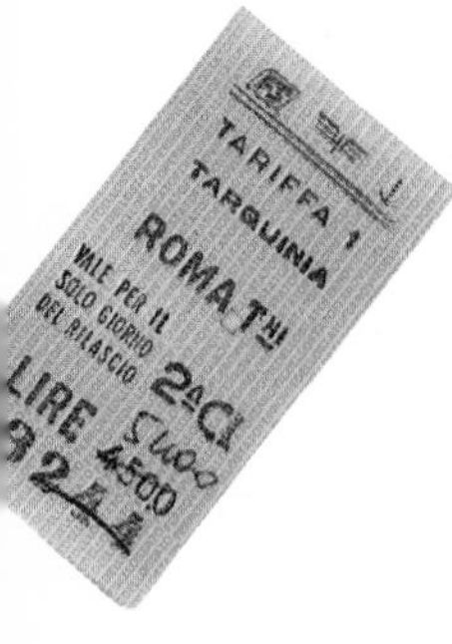

The interior The mosaics of the interior are, if anything, more stunning still and are the best of their age in the city. They fall into two distinct groups. Those in the **upper apse** are Byzantine works from about 1140, probably by Greek or Greek-trained craftsmen, and show Christ and the Virgin enthroned, flanked by a solemn parade of characters: St. Peter, St. Julius, and St. Cornelius on one side, and St. Calixtus, St. Lawrence, St. Caleponius, and Innocent II on the other. Notice the caged birds below, which are a neat piece of iconography symbolizing the imprisonment of Christ's spirit in an earthly body to redeem the sins of the world.

The second group, underneath in the **lower apse,** are by Cavallini (1290) and describe several scenes from the *Life of the Virgin*. These, too, are masterpieces of the mosaic art and contain several delightful conceits. Notice, in particular, the small building under the *Nativity* labeled "Taberna Merotoria," from which flows a stream of oil – a reference to the myth of the church's site.

Much else in the interior commands attention, not the least the 22 pitted, ancient columns, that come from the **Terme di Caracalla** (see page 178) and the outstanding, if much restored **Cosmati pavement** – all patterned swirls of red and green marble. The portico's liberal sprinkling of ancient debris consists of early Roman inscriptions and decorative Christian panels.

Masterpieces of Byzantine art

Baroque interior, Santa Maria della Vittoria

▶▷▷ **Santa Maria della Vittoria**

Via XX Settembre

All else in this ponderous baroque church (1608–20) pales alongside its surfeit of decoration – perhaps the richest in Rome – and in particular when set against Bernini's notorious **Cappella Cornaro** (last chapel on the left). Designed in 1646 for the Venetian Cardinal Cornaro, it made the Baroque's taste for theatricality literal, placing the eight members of Cornaro's family in recesses on either side of the chapel. Though theater boxes developed after Bernini, this is precisely what they appear to be, and there is no doubt that the family – shown twisting in their seats – are intended to be attending a dramatic performance – in this case Bernini's statue of the *Ecstasy of St. Teresa.*

The statue shows the saint pierced by the love of God, here symbolized by the arrow of a hovering angel, an incident taken from the saint's own description of an ecstatic vision in Avila, Spain, in 1537. Fusing together architecture, sculpture and painting, the figure represents one of the touchstones of high Baroque achievement. Indeed, one writer (Barbara Harrison) said of the showpiece: "If one is going to put one's love for the baroque to the test, the place to go is Santa Maria della Vittoria."

Many have done so, and over the centuries the statue has attracted equal amounts of praise and scorn. The chief complaint of the detractors is largely moral, the ecstasy of the saint, sublimely expressed, being too easily misconstrued as earthly, rather than divine. Bernini's intentions, Catholic that he was, were doubtless honorable, but the charge of secular titillation is easily made. "I feel within myself, if I may say, a kind of mental blush," said an 18th-century cleric. "Certainly the most unfit ornament to place in a Christian church that can be imagined," added a 19th-century Englishman. Others, however, recognized the genius of the piece, notably Stendhal, who wondered whether "the Greek chisel produced anything to equal the head of St. Teresa."

St. Teresa (1515–82) was a writer and mystic who refounded the Carmelite order of nuns. The personal account of her ecstasy is loaded with potent and ambiguous imagery: "In his hand I saw a great golden spear, and at the iron tip there appeared to be a point of fire. This is plunged into my heart several times so that it penetrated to my entrails. . . . The pain was so severe that it made me utter several moans. The sweetness caused by this intense pain is so extreme that one cannot possibly wish it to cease. . . . "

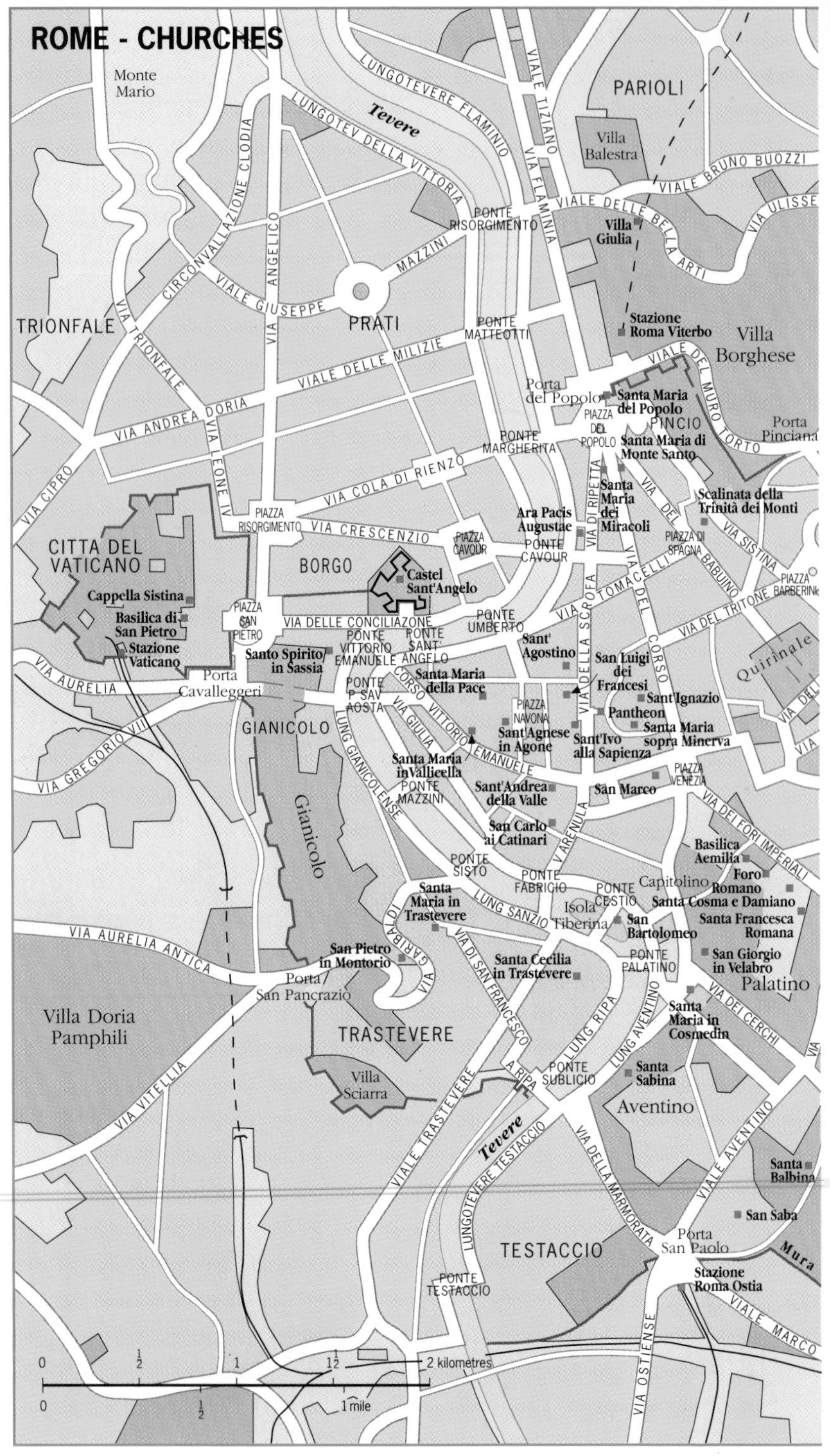
ROME - CHURCHES
Monte Mario
PARIOLI
Villa Balestra
Tevere
TRIONFALE
PRATI
Villa Giulia
Stazione Roma Viterbo
Villa Borghese
Porta del Popolo
Santa Maria del Popolo
PIAZZA DEL POPOLO
PINCIO
Porta Pinciana
Santa Maria di Monte Santo
Santa Maria dei Miracoli
Ara Pacis Augustae
Scalinata della Trinità dei Monti
PIAZZA DI SPAGNA
PIAZZA BARBERINI
CITTA DEL VATICANO
BORGO
Castel Sant'Angelo
Cappella Sistina
Basilica di San Pietro
Stazione Vaticano
PIAZZA SAN PIETRO
PIAZZA RISORGIMENTO
PIAZZA CAVOUR
Santo Spirito in Sassia
Porta Cavalleggeri
Sant' Agostino
San Luigi dei Francesi
Sant'Ignazio
Pantheon
Santa Maria sopra Minerva
Quirinale
Santa Maria della Pace
PIAZZA NAVONA
Sant'Agnese in Agone
Sant'Ivo alla Sapienza
GIANICOLO
Gianicolo
Santa Maria in Vallicella
Sant'Andrea della Valle
San Marco
PIAZZA VENEZIA
San Carlo ai Catinari
Basilica Aemilia
Foro Romano
Capitolino
Santa Cosma e Damiano
Santa Francesca Romana
Santa Maria in Trastevere
Isola Tiberina
San Bartolomeo
San Giorgio in Velabro
Palatino
San Pietro in Montorio
Santa Cecilia in Trastevere
Porta San Pancrazio
Villa Doria Pamphili
TRASTEVERE
Santa Maria in Cosmedin
Villa Sciarra
Santa Sabina
Aventino
Santa Balbina
San Saba
TESTACCIO
Porta San Paolo
Mura
Stazione Roma Ostia
LUNGOTEVERE FLAMINIO
LUNGOTEV DELLA VITTORIA
VIALE TIZIANO
VIA FLAMINIA
VIALE BRUNO BUOZZI
VIALE DELLE BELLE ARTI
VIA ULISSE
PONTE RISORGIMENTO
CIRCONVALLAZIONE CLODIA
VIA ANGELICO
MAZZINI
VIALE GIUSEPPE
PONTE MATTEOTTI
VIALE DEL MURO TORTO
VIA TRIONFALE
VIALE DELLE MILIZIE
VIA ANDREA DORIA
VIALE LEONE IV
PONTE MARGHERITA
VIA COLA DI RIENZO
VIA CIPRO
VIA DI RIPETTA
VIA DEL BABUINO
VIA SISTINA
VIA CRESCENZIO
PONTE CAVOUR
VIA TOMACELLI
VIA DEL CORSO
VIA DEL TRITONE
VIA DELLE CONCILIAZONE
PONTE UMBERTO
PONTE VITTORIO EMANUELE
PONTE SANT' ANGELO
VIA DELLA SCROFA
VIA AURELIA
PONTE P SAV AOSTA
CORSO VITTORIO EMANUELE
VIA GIULIA
VIA GREGORIO VII
LUNG GIANICOLENSE
PONTE MAZZINI
V ARENULA
VIA DEI FORI IMPERIALI
PONTE SISTO
PONTE FABRICIO
PONTE CESTIO
LUNG SANZIO
PONTE PALATINO
VIA AURELIA ANTICA
VIA GARIBALDI
VIA DI SAN FRANCESCO A RIPA
VIA DEI CERCHI
LUNG RIPA
LUNG AVENTINO
PONTE SUBLICIO
VIA VITELLIA
VIALE TRASTEVERE
LUNGOTEVERE TESTACCIO
VIA DELLA MARMORATA
VIALE AVENTINO
PONTE TESTACCIO
VIA OSTIENSE
VIALE MARCO
0
½
1
1½
2 kilometres
1 mile

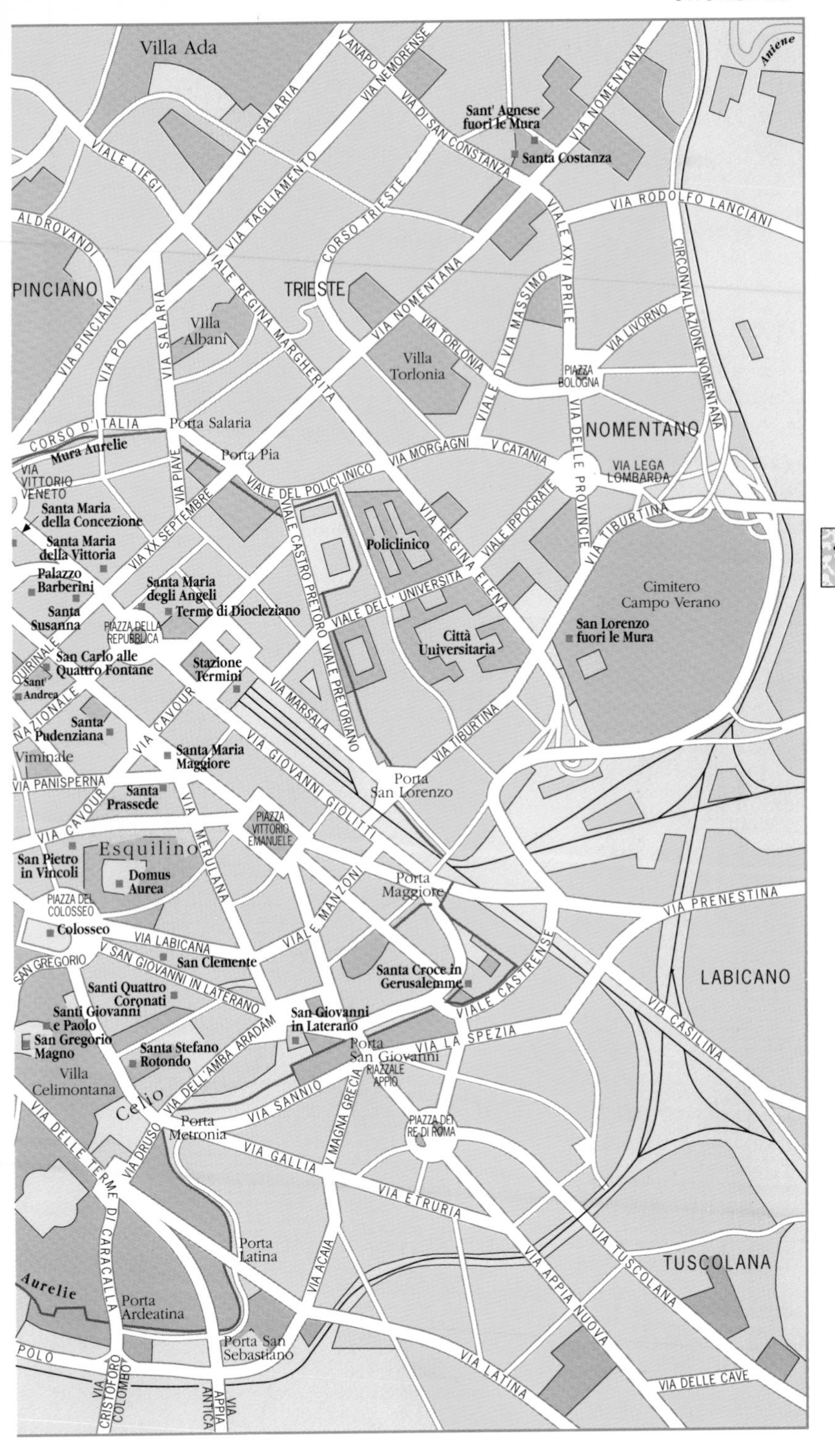
Villa Ada
Aniene
Sant' Agnese fuori le Mura
Santa Costanza
PINCIANO
TRIESTE
Villa Albani
Villa Torlonia
PIAZZA BOLOGNA
NOMENTANO
VIA LEGA LOMBARDA
Porta Salaria
Porta Pia
Mura Aurelie
VIA VITTORIO VENETO
Santa Maria della Concezione
Santa Maria della Vittoria
Palazzo Barberini
Santa Susanna
Santa Maria degli Angeli
Terme di Diocleziano
PIAZZA DELLA REPUBBLICA
Policlinico
Città Universitaria
Cimitero Campo Verano
San Lorenzo fuori le Mura
San Carlo alle Quattro Fontane
Sant' Andrea
Stazione Termini
Santa Pudenziana
Viminale
Santa Maria Maggiore
Porta San Lorenzo
Santa Prassede
PIAZZA VITTORIO EMANUELE
Esquilino
San Pietro in Vincoli
Domus Aurea
PIAZZA DEL COLOSSEO
Colosseo
Porta Maggiore
San Clemente
Santi Quattro Coronati
Santa Croce in Gerusalemme
LABICANO
Santi Giovanni e Paolo
San Gregorio Magno
San Giovanni in Laterano
Santa Stefano Rotondo
Villa Celimontana
Porta San Giovanni
PIAZZALE APPIO
Celio
Porta Metronia
PIAZZA DEI RE DI ROMA
Porta Latina
Aurelie
Porta Ardeatina
Porta San Sebastiano
TUSCOLANA
VIA ANAPO
VIA NEMORENSE
VIA DI SAN CONSTANZA
VIA NOMENTANA
VIA SALARIA
VIALE LIEGI
VIA TAGLIAMENTO
CORSO TRIESTE
VIA RODOLFO LANCIANI
ALDROVANDI
VIALE REGINA MARGHERITA
VIALE XXI APRILE
VIA DI VIA MASSIMO
CIRCONVALLAZIONE NOMENTANA
VIA LIVORNO
VIA TORLONIA
VIA PINCIANA
VIA PO
VIA SALARIA
CORSO D'ITALIA
VIA MORGAGNI
V CATANIA
VIA DELLE PROVINCIE
VIA PIAVE
VIALE DEL POLICLINICO
VIA XX SETTEMBRE
VIALE CASTRO PRETORIO
VIALE PRETORIANO
VIA REGINA ELENA
VIALE IPPOCRATE
VIA TIBURTINA
VIALE DELL' UNIVERSITA
QUIRINALE
NAZIONALE
VIA CAVOUR
VIA MARSALA
VIA GIOVANNI GIOLITTI
VIA TIBURTINA
VIA PANISPERNA
VIA MERULANA
VIALE MANZONI
VIA PRENESTINA
VIA LABICANA
SAN GREGORIO
V SAN GIOVANNI IN LATERANO
VIALE CASTRENSE
VIA CASILINA
VIA LA SPEZIA
VIA DELL' AMBA ARADAM
VIA SANNIO
V MAGNA GRECIA
VIA DELLE TERME DI CARACALLA
VIA DRUSO
VIA GALLIA
VIA ETRURIA
VIA TUSCOLANA
VIA APPIA NUOVA
VIA ACAIA
VIA LATINA
VIA DELLE CAVE
POLO
VIA CRISTOFORO COLOMBO
VIA APPIA ANTICA

163

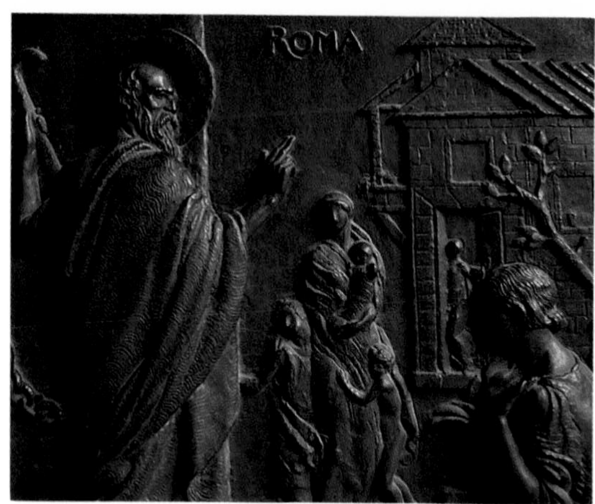

Bronze door detail from San Paolo fuori le Mura

A famous mosaic runs along the nave of San Paolo showing all 265 popes from St. Peter onward (though only the first 40 survive from the original basilica). According to Roman tradition, the world will end when there is no room for another portrait. At present – ominously – there are just eight spaces left after John Paul II.

The cloisters of San Paolo fuori le Mura

▶▷▷ **San Paolo fuori le Mura**

Piazzale San Paolo, Via Ostiense

Of all the destruction visited on Rome, the loss of the original San Paolo fuori le Mura seems the most tragically poignant. In 1823 two workmen unknowingly spilled a bucket of hot coals, and overnight a fire swept away one of the city's four patriarchal basilicas, a treasure-crammed church second only in size to St. Peter's. Following the devastation, what you see now is a building that dates almost entirely from the 19th century. Although the new church faithfully replicates the old, it is a cold, unconvincing affair, and only in the 13th-century **cloisters,** possibly Rome's most alluring, can you feel any sense of its former grandeur.

The church marks the spot in which St. Paul was buried after his execution in AD 67, a relatively civilized end merited by the apostle's status as a Roman citizen. The martyrdom occurred at *Aquae Salviae,* about 3 km from the present church. According to legend, his head bounced three times, creating three springs, now the Abbazia delle Tre Fontane in EUR.

The body was interred in the family tomb of a devout Roman matron, Lucina. In time it was covered by a *martyrium,* or chapel, soon replaced by a church commissioned by Constantine. This church proved unable to cope with the throng of pilgrims drawn to the tomb, and in AD 385 plans were drawn up for what was to become the world's largest church until the rebuilding of St. Peter's in the 16th century.

With its mosaics and countless works of art, San Paolo was also the city's most splendidly decorated church, despite an outlying position that made it particularly vulnerable to attack. During a raid in 846, the Saracens collected five tons of gold and silver (all later lost off the Sicilian coast) and looted Paul's tomb – leaving the still-delicate question of whether the saint's relics now remain under the high altar. What does survive is the altar **canopy,** a superlative piece of sculpture by Arnolfo di Cambio (1285).

▶▶▶ San Pietro

Piazza San Pietro

It would be hard to visit Rome and not see St. Peter's, the most famous church in Christendom and Catholicism's most sacred point of pilgrimage. Few people are unimpressed by the monumental scale of the enterprise, but many come away disappointed by its chill interior – which for a church of this fame is all but empty of great art and, if truth be told, of any abiding intensity of religious sentiment.

St. Peter's crucifixion is traditionally held to have occurred in AD 64 or 67 in the imperial gardens on the Vatican hill. Following his death, his followers reputedly buried him in a well-known cemetery. The current high altar supposedly marks the site of the saint's actual tomb, a supposition recently reinforced by persuasive archaeological work below the church.

St. Peter's is the largest church in the world — 610 feet long and 151 feet high in the nave (390 feet — in the dome) and able to accommodate a congregation of 60,000. Markers in the central aisle show the lengths of other great churches in comparison, though they are of dubious accuracy, the size of Milan's cathedral, for example, being 66 feet too short.

History The first St. Peter's for which records survive was built by Pope Sylvester I in AD 326 with the backing of the Emperor Constantine. This ancient basilica was to survive for over 1,000 years, being added to and richly embellished. By 1452, however, it was in such an advanced state of disrepair that Nicholas V resolved to build an entirely new church – but it was to be another 50 years before Julius II issued the final order for the old church's ultimate destruction.

Construction was to progress in fits and starts for some 120 years. The period's leading artists and architects all strived to achieve what was intended to be the pinnacle of Renaissance endeavor, but what eventually emerged was more a monument to the shortcomings of compromise.

Dwarfed by the architecture of Piazza San Pietro

Climbing the world's highest brick dome may be your most abiding memory of St. Peter's. Views of the city and the open countryside beyond are breathtaking. You may need to line up to take the steps or elevator to the first stage on the church terrace (café, souvenirs, and toilets) and then the steps to the higher drum and gallery — the dome's first stage. A long, steep and narrow one-way staircase then climbs between the dome's inner and outer shells to the tiny lantern on the summit. *Open:* daily 9–5. Admission charge.

Julius II employed **Bramante** as his master builder, charging him both to design a new church and to supervise the destruction of the old one – a heresy that earned him the nickname *ruinante* (destroyer) from Raphael for demolishing treasure in the basilica that was both sacred and redeemable. Bramante's scheme envisaged a church built as a Greek cross, a great central dome and a quartet of flanking cupolas. During building, his reputation was muddied by accusations of mafia-style misbehavior; nevertheless, when he died in 1516, four central pillars and the dome's vast supporting arches had been completed.

A fierce competition then emerged to complete the church, won by Antonio da Sangallo in 1539 with a plan – a dismal one in retrospect – that involved a fresh start using a Latin cross as the central theme. It was an unqualified disaster, and in 1546 Paul III called in the great Michelangelo to salvage the mess. The sculptor, then 72, reluctantly agreed, but only on condition that he would be given a free hand, in return for which he would work gratis until his death. To the authorities' consternation he simply demolished Sangallo's work and substituted a plan that returned to Bramante's first principles. The only major alteration was to be the dome, which he intended to raise higher than Bramante's – a copy of the Pantheon – to emulate Brunelleschi's cupola on Florence's cathedral.

When Michelangelo died in 1564, the drum and its distinctive twin columns and garlands had been completed. Subsequently, however, **Giacomo della Porta** (1590) was to alter the eventual profile and take the dome higher still.

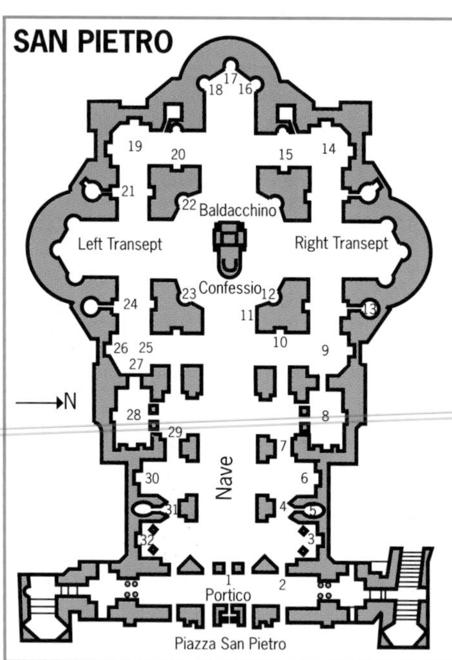

1. Main entrance
2. Porta Santa
3. Cappella della Pietà
4. Monument to Queen Christina of Sweden
5. Cappella del Crocifisso
6. Cappella di San Sebastiano
7. Monument to Countess Matilda of Tuscany
8. Cappella del Santissimo Sacramento
9. Cappella Gregoriano
10. Mosaic of the Communion of St. Jerome
11. Statue of St. Peter
12. Statue of St. Longinus. Entrance to the Sacre Grotte Vaticane
13. Entrance to the Dome
14. Cappella di San Michele
15. Mosaic of St. Peter raising Tabitha
16. Tomb of Urban VIII
17. Chair of St. Peter
18. Tomb of Pope Paul III
19. Cappella della Colonna
20. Mosaic of St. Peter healing the paralytic
21. Monument to Alexander VII
22. Statue of St. Veronica
23. Statue of St. Andrew
24. Monument to Pius VIII
25. Cappella Clementina
26. Tomb of St. Gregory the Great
27. Monument to Pius VII
28. Cappella del Coro
29. Monument to Pope Innocent VIII
30. Cappella della Presentazione
31. Monument to the Last Stuarts
32. Baptistery

Inside San Pietro

Popes long suspected the existence of an ancient tomb below St. Peter's high altar, but all had feared to disturb the ground out of respect, superstition or the dread of finding St. Peter's relics missing. The Saracens were known to have raided St. Peter's in 846, and parts of the earliest crypt had been clearly desecrated. Pius XII was the first to consent to excavations in 1939, and work continued through the war, uncovering a perfect street of early pagan and Christian tombs.

In 1605 Paul V asked **Carlo Maderno** to redesign the church yet again, leading to the restoration of the Latin cross rejected by Michelangelo. The restoration involved pushing a long nave out to the old Piazza San Pietro and the addition of the present facade (1612), much criticized over the years for obscuring the dome from below. However, it was **Bernini**, appointed the interior's chief architect, who came up with the doomed idea of adding twin towers to the facade's flanks. These towers were so appalling that they eventually had to be leveled to the facade's height – thus increasing its width.

Eventually, on November 18, 1626, the 1,300th anniversary of the old church, Urban VIII consecrated the new St. Peter's.

Portico St. Peter's grand portico has five entrances. **Porta Santa**, on the extreme right, is opened only every 25 years in Holy Years. The other doors are modern bronzes, all except the **central doors** (1433-45), which were saved from the old church. Cast to commemorate the Council of Florence in 1439, the figures depicted are visitors to the council (Africans, Ethiopians, Greeks) with the Virgin, Peter, Paul and Eugenius IV. Above the main doorway are fragments of a renowned but much restored fresco by **Giotto**, the *Navicella,* also rescued from the old basilica, and showing the Apostles' ship in a storm and Christ walking on the water. On the portico's extreme right stands an equestrian statue of

Bernini's St. Peter Enthroned

Canova's monument to the Stuarts

The most exciting discovery during excavations was the skeleton of an elderly, powerfully built man, along with a vast horde of coins of different ages and countries. There were also marks of interference – perhaps made by the Saracens, who may have looted the tomb but left the body alone. Though a cranium was found in another niche, this frame was headless, and St. Peter's skull has supposedly been venerated for over 1,000 years in San Giovanni in Laterano.

Constantine by Bernini, mirrored by another of *Charlemagne* on the left.

Above the center of the portico is the benediction **loggia** from which the popes give their blessing at special festivals and where new popes, saints and beatifications are proclaimed.

Interior Superlatives hardly do justice to the interior's overwhelming size, which can hardly fail to impress. You could wander for hours exploring the nuances of each papal tomb, every third-rate monument, and the avalanche of chill Baroque artifice, but in practice it pays to be selective and to hunt out the highlights or the points of arcane historical interest.

Right-hand aisle The church's most famous work is Michelangelo's *Pietà* (1499), now behind glass in the first chapel after a vandal's attack in 1972. It was completed when the artist was only 25 and is his only signed work, Michelangelo having been moved to add his name when he overheard onlookers disputing its authorship. The name is carved in the hem of the cloth across the Virgin's breast.

The third chapel, the Cappella del Santissimo Sacramento, has a fresco of the *Trinity* by Pietro da Cortona, a bronze grille by Borromini, and an altar tabernacle by Bernini – a miniature copy of Bramante's Tempietto in **San Pietro in Montorio**. At the end of the aisle by the last pillar is a statue of St. Peter, its right foot caressed by millions since 1857 when Pius IX granted a 50-day indulgence to anyone kissing it after confession. The authorship is now in doubt, but it was long attributed to the Florentine, Arnolfo di Cambio. To its right, around one of the four great pillars of the dome, is a Bernini statue of *St. Longinus,* the soldier who pierced Christ's side at the Crucifixion and was later converted.

High altar and baldacchino Located over the presumed tomb of St. Peter, it is for papal use only on special occasions. Below, steps lit by flickering oil lamps lead to Maderno's *confessio*, graced with a statue of *Pius VI* (1820) by Canova. Above is Bernini's **baldacchino** (1624–33), a monumental bronze canopy as high as the Palazzo Farnese (49 feet) and infinitely more ornate. The Barberini symbol, the bee, swarms over the monument, though the offensive self-glorification is redeemed by a touching story. It is said that Urban commissioned the piece in thanks for the recovery of a young niece who had almost died in childbirth – a tale perhaps borne out by the female heads and beaming baby on all but two of the plinths' coat-of arms.

Apse Bernini's inspired way with bronze is also on show in the apse, which is dominated by his *Cathedra Petri* (Chair of St. Peter, 1656–65) designed to encase a wood and ivory chair reputedly used by St. Peter to deliver his first sermon to the Romans. When it was removed in the 1970s, it was found to be two chairs cobbled together – one from the 3rd century, the other from the 9th; a copy is on display in the church Treasury.

Alongside are two of the church's most diverting tombs: to the left is the Tomb of Paul III (1551–75) by Giacomo della Porta, whose winsome figure of Justice was said to be the pope's alluring sister, Giulia. Her charms so distracted pilgrims that she was covered in drapery in the last century. One Spanish student was said to have hidden in the church to make love to it and was found dead alongside it the next morning. To the right is the **Tomb of Urban VIII** (1642–47) by Bernini, praised in its day, and the model for Baroque tombs and monuments all over Europe.

Left-hand aisle A clutter of papal tombs lines the left aisle, one or two with arresting works of art. The first, the Cappella della Colonna, has a relief by Alessandro Algardi, *St. Leo Turning Attila away from Rome* – Leo is reputed to have threatened Attila with a fatal nosebleed if he entered the city; Saints Peter and Paul are shown translating the threat. Beyond it, before the left transept, is Bernini's late Tomb of Alexander VII (1672–78), complete with hourglass and Death as a skeleton emerging from curtains. Past the transept and pillar is Algardi's Tomb of Leo XI de' Medici – honored despite his pontificate lasting only 27 days – followed by the Cappella del Coro and bronze grilles by Borromini. Close by, a pillar frames the Monument to Innocent VIII by Pollaiuolo, the only monument from the old basilica transferred to the new church. The blade he holds is said to be part of Longinus's spear.

On the last pillar before the Baptistery and the entrance to the church stands the monument of most interest to British visitors – Canova's **Monument to the Last Stuarts** – that is, to the Roman Catholic claimants to the British throne, exiled and buried in Rome: James, Charles, and the Old and Young Pretenders.

The greatest artistic treasures in St. Peter's have been moved to the Vatican Museums (see pages 184-97). The church's own nine-room treasury contains more modest gifts made to the church over the centuries by popes, emperors, and kings. These gifts are mostly religious ornaments – relics, chalices, vestments, manuscripts, and the like – but there are also more substantial pieces and a few tantalizing relics from the old basilica. *Open:* May to September, 9–6; October to April, 9–4:30. Admission charge. Entry is by the Monument to Pius VIII at the top of the left aisle.

Interior, San Pietro

Bramante's classical Tempietto

Buried without memorial under the steps of San Pietro's altar is Beatrice Cenci, immortalized in numerous paintings and Shelley's famous drama *The Cenci* as a symbol of the human spirit in revolt against tyranny and injustice. Beatrice was tortured and executed with her mother and brother in 1599, accused of the unsolved murder of her monstrous father. She reputedly hired someone to kill him, provoked, it is said, by his repeated incestuous assaults.

▶▷▷ San Pietro in Montorio

Via Garibaldi–Gianicolo

This church's claim to be built on the site of St. Peter's crucifixion is dubious – the apostle was probably martyred in Nero's *circo* (stadium) on the Vatican Hill – but it is deservedly famous for the **Tempietto,** a small temple built on rigidly classical lines by **Bramante** in 1502.

The present building was commissioned by Ferdinand and Isabella of Spain in 1481, taking its name (literally St. Peter on the Golden Mountain) from *Mons Aureus,* or Monte d'Oro, the name given to the **Gianicolo** in earlier times. Inside, the first chapel has **frescoes** by Sebastiano del Piombo (Michelangelo provided the drawings for the *Flagellation*) and next to it a *Coronation of the Virgin* by Baldassare Peruzzi. Both are overshadowed, however, by the Tempietto, which you find outside in a courtyard to the right. Though small – it holds only 10 people – it is one of the city's key Renaissance buildings and one of the period's earliest attempts to re-create a classical building.

▶▶▷ San Pietro in Vincoli

Piazza San Pietro in Vincoli

San Pietro is known less for its chains (*vincoli*) than for **Michelangelo**'s monumental statue of Moses (1503–13), one of the sculptor's greatest works. Along with the flanking figures of *Rachael* and *Leah* (Jacob's wives), it was to form both the centerpiece of St. Peter's and the pinnacle of a great 42-figure tomb for Julius II. To the artist's disgust it was never finished – this "tragedy of a tomb" as he called it. Julius forced the artist to work instead on the Sistine Chapel and then died leaving funds for the tomb frozen. Later popes had no interest in glorifying a dead predecessor and kept Michelangelo busy with commissions of their own.

Moses is pictured receiving the tablets of the Ten Commandments (held under his right arm) and is watching his people dance around the golden calf, his look of divine illumination tinged with wrath at their faithlessness. Michelangelo left a subtle but famous signature in the statue – his own profile in the upper part of the beard.

▶▷▷ Santa Prassede

Via Santa Prassede, off Piazza di Santa Maria Maggiore

Santa Prassede is best known for a display of filial affection – the beautiful **Cappella di St Zeno** commissioned in 822 by Pope Paschal I as his mother's mausoleum (located on the left near the church entrance). Paschal imported Byzantine artists to cover both the shrine and the main body of the church in a series of mosaics that rank as highly as any in the city. Those in the **triumphal arch** portray Christ flanked by angels in a heavenly Jerusalem, with the Virgin, saints, and Apostles below. Those beyond, in the **apse**, show Prassede and Pudenziana (see panel) being presented to Christ by St. Peter and St. Paul, along with St. Zeno and Paschal carrying his church.

The Cappella di St. Zeno has gold-crusted walls so magnificent that in the Middle Ages the chapel was called the Garden of Paradise. The square halo of Theodora (Paschal's mother) on the left of the altar indicates that she was alive when the mosaic was finished (like Paschal's in the apse). On the right is a tiny **column**, usually covered in flowers, brought from Jerusalem in 1223 and believed to be part of the pillar on which Christ was scourged.

San Pietro was built in 432 on the site where St. Peter was condemned to death under Nero. It was to house the chains that bound Peter in Jerusalem, to which were later added the chains said to have shackled him in Rome's Mamertine prison. According to myth, the two sets miraculously fused and can be seen in a casket below the high altar.

Prassede and Pudenziana were the daughters of a Roman senator called Pudens, an early Christian and friend of St. Peter. Prassede is said to have witnessed the massacre of 23 Christians sheltering in the family home. All were tossed in a well, now marked by a porphyry slab in the church's Cosmati pavement. The saint miraculously soaked up all their blood with a sponge. Both Prassede and sponge, together with sister, are buried in the early Christian sarcophagi of the church's confessio.

Mosaics in the Cappella di St Zeno, Santa Prassede

Santa Pudenziana

Try to visit Santa Sabina between 3:30 and 5:30, when the lovely cloister in the Dominican monastery is open alongside the church. Otherwise be sure to wander among the orange trees in the park to its left, a calm, scented oasis with broad views of the city. The trees here are descendants of specimens planted by St. Dominic, one of which survives in the cloister – apparently the first orange tree in Italy.

The church alongside Santa Sabina is Sant'Alessio – almost as old as its neighbor, but ruined in the 18th century by wanton restoration. Its nave contains a curious monument to St. Alessio, who left his rich family to live in abject poverty, becoming so thin that he was unrecognized on his return home. He passed the rest of his life – 17 years – living under the stairs, eventually falling down them to his death – hence the stairs celebrated in the nave's monument.

▶▷▷ Santa Pudenziana

Via Urbana

Built between 384 and 399 over 2nd-century Roman baths, but much altered since, Santa Pudenziana is said to occupy the house of Pudens, in which St. Peter converted Prassede and Pudenziana.

Its pride and joy is a prized early-Christian mosaic in the apse, executed when the church was built and depicting a golden-robed Christ, the Apostles, and two women presumed to be Pudenziana and Prassede. Although damaged in places and cramped by later building, its delicate coloring, detail, perspective, and masterful execution are all of the highest order.

St. Peter is said to have lived in the Pudens household for seven years, and the church's other prize is part of a table he allegedly used to say Mass.

Opening times of Santa Pudenziana are variable and restricted.

▶▷▷ Santa Sabina

Via di Santa Sabina, Aventino

Santa Sabina has come down through the centuries miraculously intact. Perched high on the **Aventino**, it is privy to some of the city's most impressive and romantic views, as well as being its finest surviving 5th-century basilica.

Founded between 425 and 432 and restored in 824, it was eventually given to St. Dominic as the headquarters for the Dominican order. Little is known of Sabina, who according to myth was a wealthy Roman matron converted to Christianity by her Greek slave Seraphia. Both were martyred, later to be honored by a Dalmatian priest, Pietro d'Illiria, who commissioned the church.

Its greatest treasures greet you almost at the door – the carved **cypress panels** of the main portal, 18 of which (out of an original 28) are from the first church, thus forming the oldest wooden carving in the canon of Christian art. Each depicts separate scenes from the Old and New Testaments.

Inside, the church is breathtaking. Its pure, simple lines are almost completely unsullied by the heavy touches of the baroque. The plain wooden ceiling rests on 24 delicately fluted Corinthian **columns**, probably plundered from a pagan temple to Juno Regina that stood on the Aventine during the time of the Republic.

The windows above were pieced together from 9th-century originals and use the mineral selenite instead of glass, diffusing a soft light that beautifully illuminates the nave. Similarly reconstructed were the **choir, pulpits** and **episcopal throne**, though sadly the apse's old mosaics have long since disappeared. In their place is a painting by Taddeo Zuccari, which probably reproduces the subject of the mosaics but unfortunately also strikes the church's only discordant note.

In the nave as recompense, however, is a **mosaic tombstone**, the only one of its type in Rome. Above the main door is part of a 5th-century mosaic whose two female figures symbolize the churches of Jews and Gentiles. Its gold inscription names Celestinus I as the church's founder.

▶▷▷ **Santi Quattro Coronati**

Via dei Santi Quattro Coronati

Santi Quattro Coronati was ransacked by the Normans in 1084 and rebuilt in about 1111. To see the exquisite **cloisters,** ring the bell in the left aisle for a nun to admit you. Amid the fragments of the pre-1084 church here is the **Cappella di Santa Barbara,** dotted with medieval frescoes and supported by ancient columns. Lovelier still is the **Cappella di San Silvestro,** off the church's main courtyard (ring bell at the sign "Monache Agostiniane").

▶▷▷ **Santo Stefano Rotondo**

Via Santo Stefano Rotondo

This was at one time among the largest and most important churches in Christendom (built 468–483). The records of its magnificent decoration (all lost) suggest that it was held in high esteem. Now reduced in size and badly dilapidated, its effect still astounds, as should the interior's grisly **medieval frescoes** when restoration is complete.

▷▷▷ **San Teodoro**

Via di San Teodoro

Wedged into the slopes of the Palatino, circular San Teodoro was founded in the 6th century and built over the ruins of a Roman grain store. You descend to the entrance via a flight of steps and pretty courtyard (1705). The apse mosaic, though ancient, has been restored on a host of occasions.

Open: daily 4–6, closed Tuesday.

Santa Sabina's carved wooden door panels

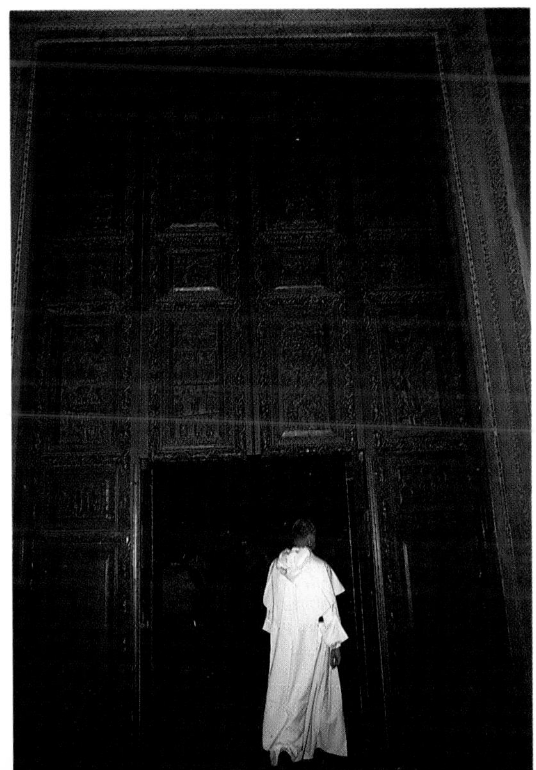

Quattro Coronati was named after four martyrs, either Roman soldiers killed for refusing to honor a pagan statue or sculptors who refused to carve a pagan idol (for which reason the church is popular with stonemasons). In either case they were killed by having an iron crown (*corona*) driven into their heads, hence the church's name.

<<... hideous paintings ... such a panorama of horror and butchery no man could imagine in his sleep, though he were to eat a whole pig, raw, for his supper. Grey-bearded men being boiled, fried, grilled, crimped, singed, eaten by wild beasts, worried by dogs, buried alive, torn asunder by horses, chopped up small with hatchets: women having their breasts torn off with iron pincers, their tongues cut out, their ears screwed off, their jaws broken, their bodies stretched on the rack, or skinned on the stake, or crackled up and melted in the fire – these are among the mildest subjects.>> – Charles Dickens, on the frescoes in Santo Stefano Rotondo, *Pictures from Italy*

The Protestant cleric William Evill (!), visiting Rome in 1870, records his impression of watching people ascend the Scala Santa: << It was a strange and suggestive, ludicrous and yet painful and depressing sight. There were reverend ecclesiastics, elderly ladies, beggars and educated gentlemen, all shuffling up together. It looked like a game – a kind of race in sacks – and one insensibly picked out a penitent to back as the winner. >> – *A Winter Journey to Rome and Back*

▶▷▷ Scala Santa

Piazza di San Giovanni in Laterano

Part and parcel of **San Giovanni in Laterano** (see pages 140–42), but separated from the main body of the church, Scala Santa (Holy Staircase) consists of 28 marble steps (now covered with wood) from Pilate's palace in Jerusalem, up which Christ ascended during his trial. On every fourth or fifth step is a brass plate with a glass center, through which are dark stains said to be the blood of Christ.

Reputedly brought to Rome by Constantine's mother, Helena, they have been an object of intense veneration ever since. In an ageless ritual somewhat bizarre to non-believers (see panel), the faithful still ascend them on their knees, gaining nine years of indulgences with every step climbed. It was here in 1510 that Martin Luther, having climbed part way on his knees, heard a voice that told him, "The just shall live by faith, not by pilgrimage, not by penance," and promptly stood up and walked back down to seek another path to salvation – Lutheranism.

At the top of the stairs is the **Sancta Sanctorum** (or Chapel of St. Lawrence), built in 1278 as the pope's private chapel and the only part of the old Lateran papal palace to survive the fire of 1308.

Open: daily 6:30–12:30 and 4–7:30. Entrance on the east side of Piazza di San Giovanni in Laterano.

▶▷▷ Scalinata della Trinità dei Monti

The Spanish Steps rise up in a glorious sweep from **Piazza di Spagna**, curve past balconies and terraces, and culminate in the twin towers of **Trinità dei Monti** (see page 182). They are at their best in May and June, decked with huge vases of azaleas in bloom. However, tawdry souvenirs proliferate, and you must watch your pockets; but it is still hard to resist at least a few minutes here.

Surprisingly, given their name, the steps were the inspiration of a Frenchman, Gueffier, the French ambassador in 1723, who also paid for them.

The Romans never had quite the same taste for drama as did the Greeks. Their cultural level was set at the opening of the Teatro di Pompey, which was inaugurated not by actors, but by the slaughter of 500 lions. Serious drama had to compete with the blood-letting of the Colosseum and soon gave way to shows of nudity, live sex, and transvestitism. In shows that required a death, condemned criminals were substituted for actors and killed on stage. Catullus's *Laureolus*, for example, relied on the vigorous torture and center-stage crucifixion of its villain.

▶▶▷ Teatro di Marcello

Via del Teatro di Marcello

An eye-catching half-circuit of arches – like a more modest Colosseum, but bizarrely overbuilt with medieval houses, the Teatro di Marcello is a major Roman landmark, best seen as you walk from **Piazza Venezia** toward the **ghetto** or **Piazza Bocca della Verità**. As a theater, rather than a gladiatorial arena, it has tended to attract less attention than has the Colosseum, but in its day it must have been almost equally impressive. Julius Caesar began the work, planning for a theater of 20,000 to upstage the (now-vanished) Teatro di Pompey, then nearing completion in the *Campus Martius* (the **Campo Marzio**). Augustus completed the project in 11 BC, dedicating it to his nephew and son-in-law, Marcellus, who was destined to be the emperor's successor had he not died before his time (in 23 BC).

By AD 235 the masses preferred the gore of the Colosseum to the culture of the theater, and the arena

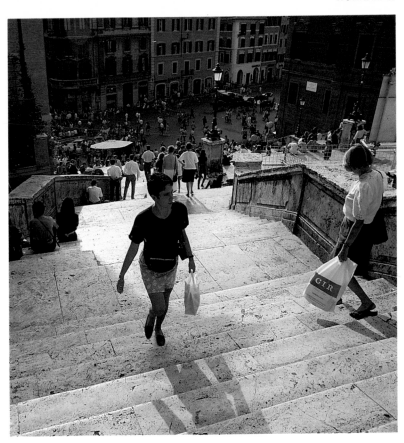

Scalinata della Trinità dei Monti

was officially abandoned. As early as the reign of Constantine (4th century), it was already being plundered of its stone to repair the nearby Tiber bridges. By the Middle Ages its strategic position on the river and near Rome's southern approaches attracted the attention of leading noble families. The Fabii, Orsini, Caetani Pierlioni, and Savelli all wove fortresses over and into its ruins, ironically the reason that anything remains at all. In 1932 Mussolini's archaeologists cleared away what by all accounts was a picturesque clutter of old shops to reveal the ancient foundations on view from the road today.

▶▷▷ Tempio della Fortuna Virilis

Piazza Bocca della Verità

Two of Rome's best-preserved temples stand not in the Roman Forum, but in the middle of **Piazza Bocca della Verità** overlooking the Tiber. In almost pristine condition and in a fine, open setting, they provide an all-but-perfect impression of how they must have looked 2,000 years ago. Like the Pantheon, they survived largely because of their subsequent consecration as Christian churches.

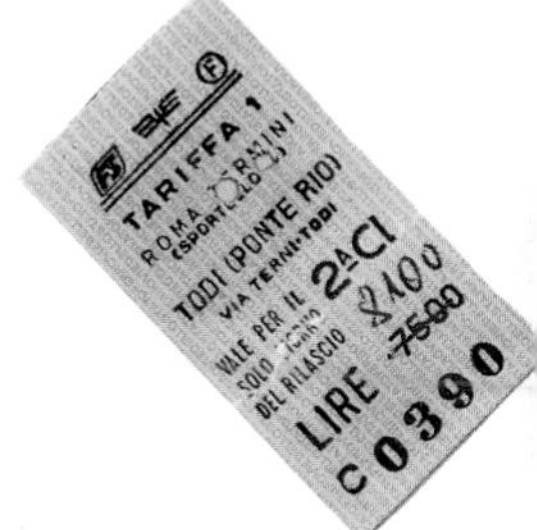

San Giorgio in Velabro lies a stone's throw from the temples and is one of this area's overlooked little churches. Velabro *(Velabrum)* was the marshy area under the Palatino where the she-wolf discovered the twins Romulus and Remus. Both the campanile and the portico date from the 12th century, and the church in places has fragments from 400 years earlier. Inside, the 13th-century altar has Cosmati marble decoration and frescoes from the same period. The church's elegant beauty makes it a favorite for Roman weddings.

Remarkably, however, Mussolini also takes much credit for their present appearance. In a typically overblown speech of 1925, he stated that "the millennial monuments of our history must loom gigantic in their necessary solitude." Within years dictatorial whim had deconsecrated the temples, stripped their medieval trappings, cleared the site, and restored their former glory. Sadly it also opened up the busy traffic junction near by.

The rectangular **Tempio di Fortuna Virilis** (the temple of "virile fortune"), dates from the 2nd century BC, its general form unmistakably aping that of its Greek antecedents. The vaunting dedication is misplaced, but no one knows the identity of the god it originally honored. Since this area was Rome's first port, it may have been Portunus, a god of harbors, a name that over the years became corrupted to Fortunus.

Also laboring under a misnomer is the circular **Tempio di Vesta**, among Rome's most evocative little ruins, which is named after its uncanny but unconnected resemblance to the Tempio di Vesta in the **Foro Romano.** It, too, dates from the 2nd century BC and was also the work of a Greek architect, but its initial dedication was to the conquering god, Hercules Victor. Here the temple is remarkably well preserved, with all but one of its 20 Corinthian columns still standing; the roof alone is a copy, the original, along with the entablature, having long vanished. It is among Rome's first marble buildings, built at a time when marble was hardly quarried at all in Rome, most – including that for the temple – being brought from Greece.

The 2nd-century BC Tempio di Vesta

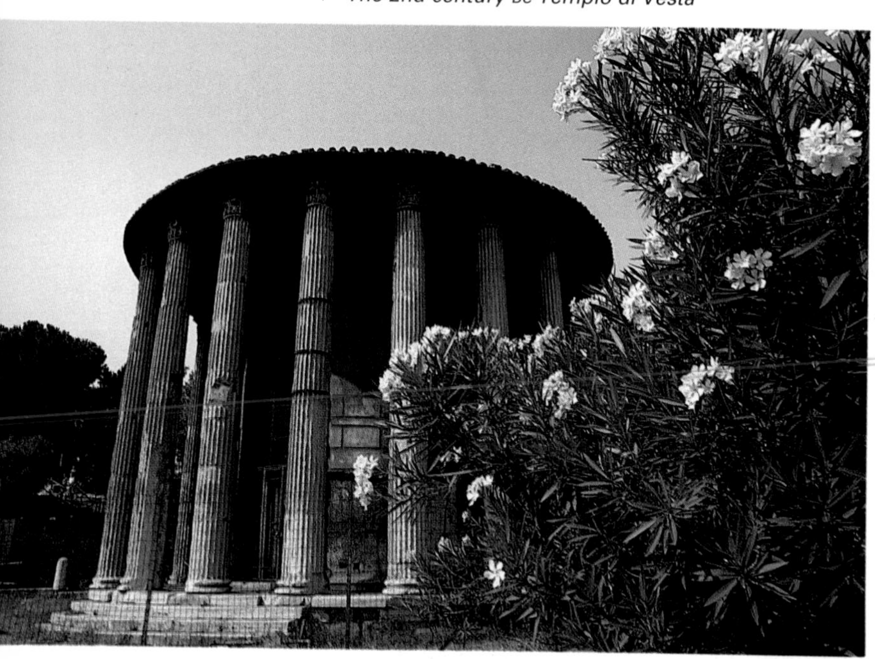

Films are one of Rome's few cultural contributions to the mainstream of Italian life and has often fixed the city in the popular imagination with films like *La Dolce Vita* and its late-1950s world of sports cars and sunglasses chic (though in truth the film was more downbeat than its popular image). Like much else with a Roman legacy, the film industry has had mixed fortunes – and has seen decidedly better days. . . .

Born in Turin, Italy's nascent film industry soon moved to Rome for its climate and ready-made locations. Its ascendancy, however, coincided with the rise of Fascism and was soon hijacked for palliative and propaganda purposes. In 1938 Mussolini opened Rome's Hollywood, Cinecittà – cinema city – with the words "cinema is our strongest weapon," having lavished a fortune to construct a modern studio. Patriotic war epics and escapist lightweight films flooded the country's cinemas in their hundreds. After Mussolini's overthrow a mob ransacked the studios, a symbol to ordinary people of how the regime had led them astray.

Rome's cinematic heyday began after the war, kicked off by Roberto Rossellini's *Roma Città Aperta*. This film was followed by other classics in the same genre like Vittorio de Sica's *Bicycle Thief*.

The boom years of the 1950s and 1960s saw an explosion of films. Federico Fellini and his crown prince, Marcello Mastroianni, ruled Cinecittà, whose reputation enabled it to grow fat on American epics like *Quo Vadis? Ben Hur, Cleopatra*, Sergio Leone's "spaghetti westerns," and a host of money-spinning potboilers and soft porn films. Pier Paolo Pasolini meanwhile chronicled the underside of Rome's 1960s expansion with films like *Accatone, Mamma Roma,* and *Una Vita Violenta.*

Rising costs and television ruined Cinecittà in the 1970s, leaving it a forlorn shadow of its former self. In the past few years, however, television has started to use the old studios and directors have returned to make major films like *Godfather III* and *The Last Emperor* – not quite reviving the studio's former glory, but at least staving off oblivion for the time being.

Some of Cinecittà's most popular outpourings in the Fascist era were the so-called *telefono bianco* films. Hundreds of these escapist, sentimental lollipops were made, which were named after the white telephone that appeared in the heroine's bedroom – symbols of the exotic Hollywood fairy tale for Italians who had never owned a telephone, much less a white one.

A scene from Roma Città Aperta, *a Rossellini classic*

Remains of Rome's most luxurious baths

The baths required huge amounts of firewood to feed the boilers that heated the saunas and steam rooms. Much was brought by tunnel to the underground furnaces from present-day Piazza Venezia. The tunnel still exists, and in the 1930s Mussolini liked to drive his Alfa down to emerge, car and all, with sudden, and no doubt ludicrous, effect on stage, as the opera festival was about to begin.

▶▷▷ **Terme di Caracalla**

Piazzale Numa Pompilio

These baths were not the largest in Rome – Diocletian's were bigger (see **Terme di Diocleziano,** page 179) – but they were by far the most luxurious. They were begun by Settimo Severo in AD 206 and all but completed by his son, Caracalla, 11 years later. In all, they could accommodate 2,000 bathers and many thousands more in the huge complex that developed close by. They continued to function until the aqueducts were cut by the Goths in the 6th century.

Although you can still gauge something of their scale from the remaining ruins, it is almost impossible to make any sense of how they were arranged or how they functioned. These days the vast arches of the central building have been restored and are most famous for summer opera performances – more often than not mind-bogglingly extravagant and often chaotic stagings of *Aida*.

Open: daily 9–one hour before dusk; Sunday and Monday 9–1. Admission charge.

Detail, Terme di Caracalla

Ancient Rome's *terme* reached huge sizes because baths for the Romans involved far more than a token immersion. They were primarily a meeting place, in the manner of a modern-day shopping mall, with gardens, libraries, sports facilities, stadiums, lecture rooms, shops, and even hairdressers. Hygiene certainly played a part, but even then water in the modern sense was conspicuous by its almost total absence. The experience was more akin to a turkish bath. You started in the *sudatoria,* a series of small saunas, and moved on to the *calidarium,* which was humid rather than hot, and where the business of cleaning took place (you were scraped rather than washed, by a slave if you could afford it). Next came the *tepidarium,* where you could start to cool off, and then the *frigidarium,* a cold-water douse and the complex's only bath in the accepted sense. If you were rich enough, there followed a rubdown with a scented towel, performed by a member of the opposite sex if you so desired. The baths were open to both sexes, but bathing took place at different times.

▶▶▶ Terme di Diocleziano–Museo Nazionale Romano

Piazza della Repubblica–Piazza dei Cinquecento

Terme di Diocleziano The remains of Diocletian's baths, once Rome's largest, have had mixed fortunes. Piazza della Repubblica was created around their curved *exadrae* to form one of the city's seedier squares; Michelangelo converted their main hall into the church of **Santa Maria degli Angeli**; and what little remained became the home of the **Museo Nazionale Romano** (see below), a repository for all antique works of art found in the city after 1889.

Piazza della Repubblica is a typical piece of 19th-century Rome, a stern, functional place whose former dignity is now decidedly tattered around the edges. Its proximity to the station tinges it with both human and architectural tawdriness, though attempts are being made to clean up the buildings and sweep away its clutter of dubious *pensione* and "adult" movie theaters. The **Fontana delle Naiadi** considerably enhances its center, and MacDonalds has opened a sleek outlet on one corner, always a sign – one way or another – of a location's changing fortunes.

Across the square, one flank is dominated by the huge brick outline of **Santa Maria degli Angeli** (see page's 180–181), an imposing facade that still manages at first glance to be totally uninviting. Nathaniel Hawthorne in his *Note-Books* of 1858 described this initial disappointment well: "The exterior of the church has no pretensions of beauty or majesty, or indeed, to architectural merit of any kind, or to any architecture whatever. . . . No one would imagine that there was a church under that enormous heap of ancient rubbish." What it does do, however, is to suggest powerfully the enormous scale of the ancient *terme*, one of the great legacies of Roman design and engineering.

Aphrodite, Museo Nazionale Romano

Fontana delle Naiadi,

Maximilian founded the **baths** in AD 298 to serve the northern parts of the city and to eclipse the **Terme di Caracalla**, which catered largely to the southern area around the Palatine and Aventine hills. By the time Diocletian finished them seven years later, they accommodated 3,000 bathers and were serviced by the gardens, libraries, sports facilities, and theaters common to all bath complexes. They survived for many centuries, a stolid monument to the building techniques, if not the aesthetic qualities, of late Imperial architecture. The aqueduct feeding the area was cut in AD 536, but as late as the 17th century, their rambling precincts were used as storehouses, monasteries, and papal prisons. It was only when the papal wreckers started to use them as quarries that large parts of the original structure disappeared.

Santa Maria degli Angeli Pius IV called on Michelangelo to convert the bath's central *frigidarium* into a church, a good choice for posterity's sake, for out of respect for the ancients, the aged sculptor did little to ruin their surviving fragments – more than could be said of his 18th-century successor, Vanvitelli, whose vigorous reconstruction and opaque Baroque decoration did much to obscure his predecessor's architectural integrity.

Watching the world go by...

Nonetheless, the church's vast, anonymous bowels at least preserve the scale of the old *terme,* though there is next to nothing in the way of art. The only work of note is a statue of St. Bruno (founder of the Carthusians, to whom the church belongs), which was so lifelike, said Clement XIV, that it refrained from talking only because of the monastic vow of silence.

Museo Nazionale Romano For artistic enlightenment you must visit the Museo Nazionale Romano (or Museo della Terme), housed in another part of the baths and among the greatest collections of antique sculpture and mosaics in the world. Restorations of its crumbling fabric have been going on for years and, as a result, many galleries are often closed. Work is also going on to cheer up its drab fittings, one of the reasons Elizabeth Bowen, in *A Time in Rome,* called this a museum to be "enjoyed on a sleepy, wet afternoon." To its credit, however, the museum's gardens do provide a setting for the sculptures similar to the one they would have had in antiquity. However, it is best to check with the churlish ticket-office staff as to which rooms are on view before you buy your ticket.

Via Nazionale was one of the roads built by Italy's new Piedmontese masters in 1870 to bring style and design to the city center. Today it is one of Rome's main shopping streets, particularly good for shoes and women's clothes. Midway down, off the street, is the *Questura,* the spot to report to if you have anything stolen or require police help – there is a special section to deal with visitors' problems.

First floor Even in the paltry fraction of the collection on show, it pays to be selective. The core of the first-floor galleries is the Ludovisi collection, bought by the state in 1906, whose centerpiece is the **Ludovisi Throne** (or altar), a Greek piece from the 5th century BC showing Aphrodite, goddess of love, being borne from the waves – one of the most beautiful pieces of sculpture in Rome. Other outstanding studies are to be found in the nine rooms of the **Great Cloister**, reputed to be Michelangelo's last architectural project before his death. Look for the *Venus of Cyrene*, possibly a copy of a Greek bronze; the *Girl of Anzio*, discovered after a storm washed away part of a villa in Anzio in 1878; an outstanding *Apollo*; and the famous Lancelotti *Discobolos,* or discus thrower, a copy of a Greek original, probably made in the 2nd century. Another masterpiece is the *Wounded Niobe*, portraying one of Niobe's children struggling to remove an arrow shot at her by Artemis.

Lancelotti's copy of a Greek Discobolos

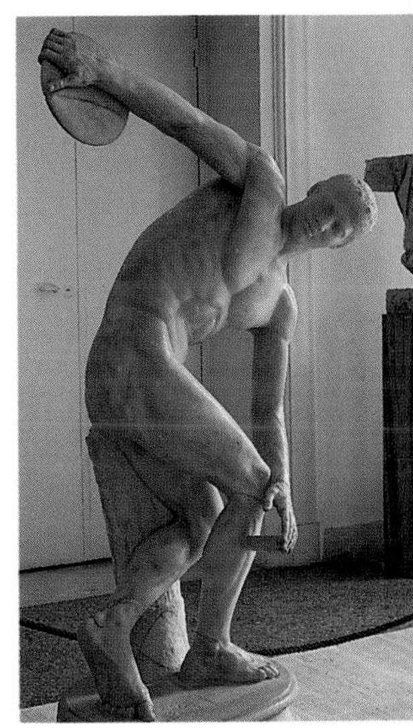

Second floor On the second floor the highlights are the stuccos and wall paintings found in an Augustan-era palace, discovered in the grounds of the **Villa Farnesina** (see pages 203–204). It was reputed to have been the house where Caesar installed Cleopatra as his mistress when she came to Rome. In a separate room are **frescoes** removed from the *Domus Flavia* on the **Palatino** (see pages 100–101) of green-shaded garden scenes, taken from an underground room reputedly built for Augustus – who was terrified of lightning – to shelter in during storms. Subsequent rooms, rarely open, contain further mosaics and paintings from the same sources.

Open: Tuesday to Saturday 9–2, Sunday 9–1. Admission charge. Entrance on the south side of the Terme complex facing Piazza dei Cinquecento.

▶▶▷ Trastevere

Every major city has a neighborhood like Trastevere, a distinct, tightly knit quarter whose seediness in time becomes the picturesque setting for restaurants, galleries and a flourishing nightlife. Here the area is on the left bank of the Tiber, bounded by the Gianicolo on one side and the Tiber on the other. The Roman dialect is at its most guttural here, and every July people turn out to celebrate the *Festa Noiantri* – "the festival of we others" – as a mark of independence.

In classical times Trastevere was close to the port, convenient for the goods shipped downstream from Ostia at the mouth of the Tiber. A mixed bag of sailors and immigrants, in particular orientals and Jews, settled here (the Jews were later forcibly settled in the **ghetto** across the river). It was also the city's artisan quarter and long maintained a tradition for small crafts workshops – a heritage that still survives, though barely, in a few of today's backstreets. By the 19th century it was the city's poorest, most violent area, and here, too, something of this legacy survives, with crime rampant in places and certain back alleys best avoided after dark.

Generally, however, its warren of streets and quiet squares are delightful to wander in during the day. In the evening you have a choice of numerous bars and restaurants, some overpriced and touristy, others still cheap and vibrant slices of old Trastevere.

▶▷▷ Trinità dei Monti

For most people Trinità dei Monti is the church on the skyline that completes the picturesque ensemble of **Piazza di Spagna** and the Spanish Steps. Its decorative effect was achieved by the facade's architect, Carlo Maderno, also responsible for the facade of St. Peter's. Charles VIII of France founded the church, but most of the work was funded by his successor, Louis XII. Napoleon later exploited the French connection by plundering most of the interior furnishings.

The Café di Marzio, Trastevere

Vatican City

■ There may be no border patrols and no duty-free shops, but the Vatican City is still an independent sovereign state. Although it welcomes you into Piazza San Pietro, San Pietro (St. Peter's), and its immense museums, the rest of the principality – all 43 hectares of it (the world's smallest state) – is a walled enclave out of bounds to all but a privileged few. . . .■

Some 200 people live and work in Vatican City (only 30 of them women), together with about 800 "foreigners" who commute in and out daily.

They are presided over by Europe's only absolute monarch, Pope John Paul II, and cocooned in a self-sufficient world with its own civil and judicial systems, shops, banks, currency, station, post office, garages – even its own helicopter pad; radio station; and newspaper, the *Osservatore Romano*. Its official language is still Latin.

The information office is in Piazza San Pietro to the right of the steps up to St. Peter's. *(Open* daily, Monday to Saturday, 9–noon, 2–5; tel: 698 4466).

As well as a wealth of pamphlets, books, stamps and souvenirs, the office provides tours of the **Vatican Gardens**. These tours should be reserved a day or two in advance. From November to February the tours run on Tuesday, Thursday and Saturday at 10 (Admission charge). Between March and October, the tours also include guided visits to either St. Peter's or the Sistine Chapel and run at 10 on Tuesday, Friday, and Saturday.

Alongside the office an orange sign marks the departure point for the special bus to the Vatican museums – its route takes a shortcut through the Vatican Gardens should you fail to make one of the tours.

Papal audiences If you wish to join the 7,000 onlookers every Wednesday, apply in writing for a free ticket to the Prefettura della Casa Pontifica, 00121 Città del Vaticano (tel: 69 82), or apply in person to the Prefettura's office – through the bronze doors in the right-hand colonnade of Piazza San Pietro. (*Open:* Monday and Tuesday, 9–1; Wednesday 9–11 – though last-minute tickets may not always be available.)

<< The Swiss Guard uniforms were designed by Michelangelo, in the medieval colors of the Medici popes (red, yellow, and blue). Recruited from Switzerland's four Catholic cantons, the guards must be between 19 and 25, at least 5'6" tall, and unmarried during their tours of duty. **>>**

The Vatican Gardens

Open: October to June, Monday to Saturday 9–2; Holy Week and July to September, Monday to Friday 9–5; Saturday 9–2. Closed on religious holidays and Sunday throughout the year except for the last Sunday of every month (winter 9–2, summer 9–5). Admission charge (but free on the last Sunday of each month). The last ticket is sold one hour before closing time. Note that the museums are open on Monday when Rome's state-run galleries are all closed.

▶▶▶ Vaticano and the Musei Vaticani

(Vatican City and the Vatican Museums)

Musei Vaticani

The 12-museum complex is the biggest in the world, with 1,400 rooms. To do them justice, however, requires more time than most people can spare, and even seeing their highlights needs a good two days.

You should probably brave the crowds and see its high spots – the **Stanze di Raffaello** and the **Cappella Sistina** and then visit the remaining galleries (7 km of walking in all) according to whether you are interested in Etruscan art, classical statuary, archaeology, Egyptian artifacts, Renaissance painting, books, maps, manuscripts, tapestries, furnishings, or any other of the museums' myriad treasures.

The four color-coded routes laid out to ease the crowds are difficult to follow in practice. Instead, use the map in conjunction with the itinerary below to find the highlights. Leave time for the museums at the end, overflow galleries for the Vatican's avalanche of artifacts that are often overlooked.

Museo Gregoriano Egizio

The eight superbly remodeled rooms of the Egyptian museum contain mummies, sarcophagi and monumental statues dating from 3000 to 100 BC. The more

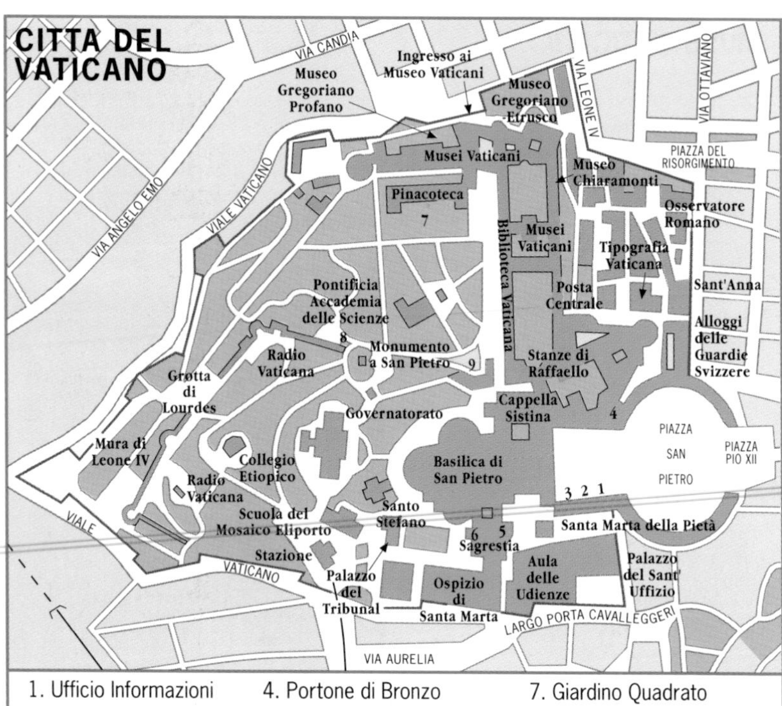

1. Ufficio Informazioni
2. Ufficio Postale
3. Arco delle Campane
4. Portone di Bronzo
5. Ufficio Scavi
6. Museo Storico Artistico
7. Giardino Quadrato
8. Fontana dell'Aquilone
9. Fontana del Sacramento

outstanding pieces include Room V's sandstone *Head of the Pharaoh Mentuhotep* (20th-century BC) and its looming figure of *Queen Tuia*, mother of Rameses II. Of most general interest are the exhibits of Room III – Roman imitations of earlier pieces, mainly taken from the Villa Adriana at Tivoli (see pages 214–215).

Museo Chiaramonti

This wing contains a vast but mixed offering of antique Greek and Roman busts, urns, portraits, and sarcophagi that are too indigestible for all but specialist tastes. Sheer quantity here is the museum's most impressive angle, and for quality you are better off in the Museo Pio-Clementino (see below).

Museo Pio-Clementino

Arranged by Popes Clement XIV (1769–74) and Pius VI (1775–99), this museum contains the cream of the Vatican's immense collection of classical sculpture. Note that the flow systems introduced to relieve congestion push you through its galleries backward, from Room XII to Room I.

Highlights include Room XII's 3rd-century BC *Sarcophagus of Lucius Cornelius Scipio* and Room X's *Apoxyomenos* (The Scraper), a 1st-century Roman copy showing an athlete scraping oil from his body after a wrestling match. Room VIII, the Cortile Ottagono,

To reach the Vatican museums take a 64 bus from Termini, Piazza Venezia or anywhere on Corso Vittorio Emanuele to Piazza San Pietro, where a special bus runs from the tourist office to the museums (daily every half-hour, 9–2 except Sunday and Wednesday). Or walk from Piazza San Pietro on Via di Porta Angelica and Viale Vaticano (15 minutes). Alternatively take an 81 bus from the Colosseum or Piazza Venezia to Piazza del Risorgimento, just five minutes' walk from the entrance. The nearest metro station is Ottaviano (15 minutes).

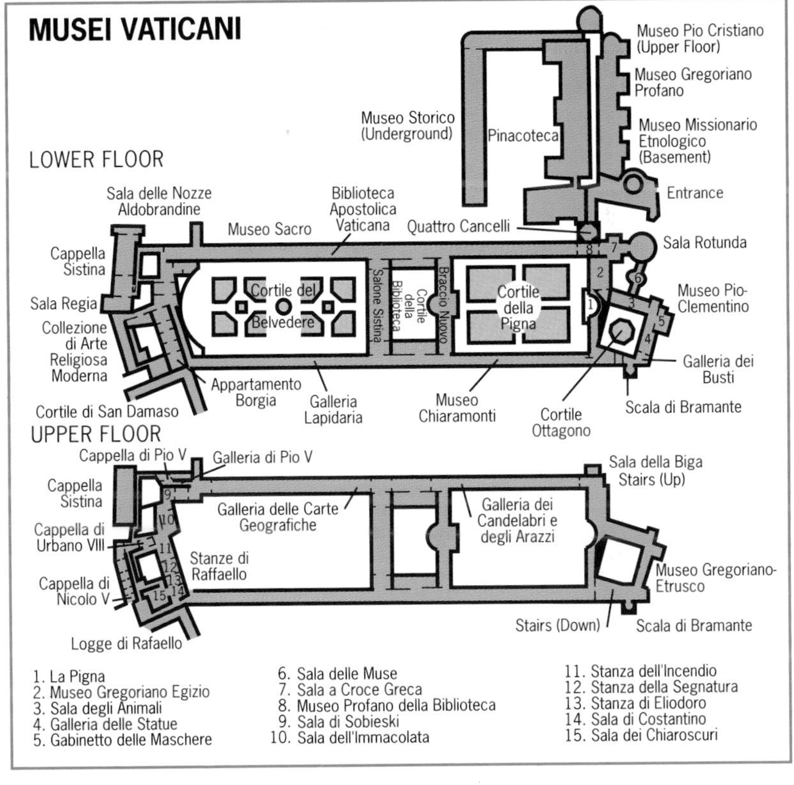

Feeding time in the Piazza San Pietro

houses the *Apollo Belvedere*, a magnificent Roman copy (AD 130) of a Greek bronze (c 330 BC). The young god, long an ideal of male beauty, is shown following an arrow he has just shot. In the 1970s a diver stumbled across the original, now housed in a museum in Reggio Calabria.

Next to the *Apollo* is one of the world's most famous statues, the **Laocoön.** Carved in 50 BC by sculptors from Rhodes, it shows the Trojan priest of Apollo, Laocoön, and his two sons fighting with sea serpents. The group was wrongly reassembled by Michelangelo (who was also responsible for restoring a part of it) until a vital missing link (an arm) was found in a Roman antiques shop in 1906.

The courtyard's other niches display another Roman copy, a version of Praxiteles's lovely *Hermes,* shown with a cloak thrown over his left shoulder, together with two bronze *Boxers* and *Perseus with the Head of Medusa* by Antonio Canova.

The room alongside is the Sala degli Animali, a sculptural zoo of antique pieces and creatures made for Pius VI in the 18th century. Room V, the Galleria delle Statue, boasts the *Apollo Sauroktonos*, a copy of a 4th-century BC original by Praxiteles, portraying Apollo about to kill a lizard, and the renowned **Candelabri Barberini,** a pair of 2nd-century lamps from the Villa Adriana at Tivoli (see pages 214–215).

Backtracking to Room VII, the Gabinetto delle Maschere, named after masks collected from the Villa Adriana, you find the *Cnidian Venus*, a copy of an infamous nude by Praxiteles, rejected for its eroticism by the islanders of Kos who commissioned it, but eagerly bought by the Cnidians for the centerpiece of a seafront temple. Room III, the Sala delle Muse, is best known for the Belvedere Torso, a 1st-century work found in Campo dei Fiori, which though badly mutilated was much admired by Michelangelo.

Pope Leo X lent a pair of rooms in the wing now occupied by the Pio-Clementino museum to Leonardo da Vinci, ostensibly for him to use in experiments to turn lead into gold. Instead Leonardo used it as a studio to study anatomy, but was eventually turfed out after rumors that he had entertained ladies of the night with the dubious aim of improving his gynecological draughtsmanship.

Room II, the Sala Rotonda, focuses attention on the floor, which is paved with ancient mosaics from Otricoli in Umbria. Room II concerns itself with a remarkable pair of monumental sarcophagi; one, the **Sarcophagus of St. Helena,** a tomb of red Egyptian porphyry, was made for Constantine but used for his mother (4th century). Notable for its almost total lack of Christian decoration, it contrasts with its neighbor, the **Sarcophagus of Constantia** (AD 350–360), brought from the church of Santa Costanza (see page 139), which is finished with paleo-Christian motifs of lambs, peacocks, and grape harvests.

Museo Gregoriano-Etrusco

This gallery's 18 rooms contain some of Italy's finest Etruscan artifacts (Rooms I—IX), mostly taken from the old cities of southern Etruria like Cerveteri (see page 220) and Tarquinia (see page 221). If the Etruscans appeal, be sure to visit the Museo Nazionale Etrusco at the **Villa Giulia** (see pages 204–205).

Room II presents finds from the 7th-century BC **Tomba di Regolini-Galassi**, unearthed at Cerveteri in 1836 and largely reconstructed in the museum. All the gold ornaments and tomb furniture found are on display, though none individually compares with the bronzes of Room III, and in particular with the 4th-century **Mars of Todi,** a figure grand in both scale and accomplishment. Room XII, the so-called room of the Greek originals, houses examples of the Greek art that heavily influenced Etruscan culture. Outstanding are the 5th-century BC **Head of Athene**; pieces of the Parthenon frieze; and the funeral *stele,* or headstone, showing a servant and a young athlete.

Also among the highlights is the black-figured amphora of *Achilles and Ajax playing Morra,* a delicately drawn game of dice dating from about 530 BC.

Vases quickly become wearisome, but try to hunt out *Hermes Stealing the Cattle of Apollo* in the same room and *Apollo Sitting on the Delphic Tripod* in Room XIV. The remaining four rooms contain fragments of Greek statues and reliefs.

Sala della Biga

Visit this room before returning to the entrance and the long haul down the galleries to the Sistine Chapel and the Raphael rooms. It houses a *biga,* or two-horsed chariot, reassembled from a 1st-century original in the 18th century. In its day it may have been a votive offering to the god Cere, but for years afterward it formed part of an episcopal throne in the church of San Marco (see page 148).

Galleria dei Candelabri

This is the first link in Bramante's 1,312-foot triple gallery, once open to the air, now windowed, and built to link disparate parts of the papal palace. Each section is decorated in different styles, in this case with ancient marble candelabra, which are ranked in pairs amid various pieces of classical sculpture and sarcophagus reliefs.

Byron made an impassioned plea on behalf of the Laocoön sculpture:
<< Or, turning to the Vatican, go see Laocoön's torture dignifying pain –
A father's love and Mortal's agony
With an immortal's patience bending: – Vain
The Struggle: vain, against the coiling strain
And gripe, and deepening of the dragon's grasp,
The old man's clench: the long envenomed chain
Rivets of the living links, – the enormous asp
Enforces pang on pang, and stifles gasp on gasp. >>

A Swiss Guard in Medici colors

Galleria degli Arazzi
The gallery's central portion is colored by glorious tapestries. Those on the left wall (describing the *Life of Christ*) are 16th-century Belgian works, but were woven to the design of Raphael's pupils – and are thus known as the "New School" to distinguish them from the "Old School" Raphael originals in the Pinacoteca (see pages 196–197). The hangings on the right wall are from a 17th-century Roman workshop and were commissioned by Cardinal Francesco Barberini to honor his uncle, Pope Urban VIII.

Galleria delle Carte Geografiche
When you have forgotten much else in the Vatican museums, there is a good chance you will remember the gorgeous corridor of **maps** in the last 328 feet of the gallery. Compiled in 1580, and beautifully painted in colorful 3-D, the 40 panels show all the papal lands of the time and most of Italy besides, as well as a plan of each region's principal city – that of Venice being particularly beautiful. Also included in the ceiling frescoes are episodes from the history of the area below them.

Galleria di Pio V
Little more than an annex at the end of the gallery, this serves to show off more Belgian tapestries, among them precious 15th-century weavings from Tournai with scenes of the *Baptism and Passion of Christ.*

Sala di Sobieski
An appendage to the previous room named after the huge painting showing John III Sobieski, king of Poland, helping to defeat the Ottomans at Vienna in 1683.

Sala della Concetzione
This is home to a forgettable display of books and manuscripts, presented to Pius IX after his proclamation on the dogma of the Immaculate Conception in 1854. Far more arresting is Michelangelo's model for the dome of St. Peter's.

Galleria delle Carte Geografiche

A fresco from the Stanze di Raffaello

Stanze di Raffaello
When Pope Julius II moved into the Vatican in 1503, he hesitated to use the Borgia apartments frequented by his ill-famed predecessor, Alexander VI. Instead he commissioned the 26-year-old Raphael to decorate a suite of four small rooms he could call his own. In doing so, he was to be responsible for one of the masterpieces of the High Renaissance and one of the highlights of any Vatican tour. Sadly, he was also expunging great work from the past, for the rooms previously had frescoes by Piero della Francesca; Andrea del Castagno; and the Umbrian, Benedetto Bonfigli.

Only two of the rooms were wholly covered in frescoes by Raphael – the others were finished on his death (1520) by pupils to the master's design.

Room I: Stanza dell'Incendio del Borgo (1514–17) The first room, but last to be painted, this was the papal dining room, by then being prepared for a new pope, Leo X. Leo chose to celebrate the virtues of his previous papal namesakes, eliciting from Raphael and his assistants a more Mannerist approach to the themes in hand. This approach meant grander gestures, more virulent color, and a greater emphasis on the human body as a vehicle of expression.

The four main frescoes depict the *Coronation of Charlemagne in St. Peter's* (by Leo III in 800); the *Oath and Self-Defense of Leo III;* the *Battle of Ostia*, at which Leo IV showed mercy to the defeated Saracens in 848; and the *Fire in the Borgo*, a fire that Leo IV – painted in the guise of Leo X – extinguished in 847 by making the sign of the Cross. The ceiling is by **Perugino**, Raphael's teacher, and is the only pre-1503 fresco to survive.

Having a drink in the Vatican Gardens

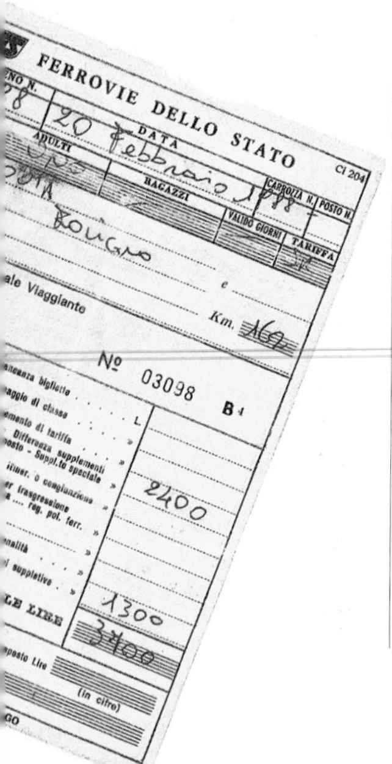

Room II: Stanza della Segnatura (1508–11) Its frescoes painted entirely by Raphael, this is the most renowned room, distilling not only the painter's genius, but the essence of High Renaissance artistic endeavor. The first room to be painted, it served as Julius's library and was the spot where papal bulls received their signature *(segnatura).* In their summation of Theology, Philosophy, Poetry and Justice, respectively, the four main paintings contain an intimidating wealth of classical and religious allusion.

The first fresco (Theology), on the long wall, is the *Dispute over the Holy Sacrament* (behind you as you enter) and celebrates the triumph of religious faith. It is divided into two areas – first the earthly domain (around the altar), with popes, bishops, cardinals and the faithful, some anonymous, others like Dante (with laurel crown) and Fra Angelico (far left) deliberately recognizable. Above, the second zone describes the heavenly sphere, featuring God the Father, Christ with the Virgin and John the Baptist, all flanked by ranks of saints, prophets, and characters from the Old and New Testaments (the latter with halos).

On the opposite wall is the *School of Athens* (Philosophy), one of the greatest Renaissance masterpieces. Set in an imaginary temple, it depicts the triumph of philosophy, the natural sciences and earthly intellectual vigor in general. To this end several of the figures are portraits appropriate to particular disciplines (though there is dispute as to precisely who is who). The majestic central figures are Plato and Aristotle (Natural and Moral Philosophy), the latter possibly a portrait of Leonardo da Vinci, with Socrates alongside. In the right foreground are Euclid, Archimedes, and Pythagoras (mathematics), with Bramante (architecture) and Xenophon (history), with Raphael (far right, behind the man in white) and Michelangelo on the stairs.

Above the window, brilliantly moulded to a difficult surface, is a painting of *Parnassus* (Poetry), which portrays Apollo surrounded by the Muses and a crowd of poets, including Homer, Dante (in profile), Virgil and Sappho on the left and Ovid and Boccaccio (both seated), with Horace and Pindar on the right.

In the lunette of the opposite window are allegorical evocations of *Prudence, Fortitude* and *Temperance,* reinforcing the glorification of canon and civil law suggested in the panels alongside (Justice). In the ceiling, Perugino's frescoes summarize the themes of the walls below, with personifications of Theology, Philosophy, Poetry and Justice.

Room III: Stanza d'Eliodoro (1512–14) The theme of the third room, a private antechamber, is of divine Providence's timely intervention to defend an endangered faith. It is worked through in four frescoes that show more drama, more power of expression and more color than the dignified panels of the Sala della Segnatura. The principal painting (on the main wall), the *Expulsion of Heliodorus from the Temple,* borrows from a tale in the Apocrypha in which Heliodorus is sent to steal the treasure of the Temple of Jerusalem and is seen off by angels and heavenly horsemen. Its more pointed allusion is to Julius II's battles to rid the papal states of foreign forces.

Leo X ascended to the papacy while Raphael was in the throes of completing the stanza, which is why the wall as you enter contains a scene ostensibly of *Leo I Repulsing Attila*. What it actually shows is Leo X advancing on a white donkey to take the allegorical glory for himself. When the piece was commissioned, Leo was a mere cardinal and was already portrayed as such in the painting (the fat figure in the red hat, left foreground). When Julius died, his place on the donkey was taken by Leo, this time in the guise of pope, and so the fresco has the dubious distinction of showing the same portly figure twice.

On the left-hand window wall is *The Deliverance of St. Peter from Prison*, a brilliantly realized trio of episodes set against a dark, nighttime background illuminated by an ethereal divine radiance. An angel is shown entering the prison, waking and unchaining Peter, and then leading him from the prison. The final panel describes the *Miracle of Bolsena,* at which a sceptical priest was convinced of transubstantiation when blood dripped from the Host onto the *corporale,* or altar cloth. The event precipitated the feast of *Corpus Domini* and the building of Orvieto's great Gothic cathedral.

Room IV: Sala di Costantino (1517–24) None of the four frescoes here on scenes from the life of Constantine is by Raphael, and only one panel, the *Victory of Constantine Over Maxentius,* is based on his drawings.

Swirling floor mosaic, Stanze di Raffaello

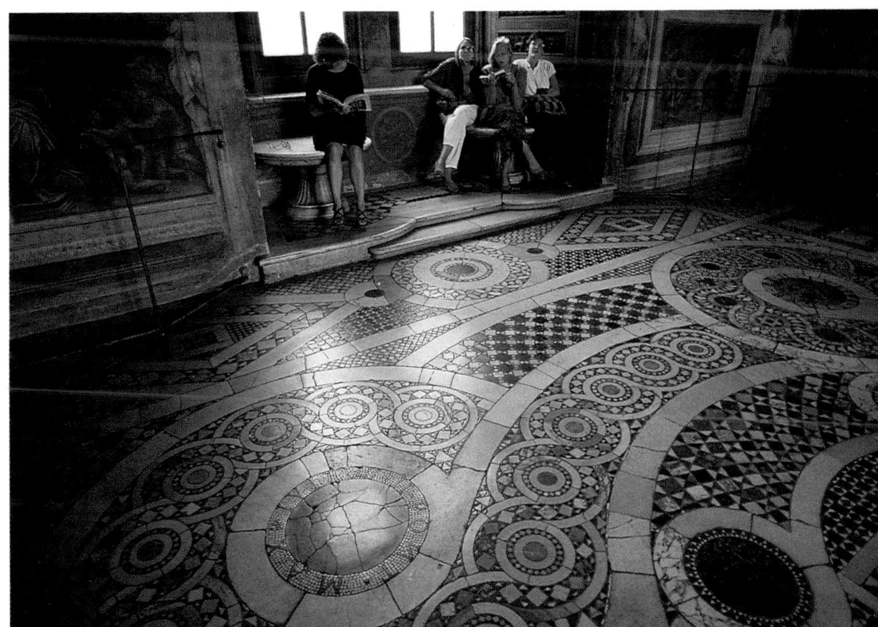

Cappella di Nicolo V
Close to the Raphael rooms, this small chapel is distinguished by the sublime frescoes of Fra Angelico showing scenes from the *Life of St. Stephen and St. Lawrence* (1447–51).

Appartamento Borgia
Named after the Borgia pope, Alexander VI, who created a palace within a palace (1492–1503) for his cronies and infamous family, this building contains a room, the Sala della Sibilla, that is thought to be where Cesare Borgia murdered his sister Lucrezia's husband, Alphonse of Aragon. Such dark doings failed to deter later popes, who used it largely as their home for the next 100 years. The popes perhaps liked the outstanding **frescoes** (1492–95) by Pinturicchio (and pupils), those in Room V (Sala dei Santi) being ranked among the artist's masterpieces. Otherwise the rooms are dim and draughty shadows of their former selves.

Biblioteca Apostolica Vaticana
Other libraries may have more books, but none has books as splendid as those in the Vatican library, by general consent the world's finest. The most precious books reside in an underground bunker, but those on display – in the lower corridor of Bramante's long gallery and in the Salone Sistina – still include handwritten manuscripts by Petrarch, Michelangelo, Luther, Thomas Aquinas, and others, as well as beautiful decorated manuscripts, biblical codices, printed scrolls, parchments, and ancient papyri.

Collezione di Arte Religiosa Moderna The Vatican does not shirk its responsibilities to modern art, devoting 55 rooms to over 800 works of recent religious art. Some are displayed close to the Raphael rooms. The roll call of artists represented includes Rodin, Dali, Modigliani, Matisse, Kandinsky, Vlaminck, Ernst, Munch, Shahn, and dozens more. Sadly, there is also much dross, a side to the collection described by *Time* magazine as "something between a pork barrel and junk pile."

The Biblioteca Apostolica Vaticana

A sibyl on the ceiling of the Cappella Sistina

Cappella Sistina
You may be prepared for the artistic sublimity of the Sistine Chapel, but you may not be ready for the enormous, unruly throng that jostles and pushes for a better view of its famous ceiling. Whatever else this hallowed spot may be, it is not a place for quiet and solitary contemplation.

Side walls Crowds or not, this is an essential sight. The huge barn of a chapel was built for Sixtus IV between 1475 and 1480. Decoration on the lower walls (1481–83) began as a joint effort of leading painters, including Perugino, Botticelli, Ghirlandaio and Rosselli, assisted by Pinturicchio, Piero di Cosimo, della Gatta and Luca Signorelli. In any other setting their efforts would be extravagantly admired, but in the shadow of Michelangelo's ceiling and *Last Judgment,* most people turn a blind eye. From the chapel's entrance, the panels on the left wall describe scenes from the life of Christ; those on the right wall describe episodes from the life of Moses. Counting from the entrance, the most celebrated of the left-hand frescoes are Ghirlandaio's *Calling of the Apostles* (3) and Perugino's *Christ Giving the Keys to St. Peter* (5); the most arresting on the far wall are Botticelli's *Moses Kills the Egyptian* (2), with the Burning Bush and other scenes, and the *Punishment of Korah, Dathan and Abiron.*

Ceiling For 20 years after the frescoes were painted on the walls, the ceiling remained a simple blue coffer decorated with silver and gold stars. In 1508, however, Michelangelo took up Julius II's commission to cover it with something more prepossessing. From the outset the artist was reluctant to take the commission, painting in Michelangelo's eyes being a less noble pursuit than sculpture. In truth he was more inclined to work on Julius's tomb, a project already under way but to the sculptor's eternal chagrin, one never to be completed (see **San Pietro in Vincoli**, page 170).

The *Last Judgment* aroused controversy even before it was unveiled, partly for its beardless Christ, but mainly for the almost unrelieved nudity of its 391 figures. Particularly outspoken was Biago di Cesena, the pope's secretary, whom Michelangelo painted in the right-hand corner of hell with ass's ears, and Pietro Aretino, a satirist and one of the artist's worst critics, who was painted as St. Bartholomew (below and to the right of Christ), clutching a human skin with the "flayed" portrait of Michelangelo.

In 1564, the year of Michelangelo's death, the zealous Pius V had leaves, loincloths, and breeches draped over the more "explicit" of the chapel's nudes. Some of these have been removed in the recent restoration, though in many cases the offending parts were found to have been permanently effaced by the painter concerned, the hapless Daniele da Volterra (a pupil of Michelangelo).

In 1985 the Vatican authorities decided to remove the centuries of accumulated grime and candle soot from the Sistine Chapel. The enterprise was paid for by the Nippon Television Network of Tokyo in return for full television and picture rights for years to come. The process has been racked by controversy, with some claiming the vibrant coloring revealed – or guessed at – is a travesty of Michelangelo's intentions, others that the patina of age is a legitimate part of a painting's effect. Lay and learned opinions are still divided, and doubtless will be for years to come.

Nevertheless he quickly knuckled down, firing his assistants early on and stubbornly refusing to bow to Julius's own hackneyed ideas for the ceiling. He unveiled his masterpiece after four years – most of them spent in appalling conditions, painting mainly while lying on his back and in extremes of hot and cold (it is said after his years lying down he could read letters only on his back).

The frescoes recounted the biblical stories of Genesis and the history of humanity before the coming of Christ. They proceed in nine basic panels, to be read chronologically in the order you walk through the chapel (but painted in the reverse order). First come the five central events in the book of Genesis: *The Separation of Light from Darkness*, the *Creation of the Heavenly Bodies*, the *Separation of Land and Sea*, the *Creation of Adam*, the *Creation of Eve*. Then come *The Fall and the Expulsion from Paradise*, the *Sacrifice of Noah*, the *Flood* and the *Drunkenness of Noah*. Around them are triangular embellishments containing Old Testament figures, fleshy sibyls, six-toed prophets, and 20 *ignudi*, or nude youths, around the main panels. The lunettes above the windows portray forerunners of Christ.

Familiarity with many of these scenes from the pictures hardly dulls their impact. The sheer scale of the undertaking – 3,050 square feet of painting, over 300 individual figures – and the staggering achievement in realizing it are patently obvious. Equally so are its monumental and heroic conception, the boldness of design, and the assurance with which it is executed. You can see Michelangelo's growing confidence made manifest by comparing the restrained early scenes (the *Drunkenness of Noah*) with the simpler, larger and more daringly colored panels, such as the *Creation of Adam*. Inescapable, too, is an appreciation of his virtuoso handling of the nude (notably in the innovative *ignudi*), a key tenet of Michelangelo's thinking being that there was little, intellectual or emotional, however complex, that could not be expressed by the human body alone.

Bold design: The Creation of Adam

The Last Judgment

■ The majestic fresco that fills the chapel's rear (altar wall) is greater, if anything, than the ceiling above. Here, however, Michelangelo was painting 20 years afterward and there is much that is darker, more somber, more disillusioned in his vision of the final judgment – notwithstanding the obvious *gravitas* demanded by a theme that was never going to be bright with optimism. Whereas earlier artists had threaded the theme with the prospect of redemption and the idea of an all-loving God, Michelangelo was uncompromising in his portrait of a pitiless God visiting a fearsome, harrowing vengeance on a cowering and degenerate humanity. . . .■

Doubtless this vehemence and disenchantment reflected, at least in part, the artist's own. He was an older man – 59 when approached by Paul III in 1534 – and again reluctant to take on the commission, being still bitterly involved with Julius's tomb (and under threat of legal action from the dead pope's relatives). Rome was also rife with the confusions of the Reformation and had been sacked seven years earlier, an event that had deeply disturbed Michelangelo and dashed forever the age's Renaissance optimism. Julius II had described the young artist as "frightening": in old age, with Rome darkened, and after seven years' work on the *Last Judgment*, he must have been nothing short of terrifying.

Given this, the central figure of Christ is remarkably measured as he summons the righteous to paradise (rising powerfully on the painting's left) and consigns the damned to hell (dragged irrevocably down on the right). Around him, however, figures of the saints swarm in a frenzy and the Virgin – though initially drawn in the artist's sketches imploring mercy – seems to shrink behind her Son, impotent to intervene. Even the saved show only resigned wonder, rather than unbridled joy, at their good fortune – nothing to the expressions of the dead rising from their graves (along the bottom of the fresco) or the unbridled horror of the famous damned soul hugging himself as he approaches his doom – the only figure in the whole work to gaze out at the onlooker.

> **<<** "The *Last Judgment* looks like the canvas of a fair, painted for a wrestling booth by an ignorant coal heaver." – Guy de Maupassant, *Chroniques*. **>>**

The majesty of Michelangelo

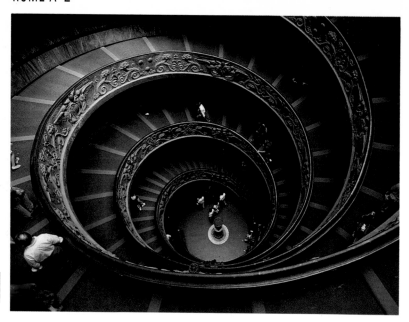

Spiraling staircase in the Vatican

Raphael's *Transfiguration* was long thought the most sublime painting in Rome. Giorgio Vasari, in *Lives of Artists,* wrote that the master had produced << figures and heads of such extraordinary beauty, so new, so varied, and at all points so admirable that, among the many works executed by his hand, this by the common consent of all artists, is declared to be the most worthily renowned, the most excellent, the most divine >>

Pinacoteca

The dire food and undrinkable coffee of the Vatican's bar do little to fortify you for Rome's finest art collection, displayed chronologically in the 18 rooms of the popes' personal picture gallery. Most of Italy's great names are here, usually painting in a religious light because the commissions were invariably drawn up to papal specifications. Here, as elsewhere, the volume of outstanding pictures is indigestible, so pick your way selectively around the main highlights.

Room I has mainly early Tuscan, Umbrian, Sienese and Byzantine pieces, all quickly eclipsed by Giotto's *Stefaneschi* triptych in **Room II**, once hung in the confessio of the old St. Peter's. **Room III** has Fra Angelico's marvelously colored *Scenes from the Life of St. Nicholas of Bari* and a triptych by the worldly monk, Fra Lippo Lippi. **Room IV** is given over to Melozzo da Forli, awarding pride of place to his famous *Sixtus IV and Platina* (the pope's librarian) and the enchanting *Angel Musicians*. **Rooms V and VI** parade a procession of 15th-century altarpieces, with a heavy complement from Carlo Crivelli, an artist from the Marche region. Alongside, **Room VII** is devoted to his neighboring Umbrians, exemplified by Perugino's *Madonna and Saints* and Pinturicchio's richly ornamented *Coronation of the Virgin*.

Room VIII is a showcase for Raphael and boasts his last painting, an exceptional *Transfiguration* (1517), chosen to hang above the artist as he lay in state. Also here are his *Madonna of Foligno* and a *Coronation of the Virgin*, together with 10 tapestries he designed for the

Sistine Chapel. **Room IX** has Rome's only Leonardo, an unfinished monochrome of St. Jerome that contrasts unfavorably with Giovanni Bellini's illustrious *Pietà* in the same room. **Room X** has a brace of outstanding altarpieces, each an early baroque statement of intent – Caravaggio's *Deposition,* Guido Reni's *Crucifixion of St. Peter,* Domenichino's *Last Communion of St. Jerome,* and Poussin's *Martyrdom of St. Erasmus.* The last rooms are a compendium of later works, with entries by Titian, Caravaggio, and Dutch and Flemish masters, rounded off with a dreary catalog of papal portraits.

Fra Angelico in the Vatican

Museo Gregoriano Profano

This is an immaculately presented collection of "profane," or pagan, art, recovered from papal property, that consists in the main of classical sculpture – reliefs, statues, funerary monuments, sarcophagi – divided between Roman originals and copies of earlier Greek models.

Museo Pio Cristiano

Split into displays of inscriptions and a general section of architecture, marbles, and mosaics tracing the growth of Christianity, this museum is best known for its hoard of Christian sarcophagi and the statue of the *Good Shepherd,* an unusual example of a freestanding early Christian sculpture.

Museo Missionario Etnologico

An anthropological display by any name, the Vatican basement is full to bursting with a vast collection of objects retrieved during the Church's missionary expeditions worldwide. All sorts of native artifacts, religious objects, and Polynesian and South American carvings stand alongside the most recent additions – the souvenirs of John Paul II's international journeys.

Museo Storico

The museums' last gasp is a historical record of the papal state, crammed with papal uniforms, weapons, carriages, flags and banners.

Congregating in the Piazza San Pietro

Little has changed in the 150 years since Charles Dickens << wandered out on the Appian Way, and then went on through miles of ruined tombs and broken walls, with here and there a desolate and uninhabited house.... Except where the distant Apennines bound into view... the whole wide prospect is one field of ruin. Broken aqueducts, left in the most picturesque and beautiful clusters of arches; broken temples; broken tombs. A desert of decay, somber and desolate beyond all expression; and with a history in every stone that strews the ground. >> – *Pictures from Italy*

▶▶▷ Via Appia Antica

For a spot so close to Rome's central maelstrom, the Via Appia Antica is a paradise of calm as close to open country as you will find in the city. Skip the long walk through the drudgery of its surrounding suburbs by taking the 118 bus from the Colosseum to its entrance at **Porta San Sebastiano** (see page 127). From here the old consular road is a joy to walk down – tree-lined, still partly paved with its Roman cobbles, and with views of ivy-clad ancient tombs and the open *campagna* unfolding as you leave the old city walls.

Tour buses run only to key sights near the beginning – the **catacombs of Domitilla**, **San Callisto,** and **San Sebastiano** (see pages 60–61) – and if you have the legs, everything thereafter is peace and tranquillity. Consider bringing a picnic or be prepared for expensive *al fresco* fare in the half-dozen or so *trattorie* on the way.

History The road was built in 312 BC by the censor Appius Claudius Caecus to link Rome with Capua and was extended to the port of Brindisi in 194 BC. This so-called queen of roads was thus Rome's main link to the south and, by implication, its main path to Imperial expansion in the eastern Mediterranean. As a consequence its main purpose was to move armies at speed – five legionnaires could march abreast across its four-meter width – but inevitably it also stimulated the growth of inns, farms, and colonies along the way. In 71 BC it was the famous spot where 6,000 of Spartacus's troops were crucified during a slaves' revolt. It became so busy that traffic jams caused Horace to observe, "For to quick travellers, it is a tedious road/But if you walk but slow,'tis pretty good," (quoted by Addison).

Present day Today it is as good as ever for the walker – but only beyond Porta San Sebastiano; before that it is an inferno. A few small churches cluster on the city side of the gate, plus the first of many tombs, the **Sepolcro degli Scipioni**, a family vault dating from 290 BC – one of the oldest on the road – but the Appia's first real point of interest is the church of **Domine Quo Vadis** (1637). This church supposedly marks the spot at which Peter, fleeing the persecution of Rome, met Christ coming the other way. *Domine, quo vadis*, he asked ("Lord, where are you going?") to which Christ replied, "I am going to Rome to be crucified a second time." At this, a shamed Peter turned back to Rome to confront his own martyrdom.

Shortly after, a right turn, the Via Ardeatina, leads to Via delle Sette Chiese and the catacombs of San Domitilla, San Callisto and San Sebastiano. Here, too, is the **Mausoleo di Fosse Ardeatine**, a somber memorial to 335 innocent Romans massacred by the Nazis in 1944 as a reprisal for a Resistance raid that killed 35 German soldiers. Back on the Via Appia, behind the Hosteria L'Archeologico is the **Torre di Romolo** (Tomb of Romulus, AD 309), an immense grave raised by Maxentius to honor his young son. Immediately beyond is the **Circo Massenzio** (AD 309), ancient Rome's last racetrack, but one that came too late to see much in

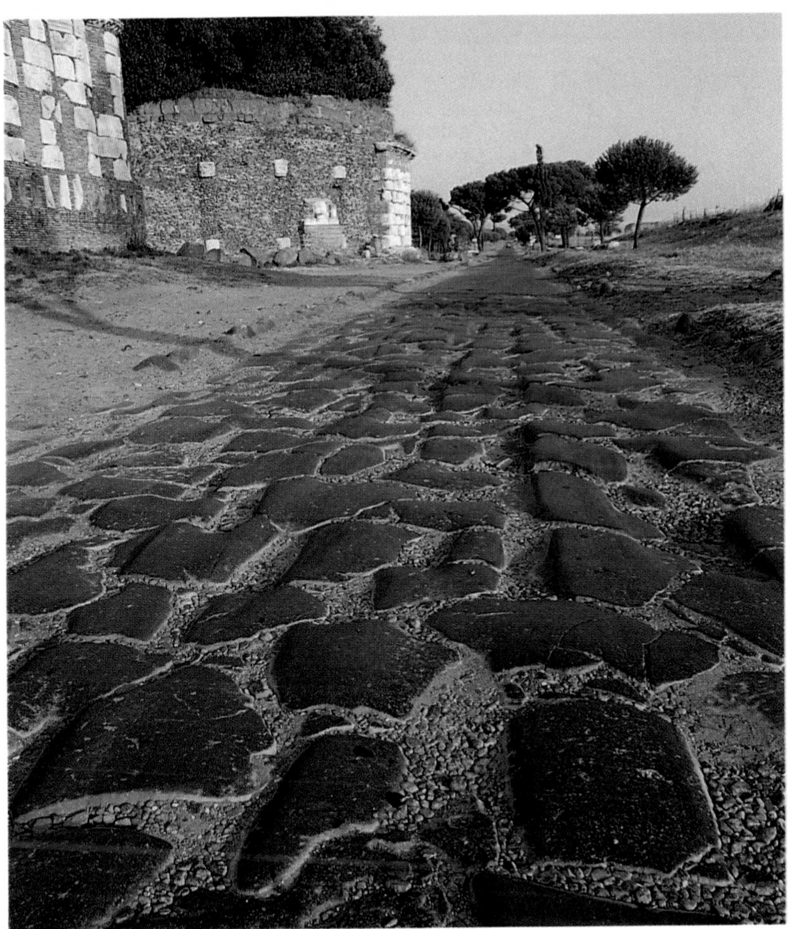

Peace on the road where armies once marched

the way of excitement. Today, in its quiet, grassy reaches, you could spend a peaceful siesta and hardly know that Rome existed. Its former central obelisk has long since found its way to the center of Piazza Navona (the tomb and circus are open Tuesday to Sunday, 9–1. Admission charge).

Farther down on the left, before the third mile marker (mile markers were placed every Roman mile on consular roads) is the Via Appia's most famous monument, the **Tomba di Cecilia Metella** (Tomb of Cecilia Metella). Not much is known of Cecilia, the daughter of Quintus Metellus Cretious and wife of Crassus, but her family must have loved her inordinately and been extremely wealthy to provide her with a tomb that, in scale, matches that of several emperors.

Beyond the tomb, the Via Appia is at its most beautiful, all open fields, crumbling tombs, cypresses, parasol pines and miles of sunny countryside, swathed in flowers in spring and sunk in silence year round.

<<Perchance she died in youth: it may be, bowed With woes far heavier than the ponderous tomb That weighs upon her gentle dust, a cloud Might gather o'er her beauty, and a gloom In her dark eye, prophetic of the doom Heaven gives her favorites – early death. . . . >> – Lines on Cecilia Metella, Byron, *Childe Harold's Pilgrimage*

Parks and Gardens

■ Rome has the lowest area of parks per head of population of any European capital and yet in few other cities are they so sorely needed. Recent studies show Rome to be the continent's noisiest city, with figures showing an average 20 decibels higher than recommended levels. . . .■

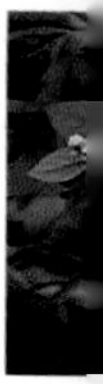

A glance at a map suggests escape lies only at Rome's fringes – in the green girdle of parks on the city's borders – the Villa Borghese or Villa Doria Pamphili. All else seems to be a thicket of roads or high-walled exclusion – no entry into the Vatican's extensive gardens, for example, or into the president's hideaway behind the Quirinale palace.

Even 30 years ago it was all very different. Then sheep grazed under the city walls and grass still grew between the cobbles of the Colosseum's side streets. Rome's cancerous growth, however, put paid to such luxuries, its suburbs sprouting and reaching out concrete tendrils into once virgin countryside. Gardens and small parks everywhere were choked with *case abusive* – houses built without a whisper of planning permission wherever bricks could be squeezed.

But a closer look at the map and a little exploration reveal a greener side to the city center. Even in the ruins of the **Roman Forum** you can find a grassy patch and few moments of quiet. Higher up, in the more secluded reaches of the **Palatino**, the **Orti Farnesini** are resplendent with wild flowers, delightful walkways, and spring-scented orange groves. Across the way, in the Colosseum's shadow, the **Colle Oppio** spreads a full-

The Villa d'Este at Tivoli

blown park over the slopes of the Esquiline hill. Locals treat it as their own, but most tourists hardly know it. Away from its café and children's playground, there is a private nook for all who want it.

The more you look, the more a pattern of sanity emerges from the apparent uniformity of concrete. South of the Colosseum a huge sanctuary of park, the **Villa Celimontana**, stretches away, all but untrodden by people who are unwilling to cross a busy road to reach it. Tucked off Trastevere's popular jungle of streets is the **Giardino Botanico**, the world's first botanical garden and one of its least visited. Behind its entrance off Via della Lungara is a lush assortment of palms and secluded corners. Up by the Spanish Steps you can escape the bedlam and the shoppers with a quick dash to the **Giardino di Pincio**, Rome's first public park. Even near St. Peter's you can take time off in the gardens around the **Castel Sant'Angelo**. If you know where to look, every popular part of the city has its sanctuary.

If you are prepared to walk a little, Rome has its bona fide parks. Nowhere is more beautiful than the **Villa Borghese**, like most of the city's parks created by popes or noble families around a summerhouse (or *villa*) as a complement to their urban *palazzo*. Farther afield, as beautiful, and if anything wilder, is the **Villa Doria Pamphili**, ranged over the slopes of the Gianicolo, whose lower reaches (the Passegiata del Gianicolo) offer a lovely, closer walk if the villa is too far.

There are any number of other outlying parks, all probably too far away to concern the casual visitor (Villa Torlonia, Villa Ada, Monte Mario). Edged on the inner suburbs, however, are other bucolic refuges that offer snatches of pastoral quiet. You may, for example, walk along the towpath of the **Tiber embankment** or sunbathe on the **Isola Tiberina** or – best of all – hike along the remarkably unspoilt **Via Appia Antica**. More eccentric diversions await in the vast open spaces of the **Campo Verano**, Rome's largest cemetery – peaceful in its own way.

Many excursions from Rome lead to some of the country's finest formal gardens (see pages 208–229). Chief among them are Hadrian's Villa at **Tivoli**, whose style was emulated in several of Rome's Renaissance gardens; the nearby **Villa d'Este**; Viterbo's **Villa Lante;** and Caprarola's **Villa Farnese**. Finally, for the *cognescenti*, there is **Ninfa**, well south of Rome near Norma, a stunningly beautiful and romantic garden woven into the ruins of a medieval village.

The perfect place to take a break

The main building in an Italian country estate was known as the casino; the Villa Borghese's is today the Galleria Borghese – which with an irony rare in Italian means literally the "little house." The later association with gambling is because this was the main recreational pastime of the villa's indolent occupants.

Sculpture in the park

▶▷▷ **Villa Borghese**

Rome's great families had a winter palazzo in the city and a summer villa in the country. This was the villa, or country estate, of the Borghese clan, laid out for Cardinal Scipione Borghese between 1613 and 1616. Today it is Rome's second largest, most easily accessible, not to say most beautiful park, but is first and foremost known for the two museums in its grounds – the **Galleria Borghese** (see pages 88–91) and the **Villa Giulia** (see pages 204–205).

It is the most bucolic respite from the city if all you want to do is walk or spend time dozing in some shady nook. The poet Rainer Maria Rilke wanted precisely these things: "To us," he recalled in a letter to a friend, "the Borghese Gardens were a familiar place of refuge . . . and we had need of a retreat, as the museums especially, with their many wretched statues, made us desolate." The walkways, woods, and lakes are big enough to find privacy, even on Sundays, when the world and his wife are here, more often than not intertwined in explicit amorous endeavor. There is also a boating lake (with a fake Greek temple), an aviary, numerous fountains, a well-known racetrack (the *Galoppatoio*), and a rather tawdry and depressing zoo. Allow a full day if you want to sample the gardens and see both museums.

Today's park bears little resemblance to Scipione's landscaped marvel, which, by all accounts, was the finest Italianate garden in the country. For a start it is much smaller – pruned by turn-of-the-century property speculation – and was remodeled in the 18th century to conform with the prevailing taste for the "natural look" of English parkland. In the 19th century it was still the favored promenade of high society, however, thanks to the Borghese's willingness to open their gates to the public. The habit was hard to shake, and a concerted campaign wrested the gardens from developers in 1902 when Umberto I bought them for the city.

(The Villa Borghese is the only Roman park officially shut at night: it is open daily 9 to dusk.)

▶▷▷ Villa Doria Pamphili

Gianicolo

Rome's largest park suffers in comparison with the **Villa Borghese** (see opposite), simply because it is far less accessible. The walk from Trastevere to the heights of the Gianicolo is a long haul, but you are repaid by vast open areas and mouth-watering views of Rome.

Accidents of circumstance have preserved much of its wilderness – it has always been too far from the center to attract development and was in private hands until as recently as the 1960s. The results are miles of walks, lakes, mature parasol pines, and enough room to call your own on most days except Sunday. If you do walk, you could take in the Gianicolo's viewpoints and **San Pietro in Montorio** en route; if not, the 44 bus from Piazza Venezia and the 75 from Termini both follow Viale Trastevere close to the park.

In nepotism's best traditions, the park was laid out for a nephew of Innocent X, the Pamphili pope, in 1650. ("Nephew" is *nipote* in Italian, hence "nepotism.")

▶▶▷ Villa Farnesina

Via della Lungara

Wonderful frescoes by Raphael, among others, and endless myths fill this elegant little Renaissance villa, one of the city's most delightful hideaways. It was built by Baldassare Peruzzi in 1511 for the wealthy Sienese banker, Agostino Chigi (but later sold to the Farnese), who like many before him made his fortune by winning the city's prize business – the papal account. The palace became the place to be seen for Rome's great and good, hosting feasts and parties in the most luxurious bad taste for popes, cardinals, high-price courtesans, diplomats, artists, philosophers, and the inevitable motley gaggle of lapdog sycophants.

Agostino Chigi was renowned for flinging the family silver into the Tiber after every course of his famous feasts, a bravura gesture of conspicuous consumption, though he failed to tell his admiring diners that a net strung below the water caught the loot for the next banquet.

The Farnesina was built, in part, over the site of Julius Caesar's country villa. Cleopatra stayed here in 44 BC, and it became her refuge after Caesar's assassination the same year. Caesar could not bring her to Rome because of his wife, Calpurnia, and instead bent the rules by lodging her outside the city limits. This hardly lessened the scandal, however, particularly because Cleopatra was accompanied by their illegitimate child, Caesarion.

Salone delle Prospettive, Villa Farnesina

Cupid and Psyche, *Villa Farnesina*

Today the villa is best known for the **Loggia of Cupid and Psyche**, once open to the garden, but now glazed to protect Raphael's 12 frescoes of *Cupid and Psyche*, painted in 1517 with Giulio Romano, Sodoma and Sebastiano del Piombo as assistants. Upstairs is Peruzzi's intriguing **Salone delle Prospettive**, an early example of *trompe l'oeil* views of Rome; a superlative collection of manuscripts and old prints; and Chigi's state bedroom, dominated by Sodoma's masterpiece, *Scenes from the Life of Alexander the Great.*

Open: Monday to Saturday 9–1.

▶▶▶ Villa Giulia–Museo Nazionale Etrusco

Viale delle Belle Arti

The Etruscans are not to everybody's taste, but if they are to yours, then the Villa Giulia's museum houses the most exhaustive collection of their art and artifacts in the world. Even if your interest is only partial, the villa itself is delightful, built in an effervescent Mannerist mode for Pope Julius III in the mid-16th century.

The Museum There is little in the way of order among the exhibits, which – since they run the gamut of an entire civilization – are necessarily varied. However, generally the main villa and its two wings are divided between the finds from northern Etruria – Veio, **Cerveteri** and **Tarquinia** (see pages 220–221) – and those from the south – Nemi and Praeneste (or **Palestrina**, see page 218). Virtually everything has been extricated from tombs, though little is morbid, for the Etruscans believed, like the Egyptian pharaohs, in leaving the dead with both their prized possessions and everything they would need – lavish or mundane – in the afterlife.

Quite the most famous piece in the museum is the ***Sarcofago dei Sposi*** – the Sarcophagus of a Married Couple, whose marital bliss is rendered in portraiture as sharp as anything carved in Rome or Greece. More expressive still are the couple's languid, reclining pose and elegant, wonderfully enigmatic smiles, reaching from beyond the grave to disarm today's onlooker (6th-century BC, from Cerveteri). Romans found it shocking that a man and a woman could be depicted on the same couch, a revealing insight into the differences between the two cultures. (Women had a high place in the Etruscan hierarchy; ancestry was traced through the female line and women were often buried alone in separate splendor.)

More to Roman taste would probably have been the museum's other great draw, the giant terracotta statues of **Apollo and Hercules**, surprisingly lively and realistic pieces from a temple at Veio (6th-century BC). Elsewhere, vases naturally play a large part, as they do in any Etruscan offering, either imported Greek originals or indigenous copies. Here, at least, you can have fun hunting for the occasionally lewd scenes, in particular the work of the so-called Pittore di Micali, the perpetrator of the famous winged phalluses in the Vatican's Museo Gregoriano-Etrusco (see page 187). Less riveting are the many musicians, dancers and sports scenes, suggesting a vigorous culture.

Pope Julius III was among the most avid of the Renaissance's collectors of classical sculpture. After his death, the statues in the Villa Giulia were removed to the Vatican in 160 separate boatloads.

Villa Giulia, home of the Museo Nazionale Etrusco

It is not all urns, however. Elsewhere there is hardly an earring, necklace, candle holder, plate, bronze or any of a huge number of miscellaneous objects, whose inventiveness and exquisite workmanship does not repay close study. Some of the best are in the treasury of the Castellani collection, locked away in a room off the central gallery of vases (Room XXII), but open on request if you leave a passport or ID with the museum guard. The quality of the gold pieces is breathtaking and, in many cases, has hardly ever been equaled since, similarly the ivory work, seen to best effect in the rooms devoted to the Praeneste excavations.

The Villa Many people who come for the Etruscans go away as pleasantly surprised by the Villa Giulia itself, one of the 16th century's most pleasing country houses. Vast in its day, with 36,000 trees in the park alone, it was built by the decidedly hedonistic Julius III to entertain boatloads of his carousing friends who were brought up-river from the Vatican. A large fortune was spent fitting it out to meet its frivolous function, part of it paid to Michelangelo as a consultant on how a small house was to be converted into a veritable pleasure dome. Also involved were Vasari, best known for his *Lives of the Artists*, but an artist and architect in his own right – though less talented than he liked to imagine. Most of the hard work was done by Ammannati and Vignola, the latter one of the leading lights of his day (see **Caprarola,** page 223), and it was he who dreamt up the wonderful *nymphaeum* – a sunken water garden to provide summer cool, fed by the springs of the Acqua Vergine. After all this, the pope never lived or slept here – beyond an occasional afternoon siesta – and had never intended to, the whole grand design having been created, like many similar villas, as a spot for a single day or evening's rest and relaxation.

Open: Tuesday to Saturday 9–2; Wednesday 9–7, Sunday 9–1.

<< . . . death, to the Etruscans, was a pleasant continuance of life, with jewels and wine and flutes playing for the dance. It was neither an ecstasy of bliss, a heaven, nor a purgatory of torment. It was just a natural continuance of the fullness of life. Everything was in terms of life. . . . The things they did, in their early centuries, are as natural and easy as breathing. . . .
>> D. H. Lawrence, *Etruscan Places*

The Etruscans

■ **"The Etruscans, as everyone knows, were the people who occupied the middle of Italy in early Roman days and whom the Romans, in their usual neighborly fashion, wiped out entirely to make room for Rome with a very big 'R'. . . . this seems to be the inevitable result of expansion with a big 'E,' which is the sole *raison d'être* of people like the Romans." – D. H. Lawrence, *Etruscan Palaces. . . .***■

The Etruscan enigma Etruscans are always mysterious in historical accounts, partly because the Romans did so much to obscure their predecessors' existence. Most of their cities were built of wood, and so they left only the contents of their tombs as a memorial, something that has long given them a reputation as a necrophilic and gloomy race. The truth was different, and much of Roman culture came from its lively and imaginative forebears.

Early settlements The Etruscans created a loose federation of cities in roughly the area between present-day Rome and Florence (known as Etruria), from which the modern name Tuscany obviously derives. They ruled all but supreme from about the 8th to the 4th centuries BC and were probably the Roman Forum's first inhabitants, draining its first swamp and providing some of the earliest kings of Rome.

Where the Etruscans came from is one of history's great mysteries, but they were probably a mixture of indigenous tribes and seafarers whose ethnic links were with Asia Minor and whose trading ties were with Greece.

A 5th-century Apollo *from the Villa Giulia*

The Etruscan legacy Much of their history and political system has yet to be understood, not to mention their language, which continues to baffle scholars – though many of its words passed into Latin and thus into most European languages. From the Etruscans, too, came the Romans' alphabet (alongside Greek elements), many of their gods and divinities, their rituals and divinations, and even their circuses and gladiatorial games. By about the 3rd century BC, these legacies – together with Etruria's cities and peoples – had been all but assimilated by the embryonic Roman state, and a separate Etruscan identity was effectively erased.

Today's evidence The Etruscans' cultural and artistic achievements, however, were high reaching and sophisticated and are on show in the excellent Museo Nazionale Etrusco (see page 204) – a collection that is vast, but manageably so, and that marshals its prize exhibits in the Villa Giulia's beautiful frescoes and decorated salons.

▶▶▷ Villa dei Medici

Viale Trinità dei Monti

A famous name, but a famous Florentine name, rather than a Roman one, which makes it apt that this palace and its gardens are closed to Romans and foreigners alike. The villa's severe, fortresslike facade, however, is too plainly on view to the left of **Trinità dei Monti** at the top of the Spanish Steps. It was built in 1540 but only bought by the Medici grand dukes in 1580, well after their golden age, though they had the grace to offer Galileo protection here when he was under house arrest by the Inquisition (1630-33). Take a special look at the round fountain outside, topped with a cannonball shot from Castel Sant'Angelo by Queen Christina of Sweden – a novel way of telling her hosts she would be late for dinner.

Open: in theory the gardens are open on Wednesday morning, 9–11 only; in practice they rarely are – check with the lodge.

Henry James called the villa's gardens << perhaps the most enchanting place in Rome," adding that they were possessed of "an incredible, impossible charm >>.

Looking up the Spanish Steps to the Villa dei Medici

The beautiful hill town of Subiaco

Rome in context Rome is the capital both of Italy and of the province of Lazio, which is bordered by the provinces of Tuscany and Umbria to the north, the Abruzzo to the east, and Campania to the south. The city's immediate hinterland is known as the *campagna,* or the countryside, while the environment beyond is bounded by the Tyrrhenian Sea to the west; the Tolfa hills and Tiber valley to the north; the foothills of the Abruzzo mountains to the east; the Albano hills to the southeast; and the broad, reclaimed flats of the Pontine marshes to the south. Until about 40 years ago, this area was little changed since classical times, but now much has surrendered to Rome's relentless suburban advance. Pockets of pristine countryside survive today, however, even close to the city, and as you shudder at the mess of ring roads; factories; and desolate, unplanned housing developments, you can also enjoy green pastures, shepherds with their flocks, ancient tufa caves, and scenes as bucolic as in the days of Cicero.

Going farther afield At first glance, there may seem few reasons to leave Rome, a city that, more than most, needs several visits to do it justice. However, for all their occasional squalor, the city's environs abound with interest, and they can make a welcome change from what may become a wearying round of churches and museums, not to mention the crowds, clamor, and oppressive heat of midsummer.

All the excursions described can be managed as day trips using public transportation. In many cases this means **bus** services operated by ACOTRAL, whose distinctive blue buses depart from different points around the city. Those for northern destinations usually leave from Via Lepanto, on the Metropolitana line A, and from Via Gaeta, just off Stazione Termini's Piazza dei Cinquecento, for points to the south. The bustle of Rome's bus terminals can appear off-putting, but once you have found the right bay, bus travel is straightforward, and fellow passengers, if not the habitually miserable drivers, are always happy to help.

Trains are more straightforward, with regular departures from Termini, and are an easy way of reaching Ostia Antica, Frascati and Tivoli, three of the most notable excursions, as well as Orvieto, Tarquinia and Cerveteri.

Cars are not strictly essential, but obviously offer flexibility and the chance to combine two or more sights, such as Subiaco and Palestrina or Viterbo and Bomarzo.

If you prefer, there are numerous organized **coach** tours to all major sites (see the individual entries and **Travel Facts** for details.

Whatever your priorities, **Ostia Antica**, Rome's ancient seaport, and **Tivoli**, site of Hadrian's Villa and the gardens of the Villa d'Este, are the two excursions that should not be missed. Thereafter, **Frascati**, the best known of the wine-producing towns in the Albano hills, is one of the most – though not deservedly – popular trips from the city. More generally, a hankering for Etruscan graves and museums can be satisfied by trips to **Tarquinia**, **Cerveteri** and the great pre-Roman temple at **Palestrina.** Garden and villa enthusiasts are best served by the **Villa d'Este** at Tivoli, **Caprarola**, **Bomarzo** and the **Villa Lante** near Viterbo. Lovers of walking should head to the **Parco Nazionale del Circeo**, **Lago di Vico**, **Subiaco** and **Bracciano**. **Viterbo** and **Orvieto**, with its glorious cathedral, are fine medieval towns, and an antidote to the Baroque mood of Rome. For more Roman ruins, Ostia Antica and Hadrian's Villa at Tivoli are the equal of anything in the city.

Down to the sea Finally, Rome is close to the sea, and many beaches can be reached as easily as any of the city's other peripheral attractions. The best spots for swimming are probably Chiarone, on Lazio's northern border with Tuscany, and the resort towns of Terracina and Sperlonga, well to the south of the city. Better-known spots, like Anzio and Rome's traditional resort, Lido di Ostia, are best avoided.

Most towns and sights have tourist offices that will provide fuller details of what each has to offer, as well as hotel information should you wish to stay overnight in any spot. You can pick up information in Rome before you set out by visiting Lazio's provincial tourist offices near Piazza della Repubblica, five minutes from Termini: Via F. Raimondi Garibaldi 7 (tel: 06/ 54 571 or 513 733).

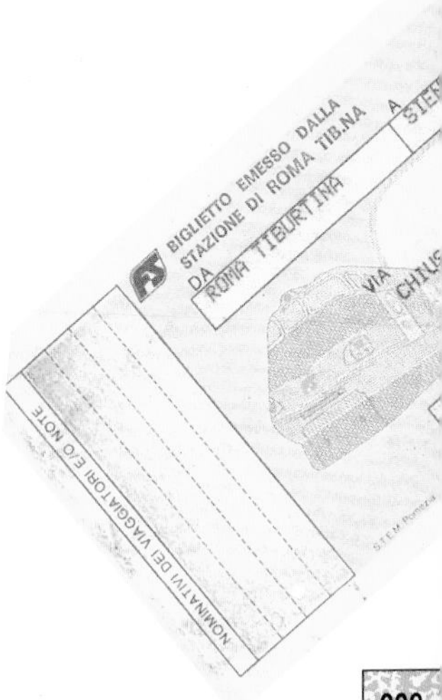

St. Benedict's cave, at Subiaco

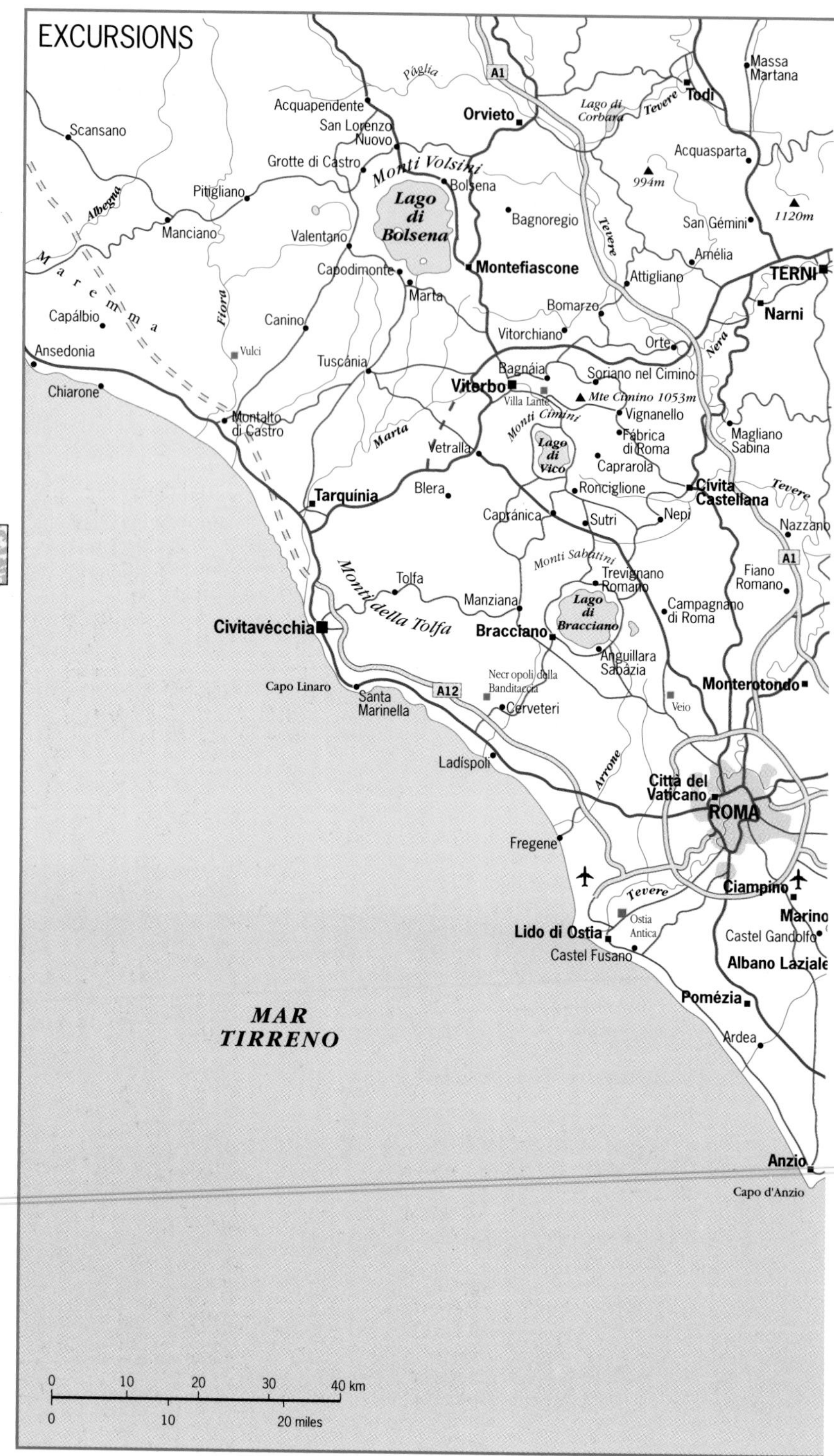
EXCURSIONS
Páglia
A1
Massa Martana
Acquapendente
Orvieto
Lago di Corbara
Tevere
Todi
San Lorenzo Nuovo
Scansano
Grotte di Castro
Monti Volsini
Acquasparta
Bolsena
994m
Pitigliano
Lago di Bolsena
Bagnoregio
1120m
Albegna
Manciano
Valentano
San Gémini
Amélia
Capodimonte
Montefiascone
Attigliano
TERNI
Maremma
Marta
Bomarzo
Narni
Capálbio
Fiora
Canino
Vitorchiano
Orte
Ansedonia
Vulci
Tuscánia
Nera
Bagnáia
Soriano nel Cimino
Viterbo
Chiarone
Villa Lante
Mte Cimino 1053m
Monti Cimini
Vignanello
Montalto di Castro
Marta
Fábrica di Roma
Magliano Sabina
Vetralla
Lago di Vico
Caprarola
Ronciglione
Civita Castellana
Tevere
Blera
Tarquínia
Capránica
Sutri
Nepi
Nazzano
Monti Sabatini
A1
Monti della Tolfa
Tolfa
Trevignano Romano
Fiano Romano
Manziana
Lago di Bracciano
Campagnano di Roma
Civitavécchia
Bracciano
Anguillara Sabázia
Monterotondo
Capo Linaro
Necropoli della Banditaccia
A12
Santa Marinella
Cerveteri
Veio
Ladíspoli
Arrone
Città del Vaticano
ROMA
Fregene
Tevere
Ciampino
Ostia Antica
Marino
Lido di Ostia
Castel Gandolfo
Castel Fusano
Albano Laziale
Pomézia
MAR TIRRENO
Ardea
Anzio
Capo d'Anzio
0
10
20
30
40 km
0
10
20 miles

Cerreto di Spoleto
Nórcia
Mte Vettore 2476m
Arquata del Tronto
Salinello
Civitella del Tronto
Giulianova
Acquasanta Terme
Spoleto
Nera
Cáscia
Corno
Monti della Laga
Teramo
Tordino
A14
Amatrice
Mte Gorzano 2458m
Montório al Vomano
Vomano
Arrone
Leonessa
Cellino Attanásio
Lago di Campotosto
Posta
Montereale
Isola del Gran Sasso d'Italia
Velino
Monti Reatini
Póggio Bustone
Stroncone
Mte Terminillo 2216m
Gran Sasso d'Italia 2914m
Penne
Gréccio
Antrodoco
Pizzoli
2570m
A24
Rieti
Cittaducale
L'Aquila
Barisciano
Appennino Abruzzese
1288m
Monti Sabini
Salto
Turano
Póggio Mirteto
Piano di Campo Felice
Capestrano
Scafa
Lago del Salto
Montópoli di Sabina
Monteleone Sabino
Aterno
Pescara
Rocca di Mezzo
Fara in Sabina
Lago di Turano
Borgorose
Pópoli
Mte. Velino 2487m
Vittorito
Montelibretti
Magliano de' Marsi
Celano
Prátola Peligna
Carsóli
Cérchio
Palombara Sabina
Tagliacozzo
A24
Sulmona
Monticelio
Vicovaro
A25
Avezzano
Pescina
Piana del Fucino
Guidonia
Pettorano sul Gizio
Tívoli
Monti Simbruini
Gióia dei Marsi
Capistrello
Canterano
Subiaco
Aniene
Villa Adriana
Scanno
Monti Tiburtini
Mte Víglio 2156m
Parco Nazionale d'Abruzzo
A1
Zagarola
Liri
Palestrina
Monti Ernici
Balsorano
Pescasséroli
Frascati
Tusculum
Fiuggi
Opi
Valmontone
Grottaferrata
Monti della Meta 2247m
Rocca di Papa
Anagni
Alatri
Sora
Lago Albano
Colleferro
Ferentino
Véroli
Alvito
L. di Nemi
Segni
Sacco
A1
San Donato Val di Comino
Genzano di Roma
Velletri
Isola di Liri
Carpineto Romano
Frosinone
Monte San Giovanni Campano
Cori
Melfa
Atina
Aprília
Cisterna di Latina
Monti Lepini
Ninfa
Norma
Ceccano
Ceprano
Sermoneta
Valvisciolo
Cassino
Sezze
Castro dei Volsci
Nettuno
Priverno
Liri
Latina
Amaseno
Pontecorvo
Pontinia
Fossanova
Lénola
A1
Sonnino
Parco Nazionale del Circeo
Monti Ausoni
Fondi
Monti Aurunci
Ausónia
L. di Fondi
Sabáudia
Mte Petrella 1533m
Terracina
Minturno
Garigliano
Sperlonga
Fórmia
San Felice Circeo
Mte Circeo 541m
Golfo di Gaeta
Golfo di Terracina
Gaeta
Mondragone

Getting there: By train, every 30 minutes from Stazione Ostiense at Piazza Porta di San Paolo (take Metro A to Piramide); journey time is 30 minutes and the ruins are 5 minutes' walk from Ostia Antica station. By metro, trains roughly hourly from Termini (25 minutes). By bus, ACOTRAL from Via Giolitti. By car, Via del Mare (the SS8) from Porta San Paolo (23 km; 35 minutes in good traffic).

Ostia Antica

Rome's ancient seaport, Ostia Antica, is Italy's best-preserved Roman town after Pompeii and Herculaneum, and the most interesting day excursion from the city (Via dei Romagnoli, tel: 06 565 0022).

History According to legend, it was here that Aeneas, forefather of the Latins, landed. In the 7th century BC, the fourth king of Rome, Ancus Martius, established a settlement at the mouth (*ostium*) of the Tiber. In about 335 BC a small fishing and trading community grew up on the site and became Rome's outlet to the sea, developing as the city grew, trading commodities from all over the Empire. With the outbreak of the First Punic War, the port also became an important naval base, and by the 2nd century boasted a population approaching 500,000.

By the 1st century, however, it was clear that the port was unable to handle the sheer volume of trade generated by the Empire, and Claudius began work on a second port, the *Portus Romae*. Gradually the new harbor began to attract more and more of Rome's shipping. The other great problem was silt, and though Trajan dredged new docks (now the site of Fiumicino airport), there was little that could be done to stop the silting-up process.

A more general decline began as Rome's own importance as a great power began to diminish. The port increasingly became a residential center, falling into virtual abandon in the 5th century with the fall of Rome. Pirate attacks and malaria sustained the exodus through the Middle Ages, by which time the sea had retreated several miles, and in 1575 a flood altered the course of the Tiber for good. Excavations began at Ostia in the 19th century and have so far revealed about half the town (some 66 hectares). The ruins themselves still offer an almost unmatched insight into daily Roman life of 2,000 years ago. The site itself is also a pleasure: covered in wild flowers, shaded by elegant parasol pines, and draped in swathes of clinging ivy. Be prepared for lots of walking and try to visit in the late afternoon to avoid the heat of the day.

Granary at Ostia Antica

The forum precincts, Ostia Antica

Looking around Any tour of the ruins starts at the Porta Romana, gateway to the Decumanus Maximus, the still-cobbled main street that bisects the town. Leading from it are innumerable side streets and the full fabric of a major Roman colony: shops and workshops, Mithraic shrines, barracks, port facilities, tombs, warehouses (*horreae*), baths, inns and domestic houses.

There are certain ruins you should make a special point of seeing. **The Terme di Nettuno** (Baths of Neptune), the first main building on the right after the Porta Romana, was built by Hadrian and preserves a series of elaborate mosaics depicting Neptune and Amphitrite. Alongside is the restored **amphitheater**, which was built by Augustus to accommodate 4,000 people, from where you can look down onto the **Piazzale delle Corporazioni.** This little square contained 61 offices of the town's shipping agents, and in front of several buildings are beautiful, black-and-white mosaics denoting the trade carried out by each – grain merchants, ships' fitters, ivory importers, rope makers and so forth. All over the town are the warehouses, some with rows of annexed shops, owned by the traders. Close by is the main forum, site of the **Capitoleum**, a temple dedicated to Jupiter, Juno and Minerva.

Of the many *domus*-type houses, the most impressive is the **Casa di Diana**, but the Casa dei Dioscuri and Casa delle Muse are also well worth a visit. Of special interest are Ostia's *insulae*, original four- or five-story apartment blocks, each well built in brick and supplied with running water and sophisticated heating and sanitation arrangements. Don't miss the captivating *thermopolium*, a Roman café, complete with marble counter, shelves to display snacks, and even wall paintings to illustrate parts of the menu. A small museum, the **Museo Ostiense**, (*open:* 9–one hour before sunset) contains statuary and other small items uncovered by the excavations.

Open: summer: Tuesday to Sunday 9–6:30; winter: Tuesday to Saturday 9–4:30. Admission charge.

Tourvisa runs all-day excursions by boat down the Tiber to Ostia Antica in the summer. A tour of the site is included and the return to Rome is by coach (tel: 06/ 495 0284).

The Lido di Ostia is Rome's traditional seaside resort, but these days it suffers from overcrowding in the summer, filthy sand and heavily polluted water. Traffic jams are severe on the approach roads from the city, the Via del Mare and Via Cristoforo Colombo, especially on Sunday. Many of the beaches are private, and every available space is covered by restaurants, bathhouses, bars, or amusement arcades. If you must bathe close to Rome, try Castel Fusano to the east of Ostia or, better still, use beaches farther afield (see Beaches and the Pontine Islands, pages 228–229).

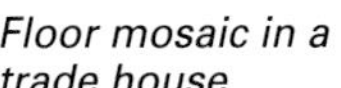

Floor mosaic in a trade house

Many companies run bus tours to Tivoli. Two of the best for the Villa d'Este are the half-day tours by American Express (tel: 06/-67 641) and CIT (tel: 06/ 479 4372). The morning tours of Carrani (tel: 06/ 482 4194) and Appian Line (tel: 06/ 464 151) include visits to the Villa Adriana.

The Villa Gregoriana is Tivoli's third and least-known sight, centered on a pair of waterfalls and a deep-cut gorge of lush vegetation. The Grande Cascata was created when the River Aniene was diverted in 1831 by Pope Gregory XVI to protect Tivoli from flooding. The smaller falls, designed by Bernini, are at the narrow head of the gorge. The remains of the Tempio di Vesta are now part of a restaurant whose belvedere affords a marvelous view of the canyon and the hills around the town. *Open*: daily 9am–90 minutes before sunset. Admission charge.

Tivoli
These days Tivoli is a lively town and the most popular day trip from Rome. It is best known for its two main tourist attractions, the **Villa Adriana** and the **Villa d'Este**, home to some of the most beautiful gardens in the world. Both spots can be very crowded, even out of season, so be sure to allow plenty of time and set out from Rome as early as possible.

Villa d'Este Located across from Tivoli's main square, Largo Garibaldi, the Villa d'Este was adapted from a convent in 1550 by Pirro Ligorio as the country retreat of Cardinal Ippolito d'Este, son of Lucrezia Borgia and the duke of Ferrara.

Now a shadow of its former self, the villa takes second place to the fountains and terraces of the formal gardens outside and the most beautiful collection of fountains in Italy. Try to visit in the evening, when the interplay of water and light produces exquisite effects.

In their heyday the fountains could boast many capricious details. The **Organ Fountain**, now sadly defunct, was capable of producing music, and the **Owl Fountain** was able to re-create bird song and the screeching of owls. Elsewhere the display is less flamboyant, but still exquisitely beautiful: the central fountain, the Fontana di Bicchierone, by Bernini, is the most elegant, though overshadowed by the scale of the **Viale delle Cento Fontane** (the Avenue of a Hundred Fountains) and its main **Fontana dei Draghi** (the Fountain of the Dragons), built in honor of Pope Gregory XIII, whose emblem was a short-tailed dragon. The most curious feature is the Rometta, which contains scale models of Rome's major buildings and a replica of the city's Isola Tiberina. It is open Tuesday to Sunday, 9 to 90 minutes before sunset. Between May and September the gardens are also open and floodlit nightly except Monday from 9 to midnight.

Villa Adriana Less visited and out of town, the Villa Adriana (Hadrian's Villa) is one of the most charming and romantic spots in or around Rome, and you could spend many peaceful hours picnicking or wandering the ruins. Although it has been plundered of treasures and robbed of stone for building over the centuries, plenty remains to evoke its once immense grandeur.

Begun by Hadrian in AD 125 and completed 10 years later, the villa's scale dwarfs the Villa d'Este – it covered an area as great as the center of imperial Rome – and makes it the largest and most sumptuous palace ever built in the Roman Empire. It was intended as a retirement home for the emperor, but illness drove him to seek healthier climes, and he enjoyed the villa for only a short while between its completion and his death three years later. His intention in the villa was partly to re-create the buildings that had impressed him during his travels, most notably the **Stoa Poikile** of Athens, the huge colonnade through which you enter, and the **Serapeum** and **Canopus**, a canal bordered by columns and statues, copied from the Temple of Serapis near Alexandria.

Fountains at the Villa d'Este

The villa is open daily from 9 to sunset except Monday; admission is charged.

Hadrian also introduced the concept, unique at the time, of scattering buildings connected by covered walkways over an area of parkland, rather than constructing in a single, central complex. The villa also contained two bathhouses, libraries, temples, praetorian barracks (the Caserma dei Vigili), a Greek theater, Imperial apartments, a stadium, and the so-called Teatro Marittimo, a small, colonnaded palace built on a private island in the middle of an artificial lagoon. This is thought to have been Hadrian's private retreat, where he could indulge his love of music, poetry, and painting. The villa even contained a beach heated from steam pipes buried in the sand and a series of underground service passages big enough to accommodate horses and carts.

The villa's original statuary was one of the finest collections in the Roman world, suggesting the grandeur the complex once possessed, but most are now in Rome's major museums. The remaining works are mainly copies, but there is a small museum on the site with a few original pieces and the latest finds from excavations that are still under way.

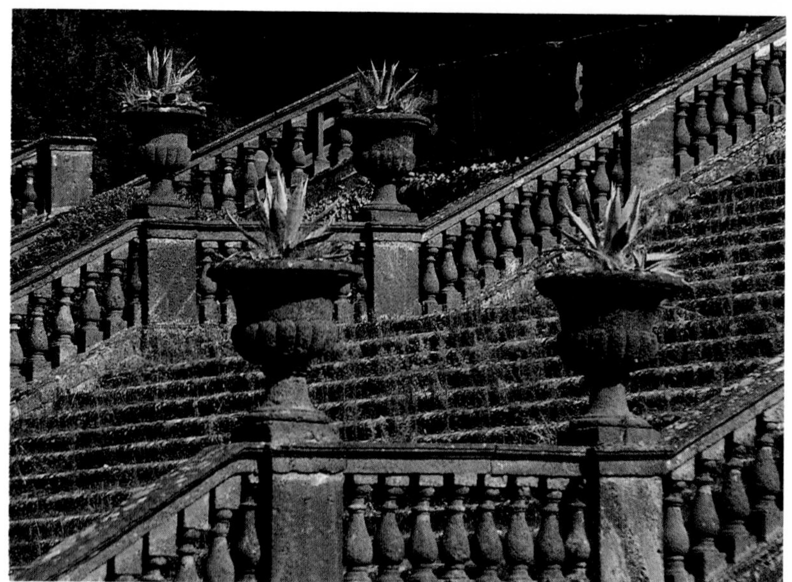

The Villa Torlonia, at Frascati

Castelli Romani
The Castelli Romani are 13 towns south of Rome, so-called because they grew up around the feudal castles of Roman patrician families or papal fortresses. All nestle in the **Collini Albani**, a 60 km chain of volcanic hills, famous for their wine; cool in summer; and dotted with lakes, fertile soil, and pockets of beautiful countryside. Sadly, many of the towns were heavily bombed in 1944, and the subsequent rebuilding and Rome's continued expansion mean that the Castelli have often been spoiled by modern development. Nonetheless they are still popular, and on weekends are crowded with Romans who come out to lunch at local trattorias.

Frascati is the most famous and most accessible of the towns, and the one to see if you are short of time or using public transportation. The air is cool after the cauldron of Rome, and magnificent views over the *campagna* can be enjoyed from the main square, Piazza Marconi. From here, too, you can see the gardens of the **Villa Torlonia**, now a park open to the public, and the grounds of the 17th-century **Villa Aldobrandini**, the main reasons, along with Frascati's well-known white wine, for a visit to the town. Country retreats have long been a feature of the Frascati countryside, and while many of its Renaissance villas are now in private hands, the ruins of Roman *Tusculum*, where Cicero once had a villa, are open and worth a brief visit (5 km).

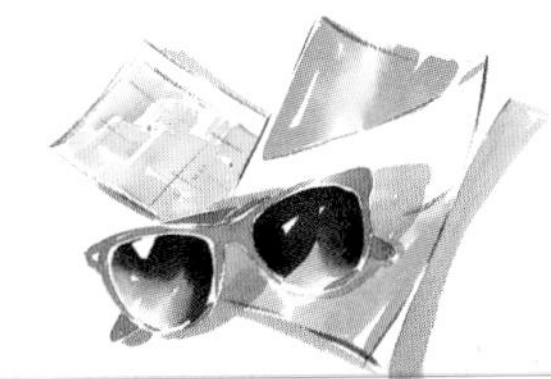

Getting there: Frequent bus and train services connect all the Castelli towns to central Rome. ACOTRAL buses leave from Anagnina (on Metro line A); trains depart from Termini.

Grottaferrata, 3 km from Frascati, is a quieter spot, best known for its 11th-century Basilian (Greek Orthodox) abbey. Monks conduct guided tours around the library; a small museum of frescoes, sculptures and icons; and the abbey church, **Santa Maria** (1025), whose Baroque interior contains a series of outstanding frescoes by Domenichino.

(*Open:* daily 9–12:30 and 4–7; some form of donation is expected.)

Marino Less attractive, though it produces some of the region's best wine, Marino is 41 km farther on.

Nemi, nearby, is reached along a panoramic road, the Via dei Laghi, and balances above the tree-sloped Lago di Nemi, the prettiest of the Albani crater lakes. The village and lake shore are famous for their strawberries.

Rocca di Papa A short diversion from the Via dei Laghi will bring you to Rocca di Papa, the highest and most dramatically situated of the Castelli towns (680 m). The upper quarter, named after a 12th-century papal fortress, is still a jumble of medieval streets and alleyways. The countryside is ideal for walking, the most tempting hike being to Monte Cavo (949 m), whose summit dominates the town and offers immense views. Part of the track follows the ancient *Via Triumphalis*.

Lago Albano, north of Lago di Nemi, is the largest of the local lakes and has two of the largest Castelli towns.

Castel Gandolfo is named after the Gandolfi family from Genoa, who built a castle here in the 12th century, but is better known for the **Palazzo Papale**, the pope's summer residence. Colorful Swiss Guards protect the palace, which was built in 1624 and drastically remodeled in this century by Pius XI. When in residence, Pope John Paul II appears at noon on Sunday to deliver a homily in the courtyard. The town has fine views down to the lake, but aside from the church of **San Tommaso**, designed by Bernini and with frescoes by Pietro da Cortona, it is uninteresting. The public lido on the lakeshore provides good swimming.

Albano Laziale Just south of Castel Gandolfo lies one of the more appealing Castelli, which grew up around the *Castra Albano*, a 2nd-century legionary camp established to defend the Via Appia.

The Lago di Nemi is also known as the *Specchio di Diana* (the Mirror of Diana). The Emperor Caligula kept two huge boats on the lake, props in the fantasy by which he declared himself the god who would wed Diana. Beautiful local girls were recruited as the goddess and forced to act out the more carnal aspects of the imperial whim. Engineers in the 1930s dredged the lake and found the remains of the boats, both of which were mysteriously destroyed by fire in 1944.

Lago Albano, the largest of the crater lakes

Getting there: by train, from Termini (40 minutes); by bus, ACOTRAL buses run every 30–45 minutes from Via Gaeta near Termini to Palestrina's Via degli Arcioni (40 minutes) from where it is a short, steep walk to the town center; by car, on the SS6, the *Via Casilina* (38 km).

Palestrina was the birthplace of the composer Giovanni Pierluigi da Palestrina (1524–94), who took his name from the town and is celebrated by a statue in its central square. Choirmaster of St. Peter's and the originator of the polyphonic mass, he also fused hymns and popular songs to produce innovative church music that combined both fun and religious decorum.

A fresco at San Benedetto, Subiaco

Palestrina

Set on the slopes of Monte Ginestro, Palestrina is known for the remains of one of Italy's great pre-Roman temples, the **Tempio di Fortuna Primigenia**, the seat of a famous oracle and temple of Fortune, mother of the gods. According to legend, the site is the oldest in Latium and was founded by Telegonus, son of Odysseus and Circe. However, archaeological evidence suggests the 7th century BC as a more likely foundation, when the ancient settlement of *Praeneste* was already established as a religious center and thriving Etruscan town. The Romans conquered the colony in 338 BC and proceeded to add further to the temple, the vast extent of which was discovered only after bombing during World War II.

Present-day Palestrina is built on six huge terraces buttressed into a steep hillside. These terraces correspond to the six original levels of the temple, traces of which are visible at every turn as you wander through the town's steep and pleasant streets. At the top of the town, in what would have been the sanctuary's top level, is the **Museo Nazionale Archeologico Prenestino**, Piazza della Cortina (open from Tuesday to Saturday 9–1:30, Sunday 9–noon, closed Monday). It is housed in the Palazzo Colonna-Barberini, which was built in the 11th century and modified in 1640 by Taddeo Barberini. The palace steps are adapted from the amphitheater annexed to the Rotunda of the temple, which was a possible site of the oracle itself. The oracle was consulted by drawing out the *sorti Praeneste* – thin, carved wooden sticks from which priests would interpret the prophesies.

The museum contains a scale model of the temple complex, fine bronze urns, numerous busts, bas-reliefs, and funerary *cistae*, or tombstones, as well as its great pride and joy, the exceptional 2nd-century BC **Mosaic of the River Nile.**

The museum ticket also admits you to the excavations on the upper terrace and the level below, the Terraza degli Emicicli. Lined with Doric columns, this is another possible site for the oracular temple. The views from here are marvelous.

Subiaco

Modern Subiaco, raised from the rubble of World War II bombing, is a long day trip from Rome, but the lovely mountain scenery close at hand and the beauty of its hill-town setting make it a worthwhile spot for an overnight stay. The site was initially a camp to house workmen building a temple nearby for the Emperor Nero. However, it is far better known as the spot to which St. Benedict retired in the 5th century. The saint spent three years here and wrote the famous Benedictine Rule, which was to be the cornerstone of Western monasticism.

Subiaco originally boasted 12 monasteries, but now only two of them survive, both a short distance from the town. The **Convento di Santa Scholastica** is the closer (Santa Scholastica was Benedict's sister), a signposted,

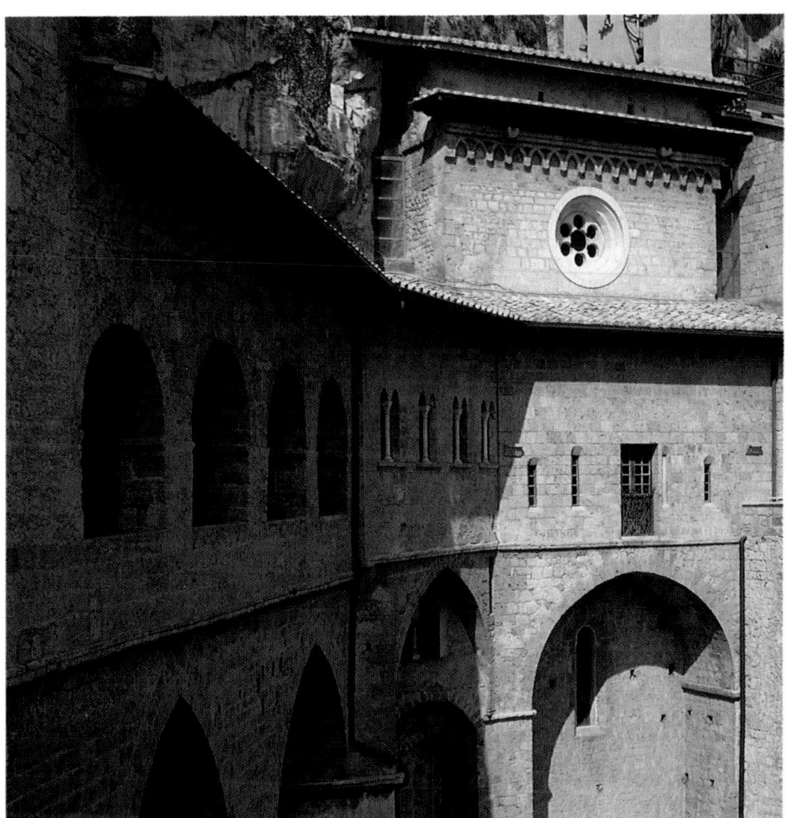

St. Benedict's original cave forms part of the lower church of the Convento di San Benedetto

25-minute walk from the center on either the road or footpaths. The buildings date from the Middle Ages, and many of their interiors have been heavily restored; the beauty of three cloisters in particular makes the journey worthwhile. The first dates from 1580 and is partly decorated with columns from Nero's villa; the second, built in 1052, is filled with flowers and vegetation and is one of the earliest Gothic cloisters in Italy; the third, dating from the 13th century, is the loveliest of the three.

Fifteen minutes' walk beyond Santa Scholastica is the **Convento di San Benedetto**. The surrounding countryside is delightful, ideal for walks and picnics. The sanctuary centers on a church divided into upper and lower levels, the higher chapel being known for a fine covering of 14th-century **Umbrian and Sienese frescoes**. The lower church is split into several levels, one of which contains Benedict's original cave, the Sacro Speco, little changed from the day he left it. A staircase winds to the **Cappella di San Gregorio**, whose walls contain an anonymous fresco of St. Francis (1210). Steps also lead from the *Sacro Speco* to a chapel used by Benedict to preach to local shepherds.

Getting there: local bus from Tivoli, or direct from Rome's Viale Castro Pretorio (2 hours/70 minutes, depending on service); by car, A24 motorway to Vicovaro exit (72 km) and country roads via Sambuci and Caterano (32 km).

If you have time in Subiaco itself, try to see the 14th-century church of San Francesco, which contains frescoes by Il Sodoma.

Etruscan tombs at Cerveteri

THE ETRUSCAN TOWNS

Cerveteri

Cerveteri, the Etruscan *Caere*, derived its wealth from minerals mined in the nearby Tolfa hills. Etruscan cities were built almost entirely of wood, so little of them survives, and present-day Cerveteri is largely medieval in appearance. About 2km north of the village is the site of the vast **Necropoli della Banditaccia** (City of the Dead), complete with streets and houses carved from the living rock. During spring and summer, special buses run to the tombs from the town's main square.

Maps are available at the entrance to the site, which is open daily, except Monday, from 9 to an hour before sunset. The bigger show tombs are near the entrance, but not all are regularly open, nor are all the graves lit, so a torch is useful. A tour can take two to four hours, depending on which tombs are open.

The earliest tombs, the *tumulus* tombs, date from about the 7th century BC and consist of vast earth-covered domes. Chambers, windows, and even beds were carved into the rock within each mound, and everyday items like food, drink, jewelry and weapons were left in the graves to provide the occupants with all they would need in the afterlife. **Tomba dei Capitelli** and the **Tumulus II** are a group of tombs belonging to one noble family. Such tombs were the prototypes for Roman graves like the Mausoleo di Augusto, Hadrian's Castel Sant'Angelo and the Tomb of Cecilia Metella.

From about the 5th century, cubic or *dado* tombs became more common – rectangular houses neatly arranged in streets and squares around the "city." At about this time, multichambered tombs gave way to graves with only one space. The best examples are on the so-called **Via dei Monti Tolfa** and **Via dei Monti Ceriti**. From the time of Caere's conquest by Rome (358 BC), the dead were mostly buried in plain, underground tombs (*hypogaea*), each with room for many dead. The best example is the **Tomba dei Rilievi**, now only intermittently open to the public.

Getting there: regular trains from Termini (1hour 10 minutes) or Roma Tiburtina (50 minutes) and connecting bus to the town center (7 km); by bus, ACOTRAL from Via Lepanto (Metro A); by car, the Via Aurelia (SS1) or A12 motorway (46 km). For coach trips to Cerveteri, contact *CIT* (tel: 06/ 479 4372). *Carrani* offer an extensive one-day "Etruscan Tour" from April to October on Tuesday and Friday (tel: 06/ 460 510).

Museo Nazionale di Cerveteri: Many of the treasures removed from Cerveteri's tombs are in Rome or foreign museums. However, some are collected in the town's museum, which is housed in the small castle built for the Orsini family in the village's central Piazza Santa Maria. In particular, there is a fine collection of Greek and Greek-style vases *(open: 9am–2pm, closed Monday)*.

Tarquinia

Ancient *Tarquinii* was one of the three major Etruscan cities – the other two being *Caere* and *Vulci* – and was the cultural, artistic and probably political capital of the civilization as a whole. Founded in the 10th century BC, its population touched 100,000, declining from the 4th century BC with the growing influence of Rome.

Some of the richest treasures of the Etruscan world have been removed from Tarquinia. Inevitably, most have gone to Rome or to private collections, often after having been stolen by grave robbers, the so-called *tombaroli*, who are still active in the area. However, some are collected in the town's small museum, the **Museo Nazionale Tarquiniese**, which is housed in the handsome 15th-century Palazzo Vitelleschi in the main street (*open:* Tuesday to Saturday 9–2, Sunday till 1; closed Monday). Pride of place goes to the famous **winged horses**, delicately carved terracotta pieces that probably originated from the frieze of an Etruscan temple.

However, it is Tarquinia's graves, the **Necropoli di Monterozzi**, located on a plateau east of the town, that deserve most of your time. The first of the tombs are about 15 minutes' walk from the museum, but others are a good deal farther, and it can be worth taking a taxi or one of the museum's guided tours. Over 6,000 graves have been uncovered since excavations began in 1489, and there are many more still to be explored. The graves are open in rotation, with the tombs open on a given day listed in the museum ticket office.

The great attraction of Tarquinia's tombs is the **wall paintings** that decorate many of the more lavish tombs. The earliest frescoes (7th century BC) show mythical and ritualistic scenes, but later graves contain tableaux of everyday Etruscan life. Some of the best are the **Tomba dei Leopardi**, with scenes of a banquet, and the **Tomba degli Auguri**, which depicts a funeral ceremony and assorted games. Try also to see the **Orco**, **Caccia**, **Leonessa**, and **Pescia** tombs. All are marvelously colorful, evoking the vitality and sophistication of the Etruscans' mysterious culture.

Getting there: regular express trains from Termini (1 hour, 10 minutes) and connecting bus to the town center; eight buses daily (2 hours) from Via Lepanto (Metro A); by car, A12 motorway to SS1 junction, 12 km south of Tarquinia.

A Roman aqueduct still stands at Tarquinia

Getting there: by train, on the private Roma-Nord line from Stazione San Pietro near Piazzale Flaminio (2 hours); by bus, ACOTRAL from Piazzale Flaminio (1 hour, 30 minutes) or RAMA from Piazza della Repubblica; by car, A1 motorway to Orte exit and SS204 dual carriageway (110 km). Tourist office: Piazza Caduti 16 (tel: 0761/ 226 161).

▶▶▷ Viterbo and the Villa Lante

Viterbo's ugly outskirts are a modern sprawl, but the impressively walled town center, though shabby in places, is well preserved and rich with medieval interest. The town was originally an Etruscan center, eventually colonized by the Romans in 310 BC. For a time in the Middle Ages it rivaled Rome in importance and was the official city of residence for several popes. Today it is a provincial capital and the largest town in northern Lazio.

The heart of the town is **Piazza del Plebiscito**, flanked by two fine civic palaces, the 13th-century **Palazzo del Podestà** and **Palazzo Comunale** (1460). Even more impressive historic buildings line the nearby **Piazza San Lorenzo**, built on the site of an old Etruscan acropolis. Most striking is the 13th-century **Palazzo Papale** (Papal Palace), overlooking the gorge that cuts into Viterbo. The town's lovely Romanesque cathedral stands opposite.

Walk through the warren of medieval streets in its oldest quarter, the **Quartiere di San Pellegrino**. As well as old town houses, the area contains the town's most handsome-looking church, **Santa Maria Nuova**.

Before leaving, see **Santa Maria in Gradi** and its beautiful cloister, the 13th-century **San Francesco**; the small Etruscan museum in the town's **Rocca** (castle); and **San Sisto**, which dates partly from the 9th century and has an altar made from 5th-century sculptural fragments. **Santa Rosa** contains the wizened remains of St. Rosa, Viterbo's 13th-century patron saint.

The **Villa Lante** at Bagnaia, 5 km east of Viterbo, is one of the most beautiful gardens of the Italian Renaissance (*open:* Tuesday to Sunday 9–noon). It is considered the masterpiece of the great architect Giacomo Barozzi da Vignola. The streams, low hedges, parterres and fountains were intended to symbolize the course of a river from its source to the sea, but can be seen only in the company of a guide, who may activate the *giochi d'acqua*. These "water jokes" were a favorite of 16th-century architects and through secret trigger mechanisms could be made to drench the cardinal's guests with water from a hidden source. Adjoining the gardens is a **park** through which you can wander unaccompanied.

The lovely Renaissance garden at Villa Lante

Caprarola's star attraction: the Palazzo Farnese

Caprarola and Lago di Vico

The **Palazzo Farnese** is one of the highlights of Italian Mannerism and the sole reason for visiting Caprarola, a charming little village. Designed by Vignola, one of the most accomplished architects of the late Renaissance, the palace was built over an earlier, pentagonal fortress constructed in the 1520s by Sangallo the Younger.

The interior highlights include a massive, leaden spiral staircase and the **Sala del Mappomondo**, beautifully decorated with huge painted maps of the world and a glittering ceiling fresco of the constellations. Sometimes crude and often vulgar frescoes by the brothers Zuccaro line most of the apartments. Guides will show you the faded central courtyard and demonstrate some of the uncanny acoustic tricks and echoes built into several of the rooms.

To the rear of the palace are a summer and winter garden, and beyond these is a park, in parts open to the public, but elsewhere it is reserved as the summer residence of the Italian president. This park contains a small "secret garden" and an enchanting summerhouse called the **Palazzina del Piacere** – the "Little Palace of Pleasure."

The **Lago di Vico**, just west of Caprarola, is one of the smallest, wildest and loveliest of the lakes around Rome. It nestles in the cone of an extinct volcano and is ringed by steep, wooded hills, the remnants of the old volcanic cone. On the northern shore Monte Venere (2,749 feet), a younger, but similarly extinct, volcano pokes through the crater. The lake is clean and delightful for swimming, and there is plenty of scope for gentle walks on the shore and in the hills. The surroundings are also pristine and are partly protected by a nature reserve, the **Riserva Naturale Lago di Vico**. Car drivers can follow a circular **scenic road**, the *Via Ciminia* around the rim of hills above the lake.

Getting there: by train, from Stazione San Pietro to Viterbo, and local buses to Caprarola via Lago di Vico; by bus, ACOTRAL from Via Lepanto (Metro A) to Caprarola; by car, to Viterbo on the Via Cassia (SS2) or A1 motorway via Orte and the SS204.

A monster at the Parco dei Mostri

Getting there: by train, from Termini to Attigliano-Bomarzo and then a 30-minute walk; by bus, ACOTRAL service from Via Lepanto (Metro A), or by one of four daily buses from Viterbo; by car, A1 motorway to Attigliano exit and follow signs for Bomarzo village (95 km). A trip to Bomarzo is best combined with a visit either to Viterbo or to Orvieto.

Bomarzo

The tiny and forlorn village of Bomarzo is a cluster of houses built in the local, rather gloomy *peperino* stone. The main point of a visit to Bomarzo is the **Parco dei Mostri** (Monster Park). It is signposted from the village and is about 10 minutes' walk.

The park is an extraordinary place, full of tangled and overgrown vegetation and dotted with a menagerie of vast and grotesque statues. It was built in 1552 by the hunchbacked duke of Orsini, and to this day no one is sure whether the Sacro Bosco (Sacred Wood), as he called it, was intended as a complex allegory or as a demented and surreal joke; Salvador Dali loved the place and made a film here.

The park's deliberate vulgarity was probably conceived to parody Mannerism, the artistic taste of the day, which glorified Arcadian retreats from society and art's apparent "triumph" over nature. However, its fantastical statues also sought to copy Mannerism's deliberate sensationalism, and many took as their inspiration Aroisto's *Orlando Furioso*, a popular epic of the day that told a tale of lost sanity. The giant warrior at the entrance tearing an adversary in half is borrowed from the story, as is the figure deeper in the park who pours Orlando's brains down the trunk of an elephant. Numerous other moss-covered carvings scatter the wood – dragons, nymphs, a whale, tortoises, and all manner of unearthly creatures – as well as a Doric temple that perversely compromises all classical conventions. Even its floor is steeply inclined and gives the impression of walking across the deck of a ship in a rough sea.

The Parco dei Mostri is quickly becoming one of Lazio's more notorious attractions, and its commercial potential is uncoubtedly being exploited to the full by its present owners. An adjacent small park offers a playground, goats, peacocks, and tame deer, as well as a pleasant café and shop. The park is open daily from 9 to sunset.

Orvieto

The ancient hill town of Orvieto, visible for miles around, sits on a table-top block of volcanic rock that rises over 984 feet from the valley below. The town is noted for its magnificent views, its white wine, the finest Gothic cathedral in Italy, and a variety of interesting medieval streets, churches and monuments.

The town's rock, or *rupa*, has been inhabited since Neolithic times and was the site of *Volsinii*, one of the Etruscans' 12-strong federation of cities.

The dark, brooding old town is dominated by the **duomo** (cathedral), a glorious building that took over 300 years to complete. It was started in 1293, partly as a monument to papal power, but also supposedly to commemorate the Miracle of Bolsena (1263) in which the Host started to bleed during a celebration of Mass in the nearby town of Bolsena. The glittering facade is covered in sculptures, bronzes, mosaics and countless architectural details and is best known for the **bas-reliefs** at its base by the Sienese sculptor and architect, Lorenzo Maitini.

The interior is decorated in the stripes of green-and-white marble that distinguish the Pisan-Romanesque cathedrals of Siena, Pisa, and Florence. However, the **Cappella di San Brizio** in the south transept contains *The Apocalypse*, a magnificent fresco cycle started by Fra Angelico and completed by Luca Signorelli in about 1501.

The town is full of other interesting monuments: the churches of **San Domenico**, with Arnolfo di Cambio's *Tomb of Cardinal Braye*; tiny **San Lorenzo**; **Sant' Andrea**; the 11th-century **San Giovenale**, which preserves beautiful early frescoes; and in the cathedral square the **Museo del Duomo**, crammed with works of art donated to the duomo, and the **Museo Etrusco**, a comprehensive collection of items removed from the town's Etruscan tombs. Finally there is the **Pozzo di San Patrizio**, a huge, 203-feet well with a spiral staircase down which you can walk.

The glittering façade of the cathedral at Orvieto was created by Lorenzo Maitani in the early 14th century

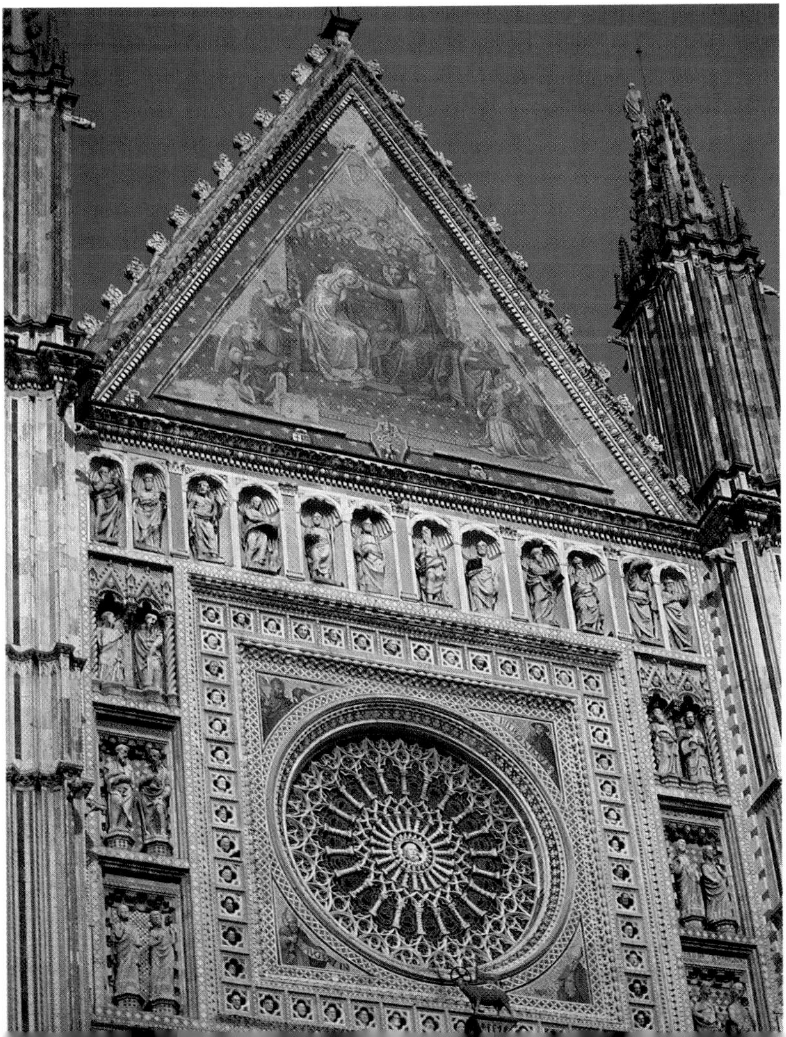

Getting there: by train, from Termini (90 minutes) and connecting bus from Orvieto Scalo to the old town; by car, A1 motorway north to Orvieto exit.

Getting there: by train, from Termini to Terracina and local bus to Sabaudia; by bus, ACOTRAL from Via Gaeta to Latina, and local bus to Sabaudia; by car, SS148 via Latina (65 km).

The Park Information Center is 1 km northeast of Sabaudia at Via Carlo Alberto 107 (tel: 0773/ 57251).

Parco Nazionale del Circeo

A perfect antidote to the clamor of Rome, the **Parco Nazionale del Circeo** is the smallest of Italy's five national parks and was created in 1934 to conserve part of a classic tract of Mediterranean coastline during the drainage of the Pontine marshes. It centers on the garden town of Sabaudia, one of several urban centers specially created by Mussolini to colonize the reclaimed marshland.

In a small area the park manages to collect a beautiful variety of landscapes: lakes, beaches, forest, *maquis,* 30 marine caves and cliff-edged mountains. It also contains a rich archaeological heritage in the shape of Roman and prehistoric remains. All but a couple of integral reserves are open to visitors, and the Visitors' Center has maps and well-presented audiovisual displays.

More serious walkers should climb Monte Circeo, at the park's southern tip, to get magnificent views over the lagoons and beaches that line the 32-km bay to the north. A minor road offers a glorious scenic drive past white-sand beaches and emerald-green stands of the distinctive umbrella pine. You can also take enjoyable boat trips from Sabaudia.

Naturalists, botanists, bird-watchers and nonexperts alike should have few problems seeing a wide variety of flowers and wildlife. Numerous birds are attracted to the area's woods, lakes and marshes all year round (a total of 230 species have been recorded), including occasional rarities during the spring and autumn migrations. You may see the dazzling golden oriole, great spotted woodpecker, little egret, spoonbill, collared pratincole, and waders such as wood sandpiper and marsh sandpiper. Terns, gulls and ducks are also present, and winter sees the arrival of many wildfowl and coot.

Animals, such as wild boar, roe deer and pine marten, thrive in the park's scrub and mixed oak woodlands. Near the sea, beaches and dunes are colonized by maritime plants like cottonweed, sea knotgrass, and rock samphire. Inland the *maquis* supports thyme, rosemary and juniper, cistus, broom and dwarf fan pines. In sunnier glades heathers and strawberry trees flourish, as do rarities like brown bee orchids, tongue orchids and woodcock orchids.

Great spotted woodpeckers are familiar visitors

Lago di Bracciano

Contained in a large, broad-rimmed volcanic crater, Lago di Bracciano is the closest of northern Lazio's lakes to Rome, and though the scenery is never more than just pleasant, it is still a favorite retreat for weekending Romans. Many come to eat in the overpriced fish restaurants that line the shore or to promenade around Bracciano, the area's main center.

The town is dominated by the **Castello Orsini-Odelscalchi**, an imposing, five-tower fortress built in the 15th century and still owned by the Odelscalchi family. It is open to the public, in the company of a guide, daily except Monday from 10–noon and 3–5. A number of rooms still contain their original frescoes, painted by the Zuccari brothers; an assortment of busts (some by Bernini); family heirlooms; and a rusting collection of armor and fearsome medieval weaponry. The view from the ramparts is worth the admission price on its own.

You can swim at the sandy Lido di Bracciano below the town and at several points around the lake shore. Boat trips run onto the lake between June and September, and rowing boats and pedalos are available for hire.

A scenic road encircles the lake, a round-trip of 35 km, and passes the bustling resort of **Anguillara** and the picturesque village of **Trevignano**. Here see the ruins of the Orsini castle and the church of **Santa Maria Assunta.**

About 6 km east of the lake is the **Museum of the Italian Airforce** (*open:* daily except Monday 9–5; free), which houses a variety of sea planes, fighters, racing planes, and flying memorabilia.

Before returning to Rome, car drivers may combine a trip to Bracciano with a stop off at **Veio**, in its day the largest of the 12 cities in the Etruscan federation. The hilltop site has its own beauty, and there are plenty of secluded spots for picnics. Archaeological attractions include the remains of the Temple of Apollo, the most important example of an Etruscan temple yet found, and the **Tomba Campana**, which contains very early examples of Etruscan tomb paintings.

Getting there: by train, from Stazione San Pietro on the private Roma-Nord line to Bracciano (30 minutes); by bus, ATAC bus 201 from Piazzale Flaminio to Isola Farnese and Veio (17 km); ACOTRAL bus from Via Lepanto (Metro A) to Bracciano; by car, the SS2 *Via Cassia* (39 km).

■ Exhausted by sightseeing and Rome's frenetic pace, you may be tempted to escape the city and find sun, sea and tranquillity on a beach somewhere. Sadly, this is an impulse shared by huge numbers of Romans, and the beaches close to the city, which is only 32 kilometers from the coast, are without exception crowded, commercialized, and polluted. However, quite short journeys either north or south, all manageable as day trips, will take you to resorts and beaches where the water is clean and the pace of life is slower. . . .■

There are daily hydrofoils to Ponza from Anzio and Formia, a town east of Gaeta, and daily ferries from Formia (2 hours 30 minutes) and Terracina, with extra sailings in summer. Daily ferries and hydrofoils cross to Ventotene from Formia, and a hydrofoil service also runs between Ponza and Ventotene (daily except Sunday).

Lido di Ostia is Rome's traditional seaside spot, but a seething mass of humanity competes for space on its filthy public beach. The promenade, or *lungomare*, for miles to the south is dense with neon signs, and all of it is built over with bars, arcades and pizzerias. As elsewhere, many of the better beaches have been leased out in strips to the so-called *stabilimenti*, private bars and beach houses where you pay an entrance fee for the privilege of modest privacy and raked sand.

North of Rome The well-known resorts north of Rome like **Fiumicino**, **Fregene** and **Ladispoli** are more or less carbon copies of Ostia, albeit less crowded ones. The coast begins to improve only in the more amenable villages of **San Severo** and **Santa Marinella**, south of Civitavecchia. These are modest resorts without too much development. Civitavecchia is an ugly industrial port that spills over into the coastline to its north.

According to health and safety tests, the water here still fails to come up to safe standards for bathing. Only on Lazio's northern border, 120km from Rome, does it meet the standard, and it is to **Chiarone** that you should head for the finest sea and beaches in this part of the region. A few Grosseto-bound trains stop daily at the little hamlet, just 90 minutes from Termini, from where it is 10 minutes' walk to undeveloped beaches.

South of Rome Trains also connect you easily to the resorts south of Rome, where generally the water is cleaner and the coast is more beautiful. **Anzio**, the Allied army beachhead in 1944; nearby **Nettuno**; and the ribbon of neighboring lidos should be passed over in favor of the more distant destinations. The coast that abuts the **Parco Nazionale del Circeo** has some marvelous beaches and lagoons, as well as a chic fishing-village resort in the shape of **San Felice Circeo**, which has sandy beaches and a picturesque mountain backdrop. Some 15 km farther south, the town of **Terracina** is split into an interesting medieval quarter on the hill and a bustling modern resort near the sea.

The coastline beyond Terracina is the prettiest in the

region, studded with cliffs, bays and a succession of small beaches signposted from the main road (the SS 213). By far the best spot to stop is **Sperlonga**, which manages to retain its charm, thanks to its Greek-looking whitewashed houses and its position high on a rocky promontory. **Gaeta** to the south is spoiled by its role as a large naval port.

The Pontine Islands Although they are too far from Rome for a day trip, this volcanic archipelago south of Terracina contains some of the most beautiful and least known of Italy's many islands. July and August are inevitably busy months, but at other times of the year you should find the main islands, **Ponza** and **Ventotene**, wonderfully peaceful. The town of Ponza is a delightful, pastel-colored fishing village, close to beaches and clear water. Elsewhere the island is lush and green, with plenty of scope for walking.

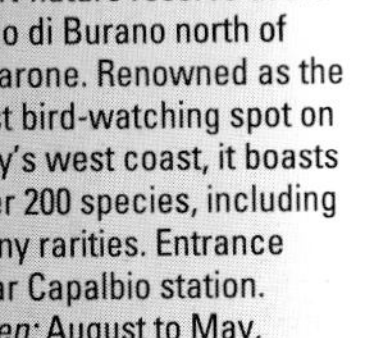

Naturalists should visit the WFN nature reserve at the Lago di Burano north of Chiarone. Renowned as the best bird-watching spot on Italy's west coast, it boasts over 200 species, including many rarities. Entrance near Capalbio station. *Open:* August to May, Thursday and Sunday only; guided visits at 10 and 2.

Ponza, one of the main Pontine Islands

Drives

Etruria and Northern Lazio

1 Lago di Bolsena and the Maremma
(155 km; 2 days).

Start at Tarquínia.
Tarquínia is the old heartland of the Etruscans, known for its Etruscan tombs and fine little museum of Etruscan artifacts (see page 221).

Take the minor road northeast 29 km to Tuscánia.
Tuscánia is a little-known walled village with a small archaeological museum and two superlative Romanesque churches – Santa Maria Maggiore and San Pietro, one of the most important of its age in Italy.

Take the minor road north to Marta on Lago di Bolsena (15 km). Follow lake road to Bolsena.
A circuit of **Lago di Bolsena**, cradled in an old volcanic crater, takes you past **Marta** and **Capodimonte,** each with gently shelving beaches. Capodimonte has a fine castle, the Castello Farnese, perched on a tree-lined peninsula. Boat trips go out to the Isola Bisentina, an idyllic, pastoral little island in the lake. Medieval **Bolsena** is the best place to find a hotel, with the chance to wander to the 14th-century castle and the old churches of Santa Cristina and San Francesco.

The Villa Lante in Bagnaia

Follow N2 north from Bolsena to San Lorenzo (11 km).
On the lake, **San Lorenzo** is an 18th-century hill town organized around an octagonal piazza.

From San Lorenzo a worthwhile diversion takes you into Tuscany and a trio of crumbling villages: Pitigliano, Sorano and Sovana. The last is home to Santa Maria (a medieval church), a magnificent duomo and Tuscany's best Etruscan tombs.

Take N312 west to Tarquínia (detour after 42 km to Vulci).
The drive back to Tarquínia takes you through the southern edge of the **Maremma**, an area almost unpopulated until this century because of malaria. Vulci has more Etruscan remains in its small Museo Nazionale.

2 Monti Cimini and Lago di Vico
(140 km; 2 days)

Start at Viterbo. Take the minor road east, signposted to Soriano; reach Bagnáia after 2 km.
On your way from **Viterbo**, stop at the **Villa Lante** in Bagnáia, a Renaissance garden designed in the 1560s by Vignola, the leading architect of his day.

Detour north from Soriano, 4 km east of Bagnáia, for Vitorchiano, or continue 12 km east to Soriano. After Soriano go south to Lago di Vico.
Vitorchiano's cluster of medieval houses clings to a crag of volcanic tufa. **Soriano** is dominated by the Castello Orsini and the gateway to the Monte Cimino, the remains of an old volcanic crater. You can drive around its rim and drop down to the **Lago di Vico**, a lovely lake edged by wooded hills and a protected *Riserva Naturale.*

From the lake road, detour to San Rocco and follow signs to Caprarola.
Caprarola has another Vignola masterpiece, the Villa Farnese.

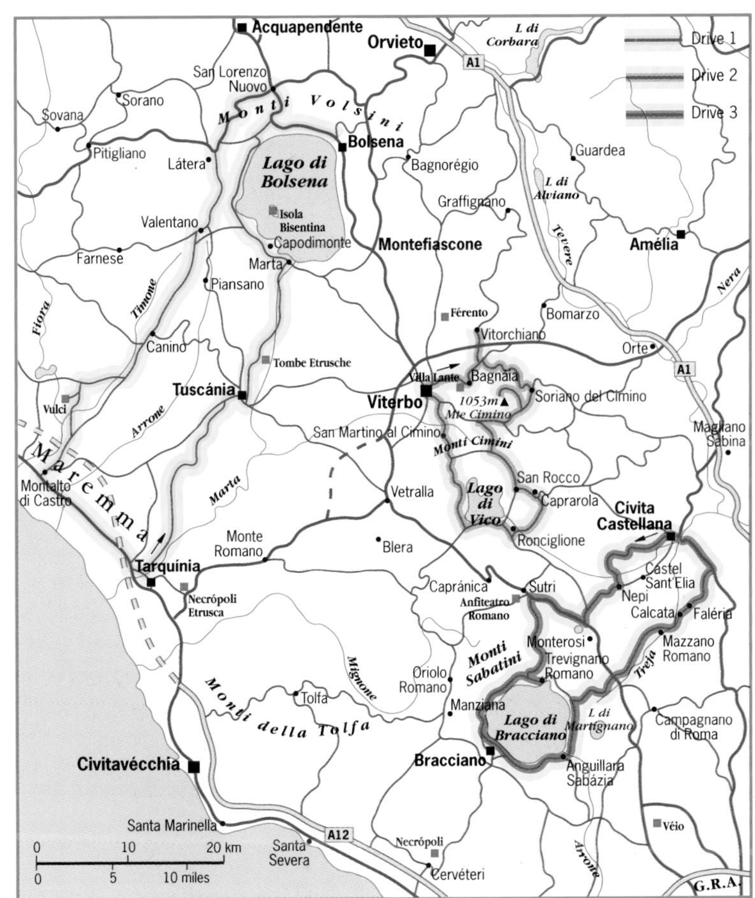

Ronciglione is 6.5 km south of Caprarola on minor roads.

Ronciglione's medieval core hangs precariously over a gorge, a good overnight stop before the drive on to **San Martino**, another hilltown.

Follow the lake road (west shore) to San Martino.

3 Lago di Bracciano
(150 km; 2 days)

Start at Cívita Castellana. Take N331 west to Nepi (12 km). Continue for 6 km on N331, then turn right on N2: 8.5 km to Sutri.

Sprawling **Cívita Castellana** should not detain you long; make for the villages of **Nepi** and **Sutri**. Nepi is renowned for the Basilica of Sant'Elia, with 8th-century remains. Sutri has a rare Etruscan amphitheater carved from the living rock. Be sure to see the ancient church of Madonna del Parto, probably converted from Etruscan tombs and a Mithraic temple.

From Sutri take minor roads south 13.5 km for Trevignano and follow the lake road 10 km west to Bracciano.

The lake at **Bracciano** is less appealing than some, but the town has a castle. Take the road northeast along the Treja River, a gorge studded with crag-top villages like **Calcata**, infamous for its inhabitants' unconventional lifestyles. **Faléria**, at its head, has an imposing castle. The area is protected by a reserve, the Parco Valle del Treja.

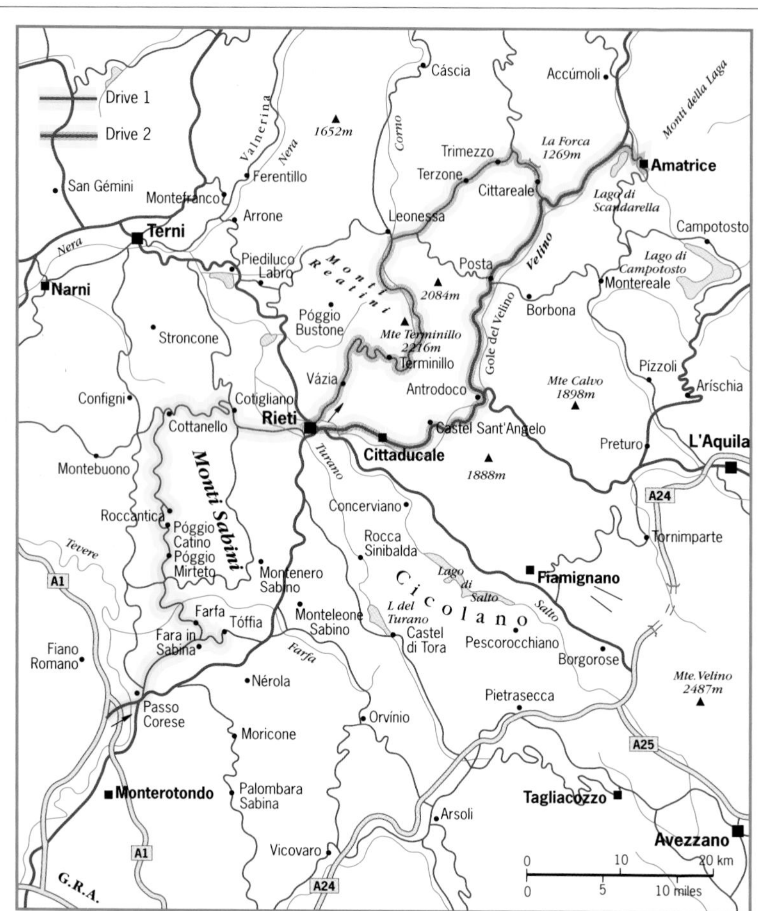

Rieti and the Mountains

1 The Sabine Hills

(150 km; 1–2 days)

Take A1 motorway north from Rome to exit 2 (Fiano Romano). Follow N4 6 km to Passo Corese, then minor roads 14km northeast to Fara, Tóffia, and Farfa.

Ancient seat of the Sabines, an early tribal rival of the Romans, the hills northeast of Rome are crammed with little villages that are increasingly being bought up for their holiday homes. Leave the ugly Via Salaria, the old consular road used to trade salt (*sale*), at **Passo Corese** and make for **Fara**, an attractive hill town of cobbled streets. In **Tóffia** the churches of San Lorenzo and Le Stimmate have patches of fresco and old carvings. The well-signed Farfa, known for its rambling abbey, once one of the most powerful in Europe, is the highlight of the tour. The restored complex has many treasures, most of them collected in its church and new **museum**.

From Farfa take the minor road north via Póggio Mirteto (6 km) to the turnoff (20 km) for Roccatina. Then return to the road and continue to Cottanello, 10 km farther north.

The church of the Assunta at **Roccatina** is crammed with medieval paintings, as is the interesting San Cataldo at **Cottanello**, a village known for the mines that produced the pink marble of many Roman monuments.

From Cottanello continue east via Contigliano to Rieti (27 km).

2 Rieti and the Mountains
(160 km; 2 days)

Start at Rieti.

Rieti is the plumb geographic center of Italy, a lively town with few interesting monuments – only the central square and its cathedral merit a quick look.

Take N4 east of Rieti. After 11 km turn left on N4bis for Terminillo (21 km). Then take the minor road north to Leonessa (14 km).

Monte Terminillo is Rome's nearest ski resort, but in summer it is a breezy mountain spot. Isolated **Leonessa** is shadowed by hills and dominated by the church of San Pietro. It is a good spot to strike north to the wilder reaches of Umbria and its hill towns.

From Leonessa follow the minor road east via Terzone (13 km) and Trimezzo (19 km). Turn south 2 km after Trimezzo to N4 via La Forca pass (1,269 m) and Cittareale. Follow N4 and N577 to Amatrice.

The diversion to **Amatrice** is worthwhile for the scenery of the Gole del Velino and the high Monti della Laga, which rises behind the town.

Return to Rieti from Amatrice via Antrodoco and Cittaducale.

Antrodoco is frequented for its pungent sulphurous *terme* and for its austere medieval backstreets. **Cittaducale**'s churches and monuments are historically more interesting.

3 The Abruzzo
(130 km; 2–3 days)

Start at Sulmona.

The mountains of the Abruzzo, the region east of Rome, provide the area's wildest and most beautiful scenery. They are protected by a well-run national park, with plenty of marked paths, and a **Park Center** at Pescasséroli (which has some of the park's famous wolves in semi-captivity.

> *EPT (Provincial Tourist Office), Via Cintia 87, Rieti (tel: (0746) 41 146).*

Allow at least a day to explore some of the area on foot and time to meander around its obscure mountain lanes, all of them highly scenic.

For a tour of the central park area, start at **Sulmona** and head for **Anversa** and the winding road south to **Scanno**.

Take N479 to Anversa (15 km), then N479 to Scanno, and continue to Villetta Barrea (27 km) .

The whole drive is magnificent, but at **Villetta Barrea** you enter the park proper.

From Villetta Barrea turn west on the N83 10 km to Opi. Continue west 5.5 km to Pescasséroli.

Opi, and to a greater extent **Pescasséroli** are the park's main exploring bases.

Continue north to Pescina for the A25 motorway and the return to Rome.

Southern Lazio

1 The Sea to the Mountains

(120 km; 1–2 days)

This trip may be combined easily with an exploration of the Abruzzo by starting at Sora. Otherwise commence at Gaeta.

Gaeta is a lively seaside resort, but also at heart a colorful medieval town.

Take the N360 from Gaeta to Ausónia (26 km), then continue on N360 to Cassino (20 km).

At **Ausónia** detour for the fresco-covered church of Santa Maria del Piano delle Fratte. At **Cassino** the most famous sight is the Benedictine abbey of Montecassino, rebuilt after World War II.

Follow the N509 north to Atina (15 km) and take the N627 west to Sora (20 km).

The road climbs toward the foothills of the Abruzzi, passing **Atina,** with its ruined medieval churches, and the lofty village of **Cámpoli**. Divert to Posta Fibreno for its bucolic lakeside setting. From here either head north into the rugged Abruzzese mountains or drive on to **Sora** to push farther west or to take the return trip to Rome.

2 Villages of the Monti Ernici

(160 km; 2 days)

Start at Sora. Take minor roads southwest or N82/214 to Abbazia di Casamari (15 km) and then minor roads west to Alatri (20 km).

Leave industrial **Sora** for a ride into the desolate hills of the Monti Ernici. The **Abbazia di Casamari** is a stolid 11th-century monastery founded by the Benedictines. **Alatri** has a wealth of medieval monuments and fine views of the surrounding hills, which away to the northeast shelter the **Certosa di Trisulti**, a 13th-century abbey with an abundance of Baroque decoration. **Collepardo,** en route, is another eye-catching village worth a look.

From Alatri follow N155 to Fiuggi, 20 km to the west, then 26 km northwest to Subiaco, or take the N155 southwest to reach Anagni (15 km).

Hilltop **Fiuggi** is a medieval ensemble largely unspoilt by modern accretions. From here, you may head through gorgeous country to **Subiaco** or to **Anagni** (a good overnight stop), once the domain of the Catani family popes, who were responsible for its fine monuments. The duomo (1077) is one of Lazio's greatest Romanesque buildings, next to a freestanding campanile and full of old frescoes.

Take N6 east (13 km) to Ferentino.

Ferentino has more than its share of early medieval buildings. Frosinone gives motorway access for the trip to Rome.

3 The Monti Lepini
(175 km; 2 days)

Start at Frosinone.

Frosinone provides the start of a meandering trip that takes you toward two key Rome excursions at Palestrina and Tívoli.

Take the N156 south from Frosinone to Priverno (26 km).

The old Roman colony of **Priverno** is now home to a Gothic central piazza, but it is better known for the **Abbazia di Fossanova** nearby, a 12th-century Cistercian abbey.

From Priverno take the N609 north and after 4 km turn west on minor roads to Norma and Sermoneta (28 km) via Sezze.

The austere abbey at Valvisciolo is easily seen on the way to the glorious villages of **Sermoneta** and **Norma**, each full of medieval nooks and crannies. Norma is a breathtaking site, perched on an eagle's nest crag. Behind it are the dramatic Monti Lepini.

Take the winding road south out of Norma for Ninfa (8 km).

Ninfa, in the valley below, is perhaps Lazio's most romantic spot. It consists of an abandoned medieval hamlet, with streams and a semi-wild garden woven into its ruins.

Follow lanes northwest via Cori (12 km) and Giulianello (19 km) to Velletri (29 km).

Velletri is the gateway to the Castelli Romani, themselves worth a visit on the way to Palestrina.

Shopping

Rome is not a shopping city to compare with London, Paris or New York, but it still has much to satisfy the wealthy or discerning shopper. Best known as one of the world's finest centers for luxury goods, its silks, leather, jewelry, shoes and accessories are of the highest quality, with high fashion, or *alta moda*, also well to the fore.

Exclusive names and luxury goods cluster in the grid of streets around Via Condotti, Via Frattina and Via Borgognona. For those on a tighter budget, the key shopping street for clothes, shoes and accessories is Via del Corso and to a lesser extent Via Nazionale, Via del Tritone, Via Cola di Rienzo, and the areas around Campo dei Fiori and the Fontana di Trevi.

Antiques shops are concentrated on Via Babuino and Via Monserrato, which have breathtaking pieces and prices to match; on Via Giulia, whose shops specialize in furniture; and on Via dei Coronari, whose workshops once made rosaries for pilgrims en route to St. Peter's and now offer items a touch below Via Babuino in quality and cost. Lesser shops and bric-à-brac stores also line Via Margutta, Via dei Banchi Nuovi and Via delle Carrozze.

China, fabrics and linen For china try Ginori, Via Condotti 87, or the 100-year-old Cavatorta, Via Veneto 159. Mouth-watering fabrics, bed linen and Italy's best silk fill the emporia of Bises, Via del Gesù; Cesari, Via del Babuino; and Meconi, Via Cola di Rienzo 305.

Market bargains: Porta Portese

Designer clothes All the top names in men's and women's fashion are concentrated around Via Condotti (Via Babuino, Piazza di Spagna, Via Borgognona and Via Frattina).

Shoes, gloves and leather goods Shoe shops almost outnumber food shops in Rome. High-quality shoes – Gucci, Ferragamo, Rossetti, Salato and Beltrami – all are on or around Via Condotti. For the outlandish, try Santini, Via Frattina 120; the plain ordinary can be found in the shops of Via Nazionale. For **gloves**, there is only one place you need visit – Sergio di Cori, Piazza di Spagna 53 – which stocks every glove imaginable. The same applies to Calza e Calze, Via della Croce 78, a tiny shop crammed with all the **tights, stockings and socks** conceivable. **Leather goods** are available on almost every street, but for reasonable and good-quality ware, try Ceresa, Via del Tritone 118 and Volterra, Via Barberini 102.

Specialist shops For **stationery**, visit Vertecchi, Via della Croce 38 and 70 and Pineider, Via Due Marcelli 68, and Via della Scrofa 7a. Buy **records, tapes and CDs** at Ricordi, Via del Corso 506, and **children's clothes** at La Cicogna, Via Boccea, and Tablo, Via della Croce 84. For **toys** (cuddly), try Al Sogno, Piazza Navona 53, stuffed with absurd cuddly creatures; for educational toys, try Città del Sole, Via della Scrofa 65/Piazza della Chiesa Nuova 20.

Shoppers on Via Condotti

Department stores The grandest of the department stores is La Rinascente, at Piazza Colonna (men's and women's clothes only) and Piazza Fiume, and tourists receive a 10 percent discount when they show their passports. Coin, Piazzale Appio, five minutes from San Giovanni in Laterano, is best for clothes and Italian kitchenware; Standa, at Via Cola di Rienzo, is cheap and popular, while UPIM, in Piazza Santa Maria Maggiore, Via del Tritone and elsewhere, is Italy's answer to Woolworth's. The central stores are open all day from 9:30 to 7:30.

Books, maps and guides Italy's largest **bookshop** is Rizzoli, Galleria Colonna, Largo Chigi 15. As well as Italian titles, it has a good selection of maps, guides, and books in English. For specialist English-language bookshops, visit the Lion Bookshop, Via del Babuino, or the Economy Book Center, Via Torino 136, which also has a large selection of secondhand books. Libri & Stampe, Lungotevere Tor di Nona 30, has antique books and prints; Libreria San Silvestro, Piazza San Silvestro 27, has a large stock of reasonably priced art books.

Food and wine You are best off visiting one of Rome's several markets (see page 135), though Rome is also still full of small, neighborhood shops, many stacked floor to ceiling with Italian delicacies. The gastronomic heart of the city, however, is Via della Croce, home to a string of luscious delicatessens. In the same street, at No. 76, is the Enoteca Isabeilli, one of the loveliest shops in Rome, with a turn-of-the-century interior, marble fountain, and a reasonably priced selection of wines and olive oils. You can buy wine by the glass and drink it at a couple of tables at the rear of the shop. Other fine wine shops that are worth visiting include the Enoteca Buccone, Via di Ripetta 19, and La Grapperia, Via della Lupa 17, home to over 400 different types of grappa.

Food and Drink

After their families, and perhaps their cars, eating is the Romans' main preoccupation. Most of their traditional titbits, however – the stuff of poverty and simple peasant cooking – may appear unappetizing to outsiders: brains, tripe, salt cod, chick peas, pigs' trotters, veal and offal, but more conventional staples from most Italian regions can be found in the city's restaurants. Dining out for most Romans is all the nightlife they need, and a summer evening's meal alfresco can be one of the city's most pleasant experiences.

Eating out Trastevere and the streets around Piazza Navona contain the city's highest concentration of **restaurants**, though few areas are without their neighborhood **trattorias** and **pizzerias**, and it is in these – away from the obvious tourist areas – that you will enjoy your liveliest and most reasonably priced meals. It is as well to be aware that in Rome smart and expensive restaurants are no guarantee of good cooking. This said, while neither Rome's restaurants nor its cuisine are in Italy's first rank, there are a few high-class establishments that serve fine Roman and Italian cuisine. Do not overlook **bars** as a source of cheap snacks, and it's acceptable to have a pizza or single course of pasta. Additions to the bill (*il conto*) will probably include 10–15 percent service (*servizio*) and a bread-and-cover charge (*pane e coperto*) of about L2,000 per person. Tourist menus may seem cheap and tempting, but they are usually a bad sign, and the food is invariably poor.

Food and wine – part of the Rome experience

Eating out is a social occasion in Italy

Main meals Breakfast is a straightforward, stand-up affair of a sweet and sometimes cream-filled croissant (*un cornetto*) and coffee (*cappuccino* or the milkier *caffè latte*). Lunch (*pranzo*) these days is not the extended, overblown affair it once was, and many Romans eat a bar snack or light pasta, saving over-indulgence for the evening meal (*la cena*), usually eaten between 8 and 9. Traditionally dinner runs through hors d'oeuvres (*antipasto*), a course of soup; risotto, polenta, or pasta (*il primo*); a meat or fish course (*il secondo*); dessert (*dolce*); and an *espresso* or bitter digestif (*amaro*) to round things off.

Specialities Roman *antipasti* are like any other – olives, ham, salami, and more rarely omelets; vegetables; and marinated mushrooms, artichokes, and eggplant. Favorite pastas with a Roman flavor, though by no means unique to the city, include *bucatini all'amatriciana* (tomato sauce, salt pork, chilli peppers), *spaghetti alla carbonara* (egg, bacon, pepper, and cheese), *gnocchi* (small potato-based dumplings with butter, tomato, or meat sauce, traditionally made only on Thursday), and *penne all'arrabbiata* (tomato sauce laced with chilli pepper). Rome's classic soup is *stracciatella*, an all-too-often insipid mix of clear broth, egg, pasta and cheese.

Unless you are on the coast, fish in most restaurants will be frozen (*surgelato*) or expensive, so meat is usually a better option. The best-known Roman specialties are *saltimbocca alla Romana* (veal scallops with ham and sage, cooked in wine and butter) and *involtini* (rolls of meat simmered in a sauce of oil, ham, celery, and carrots). Also look for a wide range of simply grilled meats, especially lamb (*agnello*) and steak (*bifstecca*). Tripe (*trippa*), brains (*cervelli*), oxtail (*coda*), and other imaginatively cooked offal are available on most menus for the more adventurous. Another local favorite is fresh peas cooked with pieces of ham (*piselli al prosciutto*).

For vegetarians Rome has only a couple of vegetarian restaurants, but leaf and other vegetables (*contorni*), delivered daily from the Roman *campagna,* abound and are of high quality. Rocket (*rucola* or *rughetta*) is common, and spinach (*spinaci*), sometimes eaten cold, almost ubiquitous. Asparagus (*asparagi*) is always good, as are the famous purple Roman artichokes, especially as *carciofi alla giudia* (artichokes flattened and deep fried), a recipe handed down from the city's Jewish population.

Italian restaurants often fall down at the dessert stage, and Rome's are no exception. Generally it is best to play safe with fresh fruit (*frutta*) or a fruit salad (*una macedonia*), rather than try the industrial puddings made off the premises. The most common cheese (*formaggio*) is *pecorino,* made from sheep's milk and usually available in mild, medium or mature versions; *caciotta,* made from sheep's and cow's milk, is also common. Most people follow the Romans' own example and leave the restaurant to buy an ice cream (*un gelato*) as part of a late-evening stroll.

Pizza – tasty, filling and cheap

Drinking Rome's local wines are the amber-colored *biancchi* of the Castelli Romani, often served in the city's *trattorie* straight from the barrel. Of these wines, *Frascati* is the most famous, though in practice most of the wines from the region – the ring of volcanic hills south of the city – are similar in character. No one pretends they are of vintage quality, but for simple meals or picnics they are more than adequate. Up-market restaurants should have reasonable wine lists, but few non-Italian wines.

It is a Roman custom to take a refreshing glass of *prosecco,* a cheap but perfectly good sparkling wine from Italy's Veneto region, at almost any time of the day – ask for it by name: *un bicchiere di prosecco, per favore.*

For wine bars, try the bustling Cul-de-Sac, Piazza del Pasquino 73; the intimate Enoteca Piccola, Via del Governo Vecchio 75; or the relaxed Enoteca Cavour, Via Cavour 313.

Water Rome's tap water is perfectly safe, but all Romans take mineral water (*acqua minerale*) with their meals, either fizzy (*gassata*) or still (*non gassata*). Ask for either a liter (*un litro*) or half a liter (*mezzo litro*).

Nightlife

Rome's *dolce vita* days are largely over, and nightlife for many Romans involves eating or enjoying late summer evenings at pavement cafés. Most places stay open until the late hours from June to September. However, plenty of night spots exist for the keener gambler, though some may strike you as overexpensive and outdated. Cultural entertainment is what you would expect of any capital city, though non-Italian speakers will find film and theater choices severely limited.

Classical concerts and recitals The **Accademia di Santa Cecilia** stages concerts by its own and visiting orchestras at the auditorium in Via della Conciliazione 4 (tel: 654 1044) or at its smaller headquarters in Via dei Greci 18 (tel: 678 3996). The **Accademia Filarmonica**, Via Flaminia 118 (tel: 360 1752), usually performs at the Teatro Olimpico, Piazza Gentile da Fabriano 17; the **RAI Orchestra** offers Saturday evening concerts at the Foro Italico, Piazza Lauro de Bossis (tel: 368 6625); and there are free sponsored Sunday recitals, the best known of which are Italcable at the Teatro Sistina, Via Sistina 129 and Alitalia at the Teatro Brancaccio, Via Merulana 244. The **Oratorio del Gonfalone** offers baroque, chamber and choral recitals at Via del Gonfalone 32A (tel: 687 5952). A host of classical music can also be heard free of charge throughout the year in Rome's churches.

Accessible culture on the Piazza Navona

Where the trendies go: The café of the moment for those in the know is Bar della Pace off Piazza Navona. The beautiful 19th-century interior is set off by marble, mirrors and plants, but most of the city's gilded youths prefer to cram the spread of tables on the cobbled street outside. The Hemingway nearby, at Piazza delle Coppelle 10, is a more languid and exclusive rendezvous, frequented by visiting stars and children of the rich and famous. Gilda, in Via Mario dei Fiori 97, is the stylish nightclub they go on to later.

Opera and ballet events are held at the **Teatro dell'Opera**, on the corner of Via Torino at Piazza Beniaminio Gigli 1 (tel: 46 364; in English on 6759 5725). The season runs from November to June and tickets (priced from L5,000) can be reserved by mail or bought two days before performances. The box office is open 10–1 and 5–7 and is closed on Monday. Lavish open-air performances are given at the Terme di Caracalla from June to September, though the quality of singing usually takes second place to a rowdy, carnival atmosphere. Tickets (from L25,000) are available from the Teatro dell'Opera box office or at the Terme on the day of performance (8–9PM).

Ballet in the city revolves around the **Rome Opera Ballet**, though leading international companies and stars often visit the city, and there are several small experimental troupes; check daily listings for details.

Films Only one movie theater regularly shows English-language films, the venerable and much-loved **Pasquino**, hidden in Vicolo del Piede off Piazza Santa Maria in Trastevere (tel: 580 3622). Programs of first- and second-run films change every few days, and there is a popular late-night screening of old classics. All other mainstream movie theaters show dubbed films, though film buffs should hunt out arts theaters (*cinema d'essai*) where original-language films are shown. The best are **Grauco Cineclub**, Via Perugia 34 (tel: 755 1785) and the **Labirinto**, Via Pompeo Magno 27 (tel: 312 283).

Rock, pop, jazz and Latin The best jazz clubs are **Big Mama's**, Vicolo San Francesco a Ripa 18 (tel: 582 551); the **Saint Louis**, Via del Cardello 13a (tel: 474 5076); and **Music Inn**, Largo dei Fiorentini 3 (654 4934). For folk and blues try the more intimate **Folkstudio**, Via Gaetano

Nightlife, good food, and fresh air, all in one

Acropolis disco – one of Rome's best

Where the rich and famous go: Many of the city's élite keep a low profile these days and prefer a quiet dinner to the hedonism of Rome's heyday in the 1950s. If they do go out, it is to the Bella Blu, Via Luciani 21, a highly exclusive nightclub, or to the legendary Jackie O, Via Boncompagni 11, not as glamorous as it was, but still particular about whom it lets in. For more intimate evenings they may choose the Tartarughino piano bar at Via della Scrofa 2, a tiny enclave of exclusivity with exacting dress standards.

Sacchi 3 (tel: 589 2374) and for a pot-pourri of jazz, folk, blues and Afro-Latin on different nights, there are **Café Latino**, Via Monte Testaccio 96 (tel: 574 4020); **Alexanderplatz**, Via Ostia 9 (tel: 359 9398); **Grigio Notte**, Via dei Fienaroli 30b (tel: 581 3249); and the **Blue Lab**, Vicolo del Fico 3 (tel: 687 9075). Rock and pop events are confined mainly to large arenas like the Paleur sports hall or the Flaminio football stadium – check the press for details – but for nightly live bands, the most authentic spots are **Melvyn's**, Via Politeama 8, in Trastevere and the outlying **Uonna Club**, Via Cassia 871.

Nightclubs and discos Rome's nightclubs and discos for young and old alike are stylish and sumptuously decorated palaces where dressing up is very much de rigeur. Entrance can cost anything up to L40,000 for the top spots. The best are **Black Out**, Via Saturnia 18; **Le Stelle**, Via Beccaria 22; **Krypton**, Via Schiaparelli 29–30; **Piper**, Via Tagliamento 9; **Hysteria**, Via Giovannelli 3; **Veleno**, Via Sardegna 27; and the **Acropolis**, Via Luciana 52. Good smaller clubs include **Yes! Brazil**, Via San Francesco a Ripa 103, and **La Makumba**, Via degli Olimpioncini 19, both with a strong African and Latin bias. Be warned, however, that many clubs come and go with alarming rapidity.

The Botteghino agency delivers theater and concert tickets to your hotel (tel: 678 3750).

Open: Monday to Saturday, 10–6. For tickets to rock, pop and jazz concerts, visit the central Orbis agency opposite Santa Maria Maggiore at Piazza Esquilino 37 (tel:482 7403).

Open: Monday to Saturday, 10–6.

For listings information buy *La Repubblica*, one of Italy's leading newspapers, whose Saturday edition has a free weekly listings booklet called *Trovaroma*.

Otherwise *La Repubblica* and *Il Messagero*, Rome's daily paper, carry more limited daily listings.

Accommodations

The exclusive Lord Byron (see Directory)

Rome has the range of accommodations you expect of any great city, from the squalid *pensione* around the railway station to the grand monuments to luxury and elegance on Via Vittorio Veneto. Despite many centuries of catering to visitors, it falls short in the middle price ranges, lacking hotels with real character in this category. Most of the best choices, unfortunately, are well known and booked months in advance by faithful patrons. Appearances can be misleading, and many crumbling stucco facades hide interiors of considerable elegance. Rooms can often be on the small side, however, even in the grander hotels. Decide whether you want to save money by staying a little way out of the city; peripheral hotels may be quieter, cooler, and cheaper, but a lot of time is wasted commuting back and forth. For long-term stays, self-catering apartments (*residenzie*) are available, but for these you should obtain a list from the Italian State Tourist Office.

Noise Wailing sirens, the scream of motor scooters, domestic arguments, car horns, buses, early-morning street cleaners, late-night bars and restaurants . . . surveys rate Rome the noisiest capital in Europe, and to make the cacophony worse, the noise is all crammed into narrow streets and amplified by tall buildings. You will not escape the racket entirely unless you patronize an expensive, sound-conditioned hotel or flee the city center altogether. You could save yourself a few decibels, however, by avoiding main thoroughfares and the area around Termini in favor of spots near the parks or in more obscure back streets. Ask for rooms either away from the front of the hotel or facing a central courtyard.

Booking Rome's peak season is between Easter and October, but the city's hotels always seem to be well booked. Worse, budget accommodations and the better hotel choices are well known, so advance reservations are recommended for whatever price category you are aiming for. Before your trip the Italian State Tourist Office in your home country will help with booking. In most cases a deposit is required, for which an international money order is useful, available from post offices. In the city always phone ahead to confirm bookings (most receptionists speak some English). If you arrive without a reservation, get to the hotel early in the morning; by afternoon most of the spare rooms will have been snapped up. Do not accept offers from the hotel touts at Termini. Under desperate circumstances, use the local tourist offices, which will call around for you, though you may have a long wait and end up with a room a long way from the center.

Prices Italy's hotels are classified into five categories, from one-star (basic) to five-star (luxury), and the prices each can charge are set by law and must be displayed in each room. Prices for different rooms, however, can vary within a hotel, so if a room is too expensive, do not be afraid to ask if they have anything cheaper. New European Community regulations may alter things.

Prices are high in Rome. For the hotels listed as Expensive in the Directory, expect to pay between L250,000 and 500,000 for two people in a double room. Moderate rates are roughly L100,000–250,000, and Budget from L50,000–100,000.

If you need to use the tourist offices' accommodations service, try to avoid those at Termini, where lines are immensely long. Instead use those at Fiumicino airport (tel: 601 1255); the Roma-Nord service station on the A1 motorway (tel: 691 9958); the Roma-Sud Frascati service area on the A2 motorway (tel: 942 0058); or the EPT, Via Parigi 5 (tel: 463 748).

Single rooms cost about two-thirds the price of double rooms, and to add an extra bed to the room puts 35 percent on the bill. Most hotels do not admit to a low season, though some will offer reduced rates between November and March. Taxes and service charges are included in the room rate, but hotels can charge supplements for air-conditioning (as much as L25,000 a day) and for showers (in cheaper places), and some will insist that you pay for breakfast whether you want it or not (around L5,000).

Accommodations areas The biggest concentration of cheap accommodations is in the streets north and south of the station: Via Amendola, Via Marghera, Via Palestro, Via Magenta and Via Principe Amedeo. Some spots are sleazy and others overpriced for the standards they offer, but if you are desperate, in a hurry, or on a budget, this is the best area. Ideally, however, the best area to stay is the city's medieval heart around Piazza Navona, the Pantheon and Campo dei Fiori. Both surroundings and accommodations are convivial and convenient, but although there are hotels in all categories, their number is small.

More establishments cluster around the Piazza del Popolo and Piazza di Spagna, still a pretty and central quarter. Most hotels here are small and moderately exclusive spots, a degree or two lower in standards than the first-class luxury hotels that concentrate around Via Vittorio Veneto and the area south of Villa Borghese. Hotels close to the Vatican and St. Peter's are quiet, but some distance away from the rest of the city.

Comfort in the Hotel Sistina (see Directory)

Itineraries

Week's Itinerary

Day one

Morning	Forum
	Campidoglio
	Colosseum
	Lunch (Colle Oppio). Walk (5 minutes)
Afternoon	Colosseum
	San Clemente
	San Giovanni in Laterano

Day two

Morning	Castel Sant'Angelo (Borgo)
	St. Peter's
	Lunch (Parco Adriano). Walk (10 minutes)
Afternoon	Vatican Museums

Day three

Morning	Piazza Navona (Campo dei Fiori)
	Santa Maria sopra Minerva
	Sant'Ivo
	Colonna di Marco Aurelio
	Lunch. Bus from San Silvestro (10 minutes/30 minutes' walk)
Afternoon	Trastevere
	Santa Maria in Trastevere
	Santa Cecilia
	Villa Farnesina (Palazzo Corsini)
	Isola Tiberina
	Gianicolo (San Pietro in Montorio)
	Villa Doria Pamphili (Park/Walk)

Day four

Morning	Fontana di Trevi (Via Condotti)
	Piazza di Spagna
	Villa Borghese. (Park/Walk)
	Galleria Borghese
	Lunch (Villa Borghese). Walk (10 minutes)
Afternoon	Piazza del Popolo
	Ara Pacis Augustae
	Palazzo Borghese
	Campo dei Fiori (Palazzo della Cancelleria)

Day five

Free day	Excursion (Frascati, Orvieto, etc.)
	Shopping: Mercato di Piazza Vittorio
	Revisits (Forum, Vatican Museums)
	Longer (bus) trips (Sant' Agnese, Santa Costanza, etc.)
	Tram (2-hour circular trip of city)
	Rest and relaxation

Day six

Morning	Aventino
	Circo Massimo (Protestant Cemetery)
	Terme di Caracalla
	Via Appia Antica
	Lunch (Via Appia Antica). Bus Piazza Venezia

Afternoon	Palazzo Doria–Pamphili
	Palazzo Colonna
	Mercati Traianei
	Santi Apostoli
	San Pietro in Vincoli
	Domus Aurea/Colle Oppio
	Santa Maria Maggiore

Day seven

Morning	Villa Giulia (Walk/Park)
	Via Veneto (Santa Maria della Concezione, etc.)
	Palazzo Barberini
	Lunch (Palazzo Barberini gardens)
Afternoon	Terme di Diocleziano–Museo Nazionale Romano
	San Lorenzo – bus from Stazione Termini
	Bus (20 minutes) from Stazione Termini to Piazza Bocca della Verità and Aventino

Weekend's Itinerary

Saturday

Breakfast	Campo dei Fiori (Piazza Farnese, Via Giulia, etc.) Walk (30 minutes) the ghetto, Isola Tiberina, Piazza Bocca della Verita (Aventino) to the Campidoglio
Morning	The Campidoglio
	The Roman Forum
	The Colosseum
	San Clemente
	San Giovanni in Laterano
	Lunch (Colle Oppio). Walk (30 min) – Foro di Traino, Piazza Venezia, etc. to Fontana di Trevi
Afternoon	Fontana di Trevi
	Colonna di Marco Aurelia
	Santa Maria sopra Minerva
	Pantheon
	Piazza Navona
	Walk (Via Coronari, Via Governo Vecchio, etc.) (Shopping – Via del Corso, Via Condotti)
Evening	Walk/bus to Trastevere (Ponte Sisto)
	Santa Maria in Trastevere
	Santa Cecilia, etc.
	Dinner in Trastevere

Sunday

Breakfast	Piazza Navona. Walk (30 minutes) to Castel Sant'Angelo via Ponte Sant'Angelo
Morning	Castel Sant'Angelo
	St. Peter's
	Vatican Museums
	Lunch
Afternoo	Walk to Piazza del Popolo
	Piazza del Popolo (Villa Borghese)
	Pincio (Walk)
	Piazza di Spagna

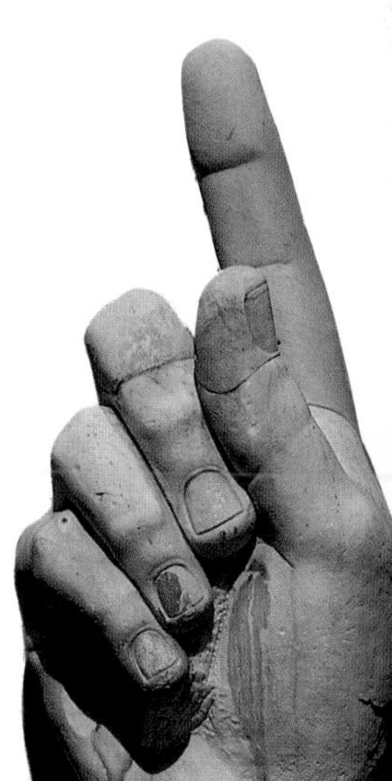

■ Rome's festivals are less extravagant nowadays. Long vanished are the bacchanalian revels of ancient Rome, the honoring of pagan gods, and the high spirits of *carnevale* that survived until the last century. For precise dates and details of minor events, contact the EPT tourist office, Via Parigi 5 (tel: 463 748). *Open:* 8:30–7 (closed Sunday). . . .■

January January 5–6: *Befana.* Raucous conclusion to Christmas children's fair in Piazza Navona. January 17: *Festa di San Antonio Abate.* Animals blessed in special service at San Eusebio all'Esquilino.

February *Carnevale.* Sunday–Tuesday before Lent. Children dress up; some street celebrations (especially Via Nazionale and Via Cola di Rienzo); restaurant parties on Martedi Grasso (Shrove Tuesday).

April Good Friday: Stations of the Cross with the pope at candlelit Colosseum. Easter Sunday: Papal blessing at St. Peter's. Late April: *Festa della Primavera.* Spanish Steps are decorated with flowers. April 21: Rome's official birthday – Campidoglio lit by flaming torches.

May Early May: International horse show at Piazza di Siena in the Villa Borghese. Rose Show at the Via di Valle Murcia on the Aventino. Antiques fair in Via dei Coronari. Open-air art exhibition in Via Margutta.

June First Sunday in June: *Festa della Repubblica.* Large military parade in Via dei Fori Imperiali. June 23–24: *Festa di San Giovanni* – snails and suckling pig eaten in gastronomic festivities at Piazza San Giovanni in Laterano. June 29: *Festa di San Pietro.* Patron saint of Rome celebrated in solemn services in St. Peter's.

July *Festa di Noiantri.* Commercialized Roman feasting, wine and festivities in Trastevere. Open-air opera season in the Terme di Caracalla (also in August). Open-air concerts at Ostia Antica. *Tevere Expo:* Italian products in stalls along the Tiber near Ponte Sant'Angelo.

August August 5: *Festa della Madonna della Neve.* Services in Santa Maria Maggiore. August 15: *Ferragosto* (Assumption). Main midsummer holiday.

September September 23–October 7: Torch-lit street and craft fair in Via dell'Orso. Second Tevere Expo.

October Wine festivals in Castelli Romani.

November November 22: *Festa di Santa Cecilia.* Special service at Santa Cecilia in Trastevere and the Catacombe di San Callisto.

December *Presepi* (antique Christmas cribs) in many churches. December 8: *Festa della Madonna Immacolata*, religious service in Piazza di Spagna, sometimes attended by the pope. December 12–January 6: Children's fair in Piazza Navona, culminating in *Befana* ("the witch") festival on the eve of Epiphany. December 24: Special midnight Masses in churches, especially Santa Maria Maggiore and Santa Maria d'Aracoeli. December 25: Mid-morning papal Mass at St. Peter's.

Winter in Rome, and for three short months the city is at its best. So much of the Roman experience seems bound up with summer – sunny blue skies, café life, alfresco eating, the cool of church interiors – that it requires a leap of imagination to picture it any other way.

Autumn is over when the windows of buses are suddenly no longer open to the breeze. In November the public heating is officially switched on, and by about the same time the great procession of tour buses beyond the Colosseum has dwindled to a trickle. Churches and museums fall empty, and only the Sistine Chapel concentrates sightseers with the intensity of summer.

Everybody has a little more space, a little more time. The city in winter becomes almost a normally functioning metropolis. The dog days of August are gone, so, too, the rumbling storms and lethargic humidity of April and September. Nights are crisp, even bitterly cold, and days are usually clear with blue skies.

Once a decade, perhaps, the impossible happens, and it snows, transforming Rome into the most beautiful city in the world. Chestnut sellers materialize on street corners, and hot chocolate appears again on the counters of bars. Persimmons come into the shops, along with the first Sicilian oranges and the traditional cakes and sweets of the Roman Christmas. Stores roll out red-and-green carpets over entire pavements, and during December Piazza Navona is filled with stalls for the traditional Christmas *festa*.

January passes quietly into February. Then before you know it, strangers are suddenly wandering the streets, disgorged from a line of tour buses that appear as if by magic in the week before Easter. Rome girds itself and then wearily begins its decline into summer madness.

A Swiss Guard in Vatican City

Arriving

Passports and visas U.S. citizens need a valid passport to enter Italy for stays of up to 90 days. First-timers should apply in person five weeks before departure to one of the 13 U.S. Passport Agency offices. Also, local county courthouses, many state and probate courts and some post offices accept applications.

Necessary documents are (1) a completed passport application (Form DSP-11); (2) proof of citizenship (certified birth certificate issued by the Hall of Records of your state of birth, or naturalization papers); (3) proof of identity (valid driver's license or state, military or student ID card with your photgraph and signature); (4) two recent, identical, two-square-inch photographs (black-and-white or color head shot with white or off-white background); and (5) $65 for a ten-year passport (those under 18 pay $40 for a five-year passport). Check, money order or cash (exact change) are accepted. Passports are sent in 10 to 15 business days.

You may renew in person or by mail. Send a complete Form DSP-82; two recent, identical passport photographs; your current passport (if it's less than 12 years old and issued after your 16th birthday); and a check or money order for $55.

By air All scheduled international and most domestic flights arrive at Aeroporto Leonardo da Vinci, 36km southwest of the city center, referred to more commonly by Romans as Fiumicino, the town nearest the airport (tel: 3640 or 60 121).

Charter flights use the smaller military airport, 16km southeast of the city at Ciampino, Via Appia Nuova (tel: 4694 or 724 241).

Private planes use Urbe on the Via Salaria (tel: 812 0524).

Fiumicino (Leonardo da Vinci) deals with heavy inbound and outbound air traffic, so be prepared for delays and congestion. The airport boasts all the facilities you would expect, including restaurants, bars, shops, a bank, a bureau de change, a hotel information desk, and car rental desks. Ciampino has similar facilities on a more modest scale, though improvements are in progress and there are plans to raise the airport's status to rival that of Fiumicino.

The quickest and cheapest way to reach the city center from Fiumicino is on the new railway line from the international terminal to the Metropolitana (subway) station at Ostiense. Trains leave every 15 minutes. At Ostiense you have a five-minute walk across the station to connect with the subway train that runs to the central railway station, Stazione Termini. Allow 50 minutes for the journey. Note that the widely advertised ACOTRAL bus service from the airport to Termini runs only at night.

Metered taxis are also available but can prove expensive if you get stuck in traffic. The 36-km trip should take about 30 minutes, but in peak times it can take two hours. There is a surcharge to the meter fare, and you should expect to pay around L60,000 for the whole journey. For the same price – and with the bonus that it is guaranteed before you start – you can hire a chauffeur-driven limousine from the SOCAT desk in the international arrivals terminal: Look for the yellow signs saying "Car with Driver." Do not accept rides from unlicensed cars (see **Public Transport**) and keep an eye on your luggage at all times in the airport.

A half-hourly ACOTRAL bus runs from Ciampino to the subway station at Subaugusta, where there are connections for Termini. Allow at least an hour for the journey.

By train Most national and international trains arrive at and depart from Stazione Termini, Piazza dei Cinquecento (tel: 4775) (known simply as Termini), which is centrally placed for all parts of the city.

Rome's other four stations are of marginal use to most visitors: Trastevere, on Viale Trastevere, handles a few trains to Tuscany, Umbria and Lazio; Roma Nord, off Piazzale Flaminia, serves the private line to Viterbo and northern Lazio;

Tiburtina, on the east side of the city, and Ostiense serve some long-distance north–south trains that stop in Rome during the night. Ostiense is

TRAVEL FACTS

the station for trips to Ostia Antica. Termini is always busy and can appear chaotic and intimidating to the first-time visitor. It is, however, a modern and efficient terminus, with shops, bars, a post office, telephones, newsstands, a pharmacy, and bureau de change kiosks. Many are crowded and some, such as the Albergo Diurno, or day hotel, – for toilets, showers, and so on – are not in the main lobby but downstairs in the station's lower levels. Left-luggage facilities are alongside Platform 1, on the extreme right of the station. There are also full-ticket and reservations facilities for national, international and discounted student tickets, as well as *couchettes* and sleepers. Dozens of buses leave for all points of the city from the front of the station, and Termini is also the intersection of the subway.

By car Car travelers will probably approach Rome on the Autostrada del Sole motorway, designated as the A1 on the Florence–Rome section to the north and the A2 on the Rome–Naples section to the south. The other main approaches to the city are the A12 motorway from Pisa on the west coast and the A24 from the Abruzzo and Adriatic coast in the east. All join the main Rome ring road, the Gran Raccordo Anulare (GRA), an extremely busy and dangerous two-lane highway (currently being widened to three lanes in places), with some 30 exits leading into the city and to the outer suburbs. Traffic jams of several miles are common at rush hour. The best way to enter the city center is to follow "Roma Centro" signs at the Aurelia or Appia exits north and south of the GRA, respectively.

Audiences with the pope
These are usually held on Wednesday. For tickets to a general audience, apply to the Prefettura della Casa Pontifica: 00120 Città del Vaticano(6982). Do this no later than 2 days and no earlier than 1 month before the date you wish to attend.

Camping
Camping is not the way to spend a night in Rome; all the city's main sites, listed in the **Accommodations** section (pages 279–80), are well

Looking down on the crowds from Trinità dei Monti

out of the city, and none is particularly cheap or salubrious. All have water, electricity and toilet facilities, and the majority are open all year.

Tourist offices have full details and current prices for sites, but if you are camping extensively, it is worth investing in the widely available *Campeggi e Villaggi Turistici*, a full rundown of sites in Italy published by the Italian Touring Club (TCI). You can obtain a free and less detailed list and make bookings in advance from the *Centro Internazionale Prenotazioni Federcampeggio*, Casella Postale 23, Calenzano, Florence (tel: (055) 882 391). Bookings can also be made direct to the campsite, but none of the Rome sites is busy enough to make reservations essential. Rough camping outside official sites – in the parks, for example – is not recommended and is usually illegal.

Children

Italians welcome children of all ages, and ample accommodation is made for them. All but budget hotels accept them unquestioningly, and it is perfectly normal to take even young children to restaurants in the evening. Diapers, accessories, and baby foods are all widely available, and shopkeepers will happily recommend Italian brands. Children under four ride free on buses, trams and trains and have free admittance to museums and galleries.

Children between four and 12 qualify for half-price reductions. The main dangers for children are the traffic – especially in the center's narrow streets, getting lost in crowds, and the unfenced banks of the Tiber on the Isola Tiberina.

Ice cream and pizza are obvious ways to spoil or placate children, and many of the key sights should capture youthful imaginations:

the Colosseum
Castel Sant' Angelo and its dungeons
the Trevi Fountain
the zoo in Villa Borghese
carriage rides from Piazza di Spagna
boat trips on the Tiber, or the modest and somewhat tatty Wax Museum on the eastern side of Piazza Venezia (*open:* daily 9–9).

Parks and zoos Most of the parks are appealing, the key attraction being the permanent funfair known as Luna Park at EUR, Via delle Tre Fontane (tel: 592 5933).

It is large and well equipped, if old-fashioned and overpriced, but the emphasis is on family amusement, so in addition to a famed Ferris wheel and roller coaster, there are a boating lake, miniature golf course, cafés and bars.

The park on the Colle Oppio, across from the Colosseum, has a roller skating rink and small playground.

The best open space for energetic youngsters is the Villa Ada, west of the Via Salaria, where they will find two playgrounds, a roller rink, areas for biking and skateboarding, ponds and wooded slopes.

Pony rides are given in Villa Glori, north of Villa Borghese, and pony-cart rides in Villa Balestra.

In the Villa Borghese you can rent boats or visit the small zoo, the Giardino Zoologico (tel: 870 564). The zoo is open all year (except on public holidays), 8:30–sunset, year-round, with free admission for

Symmetrical beauty in the Vatican Gardens

children. Check the feeding times, which are posted near the entrance.

Theaters and shows In summer parks and piazzas host numerous outdoor events specifically for kids, and from mid-December to January 6, there is a children's fair daily in Piazza Navona.

Puppet shows are presented in English each weekend at the Teatro dei Satiri, Via Grotta Pinta 19 (tel: 686 5352/589 6201), and the Teatro Crisogono, Via San Gallicano 8, off Viale Trastevere, has Sicilian puppet shows at 5pm on Thursday, Saturday and Sunday.

Theaters put on special children's matinees, but shows are invariably in Italian.

There is a children's movie theater at Via della Pineta 15 (tel: 863 485) and a planetarium on Via Giuseppe Romita.

Time for relaxation on the Piazza del Popolo

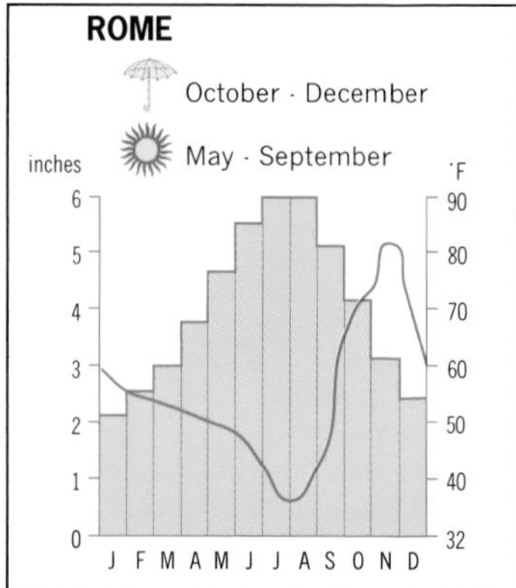

Weather Chart Conversion
25.4mm = 1inch
°F = 1.8 x °C + 32

Climate
Rome's weather is more fickle than most Mediterranean cities. Rainfall is greater than London, thunderstorms can flood streets in August, and you can bask in sunshine at Christmas. Generally, however, conditions are predictable. You can expect stifling heat during July and August – up to 100°F – often accompanied by the notorious humidity, which can strike at any time of the year. The *scirocco,* a scorching wind from North Africa – called Colonel Qaddafi's weather – can raise temperatures and humidity from April through October. Winter is short and crisp, with temperatures reaching freezing, though snow has been known only once in the past decade. Spring starts any time from mid-March and is short and delightful, though April and May can be muggy. Autumn, too, can produce perfect days, cool and bright, but also weeks of wet and wind. The panel chart gives a rough idea of what to expect: Summer temperatures can be higher than the averages given here.

Crime
The sheer number of visitors to Rome makes them an obvious target for the unscrupulous, and all sorts of horror stories are told of the unwitting tourist fleeced by Rome's criminal classes. Few such stories have much basis in fact, and while

Rome has its fair share of crime, like any other major metropolis, common sense and a few precautions will keep you safe.

- Always carry money and valuables securely in a belt or pouch – never in a pocket.
- Wear your camera, never put it down on café tables and beware of strap-cutting thieves.
- Do not flaunt valuables – better still, do not take them with you.
- Leave all jewelery in the hotel, especially chains and earrings, which may be snatched.
- Women should hold shoulder bags across their front as the Romans do, never just hung over one shoulder, where they can easily be rifled or grabbed.
- Be especially careful of pickpockets on crowded buses – the 64, always full of tourists on their way to St. Peter's, is notorious.
- Light-fingered experts are also at work among the big crowds at papal addresses on Wednesday and Sunday in St. Peter's Square.
- Be wary of the small but completely determined gypsy children who may jab a piece of cardboard in your midriff and rifle through your pockets. They move in groups and can be extremely persistent; hang on to everything you have, raise your voice, and resist as forcefully as you can.
- Key areas for extra vigilance are where tourists and shoppers congregate:

the Colosseum
St. Peter's
Via Vittorio Veneto
Largo Argentina
Via dei Fori Imperiali
Via del Tritone
Via del Corso

- At night avoid parks, peripheral parts of Trastevere, trysts in the ruins, and the area around Termini.

Report any theft to your hotel, and register the fact to the police at the *Questura,* Via San Vitale 15 (tel: 4686), which has a special department to deal with tourists' problems.

If you lose your passport, first report to the police, then contact your consulate or embassy.

Michelangelo's Moses, *San Pietro in Vincoli*

Customs Regulations

You may bring home up to $400 of foreign goods duty-free, provided you've been out of the country for at least 48 hours and you haven't made an international trip in the past 30 days. Each member of the family, regardless of age, is entitled to the same exemption; exemptions may be pooled. For the next $1,000 of goods, a flat 10% rate is assessed; above $1,400, duties vary with merchandise. Travelers 21 or older are allowed one liter of alcohol, 100 cigars (non-Cuban), and 200 cigarettes, and one bottle of perfume trademarked in the United States. Antiques and works of art over 100 years old are duty-free. Exceed these limits, and you'll be taxed at the port of entry and additionally in your home state. Gifts under $50 may be mailed duty-free to stateside friends or relatives, with a limit of one package per day per addressee. Perfumes over $5, tobacco, and liquor are prohibited. For "Know Before You Go," a free brochure detailing what you may and may not bring back into this country, contact the U.S. Customs Service (1301

Constitution Ave., Washington, DC 20029, tel: 202/927–6724).

Disabled Travelers

Rome is not an easy city for people with physical disabilities – streets are narrow and car-crowded – though facilities are slowly improving and the staff at airports, and places of interest is always willing to help. Vatican City, by contrast, has more elevators and ramps, and some up-market hotels have rooms for guests with disabilities. Thanks to a press campaign, certain high-speed trains now have wheelchair facilities. Rest rooms suitable for wheelchairs are available at Fiumicino and Ciampino airports, Termini (adjacent to Platform 1), and EUR metro stations, Metro Nazionale and the south side of Piazza San Pietro.

Restaurants present few problems, though it is a good idea to call ahead to reserve a convenient table.

Unfortunately, the city's sights are more difficult to negotiate: Most churches and museums have steps somewhere. The tourist office will provide full details of accessible sights. The more straightforward are:

the Roman Forum
the Pantheon
San Giovanni in Laterano
Santa Sabina
San Prassede
the Terme di Caracalla

Slightly more tricky are these:

the Colosseum
the Museo Nazionale Romano
the Villa Giulia
the Museo Nazionale d'Arte Orientale

General information on traveling abroad can be obtained from the following:

Australia: ACROD, 33 Thesigner Court, Deakin, ACT 2600 (tel: 06/282 4333)
Canada: Canadian Rehabilitation Council for the Disabled, 45 Sheppard Avenue E, Suite 801, Toronto, Ontario M2N 5W9 (tel: 416/250 7490)
Eire: The Disabled Drivers Association of Ireland and the Irish Association of Physically Handicapped People, Ballindine, County Mayo
New Zealand: Disabled Citizens' Society, Inc., PO Box 56-083, Dominion Road, Auckland 3
UK: Mobility International, 8 Borough High Street, London SE1 1JX (tel: 071/403 5688), and RADAR, 25 Mortimer Street, London W1 (tel: 071/723 4004)
U.S.: Information Center for Individuals with Disabilities, Fort Point Place, 1st Floor, 27-43 Wormwood Street, Boston MA 02210 (tel: 617/757–5540)

Moss Rehabilitation Hospital Travel information Service (1200 West Tabor Rd., Philadelphia, PA 19141, tel: 215/456–9603, TDD tel: 215/456–9602) provides information on tourist sights, transportation, and accommodations in destinations around the world for a small fee. They also provide toll-free telephone numbers for airlines with special lines for the hard of hearing.

Travel Industry and Disabled Exchange (TIDE, 5435 Donna Ave., Tarzana, CA 91356, tel: 818/368–5648) publishes a quarterly newsletter and a directory of travel agencies catering to the disabled. Annual membership is $15.

Mobility International USA (Box 3551, Eugene, OR 97403, voice and TDD tel: 503/343–1284) is an internationally affiliated organization with 500 members. For a $20 annual fee, it coordinates exchange programs for disabled people around the world and offers information on accommodations and study programs. It also publishes *A world of Options for the 90s*, a guide to international exchange and travel for people with disabilities (send $16 to the address above).

The **Society for the Advancement of Travel for the Handicapped** (SATH, 347 5th Ave., suite 610, New York, NY 10016, tel: 212/447–7284, fax 212/725–8253 provides information on and lists of tour operators specializing in travel for the disabled. Annual membership is $45, $25 for students and senior citizens. Send $2 and a SASE for information on specific distinations identification. Permits are available for a small fee through local offices of the American Automobile Association (AAA).

Fishing beneath the "Breezy Maniacs" ranged along the Ponte Sant'Angelo

The Project Phoenix Trust publishes a guide to Rome (and Florence) based on the personal experiences of disabled travelers; write to
Mrs. V. Saunders
Project Phoenix Trust
56 Burnaby Road
Southend-on-Sea
Essex, UK
(tel: 0702/466412)

Driving
Everything argues against driving in Rome – congestion, narrow streets, access restrictions to the city center, bad driving, bad roads, dreadful road manners, thefts, almost non-existent legal parking, and double or triple street parking. However, if you must bring a car into Rome, remember the following:
Documents Drivers licenses issued in the United States are valid in Italy. You must also have Green Card insurance and should also consider taking out an International Driving Permit before you leave, to smooth

Rules and regulations Italian traffic rules are allied to the Geneva Convention, and accordingly Italy uses internationally agreed road signs.

When driving in Rome, the main rules that you must remember are: drive on the right and give way at intersections to vehicles coming from your right.

The speed limit in built-up areas is 50 kph (31 mph), but many local drivers ignore it. Outside urban areas the limit is 90 kph (56 mph), and on motorways (autostrada) it is 130 kph (81 mph) for vehicles over 1100cc. Carrying warning triangles and wearing front-seat seat belts are compulsory in Italy.

For information on routes, road conditions, gas stations, spare tires and garages that repair foreign cars, contact the Automobile Club d'Italia (ACI), Via Marsala 8 (tel: 49 981). ACI's emergency breakdown phone number is 116; for the ACI-Rome Service Center, call 4212. For extra information, try the Automobile Club di Roma, Via C Colombo 261 (tel: 5106).

Accidents and breakdowns If you break down, put on hazard warning lights and – if appropriate in a congested street – place a warning triangle 50 m behind the car. Then call the ACI (tel: 116), giving the operator your location, car registration and make.

The car will be towed free to the nearest ACI-affiliated garage or elsewhere for a fee.

The service is available to any visiting motorist driving a foreign registered vehicle.

ACI offices also tell you where to obtain spare tires for your type of vehicle.

If you have an accident call the police (tel: 113) and do not admit liability or make statements that may later incriminate you.

Ask witnesses to remain and to make a statement to the police, and exchange names, addresses, car details and insurance companies' names and addresses with other drivers involved in the accident.

- Never leave valuables in your car and, if possible, remove car radios and stereo systems. If your car disappears, it may not have been stolen but towed away because it was blocking traffic. Call the Vigili Urbani (tel: 67 691) to find out where it is.

Gasoline Italy is one of the most expensive countries in Europe in which to buy gas – the price at press time was about L1,500 a liter (L6,750 a gallon).

If you are arriving in Italy with a car rented elsewhere in Europe, you are entitled to a 15 percent discount on gas (supergrade and leadfree) and highway tolls; an additional benefit is free breakdown and replacement car concessions. Coupons and vouchers for these discounts are not available in Italy and are best obtained from the Italian State Tourist Office in your home country. They are also available at ACI offices on a few Italian frontier posts. Only the issuing office can make refunds, and passports and vehicle-registration documents are necessary to make the purchase. There are no discounts for tourists renting a car in Italy.

Gas stations in Rome usually amount to no more than a couple of pumps on the pavement; most follow normal shop hours and are closed on Sunday.

Riding out in style, with the rest of Rome's formidable traffic

Car rentals Most major car-rental companies are represented in Rome, and visitors are advised to make a reservation in advance. Usually, you must be over 21 years of age (25 in some cases) to rent a car, and restrictions may apply to drivers over 60. Your current driver's license is usually acceptable, but some require an International Driver's Permit, available through an Automobile Club (AAA or CAA) office.

For reservations call:
Avis (tel. 800/331–1212);
Budget (tel. 800/527–0700);
Dollar (tel. 800/800–40000);
Hertz (tel. 800/654–3131);
National (800/328–4567).

Riding a scooter is a good, if life-endangering way of seeing Rome and is the means by which most young Romans get about the city. To rent one of the whining *vespas* (literally "wasps"), you must be over 21, have a driver's license, and leave your passport as a deposit. Try Scoot-a-long, Via Cavour 302 (tel: 678 0206); Scooters for Rent, Via della Purificazione 66 (tel: 465 485); and St. Peter Rent, Via di Porta Castello 43 (tel: 687 5714)

Electricity
The current is 220 volts AC, 50 cycles, with plugs of the two "round"

pin type. In older hotels and houses you will find two-pin plugs of different specifications, but adapters are widely available.

Embassies
All major countries are represented by an embassy in Rome. Embassies include
Australian Embassy: Via Alessandria 215 (tel: 832 731)
Canadian Embassy: Via G Bastia de Rossi 27 (tel: 855 341)
Irish Embassy: Largo Nazareno 3 (tel: 678 2541)
New Zealand Embassy: Via Zara 28 (tel: 851 225)
UK (British) Embassy: Via XX Settembre 80a (tel: 475 5441)
U.S. (American) Embassy: Via Vittorio Veneto 119a (tel: 46 741)

Emergency Telephone Numbers
Police, ambulance, fire 113
Red Cross 5100
Local police (Carabinieri) 212 121
Police headquarters (Questura) 4686
Car breakdown 116
English-speaking doctor:
Salvator Mundi International Hospital, Viale delle Mura Gianicolensi 66/67 (tel: 586 041)
English-speaking dentist:
Dental Hospital G. Eastman, Viale Regina Elena 287 (tel: 491 949)
Samaritans 678 9227 (Open: 7:30AM–10:30PM)

Etiquette
- Do not wear shorts, short skirts or skimpy tops into churches.
- Do not intrude while church services are in progress.
- Many churches forbid the use of the flash with cameras or the taking of photographs altogether.
- Italians smoke a good deal more than most, and there are still few no-smoking areas in restaurants and public places. Smoking is banned on buses and the metro.

Glossary of Artistic and Architectural Terms

aedicule:	decorative niche framed by columns
ambo:	simple medieval pulpit, often with marble inlay
anfiteatro:	amphitheater
apse:	semicircular recess behind church altar
architrave:	a supporting beam above a column
atrium:	inner entrance court of early house or church
baldacchino:	a canopy on columns,usually over a church altar
basilica:	originally a Roman administrative building. Later used in churches. Distinguished by a lack of transepts
battistero:	baptistery
caldarium:	steam room of a Roman bath
campanile:	bell tower
campo:	square
camposanto:	cemetery
cantoria:	choir loft
capital:	top of a column
cappella:	chapel
cartoon:	preliminary sketch for a fresco or tapestry
caryatid:	carved female figure used as a column
chancel:	part of church containing altar

Fountain and facade: Sabatini on Piazza Santa Maria (see Directory)

chiaroscuro: exaggerated light and shade effects in a painting
chiesa: church
chiostro: cloister
ciborium: tabernacle or casket for the host on or behind the altar
clivus: Latin word for street on a slope
colombarium: part of a tomb, with wall niches for the dead
comune: administrative department of an Italian town, city or village
confessio: crypt beneath a church's high altar
cornice: top of a classical facade
cortile: courtyard
cosmati: colored marble inlay
crypt: burial place of a church, usually under the altar
cupola: dome
diptych: two-panel painting
entablature: section of a classical building above the capital and below the cornice
exedra: a semicircular recess
fresco: wall painting
graffito: incised decoration on a building or wall

Ancient Rome lives on: impressive remains of the Roman Forum

horrea: Roman workshop or warehouse
insula: old Roman multistory building
intarsia: mosaic or inlay work in wood or stone
loggia: roof-gallery or outside balcony
lunetta: semicircular space above door, window or vaulting
matroneum: women's gallery in early churches
narthex: vestibule of a church nave: central space of a church
palazzo: palace, large house or apartment building
pendentives: four curved triangular elements on piers supporting a dome or cupola
peristyle: courtyard surrounded by colonnades
piano nobile: main floor of a palace
pietà: image of the Madonna mourning the dead Christ
pinacoteca: picture gallery
porta: gate
portico: covered doorway
predella: small panel below main part of an altarpiece
presepio: Christmas crib
sinopia: wall sketch for a fresco
stele: vertical headstone
teatro: theater
tempio: temple
terme: baths
torre: tower
transept: traverse arms of a church
tribune: raised gallery in a church or the apse of a basilica
triptych: painting on three panels
trompe l'oeil: tricks of perspective in a work of art

Health
Vaccinations are unnecessary for entry into Italy unless you are traveling from a known infected area. Full travel and health insurance is

very strongly recommended (to cover, for example, repatriation costs, that may be enormous). Canadian nationals are covered by their country's health insurance for treatment in Italy.

For minor ailments and injuries visit a pharmacy (see **Pharmacies**), where the staff is well trained. If for any reason you need to buy prescription drugs, have your doctor write a prescription using the drug's generic name; brand names usually vary from country to country. You will have to pay a percentage of the cost of a medicine prescribed by a doctor, as well as a fixed charge per item.

Water in Rome is perfectly safe to drink, and blisters, heat and sun problems – perhaps with the odd stomach upset – are likely to be the worst problems you will encounter.

If you need a doctor, ask first at your hotel or consult the local Yellow Pages under *Unita Sanitaria Locale*. If you want a private doctor or a hospital where English is sure to be spoken, call the Salvator Mundi International Hospital, Viale delle Mura Gianicolensi 66/67 (tel: 586 041).

The **International Association for Medical Assistance to Travelers (in the U.S.:** 417 Center St., Lewiston, NY 14092, tel. 716/754–4883) offers a free worldwide list of approved physicians and clinics whose training meets British and American standards.

If you need an ambulance, call the Italian Red Cross (tel: 5100) or the emergency services number – 113.

If immediate medical assistance is required, the following hospitals offer 24-hour first aid and emergency services:

Fatebenefratelli, Isola Tiberina (tel: 58 731)

Policlinico Gemelli, Largo Gemelli 8 (tel: 33 051)

Policlinico Umberto I, Viale del Policlinico 1 (tel: 4997 492 341)

San Camillo, Circonvallazione Gianicolense 87 (tel: 58 701)

Two sides of Roman life: paths cross briefly beneath the columns of the Pantheon

Sant'Eugenio, Piazzale dell'Umanesimon (EUR) (tel: 592 5903)

San Filippo, Via Martinotti 20 (tel: 33 061)

San Giacomo, Via Canova 29 (tel: 6726)

San Giovanni, Via Ambra Aradam 8 (tel: 77 051)

Santo Spirito (near the Vatican), Lungotevere in Sassia 1 (tel: 650 901)

Language

Italian in the mouth of a Roman can be incomprehensible – even to native speakers. Nonetheless, you should be able to make yourself understood, and Italians respond very warmly to foreigners who make an effort, however poor, to speak their language.

Younger Romans may nowadays know a smattering of English, and in the more up-market hotels and restaurants you should, of course, have few problems.

Almost all Italian words are pronounced exactly as they are written, with each vowel and each consonant sounded. Consonants are the same as in English, except for c when followed by **i** or **e**, when it becomes the soft **ch** of "children"; otherwise, **c** is hard, as in the English "cat."

The same applies to **g** when followed by **i** or **e** – soft in *giardino*, as in the English "giant"; hard in *gatto*, as in "gate."

Words ending in **o** are almost always masculine gender (plural: **i**); those ending in **a** are feminine (plural: **e**).

Days of the week
Monday lunedì
Tuesday martedì
Wednesday mercoledì
Thursday giovedì
Friday venerdì
Saturday sabato
Sunday domenica

Months of the year
January gennaio
February febbraio
March marzo
April aprile
May maggio
June giugno
July luglio
August agosto
September settembre
October ottobre
November novembre
December dicembre

Music making has always been an integral part of Italian life

Numbers
one uno
two due
three tre
four quattro
five cinque
six sei
seven sette
eight otto
nine nove
10 dieci
11 undici
12 dodici
13 tredici
14 quattordici
15 quindici
16 sedici
17 diciasette
18 diciotto
19 diciannove
20 venti
30 trenta
40 quaranta
50 cinquanta
60 sessanta
70 settanta
80 ottanta
90 novanta
100 cento
101 cento uno
200 duecento
1,000 mille
2,000 due mila
1,000,000 milione

Basic vocabulary
yes sì
no no
maybe forse
OK/alright va bene
please per favore
thank you grazie
good morning buon giorno
good afternoon/good evening buona sera
good night buona notte
morning mattino
afternoon pomeriggio
evening sera
night notte
early presto
late tardi
yesterday ieri
today oggi
tomorrow domani
next week la settimana prossima
last week la settimana scorsa
here qui/qua
there lì / la

small piccolo
large grande
nothing niente
what? che?
who? chi?
where? dove?
when? quando
why? perchè?
how? come?
how much is it? quant'e?
expensive caro
good buono
bad cattivo
beautiful bello
ugly brutto
well bene
badly male
with con
but ma
and e/ed
very molto
all tutto
near vicino
far lontano
on the left a sinistra
on the right a destra
straight ahead diretto
slow piano
fast presto/rapido
hot caldo
cold freddo
up su
down giù
open aperto
closed chiuso
entrance entrata
exit uscita
free libero
how are you? come sta?
very well, thank you benissimo, grazie
Do you speak English? parla inglese?
I would like . . . vorrei . . .
Do you have . . . ? avete . . . ?
Is there . . . ? c'e un . . . ?
What time is it? che ore sono?
I'm sorry mi scusi
I don't know non io so
I don't understand non capisco
excuse me (to attract attention) senta
excuse me (on a bus, train, etc.) permesso
not at all/you're welcome prego
help aiuto

Lost Property
Report losses first to your hotel and

Sightseers stroll by the church of Santa Maria in Cosmedin

then to the police at the *Questura* at Via S Vitale 15 (tel: 4686).

Rome's central lost-property office (Ufficio Oggetti Rinvenuti) is at Via Niccolo Bettoni 1 (tel: 581 6040) *open* 9–noon.

- For articles lost on buses or trollies, apply to the main ATAC office, Via Volturno 65 (tel: 46 951), *open* 9–noon.
- Try also the railway lost-property office behind Termini, the Ufficio Oggetti Rinvenuti, Via Marsala 53 (tel: 4730 6682), *open* all day, 7– midnight.
- Report the loss or theft of passports to the police and then contact your consulate.
- If you lose your traveler's checks, notify the police, follow the instructions given with the checks, and inform the issuing company's nearest office.

Maps
Most tobacconists, newsstands, and bookshops sell a variety of street and touring maps, but adequate maps of Rome are available free from all local tourist offices (see **Tourist Offices**, below).

For maps of the bus, tram and metro network, contact the ATAC information booth next to Termini in Piazza dei Cinquecento.

CONVERSION CHARTS

FROM	TO	MULTIPLY BY
Inches	Centimeters	2.54
Centimeters	Inches	0.3937
Feet	Meters	0.3048
Meters	Feet	3.2810
Yards	Meters	0.9144
Meters	Yards	1.0940
Miles	Kilometers	1.6090
Kilometers	Miles	0.6214
Acres	Hectares	0.4047
Hectares	Acres	2.4710
U.S. Gallons	Liters	3.7854
Liters	U.S. Gallons	0.2642
Ounces	Grams	28.35
Grams	Ounces	0.0353
Pounds	Grams	453.6
Grams	Pounds	0.0022
Pounds	Kilograms	0.4536
Kilograms	Pounds	2.205
U.S. Tons	Tonnes	0.9072
Tonnes	U.S. Tons	1.1023

MEN'S SUITS

U.K.	36	38	40	42	44	46	48
Rest of Europe	46	48	50	52	54	56	58
U.S.	36	38	40	42	44	46	48

DRESS SIZES

U.K.	8	10	12	14	16	18
France	36	38	40	42	44	46
Italy	38	40	42	44	46	48
Rest of Europe	34	36	38	40	42	44
U.S.	6	8	10	12	14	16

MEN'S SHIRTS

U.K.	14	14.5	15	15.5	16	16.5	17
Rest of Europe	36	37	38	39/40	41	42	43
U.S.	14	14.5	15	15.5	16	16.5	17

MEN'S SHOES

U.K.	7	7.5	8.5	9.5	10.5	11
Rest of Europe	41	42	43	44	45	46
U.S.	8	8.5	9.5	10.5	11.5	12

WOMEN'S SHOES

U.K.	4.5	5	5.5	6	6.5	7
Rest of Europe	38	38	39	39	40	41
U.S.	6	6.5	7	7.5	8	8.5

Media

Most major foreign language newspapers and magazines are available on the day of issue after 2 in the afternoon at the larger newsstands (*edicole*) at
Termini
Piazza Colonna
Via Veneto
Largo Argentino
Piazza Navona

The European editions of the *Financial Times* and the *International Herald Tribune* are widely available, and most smaller newsstands hold a few main titles after the day of issue. Rome's local newspaper is *Il Messagero*, but the Center-Left *La Repubblica* and Center-Right *Corriere della Sera* both publish daily city editions. All three carry daily details of local film, theater and cultural events. *La Repubblica*'s Saturday edition contains a free supplement, *Trovaroma*, with comprehensive listings for Rome and a what's on guide for the coming week.

Italian radio and television are both deregulated, and both offer a vast range of national and local stations. However, standards are usually pitifully low, with the local networks geared mainly to advertising, pop music and old films. National stations are better, dividing about equally between the three channels of the state RAI network and the stable of channels owned by Silvio Berlusconi (*Canale 5, Rete 4* and *Italia Uno*).

Money Matters

The Italian currency is the *lira* (plural *lire*), abbreviated to L.
Notes are issued in denominations of
L1,000
L2,000
L5,000
L10,000
L50,000
L100,000
Coins come in denominations of
L5
L10
(both very rare)
L50
L100
L200
L500

Mosaics in the Basilica di San Paolo fuori le Mura

and there is a L200 telephone token (*gettone*), that is also used as a coin.

- It is now unusual to be given candy in lieu of change, as happened in the past, but small denominations are still scarce and presenting L50,000 and L100,000 can still cause problems.
- All the zeros can be confusing, so check change and all monetary transactions carefully.

Import and export Visitors are advised to contact their banks for up-to-date information. If you wish to re-export (from Italy) amounts in excess of L1,000,000 and L5,000,000, respectively, you must complete Form V2 at the customs upon entry, and this form must be shown to customs on leaving. Hold on to all receipts and stubs of any transactions in the (unlikely) case of problems when you leave the country.

Traveler's checks There are no restrictions on traveler's checks, and all major checks (Thomas Cook, American Express) as well as Eurocheques are widely recognized. You may charge up to L300,000 to each Eurocheque, and most banks will allow you to cash up to three a day.

Credit cards (*carta di credito*) are gaining in acceptance, though only the larger hotels, shops and restaurants will accept them in practice. It is not unusual to find some establishment refusing a card, even though it displays a sticker of one of the principal cards (American Express, Diners Club, Visa, Access, Mastercard). It is worth checking well before you have to pay the bill. Also be sure it is impossible for stubs to be tampered with once you have signed. Gas stations will not accept cards.

Exchange Most banks will change foreign currency and traveler's checks – look for the sign *cambio,* but lines may be long and the service laborious. Many banks are concentrated on Via del Corso, between Piazza Venezia and Piazza Colonna. Specialist exchange outlets may offer a marginally worse rate but eliminate the lines and frustration. Specialist outlets are also open outside the normal banking hours (Monday to Friday, 8:30–1:30). Many hotels will change money, and on weekends, evenings and holidays, money may also be changed at Termini, at the American Express office in Piazza di Spagna, or at the airport, where counters are open most of the night.

National Holidays
Shops, banks, offices, and schools are closed on the following days:
January 1 (New Year's Day)
January 6 (Epiphany)
Easter Monday
April 25 (Liberation Day)
May 1 (Labor Day)
June 29 (St. Peter's Day)
August 15 (Assumption)
November 1 (All Saints' Day)
December 8 (Immaculate Conception of the Virgin Mary)
Christmas Day
December 26 (Santo Stefano)

- When a public holiday falls on a Tuesday or Thursday, it is customary to make a *ponte* (bridge) to the weekend and take the Monday or Friday off as well.
- Roads and railways are especially busy on and around all holidays.

Opening Times
Shops and offices are normally open from 8:30 or 9 to 1, reopening in the afternoon at 3:30 or 4 to 7:30 or 8. Most shops are closed on Sunday and many on Monday morning, and food shops also closed on Thursday afternoon. In summer a number of stores also shut on Saturday afternoon. Bars and the odd *pasticceria,* or cake shop, are the only things open Sunday. Bars and restaurants must close by law on one other day of the week, the day being specified by a sign outside the establishment.

- A large number of shops, bars, and restaurants shut completely for a summer holiday throughout August: *chiuso per ferie* is the telltale sign.

A panoramic view of the capital from the vantage point of Trinità dei Monti

Museums and galleries are usually open from 9 to 2 and sometimes from 4 to 7, and are closed on Monday. Some open also from 5 to 8 on Tuesday and Thursday. Most close a couple hours early on Sunday and do not reopen in the afternoon. Always check on opening times before a visit, to avoid disappointment. Archaeological sites, such as the Roman Forum, tend to be open all day from 9 to 5.

Churches *open* in the early morning, at around 7am, for Mass, and close around noon, opening up again at about 4pm and closing at around 7pm.

Banks are open from Monday to Friday, 8:30–1:30, and major banks may also open from 3 to 4pm. Bureaux de change (*cambio*) are open normal office hours.
Parks open from 8am until sunset, except for the Villa Borghese, which stays open.

Termini railway station closes at 2am until the first morning trains leave at about 4:30am.

Pharmacies
Pharmacies (*farmacia*) keep the same hours as shops, but also stay open late on a rotating basis. If your nearest pharmacy is closed, it will show a list of pharmacies nearby that are open at lunchtime, on holidays or at night. You can also telephone 1921 for a recorded listing.

The following are open all night:
Brienza, Piazza Risorgimento 44 (tel: 352 157)
Cristo Re, Galleria Testa of the Stazione Termini (tel: 460 776)
De Luca (near Stazione Termini), Via Cavour 2 (tel: 460 019)
Internazionale (near Via V Veneto),

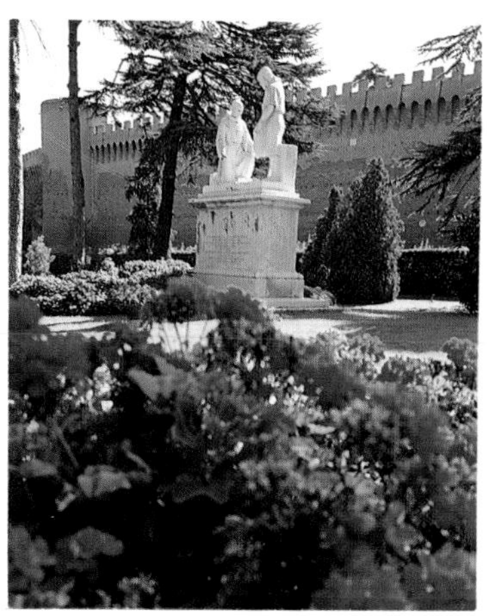

Natural and man-made ornaments on display at the Vatican Gardens

Piazza Barberini 49 (tel: 462 996)
Piram, Via Nazionale 228 (tel: 460 754)
Tre Madonne (in Parioli), Via Bertolini 5 (tel: 873 423)
Spinedi, Via Arenula 73 (tel: 654 3278)

Pharmacies sell a full range of toiletries and medicines over the counter, including some that are available only on prescription in other countries. However, if you are looking for specific British or American brands, try Internazionale or Baker and Co, Via Vittorio Emanuele Orlando 92 (tel: 460 408); Evans, Piazza di Spagna 63; or Tuccie, Via Vittorio Veneto 129 (tel: 493 447).

Places of Worship
Confession in English is heard at the Patriarchal basilicas:
St. Peter's
Santa Maria Maggiore
San Giovanni in Laterano
San Paulo fuori le Mure – all of which are open all day –
and in
San Anselmo
San Clemente
Gesù
San Ignazio
Santa Maria sopra Minerva
Santa Sabina
Roman Catholic Mass is conducted in English at the following:
San Clemente (Irish)
Via di Santo Giovanni in Laterano 45-47 (tel: 731 5723)
Sant' Isodoro
Via degli Artisti 41 (tel: 465 359)
Santi Martiri Canadesi (Canadian)
Via G.B. de Rossi
San Patrizio (Irish; Sunday 10AM)
Via Boncompagni 31 (tel: 465 716)
San Silvestro (English)
Piazza San Silvestro (tel: 679 7775)
Santa Susanna
(American; Sunday 9, 10:30AM, and noon)
Via XX Settembre 14 (tel: 475 1510)
San Tommaso di Canterbury
(English; Sunday 10AM)
Via di Monserrato 45 (tel: 654 1829)

Churches for other denominations include
Adventist (Saturday 9:30AM and noon)
Lungotevere Michelangelo 7 (tel: 311 809)
American Episcopal (Sunday 10AM)
San Pietro
Via Napoli 58 (tel: 463 339)
Anglican (Sunday 8:30 and 10AM)
All Saints
Via del Babuino 153 (tel: 679 4357)
Baptist
Rome Baptist Church
Piazza San Lorenzo in Lucina 35 (tel: 687 6652)
The Church of Christ (Wednesday 7:30PM and Sunday 9:30AM)
Viale Jonio 203 (tel: 818 4838)
Greek Orthodox Church (Sunday 10:30AM)
Via Sardegna 152
International Christian Fellowship
Via Vibio Sequestre 10 (tel: 889 0882)
Islamic Center
Via Bertolini 22 (tel: 802 258)
Jehovah's Witnesses (Sunday 9:30AM and 4, Thursday 7:30PM)
Via Romanello da Forli 14b
Jewish Synagogue
Lungotevere dei Cenci 9 (tel: 656 4648/687 5051) and Via Balbo 33
Lutheran Evangelical Church
(Sunday 10AM)
Via Toscana 7 (tel: 460 3904)
Methodist
Ponte Sant' Angelo
Piazza Santo Spirito 3
(tel: 656 8314)

Relief of the earth goddess Tellus, Ara Pacis Augustae

Methodist Evangelical Church (Sunday 10:30AM)
Via Firenze 38 (tel: 474 3695)
Mormon (Sunday 10:30 and 5)
Gesù Cristo dei Santi
Via Cimone 103 (tel: 898 384)
Presbyterian (Sunday 11AM)
St. Andrew's of Scotland
Via XX Settembre 7 (tel: 475 1627)
Russian Orthodox Church (Saturday 6PM and Sunday 7:30AM)
Via Palestro 69 (tel: 495 0729)
Salvation Army (Sunday 10:30 and 6:30)
Via degli Apuli 42 (tel: 495 6306)
Telephone to verify service times because they may vary.

Police
In an emergency dial 113, but in other cases go to the *Questura* (police headquarters) behind Via Nazionale in Via San Vitale 15 (tel: 4686). It has a special information desk to help tourists – ask for extension 2858 or 2987. At worst the police will take and validate the statement you need for your insurance company.

Police on the street are divided into three forces with overlapping responsibilities:

- The elite, semimilitary *Carabinieri*, though the butt of Italian jokes, have the best reputation and are the most efficient; they wear handsome black uniforms with red piping. For their helpline, phone 212 121.
- The *Polizia* wear blue uniforms and perform the workaday policing of the city.
- Municipal police (*Vigili Urbani*), in white helmets and Giorgio Armani-designed navy blue uniforms, mainly handle city traffic.

Police registration In theory, you should register within three days of entry into Italy. In practice no-one does it. It is not something that need worry most visitors.

Post Offices
The majority of post offices (*posta* or *ufficio postale*) are open Monday to Friday, 8:15–4 or 4:30. Most are horrendously busy from the moment they open. On Saturday and the last day of the month all offices close at noon.

The city's main post office is the Ufficio Postale Centrale
Piazza San Silvestro 00186,
open Monday to Friday 8AM–9PM and Saturday 8AM–noon (tel: 6771). It has a full range of services, including 24-hour phones, telex, and fax, and is the city's *poste restante* address (*fermo posta*). Nine other main post offices, known as *Palazzo delle Poste*, keep the same extended hours:
Fiumicino Airport
Stazione Termini
Aurelio, Via Frederico Galeotti
Bel Sitto, Piazzale delle Medaglie d'Oro
Monte Sacro, Viale Adriatico 136
Nomentano, Piazza Bologna
Ostiense, Via Marmorata
Prati, Via Andreoli 1
San Giovanni, Via Taranto

The Vatican operates its own postal services, known for its special stamps and far greater efficiency than the Italian state service. You will find an office on the right of St. Peter's (open in the morning) and one on the left (open in the afternoon), as well as a so-called mobile office in the square in front of the church (open daily 8AM–7PM).

The Vatican mail boxes are blue, as opposed to the regular Italian boxes, which are red. The slot marked *per la città* is for local mail only; that marked *alter destinazioni* is for all other destinations.

Stamps (*francobolli*) may be purchased at post offices or *tabacchi* (showing the blue T sign).

- The system's notorious inefficiency means that mail can take two weeks and over to reach its destination, so for urgent items it is worth paying extra to send them *espresso*.
- You can send a telegram from any post office or by phoning 679 5530 (24-hour service) and 47 701 for international messages.
- For other postal information, call 160.

Public Transport

Buses Short of walking, Rome's big orange buses (and the occasional tram) are the best way to see the city. The service, run by ATAC, is good – cheap, frequent, reliable, and as fast as the choked streets allow – though buses are crowded and at first glance the complexity of the route system and lists of destinations on bus stops (*fermate*) can be baffling. However, a few routes serve most of the main tourist sights (see page 270). The basic flat-fare **ticket** is valid for just one journey and must be bought before boarding the bus or tram from bars and tobacconists displaying an ATAC sticker or from green ATAC kiosks, which are located at major bus stops. The main booth and bus information office is in Piazza dei Cinquecento, in front of Stazione Termini. Tickets must be validated when you enter the bus, which you do through the rear door marked *Salita*, using the small box at the left rear of the bus. You leave the bus by the middle doors marked *Uscita*; Romans do not take kindly to people who buck the system. There is a spot fine of about L10,000 if roving inspectors catch you without a validated ticket.

If you intend to use buses frequently, you can save money by buying a block of 10 tickets (red, as opposed to the regular orange and green tickets) or by choosing a half-day ticket (*biglietto orario*), valid either from 6AM to 2PM or from 2PM to midnight.

Other tickets include

- a one-day pass
- an eight-day tourist pass (the *Carta Settimanale per Turisti*) and a one-month pass valid from the first of the month (both valid day and night for all lines in the city)
- a one-month pass valid for a single route

All are available from usual outlets and the ATAC booth in Piazza dei Cinquecento.

Buses and trams make their final trip from their head stop (*capolinea*) at midnight. Thereafter a night service takes over (*servizio notturno*), serving most of the city until 5AM.

- For bus and tram information; call either 46 951 or 469 544.

Buses out of Rome Buses to Rome's surrounding towns are run by ACOTRAL, whose information office is at Via di Portonaccio 25 (tel: 57 531). Services have different termini, depending on their destinations:

Via Gaeta/Termini for Tivoli and

Where it all began: Romulus and Remus (Campidoglio)

Bus routes
23 Termini–Trastevere
27 Termini–Roman Forum–Colosseum–Piramide
64 Termini–Piazza Venezia–Piazza Navona–St. Peter's
75 Termini–Piazza Venezia–Trastevere
81 Colosseum–Via Nazionale–St. Peter's–Vatican Museums (Piazza del Risorgimento)
93 Termini–Santa Maria Maggiore–Terme di Caracalla–

EUR
95 Piazza Venezia–Via del Tritone–Via V Veneto–Piazzale Flaminio (Piazza del Popolo)
118 Colosseum–San Giovanni in Laterano–Via Appia Antica

surroundings (tel: 460 224)
Piazza dei Cinquecento/Termini for Palestrina and surroundings (tel: 474 704)
Viale Castro Pretorio for services to eastern Lazio (tel: 492 519)
Metro station EUR Fermi for Lazio's southern coast (tel: 592 0402)
Piazzale Flaminio (north of Piazza del Popolo) for Viterbo and northern Lazio (tel: 361 0441)
Viale Giulio Cesare (near the Lepanto metro station) for Bracciano, Cerveteri and the north Lazio coast (tel: 386 196/386 406)
Metro station Anagnina for Frascati and the Castelli Romani (tel: 591 5551)

Metro Rome's subway system (*la metropolitana*) is limited to just two lines – A and B – efforts to extend them being partly hampered by the archaeological remains that work inevitably turns up and that must be analyzed before the tunnels can be continued. Trains can be immensely crowded at rush hour and stiflingly hot in summer, but provide fast transcity journeys and city center stations that serve key tourist sights.

Station entrances are marked by a large, red M, and each has a map of the stations of the network. Tickets can be bought from machines at stations (exact change only) and from the usual bars and tobacconists. Services start at 5:30AM and finish around midnight. There is a night bus service from midnight to 8AM.

Line A runs from Ottaviano in the north (near the Vatican museums) to
Lepanto Flaminio (Piazza del Popolo and the Villa Borghese)
Spagna (Piazza di Spagna)
Barberini (Piazza Barberini and Via V Veneto)
Repubblica
Termini
Vittorio Emanuele (near Santa Maria Maggiore)
Manzoni
San Giovanni (near San Giovanni in Laterano)
and then out to 12 more anonymous stations serving the outer suburbs

Line B stops at
Termini
Via Cavour
Colosseo (for the Colosseum)
Circo Massimo (near the Terme di Caracalla, Aventino and Circo Massimo)
Piramide (near the Piramide and the Protestant Cemetery)
Garbatella
San Paolo (near San Paolo fuori le Muri)
Magliana
EUR Fermi
EUR Marconi
Laurentina

● Maps showing bus and metro routes are available from the information booth in Piazza dei Cinquecento.

Taxis Yellow taxis, which may be no quicker than buses, can be hailed with difficulty on the street or found more easily in central ranks at Termini, Piazza Venezia, Largo Argentina and Piazza San Silvestro or you can call a radio taxi (tel: Radiotaxi 3570, Roma Sud 3875, le Capitale 4994, or Cosmos 8433).

Take only licensed cabs with a sign on the back saying *Servizio pubblico,* and make sure the meter is set at the starting rate. There is a charge per kilometer after that, plus several supplementary charges – you will

Cycling in Rome is a challenge, but can be worth it: cyclists take a break in the Piazza della Rotunda

pay extra per item of luggage, on Sundays and public holidays, between 10PM and 7AM; to go from Fiumicino airport to Rome, and to go from Rome to Fiumicino.

Rome's famous *carrozze* (horse-drawn carriages) are designed more to part tourists from their money than as an efficient means of public transportation. Numbers are dwindling, but there are carriage stands in Piazza Venezia, Piazza di Spagna, Via Vittorio Veneto, Piazza di San Pietro, Fontana di Trevi, Termini, and by the Colosseum.

Bicycle rental Cycling in Rome's clogged traffic is generally an unhealthy and dangerous pastime, but in parks, on the Via Appia Antica and during siesta – when cars are off the road – it can also be a pleasurable one. To rent a cycle from one of the ever- increasing number of firms you must leave your passport as a deposit.

Bicinoleggio; Lungotevere Marzio 3 (tel: 654 3394)
Collati, Via del Pellegrino 82, off Campo dei Fiori (tel: 654 1084)
Parcheggio ACI in Piazza del Popolo, Piazza di Spagna, Piazza San Silvestro and Largo Argentina
Roma Rent, Via Vespasiano 32 (tel: 310 941)
St Peter Rent, Via Porta Castello 43 (tel: 687 5714)

Senior Citizens

Travelers over 60 with identification gain free entry to Rome's state museums – Museo Nazionale Romano, Castel Sant'Angelo, Villa Giulia, Museo di Arte Orientale, and the Palazzo Barberini's Galleria di Arte Moderna and Galleria Nazionale d'Arte Antica. A 30 percent discount on the railways is available for men over 65 and women over 60 with a Carta Argenta (silver card), from mainline stations (not valid from June 16 to August 14).

The American Association of Retired Persons (AARP, 601 E St., Washington, DC 20049, tel: 202/ 434–2277) has two programs for travelers: the Purchase Privilege Program offers discounts on hotels, airfare, car rentals, RV rentals, sightseeing; and the AARP Motoring Plan, provided by Amoco, furnishes emergency road-service aid and trip-routing information for an annual fee of $39.95 per person or couple. The AARP arranges group tours, cruises, and apartment living in Europe through "AARP Travel Experience from American Express" (400 Pinnacle Way, Suite 450, Norcross, GA 30071, tel: 800/927–0111). AARP members are 50 years or older; annual dues are $8 per person or couple. AARP advises that all members can now purchase land tours through their local travel agent or any American Express office, and pay by credit card. When using an AARP or other senior-citizen identification card for reduced hotel rates, mention it when booking, not when checking out. At participating restaurants, show your card before you're seated; discounts may be limited to certain menus, days, or hours. When renting a car, ask about promotional rates, perhaps cheaper than senior-citizen discount.

Sports
Rome has four major sports centers close to the city center: the **Foro Italico** (tel: 396 4206), built by Mussolini (but upgraded for the 1960 Olympic Games) and reserved for football, swimming competitions, and major international meetings.

It is located off the Via Flaminia in the city's northern suburbs on the west bank of the Tiber; the Stadio Flaminio and Palezzetto dello Sport in the nearby **Flaminio** are used for tennis, basketball, skating, football and big competitions; the huge, domed Palazzo dello Sport at **Tre Fontane** in EUR (tel: 592 6386), another Mussolini creation, hosts many events, including basketball, hockey, swimming and tennis;and **Acqua Acetosa** (tel: 879 248), with fields for rugby, polo, football and hockey, is on the Tiber, north of Rome and close to the Villa Ada.

Participation Sports
Bicycling Roman traffic makes cycling something of an ordeal, though many parks have safe areas to ride; for serious cyclists there are tracks at the Velodromo Olimpico, Via della Tecnica; Villa Celimontana, south of the Colosseum; and at Villa Sciarra in Trastevere.
● For further information contact the *Federazione Ciclistica Italiana*, Via Leopoldi Franchetti 2 (tel: 36 851).

The South Wind blows, as depicted on the Piazza San Pietro

Boating Rowboats can be rented at Giardino del Lago in the Villa Borghese. Sailing clubs are located at EUR and at points around Lake Bracciano, 50km north of Rome, with sailing lessons and dinghies for rent from most local villages. International sailing championships take place at Castel Gandolfo, on Lake Albano, 25km south of the city.
● For more information contact the *Federazione Italiana Canottaggio,* Viale Tiziano 70 (tel: 396 6620).

Bowling Rome's best two *bocciodromi* (bowling alleys) are Bowling Brunswick, Lungotevere Acqua Acetosa (tel: 396 6696), which also has a new minigolf course, and Bowling Roma/Team Alley, Viale Regina Margherita 181 (tel: 861 184).

Fishing People you see dangling lines into the polluted Tiber are the city's optimists. For any real chance of a catch you will have to visit the lakes and rivers outside Rome – and buy a license from either the police or local tackle shop and join (for a small fee) the *Federazione Italiana della Pesca Sportiva*, Piazza Emporio 16a (tel: 575 5253).

Golf You will need to make an appointment and apply for guest membership in advance to play on any of the city's four golf courses:
Castelgandolfo Country Club, Via Nettunense, near Castelluccia (tel: 931 3084)
Acqua Santa, Via Appia Nuova 716 (tel: 783 407; closed Monday)
Olgiata, Largo Olgiata 15 (tel: 378 9141; closed Monday)
Fioranello (nine holes), Santa Maria delle Mole (tel: 600 9403; closed Wednesday)
● For information contact

Federazione Italiana Golf, Via Flaminia 388 (tel: 396 3279).

Riding Few of the riding stables (*maneggio*) outside the city are willing to allow visitors to use their facilities for just a couple of hours. The best bet for a single riding session is The Riding Club, Via di Tor Carbone (tel: 542 3998); try also the Circolo Ippico Fiano Romano, between Via Tiberina and Capena (tel: (0765) 255 019).

Swimming A few hotels have private pools; otherwise, the only outdoor public pools are the Piscina delle Rose in EUR, Viale America 20, *open:* June to September (metro line B to EUR-Marconi) and the Piscina Foro Italico at the Foro Italico, Lungotevere Maresciallo Cadorna (bus 32), *open:* June to September.

An indoor pool at the Foro Italico is open between November and May (tel: 360 1498 for details).

Sulphur baths are available at Terme Acqua Albule, Via Tiburtina, Bagni di Tivoli, 22km east of Rome (tel: 529 012).

Tennis Reservations are essential for the public courts at EUR, Viale dell'Artigianato 2 (tel: 592 4693)
Foro Italico, Via Gladiatori (tel: 361 9021)
Tennis Belle Arti, Via Flaminia 158 (tel: 360 0602) and
Tre Fontane, Via delle Tre Fontane (tel: 592 6386).

Spectator Sports

Auto racing This is held at the Valle Lunga racetrack on the Via Cassia, 34km north of Rome (tel: 904 1417).

Football Rome has two first-division, or *Seria A,* teams, Lazio and Roma, both of which are passionately followed by partisan fans. They play on alternate Sunday afternoons, September to May, at the Stadio Olimpico, Via del Foro Olimpico (tel: 399450); take metro line A to Ottaviano, then bus 32. Tickets are on sale directly from the stadium, or from *Società Roma*, Via del Circo Massimo 7 (tel: 575 151), or *Societa Lazio*, Via Col di Lana 3 (tel: 385 141).

Greyhound racing This is held at the Cinodromo, Ponte Marconi, Via della Vasca Navale 6 (tel: 556 6258).

Horse racing Flat races, steeple-chases and show jumping all take place 12km south of the city at the Ippodromo delle Capanelle, Via Appica Antica (tel: 799 3134).

Trotting can be seen at the Ippodromo di Tor di Valle, Via Mare 9 (tel: 592 683). See local press details of meetings. The main equestrian event of the year is the Rome International Horse Show, which takes place in April and May in Piazza di Siena in the Villa Borghese.

● For information write to the *Associazione Nazionale Turismo Equestre* (ANTE), Largo Messico 13 (tel: 864 4053).

Tennis The major tennis event is the Italian International Open, which takes place at the end of May at the Foro Italico.

● For details and tickets contact the *Federazione Italiana Tennis*, Via Eustachio 9 (tel: 855 894).

Student and Youth Travel

For information and discounted student travel call the Centro Turistico Studentesco e Giovanile (CTGS), Via Barberini 23 (tel: 475 6657) or the bustling CTS travel agent at Via Genova 16 off Via Nazionale (tel: 446 791/479 931).

People under 26 are eligible for BIJ tickets, reduced train travel to 2,000 European destinations, and reductions of 30 percent on Italian state railways (FS) with a *Carta Verde* rail pass, available from all mainline stations.

Air passengers aged 12 to 26 and also full-time students with international student identity cards may obtain a 25 percent discount on Alitalia fares.

Telephones

You will find public telephones, run by SIP, the state telephone company, on the street or in bars and restaurants, where they are marked with a red or yellow sign showing a telephone dial and receiver.

Most phones accept L100, L200 and L500 coins, as well as a L200 token, or *gettone*, often given as change, but that can also be purchased from post offices, bars, tobacconists and some newsstands; the oldest phones, usually in bars, often accept only these tokens.

Telephone boxes on the street are being rapidly updated to accept phone cards, or *schede telefoniche*, on sale in L2,000, L5,000 and L10,000 denominations from tobacconists or shops displaying the SIP *schede telefoniche* sticker. All the newer boxes have clear instructions for use in English.

- Local calls (*urbani*) in Rome (telephone prefix 06) rarely cost more than L200.
- The peak period is from 8AM to 1PM, and the off-peak period is from 1PM to 8PM; the cheap rate comes into effect after 10PM.
- Note that the city's telephone numbers can be anywhere between four and eight digits long and that the telephone system is currently being thoroughly overhauled, so that numbers may well be subject to change.
- Thunderstorms and bad weather can still play havoc with the somewhat antiquated system.

You can make direct international calls from all public phones, though unless you have handfuls of change or *gettoni,* it makes sense to find a card phone or use one of the metered phones (*telefono a scatti*), a soundproof cabin where you speak first and pay later. They're found in post offices, the odd bar or in the plush new SIP centers dotted around the city. These efficient and fully staffed offices are located at
Fiumicino airport
Stazione Termini
at the Postale Centrale in Piazza San Silvestro (open 24 hours) and at Corso Vittorio Emanuele.

You can make long-distance calls from more up-market hotels, but will pay a premium for the privilege.

To call abroad, first dial 00, then the country code, followed by the town or city code and the number itself. Remember to omit the first zero in any town or city code.

Country prefixes:
Australia 00 61
Canada 001
Eire 00 353
New Zealand 00 64
United Kingdom 00 44
United States 001

- To reverse charges, dial the international operator – 15 for European countries or 170 for elsewhere – ask for *una chiamata con pagamento a destinazione* or just say "reversible."
- The cheap international rate is on weekends and from 8PM to 8AM during the week.

Time

New York and Montreal are six hours earlier than Italy.

Tipping

- A 10 to 15 percent service charge (*servizio*) is added to restaurant and hotel bills, but waiters expect a small tip on top
- Taxi drivers expect 10 percent

Telephone services
Operator: 10
Police: 112
Emergency services 113
ACI car breakdowns 116
News 190
Post/telegram enquiries 160
Time 161
Weather in Rome 1911
Road reports 194/4212
Snow reports 162
Alarm call service 114

- For quick service do as the locals do and slap down a L100 coin with your receipt when ordering in a bar
- Movie and theater usherettes expect a small tip for showing you to your seat
- Always give something to custodians or sacristans for opening churches or museums out of hours or those usually closed to the public

Toilets

Except at railway stations and in the larger museums, public conveniences are scarce in Rome.

The biggest are in Piazza San Pietro in front of St. Peter's. Otherwise you must use the invariably grim facilities in bars or cafés, all in theory free – though you will be better received by the barman if you buy something first. Ask for the *gabinetto* or *bagno* and do not confuse *Signori* (Men) with *Signore* (Women). Some larger places may have an attendant and small dish for gratuities – leave around L200. The so-called *vespasiani* for men, or street-side urinals, are becoming increasingly rare.

Tourist Offices
Italy's state tourist office, the *Ente Nazionale per il Turismo* (ENIT), has its headquarters in a side street on the north side of Stazione Termini (Monday to Friday, 9–1): Via Marghera 2/6 (tel: 49 771/497 1222). It provides information on the whole country, including Rome, but for extra background on the city, visit Rome's **provincial tourist office**, the *Ente Provinciale per il Turismo* (EPT), near the Terme di Diocleziano (Monday to Saturday, 8:30–7): Via Parigi 5 (tel: 463 748). It issues free maps and plenty of information in English, including *Here's Rome*, crammed with practical information; the lively *Rome for Youth*; and a monthly list of events called the *Carnet*.

Smaller EPT branches, open daily from 8:30–7, can be found near Platform Six in the atrium of Stazione Termini (tel: 465 461/475 0078); in the Customs area at Fiumicino (Leonardo da Vinci) airport (tel: 601 1255/601 2447), and in summer in the service areas close to Rome on the A1 motorway at Area di Servizio Salaria-Ovest, arriving from Florence (tel: 691 9958), and Area di Servizio Frascati-Est, arriving from Naples and the south (tel: 946 4341).

- For excursions into Lazio and the country around Rome, contact the Lazio EPT at Via F Raimondi Garibaldi 7 (tel: 54 571/513 733).
- The American Express Travel Service, Piazza di Spagna 38 (tel: 67 641/722 801), also offers visitors help and advice (Monday to Friday, 9–5, Saturday 9–noon).
- The TCI (Italian Touring Club) has a 24-hour phone service with English-speaking operators to answer car and general travel queries (tel: 4212).
- Pilgrims and religious visitors should visit the Ufficio Informazione Pellegrini e Turisti, Braccio Carlo Magno, Piazza San Pietro (tel: 698 4466/698 4866).
- For student travel and information, call the Centro Turistico Studentesco e Giovanile, Via Barberini 23 (tel: 475 6657).

Valeting and Laundry
Although there are very few coin-operated launderettes in Rome – and those there usually insist that you leave your washing with the staff – virtually every street has an old-style cleaners (*una tintoria*), where you'll receive friendly service and clothes that come back pressed, packaged and looking new. With some encouragement you should get same-day service; most also have dry-cleaning facilities (*lava a secco*).

The skull beneath the skin: one of the reminders of mortality at the church of Santa Prassede

Accommodation

Expensive
Ambasciatori Via Vittorio Veneto 70 (tel: 47 493). Long-established luxury hotel; recently refurbished, but service and facilities are still impeccable.

Atlante Star Via Vitelleschi 34 (tel: 687 9558). Agreeable luxury hotel with growing reputation; small but comfortable and stylish rooms; superb garden terrace and views over St. Peter's.
Bernini Bristol Piazza Barberini 23 (tel: 463 051). Traditional and conservative luxury hotels opposite Bernini's Fontana del Tritone; convenient for the Spanish Steps.
Cardinal Via Giulia 62 (tel: 654 2719). Small and recently converted hotel, well absorbed into a marvelous Renaissance palace in peaceful Via Giulia.
Eden Via Ludovisi 49 (tel: 474 3551). Long-established and reliable hotel close to Via Vittorio Veneto; lowest prices in luxury class; restaurant terrace with fine views.
Excelsior Via Vittorio Veneto 125 (tel: 4708). One of Rome's top hotels; immensely polished and prestigious, but with a relaxed and appealing atmosphere; popular with Americans, actors and the rich and famous.
Flora Via Vittorio Veneto 191 (tel: 497 821). Comfortable and traditional hotel of agreeably faded elegance; large, romantically appointed rooms, some with excellent outlooks over the Villa Borghese.
Forum Via Tor de' Conti (tel: 679 2446). Converted Renaissance palace; not as splendid as others in its class, but the most convenient top hotel for the Roman Forum and the Colosseum; outstanding views of ruins from the terrace and top rooms.
Grand Via Vittorio Emanuele Orlando 3, (tel: 4709). Near Termini and Piazza della Repubblica – no longer the best location – but still among Rome's leading luxury hotels and a favored haunt of VIPs and visiting royalty.
Hassler-Villa Medici Piazza Trinit dei Monti 6 (tel: 678 2651). Captivating position above the Spanish Steps; among Rome's top three hotels; luxurious and quietly affluent atmosphere; stunning restaurant and roof terrace.
Hotel de la Ville Via Sistina 69 (tel: 6733). In the shadow of the Hassler nearby, but reliable top choice with fine panorama from the terrace and upper floors.
Hotel d'Inghilterra Via Bocca di Leone 14 (tel: 672 161). Well known and venerable; at the heart of Rome's fashionable shopping quarter; the haunt of 19th-century writers and royalty, but recently updated to 20th-century standards of taste and luxury.
Lord Byron Via G de Notaris (tel: 361 5404). Captivating and secluded top hotel, in parkland setting, away from the center in leafy Parioli; exclusive air, and perhaps most splendidly decorated of any Rome hotel; noted restaurant.
Plaza Via del Corso 126 (tel: 672 101). Famous if faded central hotel; superb Liberty/Art Deco lobby and fittings.
Raphael Largo di Febo 2 (tel: 650 881). Beautiful, ivy-clad hotel of immense style and atmosphere close to Piazza Navona; very fashionable, notably with top Italian politicians; small, plain but immaculately furnished rooms; chasing a fifth (luxury class) star, but bathrooms and service still some way short.

Moderate
Adriatic Via Vitelleschi 25 (tel: 686 9668). Standard and reliable, though not cheap, two-star choice near St. Peter's.
Alexandria Via Vittorio Veneto 18 (tel: 461 943). Above-average prices for its location, but solid, old-fashioned hotel of faded gentility with a loyal clientele.
Aventino Via San Domenico 10 (tel: 575 5231). Small villa with garden in one of Rome's greener and quieter corners; one of the city's few two-stars with wheelchair access.
Bocca di Leone Via Bocca di Leone 7 (tel: 679 8661). Cheap pensione in expensive Piazza di Spagna location.
Britannia Via Napoli 64 (tel: 463 153). Small, refitted and efficient little hotel close to Termini.
Casa Kolbe Via San Teodoro 44 (tel: 679 4974). Secluded, quiet but still central location south of the Roman Forum and west of the Palatino; wheelchair access.
Cesari Via di Pietra 89a (tel: 679 2386). Off the Corso and close to the Pantheon and Piazza Navona; fine exterior, no-frill but adequately restored interior; friendly atmosphere and faithful clientele.
Columbus Via della Concilazione 33 (tel: 686 5435). A bargain in its class; magnificent Renaissance-palace setting, gracious atmosphere and many original features; close to St. Peter's and a favorite of visiting cardinals.
Condotti Via Mario de' Fiori 37 (tel: 679 4661). Basic, but comfortable, restrained and unpretentious hotel in perfect central setting near shopping and the Piazza di Spagna.

A bird's-eye view of the Piazza Navona

DIRECTORY

Luxury at the Grand, a royal favorite

Dinesen Via di Porta Pinciana (tel: 460 932). Compact, spotless, rather old-fashioned but comfortable option near Via Vittorio Veneto and the Villa Borghese.
Doge Via Due Marcelli 106 (tel: 678 0038). Some of the most charming rooms in the two-star range; close to the Spanish Steps.
Fontana Piazza di Trevi 96 (tel: 678 6113). Convenient and central setting overlooking the Fontana di Trevi, but some rooms are noisy with the crowds and water below.
Forte Via Margutta 61 (tel: 678 6109). Endearing place in a quiet street of studios and art galleries, two minutes from the Piazza del Popolo and the Spanish Steps.
Gregoriana Via Gregoriana 18 (tel: 679 7988). Former convent, now a three-star hotel, with 19 rooms noted for Art Deco interior, created by fashion designer Erte in the 1930s.
La Residenza Via Emilia 22 (tel: 460 789). Good exploration base in a side street off Via Vittorio Veneto; among the best of Rome's three-star hotels, with facilities that deserve a higher rating; fine rooms in converted town house.
Manfredi Via Margutta 61 (tel: 679 4735). Sound choice on a sleepy back street of antique shops and galleries close to the Spanish Steps.
Marcella Via Flavia 96 (tel: 474 6451). Off Via XX Settembre between Termini and Villa Borghese; comfortable and occasionally elegant rooms, some with views, suggest a cool seclusion from the rigors of the city; fine roof terrace.
Margutta Via Laurina 34 (tel: 679 8440). Pretty hotel near Piazza del Popolo on a quiet street; cheap and central, but unexceptional rooms except for those on the top floor, which share a terrace; no restaurant.
Nerva Via Tor de' Conti 3 (tel: 679 3764). Small, straightforward two-star hotel with serviceable rooms and convenient location for the Roman Forum and Colosseum.
Nuovo Quattro Fontane e Belle Epoque Via delle Quattro Fontane 149 (tel: 481 4936). Central but reasonably quiet position near Quirinale; no great luxuries, enthusiastic rather than skilled staff and reasonable prices.
Portughesi Via dei Portughesi 1 (tel: 656 4231). Once a noted bargain, now no longer cheap, but still popular; small, recently renovated, tidily run; excellent location near Piazza Navona on a relaxed Renaissance street; fine roof terrace and views.
Rinascimento Via del Pellegrino 122 (tel: 654 1886). Thirteen-room, two-star hotel on the westerly and quieter margins of Campo dei Fiori.
Scalinata di Spagna Piazza Trinità dei Monti 17 (tel: 679 9582). Efficient, compact and well-furnished hotel; higher prices than facilities warrant, thanks to the matchless view over the city from its location at the top of the Spanish Steps; stunning roof terrace.
Sistina Via Sistina 136 (tel: 475 8867). Quiet, tidy and reliable hotel, handy for the Piazza di Spagna; lovely summer breakfast terrace.
Sole al Pantheon Via del Pantheon 63 (678 0441). Historic old three-star hotel, recently refitted but with preserved Renaissance façade; located a minute from the Pantheon.
Suisse Via Gregoriana 56 (tel: 678 3649). Long-established, well-known and often busy *pensione* in a smart setting near the Piazza di Spagna; good-size, clean rooms but not always friendly staff.
Trevi Vicolo del Babuccio 2 (tel: 678 9563). Sister hotel to the Fontana, hidden in an alley close to the Fontana di Trevi; unpretentious but pretty bedrooms.
Victoria Via Campania 41 (tel: 679 9319). A delightful and – given the fine service and refined interior – bargain-priced hotel in a quiet area near Via Vittorio Veneto and the Villa Borghese; panorama over parkland from roof terrace and upper rooms.
Villa del Parco Via Nomentana 110 (tel: 864.115). Peaceful *pensione*-style spot if you want to be out of the center (15 minutes by bus).

Budget
Abruzzi Piazza della Rotonda

69 (Pantheon) (tel: 679 2021). Slightly dog-eared rooms, noisy on the square, quiet at the back; friendly, and marvelous location opposite the Pantheon.
Alimandi Via Tunisi 8 (tel: 679 9343). Alongside the Vatican Museums; good atmosphere and facilities for its class.
Campo Marzio Piazza Campo Marzio 7 (tel: 651 4486). Simple, standard rooms in a quiet and central location.
Carmel Via Goffredo Mameli 11 (tel: 580 9921). Six rooms on a sleepy Trastevere street – an area with few places to stay.
Della Lunetta Piazza del Paradiso 68 (tel: 656 1080). Cheap, large but unprepossessing rooms; close to Campo dei Fiori and often busy.
Edarelli Via Due Macelli 28 (tel: 679 1265). Adequate but sometimes noisy rooms; handy for the Spanish Steps; optional air-conditioning.
Elide Via Firenze 50 (tel: 463 977). Intimate, amiable and family-run *pensione* on a moderately quiet street off Piazza della Repubblica.
Esty Viale Trastevere 108 (tel: 589 1202). Trastevere location close to the river; modern, adequate rooms on busy thoroughfare.
Fiorella Via del Babuino 196 (tel: 361 0597). Friendly, popular place that requires prebooking; eight spotless rooms (without bathrooms) close to the Piazza di Spagna and Piazza del Popolo.
Forti's Guest House Via Cosseria 2 (tel: 679 9390). A quiet, amiable and much-frequented spot in Prati (for St. Peter's); close to Lepanto metropolitan station.
Imperia Via Principe Amedeo 9 (tel: 475 4474). Six rooms with some original features; good budget choice.
La Rovere Vicolo Sant'Onofrio 5 (tel: 654 0739). Tucked away across the Ponte Aosta off Via Giulia; very peaceful, affable and efficient *pensione*.
Licia Via Principe Amedeo 76 (tel: 475 5293). In a big basic city block that houses eight other tattered *pensioni*.
Mimosa Via Santa Chiara 61 (tel: 654 1753). Ten rooms on a tranquil street near the Pantheon.
Navona Via dei Sediari 8 (tel: 654 3802). Eighteen basic rooms close to the Piazza Navona; run by a friendly Italo-Australian couple.
Ostello del Foro Italico Viale Olimpiadi 61 (tel: 396 4709). A no-frills youth hostel, well out of the city center; bus 492 or metro line A to Ottaviano and then bus 32 to Foro Italico.
Perugia Via del Colosseo 7 (tel: 679 7200). Small and on a peaceful side street off the Via Cavour close to the Colosseum.
Piccolo Via dei Chiavari 32 (tel: 654 2560). Quiet hotel between the Piazza Navona and Campo dei Fiori.
Pomezia Via dei Chiavari 12 (tel: 656 1371). Bargain rooms, a short stroll from the Piazza Navona.
Rasella Via Rasella 127 (tel: 462 042). Very cheap choice, just 10 minutes from the Spanish Steps.
Romano Largo C Ricci 32 (tel: 679 5851). Simple, bargain hotel close to the Roman Forum.
Rosetta Via Cavour 295 (tel: 461 598). Convenient for the Colosseum and a reasonable location on a busy street.
Smeraldo Via dei Chiodaroli 11 (tel: 687 5929). Recently redecorated, comfortable hotel, two minutes from the Campo dei Fiori.
Sole Via del Biscione 76 (tel: 654 0873). Well-known backpackers' favorite; bustling, busy rooms just off Campo dei Fiori.
Tony Via Principe Amedeo 79 (tel: 736 994). Cheap, rooms in a group of budget hotels close to Termini.
YWCA (women only) Via C Balbo 4 (tel: 460 460). Off Via Torino, 10 minutes' walk from Termini; rooms rather than dormitories; midnight curfew.

Campsites
Capitol Via del Castelfusano 45, Ostia Antica (tel: 566 2720). Open all year; near the ruins – train to Ostia Lido station and 5 bus; good facilities, including a swimming pool and tennis courts.
Flaminio Via Flaminia Nuova (tel: 327 9006). Best of Rome's sites and at 8.2km, quite close to the city center; take metro line A to Flaminio and then buses 202, 204, or 205 from Piazzale Flaminio; open all

The small and popular Portughesi

through the year.
Nomentano Via della Cesarina 11 (tel: 610 0296). Take bus 36 from Termini to Piazza Sempione, then bus 337; open March to October.
Roma Camping Via Aurelia (622 3018); 8km north of the center; take bus 46 from Piazza Venezia to Piazza Giureconsulti, then bus 246; open all year.

Restaurants

Expensive

Al Moro Vicolo delle Bollette 13; off Via del Lavatore (tel: 678 3495; reservations essential; closed Sun., Aug.) Highly popular central restaurant; brusque service, noisy and crowded, but some of the best food in the city.
Checchino dal 1887 Via di Monte Testaccio 30 (tel: 574 6318; closed Sun.). Long renowned as the place to sample the best of the usually inedible parts of an animal – tripe, brains and all the other Roman specialities; among Rome's best wine lists.
El Toulà Via della Lupa (687 3498; reservations required). High prices, highly swanky, and in many opinions Rome's best restaurant; plenty of famous faces.
Evangelista Lungotevere Vallati 24 (tel: 687 5810). A newly trendy place if you want to ogle film stars and politicians.
Hosteria dell'Orso Via dei Soldati 25 (tel: 656 4250; evenings only; closed Sun.). Rome's oldest inn – Dante slept here – and still a lovely old ambience, but extremely expensive and with a nightclub and piano bar upstairs.
Il Buco Via Sant'Ignazio 8 (tel: 679 3298; closed Mon., Aug. 15-31). Well known and long popular Tuscan-based spot close to the Pantheon; good value but hardly accommodating service.
La Fontanella Largo della Fontanella di Borghese 86 (tel: 678 3849; closed Mon., Sat. lunchtime). Tuscan food; eat outside in summer.
La Rosetta Via della Rosetta 9 (tel: 686 1002; closed Sun., Mon. lunchtime, Aug.). Specializes in fresh seafood.
L'Eau Vive Via Monterone 85 (tel: 654 1095; closed Sun., Aug.). A Rome institution, mainly for the fact the (mainly) French food is served by nuns; more than a novelty, however, and a good place to go cardinal spotting. Cheaper menu at lunchtime.
Ranieri Via Mario dei Fiori 26 (tel: 679 1592) Founded in 1865 and now better known for its old-world ambience than for its cuisine.
Relais Le Jardin Via G. Notaris 5 (tel: 360 9541; closed Sun.). Probably the spot for a once-in-a-lifetime treat for most people; elegant surroundings and superlative, cuisine. Menu is gourmet international, rather than Roman.
San Luigi Via Mocinego 10 (tel: 302 0704). Near the Vatican Museums; intimate 19th-century ambience and Neapolitan slant to the cuisine.
San Souci Via Sicilia 20 (tel: 493 504; dinner only, closed Mon., Aug. 6–Sept. 1). Immensely luxurious decor, and perhaps the best spot for a high-class intimate dinner for two; in Rome's top four, but the guitar playing can distract from the cuisine.
Vecchia Roma Piazza Campitelli 18 (tel: 686 4604; reservations recommended). Reasonably unspoiled by its popularity with tourists; great *antipasti* and seafood.

Moderate

Al Picolo Arancio Via Scanderburg 112 (tel: 678 6139). One of three fine restaurants under the same management; innovative food by Rome standards and popular with ex-patriots.
Alvaro al Circo Massimo Via dei Cerchi 53 (tel: 678 6112; reservations recommended; closed Mon. and Aug.; no credit cards). Just 12 tables and simple, high- quality cooking; excellent fresh fish and daily specials.
Da Nerone Via delle Terme di Tito 96 (tel: 474 5207). Best eating near the Colosseum; Abruzzese cooking, small and friendly trattoria atmosphere; excellent buffet *antipasti*; excellent homemade Tuscan wine.
Da Giggetto Via Portico d'Ottavia 21. Basic Roman-Jewish cuisine in old-fashioned setting and with interesting service. Closed Fri. evening, Sat. lunchtime.
Da Settimo Via dell'Arancio 50. Up-market, rather arty stable mate of the Al Picolo Arancio, but the food is excellent.
Er Comparone Piazza in Piscinula 47 (tel: 581.6249). One minute south of the Isola Tiberina; reserve a table in summer on the terrace; genuine Roman cuisine with lots of offal choices for the robust; one of the more authentic Trastevere restaurants.
Grappola d'Oro Piazza della Cancelleria 80. Close to Campo dei Fiori, and all but unknown; perhaps the archetypal old Roman trattoria.
Il Corallo Via del Corallo 10. Very popular pizzeria-restaurant near Piazza Navona; excellent if pricey pizzas and desserts; brash, lively atmosphere.
La Buca di Ripetta Via di Ripetta 36 (tel: 3612.9391). Arrive early or book for a small and deservedly popular place; simple vaguely Roman food, rustic decor, and friendly ambience.
La Canonica Vicolo del Piede (tel: 580 3845). Behind Santa

Maria in Trastevere and famous for its fresh seafood; reasonable prices and plenty of peaceful outside tables.
La Rampa Piazza Mignanelli 18 (tel: 678 2621; no reservations). Good food, reasonable prices, pleasant interior and outside summer tables make this a good basic choice.
Margutta Via Margutta 119 (tel: 678 6033). Rome's best-known vegetarian restaurant, tastefully done, with rugs, bare wood boards and lots of plants.
Mario Via della Vite 55 (tel: 678 3818). Good-value Tuscan cuisine and invariably busy, so book ahead.
Pierluigi Piazza de' Ricci/Via Monserrato (tel: 686 1302). Old Rome favorite; popular with Romans, film stars, ex-patriots and tourists alike; loud and busy, especially at Sunday lunchtime.
Sabatini Piazza Santa Maria in Trastevere 13 (tel: 582 026). A well-known and beautifully located spot, with lots of tables outside, but now expensive, full of tourists, and frequented by fake and irritating Roman "minstrels" spoiling your meal.

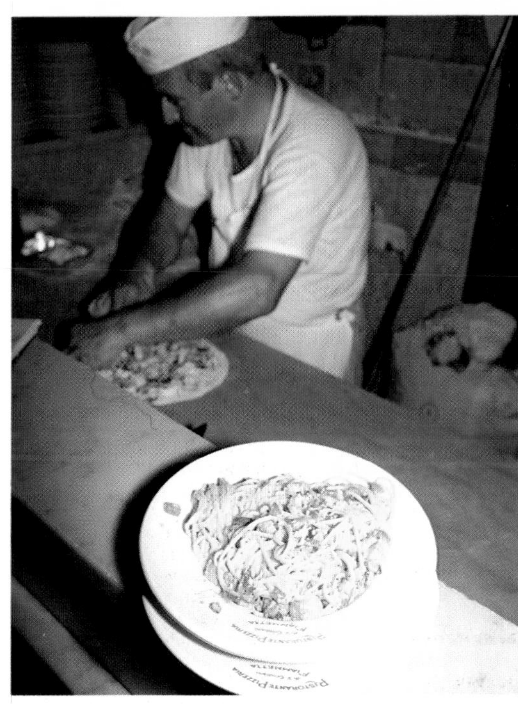

A Roman speciality: spaghetti carbonara

Budget
Africa Via Gaeta 28 (tel: 494 1077). First of Rome's new Ethiopian restaurants; cheap, cheerful and down-at-the-heels, but unusual and interesting cooking.
Al Leoncino Via del Leoncino 28. Superb pizzeria, one block off Via del Corso; wood oven and interior unchanged for 30 years.
Baffetto Via Governo Vecchio 114 (tel: 686 1617). Legendary pizzeria near Piazza Navona; busy with Romans and foreigners alike and lines are normal; amiable atmosphere and still cheap.
Chianti Corsi Via del Gesù 88. Tiny, old-style wine shop with a handful of tables for snacks and good lunches; cheap, friendly and busy.
Da Bruno Piazza San Rufino (Trastevere). Fine and functional trattoria serving basic food and snacks.
Dragon Garden Via del Boschetto (off Via Nazionale). Popular but not overly busy; probably Rome's best and most reasonable Chinese restaurant.
Filetti di Baccalà Largo dei Librari 88 (off Via dei Giubbonari). Rock-bottom prices for un-Roman menu of fried cod fillets and little else; cheap beer and wine; relaxed and always busy.
Frederico Borgo Pio. One of several cheap spots in a grid of streets east of St. Peter's; classic Rome cooking in a Felliniesque 1950s setting.
Ivo's Via di San Francesco a Ripa 157. Trastevere's top pizzeria; genuine feel, fast turnover; arrive early to avoid the lines.
La Fraschetta Via di San Francesco di Ripa 134. A few doors down from Ivo's and equally good, if slightly less busy pizzeria; excellent desserts.
Mario's Via del Moro (Trastevere). Best known and cheapest eatery in Rome; very slow service; large backpacker and foreign visitor contingent.
Pizzeria Viale Trastevere 57. Bright, no-frills pizzeria packed with noisy locals.
Popi-Popi Via delle Fratte di Trastevere. Trattoria and pizzeria with a sea of crowded outside tables in summer; otherwise a characterless interior.
Trattoria Piazza de' Renzo (Trastevere). Quiet, simple, family-run restaurant in Trastevere backwater.
Trattoria G Ficini Via Natale del Grande 10. In a side-street around the corner from Ivo's; plastic-looking frontage, but large and little-known room to the rear for cheap pizzas and solid Roman cooking.
Vino e Cucina Via Pavone, off Via Banchi Vecchi (near Campo dei Fiori). One of a dying breed of simple Rome trattorias; friendly owner and adequate food.

Index

D

P

R

Acknowledgments

The Automobile Association would like to thank the following photographers, libraries and associations for their assistance in the preparation of this book.

DARIO MITIDIERI (© AA Photo Library) took most of the pictures, with the exception of:

129 Keats' Grave – reproduced by permission of the London Borough of Camden from the Collections at Keats' House, Hampstead.

J ALLAN CASH 213 Ostia Antica 222 Villa Lante 225 Orvieto

AA PHOTO LIBRARY contributions from A Souter and P Wilson

ET ARCHIVE 206 Procession of Dignatonis, Apollo of Veio

HULTON PICTURE COMPANY 42/3 Mussolini

KOBAL COLLECTION 20 *La Dolce Vita* 177 Roma Città Aperta, *Bicycle Thieves*

MARY EVANS PICTURE LIBRARY 94 Tourists 95 Food

NATURE PHOTOS LTD 226 Great Spotted Woodpecker (J Reynolds)

ROYAL GEOGRAPHIC SOCIETY 22 Map

SCALA PICTURE LIBRARY 193, 194 *Sibilla delfica*, Sistine Chapel

SPECTRUM COLOUR LIBRARY Cover St Peter's Fountain 56 Courtyard 60 St Angelo Ceiling 195 *Last Judgement* 212 Ostia Antica

THOMAS COOK 94 Poster

ZEFA PICTURE LIBRARY (UK) LTD 16 Street scene 21 People 37 Mass in St Peters 38 St Peters, Saint Angelo 79 Francesca Romana Church 101 Musicians 124 Piazza di Spagna 133 Nuns 135 Flower Market 139 Reading 142 Baptistry 147 Sisters in Piazza Navona 207 Spanish Steps 228, 229 Ponza 248 Riding 249 Mass